STUDIES IN
THE LABOR THE
OF

STUDIES IN
THE LABOR THEORY
OF VALUE

RONALD L. MEEK

Second Edition
With a New Introduction by the Author

Monthly Review Press
New York and London

Library of Congress Cataloging in Publication Data

Meek, Ronald L.
   Studies in the labor theory of value.
   First ed. published in 1956 under title:
Studies in the labour theory of value.
   Includes bibliographical references and index.
   1. Value   2. Marxian economics.   I. Title.
[HB201.M35 1975]   335.4'12   74-7792

First Printing

Monthly Review Press
62 West 14th Street, New York, N.Y. 10011
21 Theobalds Road, London WC1X 8SL

Manufactured in the United States of America

This edition not to be sold in the United Kingdom,
the British Empire, or the countries of the
British Commonwealth, except Canada.

CONTENTS

INTRODUCTION
TO THE SECOND EDITION

This book, which was first published as long ago as 1956, has been out of print for many years. I understand, however, that there has continued to be a certain demand for it, and that this has increased somewhat during the past five years or so—as a result, no doubt, of the recent resurgence of interest in Marx, particularly among young people. The publishers have therefore suggested to me on a number of occasions that the time might be ripe for a revised second edition, and have shown remarkable patience in the face of the ill-disguised delaying tactics which, until very recently, I felt obliged to adopt.

My initial reluctance to sit down and revise the book was due in the main to the pressure of other concerns and interests, coupled with a realisation that since I had not kept up with some of the relevant literature the task of revision would probably be very time-consuming indeed. In addition, I was worried about the nature and extent of the revisions which might turn out to be necessary as a result of certain changes which had taken place in some of my political views.

When I finally came round to reading the book again, however, my worries on the latter score were considerably lessened. It was certainly true, I found, that I had rather tended to treat the labour theory of value as if it were one of the Thirty-nine Articles, and that this had led to an undue defensiveness and didacticism which now appeared somewhat quaint and old-fashioned. But it did seem to me that it was the manner of the book, rather more than the matter, which had been affected by this. In the case of most of the *major* points which now needed correction or elaboration, the reasons why they needed it had very little directly to do with politics at all.

In view of all this, I was happy to agree to a second-best solution, to the effect that the text of the book should be photographically reproduced from the original edition of 1956 without any alteration whatever, but that it should be prefaced by a new introduction which would indicate some of the main ways in which I felt the book needed up-dating and revision, and followed by an article on Marx's economic method (written in 1966 on the basis of an earlier piece dating from

1959) which summed up my attitude towards Marxian economics in general.[1] The present volume, for better or for worse, is the result.

This introduction, which makes use of several of the themes in the article at the end and carries one or two of them rather further, surveys the successive chapters of the book in some detail, in an endeavour to identify the main points which seem to me today to call for clarification, development, or alteration. I fear that the number of questions I shall ask in the introduction rather exceeds the number of answers that I shall be able to give, but I hope at any rate that the questions are the right ones, and that my asking them will stimulate further debate in this important and interesting field.

In most cases, the editions of cited works which I have used in the introduction and the article at the end are the same as the editions which I used in the original book. The most important exception to this is Marx's *Capital*: in the original book I used the Allen and Unwin edition of Volume I and the Kerr editions of Volumes II and III, whereas in the introduction and the article I have used the English editions of Volumes I, II, and III published by the Foreign Languages Publishing House, Moscow, in 1954, 1957, and 1959 respectively.

1.   *The Labour Theory of Value before Marx*

So far as the first three chapters of the book are concerned, there are only a few individual points which I would wish to develop or alter were I rewriting the book from the beginning, but there is one rather important additional theme which I would probably want to elaborate alongside the others. Let me deal first, very briefly, with the individual points, and then outline this additional theme.

In the first chapter, on value theory before Smith, I make a fairly hard and fast distinction between the "Canonist" approach on the one hand and the "Mercantilist" approach on the other. As a concession to certain of the views expressed by Schumpeter in his *History of Economic Analysis* (1954), I would now prefer to call the two stages "Aristotelian-Scholastic" and "Neo-Scholastic-Mercantilist" respectively, in order to make it clearer that certain of the *later* scholastic doctors made important positive contributions to what I call in the book the "Mercantilist" theory. I would still wish to claim, however,

---

[1] In the version reprinted here, this article was written for my *Economics and Ideology and Other Essays* (London, Chapman and Hall, 1967). I am indebted to Messrs. Chapman and Hall for allowing it to be republished in the present volume.

as against Schumpeter, that there was an essential difference between the value theories of the two stages.[1] The only other point in relation to the first chapter is that if I had known more about early French and Italian economic thought when I wrote the book, I would have emphasised that the developments described in sections 3, 4, and 5 were essentially British, and that the traditions inherited by Smith's opposite numbers in France and Italy towards the end of the eighteenth century were different in certain quite important respects.

So far as the second chapter, on Smith's theory of value, is concerned, the first point is that since I wrote the book a new set of student's notes of Smith's Glasgow lectures has been discovered.[2] This set of notes, so far as it goes, is much fuller than the set published by Cannan in 1896, and my feeling from a preliminary inspection of the manuscript is that some of my judgements in the first section of the second chapter may now be open to question,[3] although I do not think that the broad conclusions will be seriously affected. Second, if I were rewriting the book I would extend, and give more prominence to, the passage on pp. 51-3 about Smith's use of a materialist conception of history, making particular reference to his theory of the development of society through the hunting, pastoral, agricultural, and commercial stages. This "four stages" theory, as I now see it, was one of the major factors in the development of the new *science* of society which began to emerge, in France as well as in Britain, in the latter half of the eighteenth century.[4] Third, l now feel that in my account of Smith's treatment of the measure of value I may have underestimated the extent to which this treatment represented not only a stage in the development of his theory of the determination of value but also an attempt to solve the index-number problem. I do not think that this really affects the essence of my interpretation, but it does mean that it was perhaps over-simplified.

The third chapter, on Ricardo's theory of value, in which I was fortunate in being able to draw heavily on Mr. Sraffa's remarkable introduction to his edition of Ricardo's works, does not seem to me to

---

[1] I have developed this point in my *Economics and Ideology*, pp. 200-1. See also below, pp. 295-6.

[2] The new lecture notes are being edited by Professor P. Stein, Professor D. Raphael, and myself, and will, it is hoped, be published (as one of the volumes in a new edition of Smith's works and correspondence) within the next three or four years.

[3] In particular, I may have slightly underestimated the extent to which Smith, in his lectures, anticipated the concept of a natural rate of profit which was later to feature so prominently in the *Wealth of Nations*.

[4] Cf. my article on "Smith, Turgot, and the 'Four Stages' Theory" in *The History of Political Economy*, Vol. 3, No. 1, Spring 1971.

need much alteration. Were I rewriting it, however, I would try to clarify the illustration on p. 104 a little,[1] and in my account of Ricardo's theory I would lay more emphasis on the fact that Ricardo thought in terms of an intensive, as well as an extensive, margin in agriculture. Then again, being now able to look at Ricardo's discussion of the invariable measure of value from the vantage-point of Mr. Sraffa's *Production of Commodities by Means of Commodities* (1960), I would probably lay rather more emphasis on the first of the two "reasons" noted in the second paragraph on p. 112. And finally, instead of merely noting Ricardo's assumption that savings were made almost exclusively out of profits (p. 84), I would feel obliged to adduce some kind of an explanation for it.

The additional major theme, mentioned above, which I would probably now wish to develop in association with the others, arises out of my discussion in chapter 1 of the emergence of the Classical concept of a natural rate of profit on capital, and concerns an important methodological difference between the way in which Smith explained the working of the economic machine and the way in which his great contemporary Turgot explained it. During the seventeenth and early eighteenth centuries, as capitalism developed, an important distinction began to be made between money which was "passively" utilised (by lending it out at interest, or using it to buy a piece of land), and money which was "actively" utilised, either in agriculture or in "trade" (cf. below, p. 25). As the eighteenth century progressed, a further distinction came to be made, within the general category "trade", between the two separate activities of merchanting and manufacturing. Here, then, were five different ways in which a stock of money could be utilised so as to yield a revenue: lending it out at interest, using it to buy a piece of land, and employing it in order to set up as an entrepreneur in agriculture, merchanting, or manufacturing; and it gradually came to be recognised that it was in a sense *through* the utilisation of money in these ways, and in particular through the transfer of money from one use to another by its owners, in search of the highest reward, that a capitalist economic system worked.

Now all these ways of utilising money had one important feature in

---

[1] The point at issue can be seen more clearly if one imagines that industry A in my example is the gold-producing industry. Since the price of a given output of gold, or gold coins, cannot alter, it follows that when wages rise by 10 per cent, capital in industry A will lose exactly the amount which labour gains, thus lowering the rate of profit there to $9\frac{1}{11}$ per cent, and that the prices in industries B and C will then have to adjust in such a way as to yield a profit of $9\frac{1}{11}$ per cent in these two industries as well.

common: they resulted in the receipt of a revenue which was related in one way or another to the amount of money employed. This common feature seemed (at any rate to pre-Marxian writers) to warrant the use of a common term, *capital*, for money employed in any of the uses. But there was also an essential difference, both qualitative and quantitative, between the rewards obtainable from the "passive" and "active" uses respectively. The rewards from the "active" uses, it came to be postulated, were essentially associated with the employment of wage-labour, whereas the others were not; and the rewards from the "active" uses were normally higher than those from the "passive" uses. The great question was how to incorporate all these facts and distinctions into a kind of working model of the new form of society which was emerging.

The way in which Smith tackled the problem, speaking very broadly, was this. The three basic social classes, he stated, consisted of those who employed their capital in "active" uses, and who lived by *profit*; those who were hired by them, and who lived by *wages*; and those whose capital was embodied in land, and who lived by *rent* (cf. below, pp. 53-4). Profit, wages, and rent were the three primary forms of income, from which all other forms of income were ultimately derived. The mobility of capital between its two "passive" uses resulted in the establishment of a "natural" relationship between the level of interest and that of rent;[1] and, more important, the mobility of capital between and within its three "active" uses resulted in the formation of a "natural" or average rate of profit on the capital employed in these uses.[2] When it came to the question of the relationship between rent and interest on the one hand and profit on the other, however, Smith based his explanation not on the mobility of capital between its "passive" and "active" uses, but on the facts (a) that interest was "derived from" or "paid out of" profit,[3] and (b) that rent was essentially what was left over from the net product of land after the normal profit due to the capitalist farmer had been deducted.[4]

Turgot, in his *Réflexions sur la Formation et la Distribution des Richesses*, tackled the problem in a manner which in one vital respect was radically different. In Turgot's model, as in Smith's, the system worked

[1] *Wealth of Nations*, ed. E. Cannan (London, 1904), Vol. I, p. 339.
[2] Subject, of course, to differences in "the profits of different trades" arising from differences in "the agreeableness or disagreeableness of the business, and the risk or security with which it is attended" (*Wealth of Nations*, Vol. I, p. 113).
[3] *Ibid.*, Vol. I, pp. 97-9.
[4] *Ibid.*, Vol. I, p. 145.

through the transfer of capital from one use to another in search of the highest reward. But whereas in Smith's model transfers between the sphere of "active" uses and the sphere of "passive" uses (as distinct from transfers *within* each of these spheres) played little part, in Turgot's model they were of the essence of the matter. Turgot laid emphasis on the mobility of capital between *all* its five alternative uses, and explained the working of the system in terms of the manner in which the rewards accruing to capital from these different uses, in spite of the fact that they were normally unequal, were nevertheless kept in "a kind of equilibrium" by means of transfers from one use to another in response to market changes. One of the crucial results of this was that in Turgot's model the gross profit which was received by the entrepreneur who employed his capital in one of its three "active" uses, and which formed part of the supply price of his commodity, was normally fixed at a level just high enough to provide compensation for the opportunity cost incurred by him in employing his capital in the enterprise concerned rather than using it to purchase land or lending it out at interest, plus an additional amount which compensated him for the extra risk and trouble involved in employing his capital "actively" rather than "passively" and for any special abilities he might possess.[1]

Turgot and Smith were both equally aware of the importance of the interdependence of economic aggregates in a capitalist economy, and it cannot be said that Turgot's method of analysing this interdependence was inherently "better" than Smith's, or *vice versa*. As the two models stand, Smith's embodies a more accurate and direct reflection of the central socio-economic relations characteristic of a capitalist society, and is probably better fitted to analyse the process of development of such a society. Turgot's, on the other hand, lays more emphasis on the important fact that the levels of all class incomes are mutually and simultaneously determined, and is better fitted to explain (for example) why it is that the profit received from the "active" uses of capital is not lowered to the level of the rate of interest or the rent of land by means of competition between the capitalists concerned.[2]

The importance of all this, in relation to the subject of the present book, arises from the fact that Marx tended to adopt Smith's line

---

[1] Cf. my *Turgot on Progress, Sociology and Economics* (1973), pp. 23-5.

[2] All we find in Smith on this point are two or three very brief and vague statements, made more or less *en passant*, to the effect that the amount by which gross profit exceeds interest is a compensation for the "risk" and "trouble" involved in "employing the stock" (cf. *Wealth of Nations*, Vol. I, pp. 54 and 99).

rather than Turgot's. He did this, of course, for the very best of reasons: it was of the greatest importance, he believed, to counteract the idea that class incomes were in one way or another created and determined by competition—an idea which Turgot's line might at first sight be regarded as aiding and abetting. But Turgot's general methodological approach would in fact have been quite compatible with the specification of the particular institutional data and class relationships upon which Smith was concerned to lay emphasis, and the question arises as to whether present-day Marxists may not have something to learn from it. This is a point which I shall come back to briefly at the end of this introduction.

2. *Marx's Theory of Value* (1): *Methodology and Alienation*

Most of the remainder of the book (chapters 4-7) is oriented around the idea that for Marx the labour theory of value was in essence another way of saying that "the mode of exchange of products depends upon the mode of exchange of the productive forces" (below, p. 146), so that it represented a kind of crystallisation or embodiment of the methodology which he employed in his economic analysis. Chapter 4, which attempts to trace the gradual emergence of this idea in Marx's early work, and to delineate the main elements of his basic economic methodology, therefore occupies an important place in the book as a whole.

The second section of this chapter, dealing specifically with the early development of Marx's economic thought, includes an account of the celebrated manuscripts on political economy and philosophy which Marx wrote in 1844 (nowadays sometimes called the "Paris Manuscripts"). These manuscripts seemed to me, as I said (below, p. 135), to sum up an extremely important stage in Marx's intellectual development. It was in them, as everyone now knows, that Marx expounded (*inter alia*) a very interesting—if not always readily comprehensible—set of ideas about the "alienation" or "estrangement" of labour. After discussing these ideas at some length in my book, I suggested (p. 138) that although Marx's method of treatment in *Capital* was very different from that in the 1844 manuscripts, "the gap between the two approaches is not quite as wide as may appear at first sight". In particular, "the idea of the product of labour standing opposed to the producer as an alien entity survives in the vital concept of the fetishism of commodities"—a concept which I discussed in some detail in chapter 5 (pp. 174-6).

Interest in Marx's ideas about alienation has been heightened in recent years as a result of the increasing attention which has been paid not only to his 1844 manuscripts but also (and more particularly) to his so-called *Grundrisse*, a set of notes on political economy written in 1857-8 which for various reasons did not become generally accessible in the West until the 1950s and which has not as yet become available in a complete English translation. It is fairly evident, however, from certain extracts which have already been translated—in particular, from those published by Mr. David McLellan in a recent book[1]—and from the interesting account of the work as a whole given a few years ago by Mr. Martin Nicolaus,[2] that the concept of alienation plays a more extensive role in it than many of us might have expected, and that the *Grundrisse* constitutes an important link between the ideas of the 1844 manuscripts on the one hand and the economic doctrines of Marx's *Critique of Political Economy* (1859) and *Capital* (Vol. I, 1867; Vol. II, 1885; Vol. III, 1894) on the other. As a result, some of our traditional notions about the part played by "alienation" in Marx's mature economic work may well have to be revised.

I shall come back to this point shortly, but it will be convenient to deal first with a rather different though closely related matter—the old question of whether or not Marx "changed the plan" which he elaborated in the late 1850s for his proposed work on economics. The best starting-point here is Marx's letter to Engels of 2 April 1858, in which the plan at which he had then arrived for the proposed work is very clearly set out. "The whole shit", Marx indelicately wrote, "is to be divided into six books: I. Capital; II. Landed property; III. Wage labour; IV. State; V. International trade; VI. World market." The first of these six "books" (i.e., main divisions of the work as a whole), that dealing with capital, was to consist of four sections, as follows:

A. "*Capital in general*". This was to be divided into three subsections, namely (1) Value, (2) Money, and (3) Capital. (Other evidence[3] suggests that the third subsection was to be further divided into production, circulation, and the transformation of surplus value into profit.)

B. "*Competition*, or the action of the many capitals upon one another."

C. "*Credit*, where capital appears as the general element in comparison with particular capitals."

[1] *Marx's Grundrisse* (1971).
[2] *New Left Review*, no. 48, March-April 1968.
[3] Summarised by McLellan, *op. cit.*, pp. 8-11.

D. "*Share capital* as the most complete form (passing over into Communism) together with all its contradictions."

After the first "book" would come the second, on landed property; then the third, on wage labour; and finally the remaining three "books" on state, international trade, and the world market. The question at issue is whether Marx subsequently changed this plan—or rather, since it is perfectly clear that *some* alterations to it were in fact made, whether he changed it radically.

Mr. McLellan, in his book on the *Grundrisse*, argues in effect (a) that Marx did *not* "change his plan"; (b) that *Capital* was only the elaboration of the first of these six "books"; (c) that in the *Grundrisse* "Marx was led to sketch out to some extent the fundamental traits of the other five books"; and therefore (d) that the *Grundrisse*, in so far as it is the *Grundrisse* of more than the first "book", is "the most fundamental work that Marx ever wrote".[1] In other words, if we want to know what Marx would have said, had he lived to complete his work, about landed property, wage labour, etc., the only place where we can—and should—look is the *Grundrisse*, and it is in this that the latter's chief importance lies.

Let us concentrate on the crucial link in this chain of argument— point (b). Now nothing is more obvious than that *Capital* in fact contains a great deal about landed property and wage labour, which in Marx's original plan were to constitute the subject of the second and third "books" of the work as a whole. And, indeed, looking at it from the vantage-point of *Capital*, nothing appears at first sight to be odder than this original plan: how could Marx ever have contemplated starting with a section on the subject of capital (including the production of surplus value and its transformation into profit) which abstracted from a consideration of landed property and, more particularly, of wage labour? The answer, surely, is to be found in Marx's view, in his original plan, of the *relation* between the proposed first "book" and the two which were to follow. This relation is in fact outlined fairly clearly in the very letter to Engels from which I have just quoted. At the beginning of Marx's summary of his proposed section on "Capital in General" ("A" above) occurs the following paragraph:

"In the whole of this section it is assumed that the wages of labour are constantly equal to their lowest level. The movement of wages

[1] McLellan, *op. cit.*, pp. 8-11.

and the rise or fall of the minimum come under the consideration of wage labour. Further, landed property is taken as = o; that is, nothing as yet concerns landed property as a particular economic relation. This is the only possible way to avoid having to deal with everything under each particular relation."

It can reasonably be concluded from all this, I think, that Marx originally planned to begin his work with a "book" in which the basic economic processes of capitalism were analysed on two specific assumptions—viz., (i) that landed property (and therefore rent) were non-existent; and (ii) that labour-power was bought and sold at its value. This would then be followed by a second "book" on landed property in which assumption (i) was dropped and rent was brought into the picture; and by a third "book" on wage labour in which assumption (ii) was dropped and the question of "the movement of wages and the rise or fall of the minimum" was dealt with.

In the final outcome, this plan of Marx's was certainly "changed", although not in nearly such a radical way as some commentators have suggested. The general framework of *Capital* is indeed very similar to that contemplated in his proposed first "book"; but he eventually decided to remove the two assumptions *in the course of his analysis within this framework* rather than in two *subsequent* "books". Thus the first part of Volume I of *Capital* is based on the assumption that labour-power is bought and sold at its value; but this assumption is removed, and the question of "the movement of wages and the rise or fall of the minimum" is considered, later in the same volume. The whole of Volumes I and II of *Capital*, again, is based on the assumption that "landed property = o"; but this assumption is removed, and rent is brought into the picture, before the end of Volume III. So far at least as landed property is concerned there is little excuse for not noticing this "change of plan", since Marx in a letter to Engels of 2 August 1862 said specifically that he now intended after all "to bring the theory of rent already into this volume"; and in a letter to Kugelmann of 6 March 1868 he said that property in land would be one of the subjects dealt with in the "second volume".[1] Is there really very much doubt, then, that when Marx said in a letter to Engels of 15 August 1863 that he had had "to turn everything round", these alterations were what he was mainly referring to?

[1] Marx at that time, shortly after the publication of Volume I of *Capital*, still envisaged that the whole of the material which was eventually to be published in Volumes II and III would in fact appear in one volume—the "second".

If my interpretation is correct, it follows that the chief importance of the *Grundrisse* must be sought in rather different directions. It may well in the end be found to lie, I suspect, in the fact that from the perspective of this work—to use Mr. Nicolaus's words—"the often apparently 'technical' obscurities of *Capital* will reveal their broader meaning",[1] or, as I would prefer to put it, the sociological underpinning of some of the "technical" arguments which Marx developed *after* the 1850s[2] will become clearer. It is evidently also important, however, because it would appear to be the first work in which Marx elaborated his *theory* of surplus value (on the basis of the vital distinction between labour and labour-power); and last but not least because, as I have already noted above, the concept of alienation played a more important role in it than might perhaps have been expected in Marx's writing at that time.[3]

With reference to the latter point, Marx's use of the concept of alienation in some of the passages which Mr. McLellan has translated from the *Grundrisse* is very interesting indeed; and in the light of these passages I would certainly wish, were I rewriting my book today, to amend and expand the sentence on p. 138 below dealing with the connection between the ideas of the 1844 manuscripts and the doctrines of *Capital*. What is of particular interest here is the manner in which Marx in the *Grundrisse* analyses *commodity production as such*—the "second great form" of society, as he calls it, which according to his account arises out of and eventually replaces the first form, based on "relationships of personal dependence". The "universal nature" of commodity production, Marx writes, "creates an alienation of the individual from himself and others, but also for the first time the general and universal nature of his relationships and capacities". In other words, commodity production creates the conditions for the arrival of a third form of society, which will be "founded on the universal development of individuals and the domination of their communal and social productivity".[4] In the light of these (and other) passages from the *Grundrisse*, I think I would now wish to argue that *Capital*, in a very real and important sense, is in fact a book *about*

[1] Nicolaus, *op. cit.*, p. 60.

[2] I am thinking here in particular of certain arguments relating to the transformation of surplus value into profit, and to the famous reproduction schemes, which Marx described to Engels in letters dated respectively 2 August 1862 and 6 July 1863.

[3] If it should turn out that the *Grundrisse* contains more on "State", "International trade", or "World market" than *Capital* does, it will of course be important on that account as well.

[4] McLellan, *op. cit.*, pp. 67-71.

alienation—or, to be more precise, about two different but closely interrelated types of alienation between which it is important to distinguish.

The first type of alienation is that just mentioned, which is associated with *commodity production as such.* Marx's basic idea here, speaking very broadly, is that as the social division of labour is extended, and as commodity production develops, gradually dissolving and eventually replacing relations of personal dependence, human labour takes on the two-fold character of concrete (or utility-producing) labour, *and abstract (or value-producing) labour.* In its latter capacity, which it assumes only when society has entered a particular historical stage, labour becomes "a means to create wealth in general", and ceases to be "tied as an attribute to a particular individual".[1] All products and activities, as Marx puts it in the *Grundrisse,* then disintegrate into exchange values,[2] and "the individuals are subordinated to social production, which exists externally to them, as a sort of fate".[3] In such a situation, Marx writes,

> "The social character of activity, and the social form of the product, as well as the share of the individual in production, are here opposed to individuals as something alien and material; this does not consist in the behaviour of some to others, but in their subordination to relations that exist independently of them and arise from the collision of indifferent individuals with one another. The general exchange of activities and products, which has become a condition of living for each individual and the link between them, seems to them to be something alien and independent, like a thing."[4]

Thus "the social relations of individuals . . . appear in the perverted form of a social relation between things",[5] and the social action of producers "takes the form of the action of objects, which rule the producers instead of being ruled by them".[6] In *Capital,* it is true, as distinct from the *Grundrisse,* Marx does not specifically use the term "alienation" in his analysis of this state of affairs—or at any rate I have not been able to find any passage in which he makes such a use of it. But in his account of "the fetishism of commodities", which occupies

---

[1] *Critique of Political Economy* (Lawrence and Wishart, London, 1971), p. 210.
[2] McLellan, *op. cit.*, p. 65. Cf. also *ibid.*, p. 73.
[3] *Ibid.*, p. 68.   [4] *Ibid.*, p. 66.   [5] *Critique*, p. 34.
[6] *Capital*, Vol, I, p. 75. Cf. *ibid.*, pp. 80-1: "These formulae [concerning the relation between the value of commodities and the labour embodied in them] . . . bear stamped upon them in unmistakable letters, that they belong to a state of society, in which the process of production has the mastery over man, instead of being controlled by him."

a strategic position at the end of the opening chapter on commodities and in a sense sums the latter up, it is surely clear that what he is in fact talking about is this first type of "alienation".

The second type of alienation, which eventually arises out of the first, exacerbates it, and becomes as it were superimposed upon it, is that associated with the specific socio-economic institutions of *capitalist* commodity production. Here there is no need to go back to the *Grundrisse* for documentation: there are more than enough references in *Capital* itself. Under capitalist commodity production, as Marx puts it, the worker's labour is "alienated from himself by the sale of his labour-power", and is "realised in a product that does not belong to him";[1] capital becomes "an alien power that dominates and exploits him";[2] capital and land together are "alienated from labour and confront it independently";[3] and all means for the development of production "estrange from him [the worker] the intellectual potentialities of the labour-process".[4] Once again Marx's main general discussion of this second type of alienation in *Capital* is placed in a strategic position—at the end of Volume III, immediately before the last unfinished chapter on classes; and once again his analysis of it is closely associated with the concept of fetishism—in this case not the fetishism of commodities as such, but the fetishism of capital and land.[5]

The whole point of *Capital*, however, is that Marx is there concerned, not so much with lamenting the existence of these types of alienation,[6] but rather with stripping away the "mystical veil"[7] which hinders their existence (and importance) from being fully recognised. To expose this fetishism, Marx believed, one had to penetrate below the "estranged outward appearance of economic relationships"[8] to the underlying economic relationships themselves. But it was not enough to do this, as it were, *qualitatively*, or sociologically: since under commodity production the "social relation between things" which reflected the underlying "social relations of individuals" took the form of a *price* or *value* relation, the job had to be done *quantitatively* as well. It was here, of course, that Marx's version of the labour theory of value, in its capacity as a theory of price in the traditional sense, came into the picture. Under commodity production as such, this theory says in

---

[1] *Capital*, Vol. I, pp. 570-1.   [2] *Ibid.*, Vol. I, p. 571.
[3] *Ibid.*, Vol. III, p. 804.   [4] *Ibid.*, Vol. I, p. 645.
[5] See in particular *Capital*, Vol. III, pp. 803-10; and cf. *ibid.*, pp. 383 ff., where the fetishism of interest-bearing capital is discussed.
[6] "What avails lamentation in the face of historical necessity?" (*Capital*, Vol. I, p. 595).
[7] *Capital*, Vol. I, p. 80.   [8] *Ibid.*, Vol. III, p. 797.

effect, the price relations between things reflect production relations between men in so far as the latter are expressed in the different quantities of labour the men embody in their commodities. Under capitalist commodity production, these price relations between things are modified, but the modification is itself a reflection of the change which has occurred in the production relations between men, and is quantitatively determinate. With the aid of the labour theory of value, Marx believed, one could show that it was precisely *through* the working of the price mechanism, competition, and the "law of value" that the two basic types of alienation arose and persisted.

There was indeed, then, an important link between Marx's theory of value and his concept of alienation. To say that a thing possessed *value* in exchange was the same as saying that it was the product of somebody's labour in a commodity-producing society, and that its producer was therefore alienated "from himself and others". To say that the equilibrium price of a thing diverged from its *value* in the way described in Volume III of *Capital* was the same as saying that it was the product of labour in a *capitalist* commodity-producing society, and that its direct producer was therefore confronted by capital as an "alien power". But these "moral" connotations do not, I think, make Marx's theory of value, *in its capacity as a theory of the determination of the relative prices of commodities*, any the less objective—or "scientific", if one wishes to use my own rather question-begging term. Were I rewriting today the passage at the top of p. 129 below, I would certainly want to make it clearer that Marx's "vision" included not only a "principle of causation" but also a "moral" attitude towards certain of the phenomena which were caused; but there is not very much else that I would wish to alter. I would still wish to deny that Marx's theory of value actually *embodied* any particular ethical or political viewpoint, while emphasising at the same time its close *association* with the materialist conception of history—and, as I would now wish to add specifically, with the concept of alienation.

So far as the last section of chapter 4 is concerned—that dealing with Marx's economic method—there is once again little that I would actually wish to take back, although some of the points will be found to be put rather differently in the essay appended at the end of the book, which represents a later view. Provided that the reader does not get the idea from pp. 146-8—as he might well be excused for doing—that Marx wrote *Capital* just to test a hypothesis, I do not think he will be too seriously misled by this section as it stands. The distinction between the two senses of the term "relations of production" on pp. 151-2 still seems to me to be a neglected and vitally important one. And I still think I was right in laying special emphasis on Marx's "logical-historical method" (pp. 148-9): indeed, if anything I think I underestimated the extent to which Marx's economic work was guided by it.[1] And there is one related point which I might perhaps have brought out more clearly in this context. In so far as Marx's *logical* transition in *Capital* (from the commodity relation as such to the "capitalistically modified" form of this relation) is presented by him as the "mirror-image" of a *historical* transition (from "simple" to "capitalist" commodity production), Marx's procedure becomes formally similar to that of Adam Smith and Ricardo, who also believed that the real essence of capitalism could be revealed by analysing the changes which would take place if capitalism suddenly impinged upon some kind of abstract pre-capitalist society (see below, pp. 303-4). The major difference between Marx's analysis in this respect and that of Smith and Ricardo—a difference to which I now feel that I have not hitherto given sufficient attention—is that whereas for Smith and Ricardo the "early and rude state of society" which they postulated was not only pre-capitalist but also in a sense pre-historic, for Marx the system of "simple commodity production" which he postulated was the historically prior form of a definite *stage* in the development of society—the stage of commodity production in general, or as such. The coming of capitalism, therefore, while it certainly brought about the replacement of "simple" by "capitalist" production relations, did so within the general framework of commodity production as such. Indeed, as Marx said in *Capital*, "the mode of production in which the product takes the form of a commodity . . . is the most general and embryonic form of bourgeois production".[2] To understand capitalism, therefore, Marx was in effect saying, and in particular to dispel the illusions about its character which were implicit in Classical political economy, one must understand first and foremost that it is a particular type of *commodity-producing* society. If we are looking for the main reason why Marx "starts with values", and why, having "transformed" them into prices of production, he still insists that the "values" play a determining role, here surely it is to be found.

---

[1] I might have been more seized of its importance—and complexity— if I had at that time read Lenin's "Philosophical Notebooks". See Lenin's *Collected Works*, Vol. 38 (1961), pp. 178-80 and 319-20.

[2] *Capital*, Vol. I, p. 82.

3. *Marx's Theory of Value (2): The "Transformation Problem"*

Marx's version of the labour theory of value consisted essentially of a set or sequence of causal propositions concerning the qualitative and quantitative connections between production relations and exchange relations under commodity production in general and capitalist commodity production in particular. In chapter 5 of my book, I attempted to explain what these propositions in fact were and the reasoning which underlay them. There is not very much in the chapter which seems to me to be actually wrong, but if I were rewriting it today I would wish to make a number of alterations and additions.

The first point concerns the general layout of the chapter, which I now feel may have hindered some readers from seeing the wood for trees. Were I rewriting the chapter, I would wish to adopt something more like the order of treatment employed on pp. 304-11 of the essay appended at the end of the book. The summary of Marx's theory of value given there is rather too formalised and schematic to stand on its own, but the three successive logical-historical *stages* of Marx's analysis are more clearly delineated and distinguished than they are in chapter 5 of the book. In particular, the distinction between the two stages of Marx's analysis of *capitalist* commodity production is brought out more clearly. The important fact here is that in the first of these two stages, when competition among capitalists is assumed to exist within each industry but not as yet between different industries, and commodities are assumed still to sell "at their values", differences in the organic composition of capital in different industries are necessarily associated with differences in the rate of profit. It is *not* the case, I believe, as is sometimes suggested, that in this stage of his analysis Marx assumed that the organic composition of capital (and therefore the rate of profit) was everywhere the same.

Second, I would now be rather more critical of certain aspects of Marx's treatment of the quantitative side of the value problem. If Marx in fact meant what I believe he meant by the passages quoted on pp. 159-60 below, he should surely have said so more specifically. His treatment of the skilled-unskilled labour problem (below, pp. 167-73), although suggestive enough, is rather fragmentary and incomplete, and there seems little doubt that he underestimated the importance of the problem. Similarly, his failure to get down to the "transformation problem", after approaching it directly three times (below, pp. 192-3), cannot be entirely ascribed to the fact that he did not live to work over

Volume III again: part of the explanation, I now feel, must be that once again he did not fully appreciate the importance of the problem. It is no answer to these criticisms to say that Marx was more concerned with (and interested in) the qualitative side: possibly he was, but while this may explain his failure to tie up these loose ends on the quantitative side it does not completely excuse it. Any theory of value, whatever else it may be called upon to do at the same time, must surely provide a determinate explanation of the relative equilibrium prices of commodities, and to the extent that it falls short of doing so it must be open to criticism.

Third, I would want to say something more about Marx's application of the theory of value to the problem of the determination of the value of labour-power (below, pp. 183-6). While this part of his analysis may have been perfectly plausible when applied to capitalism in its competitive stage (with which Marx himself was of course primarily concerned), it seems to me to be very much less plausible when applied to contemporary capitalism, particularly in situations where a strong trade union can enforce a rise in wages and a strong monopolistic employer can pass on this increase in wages to consumers by raising prices. I am unconvinced by the attempts of some modern Marxists to get out of this by redefining "the value of labour-power" so that it becomes equivalent, in effect, to any wage which the workers happen to be getting.[1]

Fourth, I would want to say something more about the Classical assumption of constant returns to scale to an industry as a whole (under given technical conditions), which apparently underlay Marx's view that prices were determined independently of demand. The unit price of a commodity, he freely acknowledged, would be determined by "socially-necessary labour"—i.e., by the quantity of labour required under the prevailing technical conditions to produce a unit of it—only if the *total* quantity of labour devoted to the production of the commodity, and therefore the total output of the commodity, corresponded to the "social need" for it. But in his view it did not follow from this that "social need" (or demand, or utility) entered into the determination of unit prices, because he assumed that when "social need" changed, and output was appropriately adjusted, there would be no change in "socially-necessary labour" as defined above and therefore no change in the unit price (below, pp. 178-9; and cf. also pp. 35, 74, and 162). The question is simply whether the latter assumption corresponds

[1] Cf. my *Economics and Ideology*, pp. 118-19.

closely enough to reality. If it does, well and good; but if it does not, what should one do about it? Should one argue that although "socially-necessary labour" may in fact vary with demand, there is still some fundamental sense in which it can be said to *determine* prices at any given level of demand? Or should one grasp the nettle and bring demand specifically into the picture? I shall be saying a little more about this problem below.

Fifth and finally, I would want to say quite a lot more about the so-called "transformation problem", partly because (like Marx himself) I tended to underestimate its importance, and partly because a number of interesting new contributions have been made in this field since I wrote my book. Since some of the points which have arisen in the course of the recent discussions are very relevant to the question of what present-day Marxists ought to do about the labour theory of value, it may be useful if I try to summarise the basic issues in a way which will make them as accessible as possible to the non-mathematical reader.[1]

Let us start again, then, more or less from the beginning, with the following very simple value schema in three departments:

$$
\begin{array}{ccccc}
 & c & v & s & a \\
\text{I} & 20 + 80 + 80 & = & 180 \\
\text{II} & 50 + 50 + 50 & = & 150 \\
\text{III} & 80 + 20 + 20 & = & 120 \\
\end{array}
$$

Here c, v, and s have their usual meanings; and a represents simply $c + v + s$ — i.e., the total amount of past and present labour embodied in the output of the department or industry concerned. As usual, the exploitation ratio $\left(\dfrac{s}{v}\right)$ is assumed to be the same ($= 1$ in this illustration) in each industry; but the organic composition of capital $\left(\dfrac{c}{v}\right)$ is assumed to be different in each, being lower than, equal to, and higher than the "social average" in industries I, II, and III respectively.

Marx's method of transforming the values into prices was to share

---

[1] I shall assume in what follows that the reader has already had a look at the account on pp. 193-7 below, and that he therefore understands the general nature of the transformation problem and the meaning of the main symbols usually employed in its solution. In the new exposition which follows in this introduction, however, it will be convenient to use the symbols p_1, p_2, and p_3 for the price-value coefficients instead of (as in the text of the book) x, y, and z.

out the total amount of surplus value produced in the economy (150 in our example) among the three industries, in accordance with the ratio which the capital employed in each industry $(c + v)$ bore to the total capital employed in the economy as a whole $[\Sigma(c + v)]$. In the present illustration, since the ratio $\dfrac{c + v}{\Sigma(c + v)}$ is in each case equal to $\frac{1}{3}$, each industry receives $\frac{1}{3}$ of the total amount of surplus value—i.e., 50—in the form of profit. This 50 profit is added to the 100 capital employed in each industry to form, in each case, a "price of production" of 150. Thus the equilibrium price of the product of industry I turns out to be $\frac{5}{6}$ of its value; that of the product of industry II to be equal to its value; and that of the product of industry III to be $1\frac{1}{4}$ times its value. These prices bring the *rate* of profit in each industry out at $\frac{1}{2}$ (i.e., 50%).

In order to link this up with the subsequent work we shall be discussing, let us describe this operation in a rather different way. What Marx *in effect* did, we could perhaps say, was to set up and solve a system of simultaneous equations of the following general form:

$$c_1 + v_1 + r(c_1 + v_1) = a_1 p_1 \ \ldots \ (1)$$
$$c_2 + v_2 + r(c_2 + v_2) = a_2 p_2 \ \ldots \ (2)$$
$$c_3 + v_3 + r(c_3 + v_3) = a_3 p_3 \ \ldots \ (3)$$
$$r[\Sigma(c + v)] = E(\Sigma v) \ \ldots \ (4)$$

Here the subscripts 1, 2, and 3 relate to the three industries I, II, and III respectively; p_1, p_2, and p_3 are the coefficients by which a_1, a_2, and a_3 have to be respectively multiplied in order to transform them into the appropriate prices of production; r is the rate of profit, assumed to be the same in each industry; and E is the uniform exploitation ratio $\dfrac{s}{v}$. Equations (1), (2), and (3) represent the original value schema in its "transformed" price form; and equation (4) expresses the condition that the sum of the profits should be equal to the sum of the surplus values. There are four unknown quantities—p_1, p_2, p_3, and r; and on the basis of our four equations we can readily obtain solutions for them in terms of the known quantitites—the c's, the v's, the a's, and E. From equation (4), the rate of profit r is obviously equal to $\dfrac{E(\Sigma v)}{\Sigma(c + v)}$; and in the case of any particular industry—let us call it industry "j"—

$$p_j = \frac{(c_j + v_j)\left[1 + \dfrac{E\,(\Sigma v)}{\Sigma\,(c + v)}\right]}{a_j}$$

Substituting the values for the c's, the v's, the a's, and E in our original numerical illustration, we naturally get the same results as we did before: p_1 works out at $\frac{5}{6}$, p_2 at 1, p_3 at $1\frac{1}{4}$, and r at $\frac{1}{2}$ (i.e., 50%).

If we had had only equations (1), (2) , and (3) at our disposal, the best we could have done would have been to obtain a solution for the *ratio* of the three p's—i.e., for $p_1 : p_2 : p_3$. In order to obtain a solution for p_1, p_2, and p_3 in absolute rather than relative terms, and also a solution for r, we clearly need a fourth equation. Marx's equation (4), expressing the condition that the sum of the profits should be equal to the sum of the surplus values, is quite adequate for this purpose, at any rate from a formal point of view. And *in the present case* it would have amounted to exactly the same thing if we had used instead of this an equation expressing the condition that the sum of the prices should be equal to the sum of the values, since this would merely have involved adding the same quantity—$\Sigma\,(c + v)$—to both sides of (4).

To make the meaning of the solution clearer, and to pave the way for what follows, it may be useful at this stage to bring money into the picture. To say that the price of the output of industry I is $\frac{5}{6}$ of its "value"—i.e., $\frac{5}{6}$ of the total amount of labour-time embodied in it— appears at first sight to be meaningless, since prices are customarily expressed in terms of money, and not of labour-time. To give meaning to it, let us begin by assuming that before the transformation, when all commodities exchanged strictly in accordance with the quantities of labour embodied in them, they were always bought and sold for some given sum of money—£2, say—per unit of the labour-time of which they were the product. The application of the three coefficients $\frac{5}{6}$, 1, and $1\frac{1}{4}$ to the respective values of our three products, it may be argued, will then yield their prices in terms of this given sum of money. Thus the money price of output I will be $\frac{5}{6}$.180.£2 $(=£300)$; of output II, 1.150.£2 $(=£300)$; and of output III, $1\frac{1}{4}$.120.£2 $(=£300)$.[1]

This method is simple enough, but since it begs a number of questions it may be thought preferable to bring money into the picture in a different way—by assuming that it is one of the commodities included in our basic schema. Let us assume, for example, that the

---

[1] If we did not have a fourth equation, and therefore knew only that the *ratio* of the three coefficients was $\frac{5}{6} : 1 : 1\frac{1}{4}$, the three prices would obviously be indeterminate.

commodity gold, which we suppose to be the sole monetary medium, is produced by industry III, and that each unit of labour-time (past and present) employed in this industry produces, say, three gold sovereigns. The money price of the total output of industry III will then be £360, and this price will clearly be the same both before and after the transformation. Suppose, then, that for equation (4) in our system we substitute

$$p_3 = 1$$

The system will once again be determinate, and solutions for r, p_1, and p_2 can readily be obtained. In our example, r will be $\frac{1}{5}$ (i.e., 20%), p_1 will be $\frac{2}{3}$, and p_2 will be $\frac{4}{5}$. The application of the three coefficients $\frac{2}{3}$, $\frac{4}{5}$, and 1 to the respective values of the three products will then give us their prices in terms of the sum of money represented by the product of one unit of labour-time in the gold-producing industry. Thus the money price of output I will be $\frac{2}{3}$.180.£3 ($=£360$); of output II, $\frac{4}{5}$.150.£3 ($=£360$); and of output III, 1.120.£3 ($=£360$).[1]

Bearing this in mind, let us now pass to the "transformation problem" proper, which arises because Marx's method transforms only the values of *output* into prices, leaving the elements of *input* in unchanged value terms. This is clearly inadequate. Suppose, for example, that we assumed that industry I produced capital goods, industry II workers' consumption goods, and industry III capitalists' consumption goods. This would mean that the coefficient p_1, applied in Marx's method only to the output a_1, would also have to be applied to c_1, c_2, and c_3; and that the coefficient p_2, applied in Marx's method only to the output a_2, would also have to be applied to v_1, v_2, and v_3. The main question originally raised about this by certain critics of Marx was whether, under such circumstances, the necessary transformation could in fact be carried out—i.e., whether the relevant relations and conditions could be expressed in the form of an equational system which was mathematically determinate.

The simplest way of showing that they can in fact be so expressed is to begin with a "transformed" schema consisting of the three following equations:

---

[1] If we had assumed that industry II (the one with an organic composition equal to the social average) was the gold-producing industry, making $p_2 = 1$ instead of p_3, the three coefficients would of course work out at $\frac{5}{6}$, 1, and $1\frac{1}{4}$, as they did before, and the money price in each case would work out at £450.

$$c_1p_1 + v_1p_2 + r(c_1p_1 + v_1p_2) = a_1p_1 \dots (1A)$$
$$c_2p_1 + v_2p_2 + r(c_2p_1 + v_2p_2) = a_2p_2 \dots (2A)$$
$$c_3p_1 + v_3p_2 + r(c_3p_1 + v_3p_2) = a_3p_3 \dots (3A)$$

Comparing these equations with (1), (2), and (3) on p. xix above, we see that the coefficient p_1 has now been duly applied not only to a_1 but also to the three c's, and that the coefficient p_2 has been similarly applied not only to a_2 but also to the three v's.[1] Since there are four unknowns (p_1, p_2, p_3, and r), these three equations alone do not get us very far: it is easy to show that they enable us to find r, and the ratio $p_1{:}p_2$, but nothing more. To make the system fully determinate, we need, as before, a fourth equation. Now there are, as we have already seen, three possible candidates here:

(i) $r[\Sigma(c + v)] = E(\Sigma v)$

(expressing the condition that the sum of the profits should be equal to the sum of the surplus values[2])

(ii) $a_1p_1 + a_2p_2 + a_3p_3 = a_1 + a_2 + a_3$

(expressing the condition that the sum of the prices should be equal to the sum of the values)[3]

(iii) $p_j = 1$

(expressing the fact that one of the industries—industry "j"—is assumed to be the gold-producing industry)

For fairly obvious reasons, it is no longer a matter of indifference whether we use (i) or (ii): except in special cases, the answers we get will differ according to which of these two we choose.[4] My own feeling is that out of (i), (ii), and (iii) the one Marx himself would have wished to use is (ii); but at any rate from a formal point of view any one of the three is just as good as any other. Whichever we choose, we will be able to get determinate solutions for the unknowns, although the relevant formulae will naturally be much more complex than those on pp. xix-xx above.

[1] The first to appreciate that the basic equations could be framed in this relatively simple form was Winternitz, in his June 1948 *Economic Journal* article. Cf. below, p. 196, where (as I should have explained more clearly) Winternitz's S_1, S_2, and S_3 in the price schema represent the profits. Winternitz's contribution might not have been possible without the pioneering efforts of Bortkiewicz, of which I perhaps tended to be too critical in my account (see below, p. 196).

[2] The c's and v's on the left-hand side of the equation will now of course have to be expressed in *price* terms.

[3] This is the one which Winternitz used in his solution.

[4] Or, to put the same point in another way, it is now impossible (except in special cases) to obtain a solution in which the sum of the profits is equal to the sum of the surplus values *and* (at the same time) the sum of the prices is equal to the sum of the values.

Once this method of solution had been propounded, the question of its generality was bound to arise. Why should the number of industries in our schema be restricted to three? And why should it be assumed that the ultimate use of each product in the economy was invariable and predetermined by its industry of origin? Francis Seton, in a justly famous article in the *Review of Economic Studies* for June 1957, showed that "the most general n-fold subdivision of the economy, in which each product may be distributed among *several* or *all* possible uses is equally acceptable—and easily handled—as a premiss for the required proof" (*op. cit.*, p. 150). Seton began by representing the structure of the economy in an ingenious schema (in value terms), similar to the well-known Leontief input-output matrix, and then showed in effect that this system of value flows could be uniquely transformed into price terms—provided, of course, that the physical amounts of each input which entered into the production of each output were assumed to be known, and provided also (if one wished to determine the *absolute* prices, as distinct from the price *ratios*) that some "postulate of invariance" was chosen. What the latter condition amounts to is that some aggregate or characteristic of the value system which is to remain invariant to the transformation into prices has to be selected. This "postulate of invariance" plays the same kind of role in Seton's solution as the "fourth equation" plays in the other two solutions we have discussed, and may be chosen from the same three candidates as before (above, p. xxii). Since, according to Seton, there is no objective reason for selecting any one of these candidates rather than any other, the solution to that extent falls short of complete determinacy, but it is nevertheless quite adequate to provide an affirmative answer to the particular question originally raised by the critics of Marx.

But this, unfortunately, is not the end of the matter, as a number of post-Seton contributions (notably an article by Professor Samuelson in the *Journal of Economic Literature* for June 1971)[1] have clearly demonstrated. The question now at issue, speaking very broadly, is this: *what happens to the labour theory of value* when it has been "rescued" from its critics in the manner elaborated for us by Winternitz and Seton? Is it still legitimate for a modern Marxist to use a model which starts with values and surplus values, as Marx's did? And even if it is formally legitimate, is it really necessary? Could he not just as well

---

[1] This article contains an exhaustive bibliography covering all the recent contributions to the debate.

use a model which started with prices and profits—assuming of course that he could find one which allowed him to lay due emphasis on those social and economic relationships which as a Marxist he considered important? Or could he perhaps use a model which started with neither prices nor values, but with physical commodities?

In order to deal with these problems, let us first ask ourselves why it was, exactly, that Marx started with values and surplus values and then "transformed" these (in the third stage of his analysis) into prices and profits. To a non-Marxist economist, unaccustomed to the idea that a theory of value may be given qualitative as well as quantitative tasks to perform, Marx's procedure is bound to appear quite irrational. Since from a formal point of view one could just as readily start with prices and profits and "transform" them back into Marxian values and surplus values, what justification is there for doing the job in the reverse direction—or, indeed, for doing it at all?[1]

Marx felt himself justified in tackling the problem in the way he did for two closely associated reasons. In the first place, as we have already seen (above, p. xv), he believed it was important to emphasise that capitalist production was a form of *commodity* production. The first distinguishing characteristic of capitalism, Marx wrote, is "the fact that being a commodity is the dominant and determining characteristic of its products".[2] One's analysis ought therefore to begin with the commodity as such, and then proceed from this to the "capitalistically modified" commodity—this logical transition being regarded as the "corrected mirror-image" of a historical transition from simple commodity production to capitalist commodity production. Thus, since the qualitative task of the labour theory was to show how relations of exchange were determined by relations of production, one ought to begin by showing how the broad relations between men as producers of commodities determined exchange relations under simple commodity production (Stage 1—values). One should then proceed to show how this process of determination was modified as a result of the emergence of capitalist relations of production. Since the emergence of these relations was primarily dependent upon the emergence of labour-power as a commodity, and since the labour-capital relation constituted the essence of capitalism, one should go on next to analyse the latter relation as such (Stage 2—values and surplus values), in abstraction from certain market phenomena, belonging historically to a later period, which disguised the fundamentally exploitative character

---

[1] Cf. Samuelson, *op. cit.*, pp. 416-17.   [2] *Capital*, Vol. III, p. 857.

of this relation. Eventually, however, these market phenomena must obviously be brought into the picture, and one should then (but only then) proceed to Stage 3—prices and profits.

In the second place, Marx was very much concerned to combat what he called the "illusions created by competition", and in particular the idea that "wages, profit and rent are three independent magnitudes of value, whose total magnitude produces, limits and determines the magnitude of the commodity-value."[1] Again and again Marx went out of his way to attack the then-prevalent notion that it was sufficient to say that the levels of wages, profit, and rent were determined "by competition", or "by supply and demand". There must surely be postulated, he believed, some prior concrete magnitude, or set of magnitudes, which as it were preceded these class incomes and limited their total sum. This prior concrete magnitude, he argued, could only be constituted of the *value* of commodities.[2] Given the value of the finished commodities produced in the economy, and given the value of the commodities used up as means of production in order to produce them, the limit of the sum of class incomes was determined by the difference between these two given quantities of value. If the level of the average wage were taken as given, therefore, the limit of the sum of all other class incomes was necessarily determined. Thus although competition certainly brought about an average rate of profit on capital, competition did not *create* profit: the average had to be an average of *something*, and the magnitude of this "something"—aggregate surplus value—was independent of competition. Once again, therefore, it appeared that the proper order of treatment was to go from Stage 1 (values) to Stage 2 (values and surplus values), and from there to Stage 3 (prices and profits).

Given Marx's particular preoccupations, his view as to the role or roles which ought to be assigned to a theory of value, and the economic and mathematical techniques which were available to him, this way of tackling the problem still seems to me to be perfectly defensible. With the final solution of the transformation problem, however, some of Marx's particular propositions in Volume III of *Capital* become more vulnerable to criticism than they were before, while at the same time certain new perspectives for an alternative approach begin to open up.

[1] *Capital*, Vol. III, p. 841.
[2] Cf. *Capital*, Vol. III, p. 841: "In reality, the commodity-value is the magnitude which precedes the sum of the total values of wages, profit and rent, regardless of the relative magnitudes of the latter."

The point is that the theory of price (and income) determination with which we finish up at the end of the transformation process differs in certain very important respects from the one with which we started. In the value schema of Stage 2, the exchange relation between any pair of commodities A and B appears as a direct reflection of the production relation between the producers of A and B respectively, and is quantitatively determined in accordance with the respective amounts of labour embodied by these producers in their commodities. The relative prices of the two commodities depend solely on the conditions of production in the two industries concerned: given the level of wages and the exploitation ratio, nothing which happens anywhere else in the economy can affect these prices at all, and it is quite plausible to think of the level of profit in each industry as being limited by—and in a sense determined subsequent to—the price of its product. With the solution of the transformation problem in Stage 3, however, we arrive at a situation in which the relative prices of any pair of commodities can and will be affected, often in a substantial way, by things which happen elsewhere in the economy, and in which the overall pattern of relative prices and the average rate of profit are mutually and simultaneously determined. Marxian "values" can still be spoken of, if one wishes, as the "ultimate determinant" of prices, but only in the sense that the known quantities in the equations are expressed (or expressible) in terms of embodied labour—a sense which is rather more attenuated than that implied in Marx's own statement to the effect that "the price of production is not determined by the value of any one commodity alone, but by the aggregate value of all commodities".[1] Then again, Marx's proposition that "the level of the rate of profit is . . . a magnitude held within certain specific limits determined by the value of commodities"[2] now has to be very carefully qualified: in particular, it can *not* be taken to imply either that the sum of the profits will necessarily be equal to the sum of the surplus values (unless of course we decide to use this equality as our "fourth equation"), or that prices and profits are not in actual fact mutually and simultaneously determined.

The question arises, therefore, as to whether the really important things which Marx was trying to say in this part of his analysis can in fact be said in a less exceptionable way through the adoption of an alternative approach. Suppose, for instance, that we accept Marx's basic idea that we ought to start with what I have called above "some

[1] *Capital*, Vol. III, p. 202.   [2] *Ibid.*, Vol. III, p. 838.

prior concrete magnitude", but that we select for this purpose not the *value* of the commodities concerned but *the commodities themselves*. To take a very simple example, let us assume that we have a two-industry capitalist economy (wheat and cloth) in which a total of 100 workers are employed. In the wheat industry, inputs of 10 units of wheat plus 20 units of cloth plus the direct labour of 50 workers produce 100 units of wheat. In the cloth industry, inputs of 20 units of wheat plus 30 units of cloth plus the direct labour of 50 workers produce 100 units of cloth. We start, then, with the following simple schema expressing the conditions of production:

$$10 \text{ wheat} + 20 \text{ cloth} + 50 \text{ labour} \rightarrow 100 \text{ wheat}$$

$$20 \text{ wheat} + 30 \text{ cloth} + 50 \text{ labour} \rightarrow 100 \text{ cloth}$$

Let us assume that the real wage (in commodity terms) per head, which we take as given, is $\frac{2}{5}$ of a unit of wheat plus $\frac{2}{5}$ of a unit of cloth. Total real wages are thus 40 wheat plus 40 cloth. Since the total commodity inputs are 30 wheat and 50 cloth, this means that out of the aggregate output of 100 wheat and 100 cloth, there remains a surplus of 30 wheat and 10 cloth for the capitalists.[1]

Now let us transform this physical schema into *price* terms. Let p_w be the price of a unit of wheat, and p_c the price of a unit of cloth. The wage per head in price terms will then be $\frac{2}{5}(p_w + p_c)$. Let the rate of profit, assumed to be the same in both industries, once again be r. The price schema will then look like this:

$$[10p_w + 20p_c + 50.\tfrac{2}{5}(p_w + p_c)](1 + r) = 100p_w$$
$$[20p_w + 30p_c + 50.\tfrac{2}{5}(p_w + p_c)](1 + r) = 100p_c$$

To determine the three unknowns p_w, p_c, and r we obviously need a third equation, so let us simply assume that cloth is the standard in which prices are expressed and write

$$p_c = 1$$

The system then immediately simplifies to

$$(30p_w + 40)(1 + r) = 100p_w$$
$$(40p_w + 50)(1 + r) = 100$$

[1] It will be noted that if we adopt this method of expressing the conditions of production, it is only the surplus produced *over the economy as a whole* (as distinct from that in each industry) which can be unambiguously defined at this stage.

which yields the solution $p_w = 0.781$, and $r = 0.231$, or 23.1 %. The reader may check if he wishes that with these values for the unknowns everything "adds up" correctly; that the wages paid to the workers are just sufficient to enable them to buy the 40 wheat and 40 cloth which we set aside for them; and that the profits received by the capitalists are just sufficient to enable them to buy the surplus of 30 wheat and 10 cloth.[1]

It will be seen that this kind of model, even in the very simple form in which I have just presented it, bears a strong family resemblance to the "Marxian" transformation models about which I have been speaking above. Both types of model are based on the idea that one's analysis ought to start with some "prior concrete magnitude" which in one way or another limits the levels of the different forms of class income. Both of them, again, embody the notion that an explanation of prices and incomes must be sought primarily in the conditions of production rather than in the conditions of demand. And both of them, finally, involve the mutual and simultaneous determination of prices and profits in an equational system which expresses these conditions of production in price form. In the final section of this introduction I shall elaborate these points, with particular reference to the commodity production model put forward by Sraffa in 1960.

4. The Critique and "Reapplication" of the Marxian Labour Theory: The Sraffa System

Chapter 6 of the book, dealing with the critique of Marx's version of the labour theory, does not seem to me to require very much updating. If one is going to criticise a thinker like Marx, it is even more important than it usually is in such cases that one should do so for the right reasons; and most of the critics whose work is considered in this chapter still appear to me to have done so, in the main, for the wrong reasons. Nor, to my knowledge, have any of the more recent critics of the labour theory—apart from some of those who have concerned themselves with the transformation problem—added anything that is really new to the critiques of their predecessors. Thus, except for the overly apologetic passage on p. 202 and the somewhat tortuous style of parts of my account, there is not much that I would really want to alter substantially today. I would, however, wish to reformulate

---

[1] Since the values for the unknowns are given to three decimal places only, these sums will not of course work out *exactly*.

certain passages (e.g., those on pp. 215 and 229) in which it is suggested that a theory of distribution must be "based on" a theory of value. The implication of some of these statements as they stand is that one must necessarily *start* with some kind of theory of value (preferably the Marxian theory), and then work up from this, as it were, to a theory of distribution. I no longer believe that this is correct. It is certainly true that if one is going to formulate a theory of distribution one must get the relevant prices from *somewhere;* and it is also true, I believe, that one should properly start with *some* kind of "prior concrete magnitude" which limits the levels of class incomes. But, as has been suggested above and will be shown in more detail below, the "prior concrete magnitude" may be conceived in commodity terms rather than in value terms; and it is possible to erect on this basis a theoretical system, not *essentially* different from Marx's, in which prices and incomes are mutually and simultaneously determined.

The only other point of substance in connection with chapter 6 relates to my comments on the critiques of Lange and Schlesinger, which now seem too harsh. Whatever else may be said of their contributions, they did at any rate pose certain important questions which must be answered in one way or another by contemporary Marxists. Lange's critique, for example, raised in a particularly sharp way the question of whether or not an "institutional datum" can in fact be legitimately "tacked on" to a more general theory (p. 229). And Schlesinger's critique, besides identifying correctly the major difficulties inherent in the Marxian labour theory, raised in an equally sharp way the question of whether Marxists today need necessarily try to explain the pattern of prices directly in terms of "the assumed substance of economic relations" (p. 232).

The final chapter of the book, which I optimistically entitled "The Reapplication of the Marxian Labour Theory", begins with a section on the so-called "marginal revolution" which contains a rather important error of interpretation. I am not referring here to anything in the purely historical part of the narrative, which does not seem to me to require very much amendment—although I no longer think that the emphasis placed by the founders of "marginal utility" economics on the scarcity problem was in fact quite as great as I made out, or that it can be quite so easily explained,[1] and I would today wish to bring out more clearly certain positive elements (connected in par-

---

[1] In particular, I think I would wish to wind down the kite which I flew in the first two sentences on p. 249.

ticular with modern welfare economics and the economics of socialism) which were implicit in many of the early "marginalist" formulations.[1] The error I am speaking of is contained in the categorisation
of general equilibrium theory on pp. 253-6. Here I was misled by the
apologetic use to which I conceived that Walras had put his theory,
and by subsequent attempts to express it in a form which would be
independent of any "institutional datum" at all, into treating the
general method which underlay it as if it represented a kind of relapse
into pre-scientific enquiry. To put the point in another way, I tended
to argue as if the only possible type of valid *causal* statement in value
and distribution theory was one which started with some kind of
"independent determining constant" and proceeded from there to the
final conclusion by means of a simple uni-directional "*catena* of causes".
To solve the problem of value by expressing the conditions of the
mutual interdependence of economic quantities in the form of a
mathematically determinate system of equations, I suggested (p. 254),
was to solve it only in a purely formal sense—i.e., not to solve it at all.
As I now see it, however, a system of equations in which the unknowns
one is interested in are mutually and simultaneously determined *may*
be framed in such a way as to involve a clear statement of the order
or direction of determination, and *may* indeed embody a principle
of causation of a higher type than that embodied in a simple "*catena*
of causes". This confession of error, however, should definitely not
be taken to imply that I would wish to alter the general views about
neo-classical value and distribution theory which I expressed, however
imperfectly, in this section of the book.

The next section, on the operation of the "law of value" under
socialism, bears more distinct marks of the particular period in which
it was written, and of the particular controversies which were then
taking place, than any other part of the book. The argument largely
revolves around Stalin's work on *Economic Problems of Socialism in the
U.S.S.R.*, the appearance of which in 1952 had a liberating effect
whose nature and extent it may possibly be difficult for younger
readers to appreciate; and, as the curious and sadly over-optimistic
"stop press" passage on pp. 282-4 will indicate, the writing of the
section was concluded just at the time when the Twentieth Congress
of the Soviet Communist Party, at which Khrushchev's famous
denunciation of Stalin was delivered, appeared to open up a whole

[1] Cf. my article on "Marxism and Marginalism" in *History of Political Economy*, Vol.
4, No. 2, Fall 1972.

number of hopeful new perspectives. Thus this section is the product of a very odd period of history in which, for Marxists, the lid was as it were half off and half on.

For all that, there do not seem to me to be many actual errors of substance in the section as it stands, however "historically relative" its selection of issues and style of writing may appear today. I would not wish to alter the interpretation of Marx's theory on pp. 256-62; and the ideas and events described in the following pages will, I am sure, still be seen as important by future historians of the economic thought of the period. But they are likely to be seen as important in a new context, which is only occasionally hinted at in my account as it stands—that of the gradual disentanglement of the theory of socialist planning from the original Marxian theory of value. There are three more or less separate issues here, which tended to be confused in the controversies described in the book, and which still tend to be confused in similar controversies today.

The first issue relates to the question of the applicability or otherwise of the Marxian (and Classical) concept of "economic law" in a planned, fully socialist economy. For Marx, as for Smith and Ricardo, an "economic law" embodied some kind of objective necessity which imposed itself upon society, as it were, elementally and autonomously —as a by-product, certainly, of the conscious actions of millions of individual economic agents, but not as the result of any preconceived human design. Here I would myself feel that as central planning develops in a socialist economy, the range of applicability of this concept of "economic law" is bound to become smaller and smaller. For example, it will surely become less and less plausible to describe as "economic laws" all those objective economic conditions and relations of which planners must take proper account if they are to avoid getting into a mess. Even now, it seems rather unhelpful to describe as an "economic law" the necessity which planners are under to secure some kind of (unspecified) balance or proportion between different branches of the economy.

The second issue relates to the question of the extent to which prices in a socialist economy are in fact governed by the elemental laws of the market or something akin to them—i.e., broadly, by the "law of value" in Marx's sense. Here I still feel that Stalin's method of approach to this problem—via the original Marxian concept of "commodity production" and the fact of the existence of a collective-farm sector—makes good sense. Certainly, at any rate, it makes much more sense than the method of approach adopted by those more recent writers who in effect say merely that all goods which are bought and sold are "commodities" and that the "law of value" therefore necessarily applies to them.

The third issue relates to the question of whether the "law of value", in some sense or other, is useful as a guide to action when it comes to *fixing* prices in a socialist economy. My own feeling here is that while Marx's generalisations about the "balancing of useful effects and expenditure of labour" are certainly relevant as a framework of discussion in connection with the problem of pricing under socialism, these generalisations have very little to do with his "law of value"—as he himself often enough emphasised. Thus those economists who, like Novozhilov, try to generalise Marx's theory of value so as to make it describe not only how prices are autonomously determined under simple and capitalist commodity production but also how they ought consciously to be fixed under socialism, seem to me to be barking up the wrong tree—however ingenious their efforts may be, and however they may help in making the principles of rational pricing appear more palatable to planners who have been brought up on Marxian theory.

The final section of the book—the one dealing directly with the question of the "reapplication" of the law of value to the monopoly stage of capitalism—now seems to me to be open to criticism, in particular, on the grounds that (apart from one or two incidental remarks) it deals with the question of price-determination more or less in abstraction from the question of income-determination. And although I would still wish to maintain that there is nothing *essentially* wrong with the type of enquiry outlined in this section, I would now wish to urge that this enquiry should be conducted within a rather different conceptual framework—that provided by Sraffa in his *Production of Commodities by Means of Commodities*. In what remains of this introduction, therefore, I shall try to outline the Sraffa system—or, rather, to show how certain basic elements of this system could conceivably be adapted and used by modern Marxists. My demonstration will take the form of a sequence of five Sraffa-type models, linked by a kind of "logical-historical" analysis similar to that employed by Marx.[1]

We begin, as Sraffa himself does, with a model of a very simple

[1] I should emphasise right at the beginning of this exposition, as I shall also do at the end, that my own account differs to a certain extent, both in orientation and in content, from that given by Sraffa himself. In particular, Sraffa in effect skips out my second and third models.

subsistence economy which produces every year just enough to maintain itself. Suppose, for example, that the economy contains only three industries which produce wheat, iron, and pigs respectively. In the wheat industry, 240 quarters of wheat, 12 tons of iron, and 18 pigs are used as inputs to produce an annual output of 450 quarters of wheat. In the iron industry, 90 quarters of wheat, 6 tons of iron, and 12 pigs are used as inputs to produce an annual output of 21 tons of iron. And in the pig industry, 120 quarters of wheat, 3 tons of iron, and 30 pigs are used as inputs to produce an annual output of 60 pigs.[1] The commodity inputs, we assume, include not only means of production but also subsistence goods for the workers who are employed in each industry.[2] Thus we have the following overall input-output situation in physical terms—i.e., in terms of *commodities:*

240 qr. wheat + 12 t. iron + 18 pigs → 450 qr. wheat
90 qr. wheat + 6 t. iron + 12 pigs → 21 t. iron
120 qr. wheat + 3 t. iron + 30 pigs → 60 pigs

It will be noted that the total inputs of the commodities are exactly equal to their total outputs: for example, a total of 450 qr. wheat is used up in production in the three industries taken together, and 450 qr. of wheat is produced each year by the wheat industry.

When exchange begins after the harvest, the wheat producers are going to have 450 qr. wheat in their hands, 240 qr. of which has to be earmarked for the following year's input. Thus if the production of wheat is to continue at the same level in the following year, the *prices* of wheat, iron, and pigs must be such that 210 qr. of wheat will exchange for the other required elements of input—viz., 12 t. iron plus 18 pigs. Similarly, turning to the iron industry, 15 t. iron must be able to exchange for 90 qr. wheat plus 12 pigs; and, turning finally to the pig industry, 30 pigs must be able to exchange for 120 qr. wheat plus 3 t. iron. Thus, if we call the price of a quarter of wheat p_w, the price of a ton of iron p_i, and the price of a pig p_p, we can readily translate our physical schema into price terms as follows:

$$240p_w + 12p_i + 18p_p = 450p_w$$
$$90p_w + 6p_i + 12p_i = 21p_i$$
$$120p_w + 3p_i + 30p_p = 60p_p$$

[1] This model is taken from Sraffa, *op. cit.*, p. 3.
[2] In this respect the model differs from that on p. xxvii above, and also from the fifth model considered on pp. xxxviii–ix below, in both of which the quantity of direct labour employed in each industry is represented explicitly.

It will be clear that the first of these equations in effect expresses the condition that prices must be such that 210 qr. wheat will exchange for 12 t. iron plus 18 pigs; and similarly for the other two equations. There are three unknowns here (p_w, p_i, and p_p), and three equations. But since when we add the equations together the same quantities appear on both sides, any one of the equations can be deduced from the sum of the others, so that we in fact have only two *independent* equations. If we want the *absolute* prices, then, we need a fourth equation. Let us therefore take one of the commodities—iron, say—as the standard of value, and put

$$p_i = 1$$

The system of equations then becomes determinate, and elementary algebra gives us values of 0.1 and 0.5 for p_w and p_p respectively.

In order to generalise this, let us now suppose that there are k industries, whose respective commodities we label "a", "b", ..., "k"; that A is the quantity annually produced of "a", that B is the similar quantity of "b", and so on; that A_a, B_a, ..., K_a are the quantities of "a", "b" ..., "k" used as inputs by the industry producing A, that A_b, B_b, ..., K_b are the corresponding quantities used by the industry producing B, and so on; and that p_a, p_b, ..., p_k are the unit prices for "a", "b", ..., "k" which will enable production to be carried on from year to year at the same level. We will then have the following system of k equations:

$$A_a p_a + B_a p_b + \ldots + K_a p_k = A p_a$$
$$A_b p_a + B_b p_b + \ldots + K_b p_k = B p_b$$
$$\cdots\cdots\cdots\cdots\cdots\cdots\cdots$$
$$A_k p_a + B_k p_b + \ldots + K_k p_k = K p_k$$

Although we have k equations here, there are clearly only $k-1$ *independent* equations, so once again, in order to solve for the k unknowns (p_a, p_b, ..., p_k), we need another equation. As before, let us take one of the commodities—say "j"—as the standard of value, and put

$$p_j = 1$$

The system obviously then becomes determinate.

This *first model*, if one wishes, can be taken to represent an elementary form of Marx's "simple commodity production". And it is fairly easy to show that under the assumed circumstances the prices of the different commodities will, as in Marx's model, be proportionate to the different quantities of labour which have been directly and indirectly employed to produce them. For if, as we are assuming here, there is no form of income other than the "wages" accruing to the direct producers, all input-costs ultimately reduce to "wage"-costs. This means that the price of each end-product will be equal to the sum of its inputs at their "wage"-costs, which implies, if wages per head are assumed to be uniform over the economy as a whole, that price ratios will be equal to embodied labour ratios.[1]

Another point of some importance should be noted before we proceed to the second model. Sraffa is primarily concerned in his book with the analysis of the properties of an economic system in which production continues year after year without any change in the scale of any industry or in the proportions in which inputs are combined to produce its product.[2] Thus the prices in the model we have just considered can be regarded as springing directly and exclusively from what Sraffa calls "the methods of production and productive consumption", or, for short, *"the methods of production".*[3] If, however, one were concerned with the analysis of a more dynamic economy in which changes in scale were frequently taking place, and if these changes in scale were associated with significant changes in the proportions in which inputs were combined (i.e., if returns to scale were not constant), it would not of course be possible any longer to abstract from demand in this way.

Let us now pass to the second "logical-historical" stage of our analysis, and to the *second model.* Suppose that the economy we have been considering becomes capable of producing more than the minimum necessary for replacement. For example, starting from the three-industry case which we considered on p. xxxiii above, suppose that the situation changes to the following:

240 qr. wheat + 12 t. iron + 18 pigs → 600 qr. wheat.
90 qr. wheat + 6 t. iron + 12 pigs → 31 t. iron.
120 qr. wheat + 3 t. iron + 30 pigs → 80 pigs.

There is now a surplus of 150 qr. wheat, 10 t. iron, and 20 pigs, over and above what Ricardo called "the absolutely necessary expenses of

---

[1] For a simple illustration, see my *Economics and Ideology*, p. 167, footnote 20. For a more rigorous demonstration, see Sraffa, *op. cit.*, pp. 12 and 89.
[2] Sraffa, *op. cit.*, p. v.   [3] *Ibid.*, p. 3.

production", which is available for distribution. Let us assume that there is as yet no capitalist class in existence, so that this surplus is shared out among the direct producers, whose "wages" are now raised above the subsistence level which we supposed them to be at in the first model. If there are, say, 100 direct producers in all, each will receive an addition of $1\frac{1}{2}$ qr. wheat plus $\frac{1}{10}$ t. iron plus $\frac{1}{5}$ of a pig to his former subsistence "wage". We may now make out a new schema in physical terms, adding this accretion to real "wages" to the appropriate items on the left-hand side. If 40 of the producers are employed in the wheat industry, 30 in the iron industry, and 30 in the pig industry, the amended schema will be as follows:

$$300 \text{ qr. wheat} + 16 \text{ t. iron} + 26 \text{ pigs} \rightarrow 600 \text{ qr. wheat}$$
$$135 \text{ qr. wheat} + 9 \text{ t. iron} + 18 \text{ pigs} \rightarrow 31 \text{ t. iron}$$
$$165 \text{ qr. wheat} + 6 \text{ t. iron} + 36 \text{ pigs} \rightarrow 80 \text{ pigs}$$

With this change in the "methods of production", a new set of prices will now emerge. If we translate the physical schema into price terms, and, as before, put $p_i = 1$,[1] we will get values of 0.097 and 0.498 for p_w and p_p respectively. The new price ratios will still be equal to the (new) embodied labour ratios, for the same reason as before. If we wish, we can take this second model as representing a more advanced form of Marx's "simple commodity production", alluded to as a possibility by Marx himself in a passage in Volume III of *Capital*,[2] in which the workers produce a surplus which they themselves receive. The "rate of profit"—i.e., the ratio of this surplus to the "capital" employed—will under such circumstances normally be different in the case of each industry, but since the workers will still think of their income as a reward for their labour rather than as a return on the "capital" they happen to employ, this difference in the "rate of profit" will, as Marx puts it, be "immaterial", and there will be no tendency for the difference in the "rate of profit" to be ironed out through the migration of "capital" from one industry to another.

Since the generalisation of this model involves nothing new, we can proceed at once to the *third model*, in which we assume that a class of capitalists appears for the first time on the historical scene.

---

[1] We need a fourth equation here because, as before, the same quantitites appear on both sides when we add the equations together, so that there are in fact only two *independent* equations.

[2] Pp. 174-6.

Let us suppose that three separate groups of capitalists emerge, each taking over one of the three industries, operating it as a capitalist enterprise, reducing the wages of the direct producers to their former subsistence level, and appropriating the whole of the surplus as profit.[1] If we imagine that we are examining the *immediate* effects of this take-over—i.e., the effects which are experienced *before* competition between the three groups of capitalists and the migration of capital from one industry to another equalise the rate of profit on capital— it is easy to see that there will be no alteration whatever in the relevant quantities in the physical schema of our second model. The wage element in the inputs on the left-hand side will certainly be reduced to its former level, but this will be exactly balanced by the inclusion of the new profit element. Thus the prices of the commodities will remain the same as before, and price ratios will still be equal to em- bodied labour ratios. The rate of profit, however, will differ from one industry to another. If we wish, we can regard this model as analogous to that used by Marx in Stage 2 of his analysis, where commodities are assumed to sell "at their values" and the rate of exploitation is assumed to be the same in each industry, but where the rate of profit (except in the special case in which all capitals are of the same organic composition) differs from one industry to another.

We may now proceed immediately to the *fourth model*, in which we assume that as a result of competition between the three groups of capitalists, and the consequent migration of capital from one industry to another, the rate of profit is equalised over the economy as a whole. We now have to revert to the physical schema on p. xxxv above. If we again call the rate of profit r, this schema in price terms will appear as follows:

$$(240p_w + 12p_i + 18p_p)(1 + r) = 600p_w$$
$$(\ 90p_w + \ 6p_i + 12p_p)(1 + r) = \ 31p_i$$
$$(120p_w + \ 3p_i + 30p_p)(1 + r) = \ 80p_p$$

The three equations are now all independent, but since we have four unkowns (p_w, p_i, p_p, and r) to be determined, instead of only three as

[1] We assume, as Marx did at the corresponding point in his analysis, that capital subordinates labour on the basis of the technical conditions in which it finds it, without immediately changing the mode of production (cf. *Capital*, Vol. I, pp. 184 and 310). We also assume, rather less realistically, that in the first instance capitalists in each industry reckon on receiving as profit, in real terms, exactly what they have caused the workers *in that industry* to lose. In the wheat industry, for example, they reckon on receiving enough profit to enable them to purchase 60 qr. wheat plus 4 t. iron plus 8 pigs.

before, we once again need a fourth equation. Putting $p_i = 1$ as we previously did, the system immediately becomes determinate, and values of 0.11, 0.56, and 0.36 ($= 36\%$) for p_w, p_p, and r are fairly readily obtained. The new price ratios, of course, now diverge from the embodied labour ratios, but they can still be said to be determined by the fundamental methods or conditions of production.

To generalise this, we use our previous notation and arrive at the following system of k equations:[1]

$$(A_a p_a + B_a p_b + \ldots + K_a p_k)(1 + r) = A p_a$$
$$(A_b p_a + B_b p_b + \ldots + K_b p_k)(1 + r) = B p_b$$
$$\ldots \ldots \ldots \ldots \ldots \ldots \ldots \ldots \ldots$$
$$(A_k p_a + B_k p_b + \ldots + K_k p_k)(1 + r) = K p_k$$

All the k equations are independent, and, if we take one of the commodities ("j") as the standard of value and put $p_j = 1$ as before, we have enough equations to determine the $k-1$ unknown prices and the rate of profit r. It will be clear that the transition from the previous model to this one is analogous to the transition involved in the solution of the Marxian "transformation problem".

We pass now finally to the *fifth model*, in which we assume that the workers have combined and forced the capitalists to return to them some of the surplus. Wages will now include not only what Sraffa calls "the ever-present element of subsistence"[2] (which is constant), but also a share of the surplus product (which is variable).[3] Analytically speaking, what ought one to do about this? The most appropriate thing to do, Sraffa suggests,[4] would be to separate the wage into its two component parts, continuing to treat the commodities required for the subsistence of the workers as means of production along with the seed, iron, etc., and treating the variable element in the wage as part of the surplus product of the system. Sraffa, however, largely for the sake of convenience,[5] treats the *whole* of the wage as variable—i.e., as part of the surplus product. This means that the quantity of labour employed in each industry now has to be represented explicitly in our

[1] Sraffa, *op. cit.*, pp. 6–7.   [2] *Ibid.*, p. 9.
[3] In his discussion of "The General Law of Capitalist Accumulation" in Volume I of *Capital*, Marx in one place envisages a situation in which the demand for labourers exceeds the supply, so that "a larger part of their own surplus-product . . . comes back to them in the shape of means of payment" (p. 618).
[4] *Op cit.*, pp. 9–10.
[5] And also, as he says (p. 10), in order to "refrain . . . from tampering with the traditional wage concept"—i.e., the concept of the wage as a variable share in "value added".

statement of the conditions of production,[1] taking the place of the corresponding quantities of subsistence goods in our previous statements, and that profits have to be reckoned as a percentage of the total of the prices of the means of production *excluding wages*.[2] If we use the symbols L_a, L_b, . . ., L_k for the annual quantities of direct labour employed in the industries producing A, B, . . ., K, and the symbol w for the wage per unit of labour (assumed to be the same in all industries), the system of equations in generalised form will appear as follows:[3]

$$(A_a p_a + B_a p_b + \ldots + K_a p_k)(1 + r) + L_a w = A p_a$$
$$(A_b p_a + B_b p_b + \ldots + K_b p_k)(1 + r) + L_b w = B p_b$$
$$\cdots\cdots\cdots\cdots\cdots\cdots\cdots\cdots\cdots\cdots\cdots\cdots$$
$$(A_k p_a + B_k p_b + \ldots + K_k p_k)(1 + r) + L_k w = K p_k$$

Here there are k independent equations, and $k + 2$ unknowns (the k prices, r, and w). Instead of, as before, taking one of the commodities as the standard of value and setting its price equal to unity, Sraffa (again for the sake of convenience) takes the total surplus or net product of the system as the standard and sets *its* price equal to unity, so that instead of the familiar additional equation $p_j = 1$ we have the following:[4]

$$[A - (A_a + A_b + \ldots + A_k)]p_a + [B - (B_a + B_b + \ldots + B_k)]p_b + \ldots + [K - (K_a + K_b + \ldots + K_k)]p_k = 1$$

We now have $k + 1$ independent equations, but since there are $k + 2$ unknowns the system is still not determinate. The important point, however, is that if either w or r is known, the system will immediately become determinate. In particular, if we know what the wage (w) is, the rate of profit and all the prices will be determined.

Before going on to discuss the implications of this series of five models, I should once again make it clear, as I have already done above,[5] that this account diverges somewhat from Sraffa's. The historical side of my "logical-historical" analysis is something of a gloss on Sraffa; and I have included the second and third models (which do not appear in Sraffa's analysis) only in order to show how closely a sequence of Sraffa-type models may be made to mirror

---

[1] As it was in the model on p. xxvii above.
[2] Sraffa emphasises (*op. cit.*, p. 10) that "the discussion which follows can easily be adapted to the more appropriate, if unconventional, interpretation of the wage suggested above".
[3] *Op cit.*, p. 11.   [4] *Op. cit.*, p. 11.   [5] P. xxxii, footnote.

Marx's own sequence. Marx, of course, did not deal (except in occasional incidental remarks) with the situation represented in the fifth model; but the first and second models, taken together, can be regarded as corresponding to Marx's analysis of simple commodity production (Stage 1), the third model to his preliminary analysis of the origin and appropriation of surplus value (Stage 2), and the fourth model to his analysis of prices and profits (Stage 3). What I have tried to do, in effect, is to show how a modern Marxist might reformulate and develop Marx's original theory, taking as his "prior concrete magnitude" not the "values" of the commodities concerned but the commodities themselves.

Sraffa himself proceeds to develop the analysis, on the basis of the fifth model described above, by giving the wage (w) successive values from 1 to 0—a wage of 1 representing a situation in which *all* the net product goes to labour (i.e., a situation in which there is no class of capitalists and no profit), and a wage of 0 representing the other extreme in which *none* of the net product goes to labour (i.e., a situation in which there is a class of capitalists which manages to secure *all* the net product for itself in the form of profit).[1] Sraffa's main task here is to demonstrate what happens to prices and the rate of profit as the wage is reduced from 1 to 0. The key to the movement of prices lies here, as Ricardo was the first to make clear,[2] in "the inequality of the proportions in which labour and means of production are employed in the various industries".[3] As an integral part of this analysis, Sraffa formulates the notion of a "standard commodity" (to take the place of the one hitherto arbitrarily chosen as a standard) which would not rise or fall in value relative to any other commodity when wages rose and fell, and which would therefore be capable of "isolating the price-movements of any other product so that they could be observed as in a vacuum".[4] The details of this ingenious construction need not concern us here, but an interesting analogy between Sraffa's procedure and Marx's in this connection is worth noting. One of the conclusions which Marx drew, on the basis of a model like the one on p. xviii above in which the organic composition of capital in one of the industries is equal to the "social average", was that (when wages were taken as given) the average rate of profit, and therefore the deviations of price ratios from embodied labour ratios in the system as a whole, were

---

[1] These meanings of the two extreme situations follow from the fact that the value of the net product is now being taken as the standard in which the wage, as well as the *k* prices, are expressed.
[2] Cf. below, pp. 103 ff.   [3] Sraffa, *op. cit.*, p. 12.   [4] *Ibid.*, p. 18.

governed by the ratio of direct to indirect labour in this "average" industry. But Marx's conclusion, at best, could only be a provisional and approximate one, since in reaching it he had abstracted from the effect which a change in the wage would have on the prices of the means of production employed in the "average" industry. What Sraffa really does in this part of his analysis is to show that the same results can be achieved, without abstracting from this effect at all, if we substitute his "standard" industry for Marx's industry of average organic composition of capital.[1]

There are a number of other aspects of Sraffa's analysis which ought to be of considerable interest to Marxists—for example, his incorporation of land and rent into the general system; his treatment of "basic" and "non-basic" products, which raises once again the important question, discussed in particular by Bortkiewicz, as to whether the conditions of production of luxury goods enter into the determination of the price-relations of other products and the rate of profit; and above all, perhaps, his exercise in the reduction of the means of production, hitherto expressed in physical terms, to quantities of labour. In the latter connection, he shows in effect that this reduction operation can in fact be performed—enabling us, if we wish, to start with labour instead of with commodities—provided that the labour is *dated* labour, since the dating will clearly affect the rate of profit and therefore the prices of the commodities concerned. And of at least equal interest is the critique of the neo-classical theory of value and distribution which is implied in the system as a whole.[2]

The main difference between Marx's system and the one just outlined lies in the methods they respectively employ to secure determinacy. Marx's Volume I models (corresponding roughly to the first, second, and third models described above) are determinate because with the aid of the labour theory of value determinacy is secured, as it were, in each industry separately. Marx's Volume III model (corresponding to the fourth model described above) is determinate because it involves nothing more than the addition of certain magnitudes which are predetermined in the case of each separate industry and the reallocation of the total of these magnitudes among the different industries in proportions which are also predetermined. Marx was of course aware that there were important interrelation-

---

[1] On this whole question, see my *Economics and Ideology*, pp. 175-8.
[2] On this latter aspect, see Maurice Dobb, "The Sraffa System and Critique of the Neo-Classical Theory of Distribution" (*De Economist*, 118, NR. 4, 1970, pp. 347-62).

ships between elements of input and elements of output over the
economy as a whole—as witness his interest in Quesnay's *Tableau
Économique*, and his Volume II reproduction schemes which constituted
in a sense his own version of the *Tableau*. But he did not hit on the
idea that the postulation of specific input-output interrelationships
could help to make prices and incomes determinate. His Volume III
model, indeed, seems to have been based on the assumption that none
of the commodities concerned entered as inputs into the production
of any of the others. The Marxian "transformation problem", however, as we have seen, cannot be properly solved without the postulation, in one form or another, of specific input-output interrelationships.
And once the "transformation problem" had in fact been solved on
this basis, the idea was bound to arise that this method of helping to
secure determinacy could be applied not only in the final stage of the
analysis but in the earlier stages as well. All of the five Sraffa-type
models described above postulate certain specific, technically fixed,
input-output interrelationships, and all of them involve the mutual
and simultaneous determination of the unknowns on the basis of these
interrelationships.

In all this, it is true, the Marxian "labour theory of value" *as such* is
pushed into the background, in the sense that its specific quantitative
propositions emerge, as it were, only as by-products of the main
analysis. But our Sraffa-type sequence of models does essentially the
same set of jobs which the Marxian labour theory was designed to do;
it starts, as Marx's system did, with a "prior concrete magnitude"
which limits the levels of class incomes; it is based on the same view
about the order and direction of determination of the variables as
Marx's system was; it is just as well suited to the application of a
"logical-historical" method of approach; and it has the great additional
advantage that it contains a built-in solution of the "transformation
problem". And on the qualitative side, it is at least arguable that Sraffa's
procedure reflects the basic idea which Marx was trying to express in
his labour theory—the idea that prices and incomes are ultimately
determined by relations of production—more clearly and effectively
than Marx's own procedure did.

In connection with the latter point, there is one particular aspect of
Sraffa's system which will no doubt already have struck the reader
and which requires comment. It relates to the fact that in the fifth
model, where it is assumed that wages include not only "the ever-
present element of subsistence" but also a variable share of the surplus

product, the system is indeterminate. So far as the earlier models are concerned, no really serious difficulties about the determinacy of class incomes are likely to arise. In the first model, "wages" are necessarily confined to subsistence by virtue of the relatively primitive economic conditions which are postulated. In the second model, "wages" necessarily absorb the whole of the surplus because there is assumed to be no capitalist class to appropriate it. In the third and fourth models, wages can reasonably be assumed to be kept at subsistence level by the operation of some kind of "Marxian" mechanism, and the *origin* of "surplus value" (or profit) can be plausibly explained on that basis. In the fifth model, however, the division of class incomes, at least as Sraffa's system stands, is left indeterminate—a fact which may be regarded by some as constituting a defect, but which should more properly be regarded, I think, as providing an opportunity and a challenge. What is required, in order to complete the system, is some kind of ordered explanation of the factors determining the division of class incomes in the monopoly stage of capitalism. Here a whole host of difficult problems arises which I am not competent even to formulate, let alone to resolve. But the main *methodological* questions involved, I suppose, relate to (*a*) the choice between wages and profits as the independent variable; (*b*) the *scope* of the explanation—i.e., whether it is to be regarded as something complete in itself or merely as something which is as it were superadded to Marx's theory; and (*c*) the manner in which the explanation can be made to reflect—as Marx himself would have insisted—the socio-economic relations characteristic of the new stage.

In conclusion, two other points which may be of some importance should be mentioned. The first is related to the difference described above (pp. v–vi) between Smith's model of the economic system and Turgot's—the point being, as I there said, that Marx's procedure in this respect was modelled on Smith's rather than on Turgot's. When one reads what Marx has to say in *Capital* about the relation between profit on the one hand and rent and interest on the other, one is struck by the fewness of the occasions on which he alludes even indirectly to the mobility of capital between its "active" and "passive" uses. The concept of the mutual and simultaneous determination of profit, rent, and interest is virtually non-existent, and one is never quite sure why, exactly, the rate of profit is not reduced by competition to the level of the rate of interest (or to that of the rate of return on capital invested in land-purchase). If this is regarded as an important problem, the only adequate way of dealing with it, from the formal point of view, would be to extend the system of equations, thereby moving rather further towards a general equilibrium system of the Walrasian type.[1]

The second point relates to the question of the constancy or otherwise of returns to scale. The Sraffa system, as we have seen, can provide an excellent framework for the analysis of "such properties of an economic system as do not depend on changes in the scale of production or in the proportions of 'factors' ".[2] If, however, we happen to be interested also in those properties of an economic system which *do* depend on such changes, we would seem to have no option but to extend the system further in order to include a set of demand equations. Such a procedure would not mean selling the pass if "Marxian" factors were clearly postulated as underlying the demand equations, and if the system as a whole were made to embody appropriate indicators of the order of determination of the variables. Here, then, is yet another problem for those who are anxious to use "Marxian" categories and methods of analysis to throw light on the monopoly stage of capitalism. *Hic Rhodus, hic salta*!

---

[1] Sraffa can perhaps be said to have paved the way here by bringing *differential* rent (but not what Marx called "absolute" rent) into his system.

[2] Sraffa, *op.* cit., p. v.

PREFACE

THIS book really owes its origin to a long correspondence on certain matters of economic theory which the author had in 1951 with Mrs. Joan Robinson. In our discussion we found ourselves returning again and again to the question of the validity of the labour theory of value, and it soon became clear that the main hindrance to mutual understanding between us was the wide difference between our respective views on this question. The correspondence ended with each of us giving the other up as more or less hopeless, but I was left with the uncomfortable feeling that my failure to convince Mrs. Robinson that the labour theory was good sense and good science was my fault rather than hers. Surely it must be possible, I thought, to build some sort of bridge between Marxian economists and their non-Marxian colleagues so that the latter can at least be made to see what the former are trying to get at.

This book, then, was originally intended as an attempt to provide such a bridge. I felt that the adoption of a genetical approach to the labour theory might help: if one showed how it had evolved—not only over a historical period but also in the minds of individual economists like Smith, Ricardo and Marx—its general character and the nature of the job it tries to do might emerge rather more clearly. My aim was to try to persuade sincere but sceptical non-Marxian economists that the intellectual quality of the labour theory of value, and indeed of Marx's economic teaching as a whole, had been seriously underestimated by most of those on whose works they had been brought up.

As the book proceeded, however, another aim distinct from though related to this began to come into prominence. It was clearly necessary, if I was to fulfil my task properly, to show not only that the labour theory was good science in Marx's time but also that it is good science today. And this raises certain issues of great importance and difficulty. The point is that capitalism has not stood still since the time when Marx wrote: it has developed into what Marxists call its imperialist or monopoly capitalist stage, in which the economic processes which go on differ in certain important respects from those which went on in the old capitalism which Marx knew and analysed. In the new situation which has arisen, certain long-accepted Marxian economic laws no longer operate, or at least operate in new ways. Marxists argue, however, that monopoly capitalism, even though it differs in this way from the system which existed a century ago, is still capitalism, and that the basic categories of Marx's economic analysis are the key to the proper understanding of the new situation as well as of the old. But we can hardly hope to persuade others that we are right unless we ourselves actually do the job of reapplying these basic categories to the new situation, and deduce the laws of the processes of capitalism in its present stage just as convincingly as Marx did in the case of the stage in which he himself lived. And this is a job whose importance we have been slow to recognise— largely, no doubt, because we have tended to be over-optimistic about the probable duration of the monopoly capitalist period.

Within the limits of the field I had mapped out for myself it was fairly clear what had to be done in this connection. Marx had developed the labour theory of value in the context of a given set of problems and a given stage in the development of capitalism. The essence of what he said had to be disentangled from this context and reapplied to the present-day situation, taking account of everything that was new. It seemed to me that if this could be done in relation to the labour theory of value, which played such a vitally important part in Marx's analysis, the task of reapplying the remaining categories might be made a little easier. This would be so, I thought, even if—as in fact turned out to be the case—I personally was able to do little more than suggest a new conceptual framework within which research into the operation of the law of value in different historical systems, including monopoly capitalism, might profitably proceed.

The result of this is that the book as it now stands is addressed not only to my non-Marxian colleagues but also to those Marxists who are interested in the development and reapplication of the basic Marxian economic categories. My fear, of course, is that in trying to address two different audiences at once I shall succeed in appealing to neither. My hope, however, is that the book may play a small part in helping to usher in a period of coexistence between the two groups, in which accusations of dishonesty and academic incompetence will be replaced by genuine attempts to understand and evaluate one another's point of view, and in which Marxists and non-Marxists will enter into peaceful competition with one another to see who can provide the more accurate and useful analysis of economic reality.

This book has been some time in the making, and the obligations

I have incurred to those of my friends and colleagues who have discussed these problems with me are too many and various to specify in detail. I owe a special debt, however, to Professor A. L. Macfie, whose conversations over the past eight years on certain aspects of the history of economic thought have helped me to surmount many obstacles; and also to Mr. Emile Burns, Mr. Maurice Cornforth, Mr. M. H. Dobb and Mr. John Eaton, who read the book in manuscript and made valuable suggestions for its improvement. My obligation to Mr. Dobb extends far beyond this particular service: his constant interest and encouragement, and the inspiration afforded by his own work in this field, have more than anything else made the writing of this book possible. None of these, of course, must be held responsible for the arguments put forward in this book, or for any errors and mis-interpretations which remain.

I am obliged to the editors of the *Economic Journal, Economica,* the *Review of Economic Studies* and the *Scottish Journal of Political Economy* for permission to reproduce certain passages from articles which have already appeared in these journals.

Finally, I should like to thank my students, both at Glasgow University and elsewhere. If to teach is to learn, to learn is also to teach.

R. L. M.

12th November, 1955

CHAPTER ONE

VALUE THEORY BEFORE ADAM SMITH

ACCORDING to the Classical economists,[1] the main task of value theory was to explain what determined that "power of purchasing other goods" which the possession of a particular commodity normally conveyed to its owner. "Normally" was defined with reference to the prevalence of competition. Under competitive conditions, it was said, and in the long period, commodities "normally" tended to sell at prices roughly equal to their costs of production, including profits at the customary rate, although temporary deviations from this "normal" or "natural" price might be brought about by fluctuations in supply and demand. This "normal" price, equal to costs of production, was regarded as the monetary expression of the *value* of a commodity.

The majority of Western economists today would probably not be prepared to accept this definition of value; but to most of them, particularly if they have been brought up in the Marshallian tradition, it is at least not likely to appear inherently unreasonable. Indeed, so reasonable does it still appear that one is apt to forget that each of the several positions of which it is compounded had to be conquered by the early Classical economists in the face of considerable opposition and confusion. It is the first of the purposes of the present chapter to describe and account for the gradual evolution of this way of looking at value, with particular reference to the century prior to the publication of Adam Smith's *Wealth of Nations*.

What does appear unreasonable to many Western economists is the considerable emphasis which Classical political economy placed on the role of labour in the determination of value, and its stubborn refusal to grant demand and utility the status of determinants. Yet the labour theory of value was not an exotic growth: its development went hand in hand with that of the concepts I have just been

[1] The term "Classical economists", which seems to have been first employed by Marx, is widely used by present-day historians of economic thought, but only rarely in Marx's original sense. In this book it is employed, as it was by Marx, to mean the school of political economy dating from Petty to Ricardo in Britain and from Boisguillebert to Sismondi in France which "investigated the real relations of production in bourgeois society". See Marx's *Critique of Political Economy* (Kerr edn.), p. 56, and *Capital*, Vol. I (Allen & Unwin edn.), p. 53, footnote.

describing. It is the second of the purposes of this chapter to account for the evolution of the outlook which gave rise to the labour theory, and to explain its historical connection with these concepts.

1. *The Canonist Approach to the Value Problem*

Although this chapter will be mainly concerned with value theory in the seventeenth and eighteenth centuries, it is useful to start the story with Aquinas. The particular approach to the problem of value which is revealed in most of the early Canonist writings on the just price has rather more in common with the Classical theory than has the approach generally adopted by the Mercantilists. The reason is, of course, that the Canonists, like the Classical writers, generally attacked the problem of value from the point of view of man's activity as a producer of commodities, whereas the Mercantilists usually attacked it from the point of view of his activity as an exchanger of commodities.

The particular form of production in which Aquinas was predominantly interested was that which was carried on by small independent producers who sold their products on the market and purchased commodities for their own use with the proceeds. The chief problem which concerned the early Canonist writers was so to define the "value" of commodities produced and exchanged in this fashion that any divergence between this value and the actual price received and paid could be clearly disclosed as ethically unjust either to the seller or the buyer. Since the proceeds of the sale of a commodity normally accrued in the first instance to its direct producer, the idea that remuneration should be proportionate to outlay and effort in production (provided that the remuneration was weighted according to status, and provided also that the effort was properly directed) afforded a natural basis for the definition of the just price. The constituent elements of the mediaeval just price were mainly items of producers' cost—notably labour expended, but also risk undertaken, money laid out in the purchase of raw materials, costs of transport, etc.—which required to be adequately compensated for if justice was to be done. These elements in their totality made up the value or real worth of a commodity, which might differ from the subjective estimates of its worth made by either party to the exchange transaction. Generally speaking, the judge of the point of equivalence between cost and reward was conceived to be simply the common agreement or estimation of the community. This criterion, in Aquinas's time, was probably adequate to secure a rough measure of distributive justice, since in a small, static and relatively self-sufficient community the efforts made and expenses incurred by different producers could usually be directly compared.[1]

But another form of exchange was already becoming important in Aquinas's time. In Aquinas's famous discussions on "Fraud Committed in Buying and Selling", the first three of the four sections seem to deal mainly with the obligations of sellers who are also independent producers. But the fourth section deals with the case of those whose activities are directed towards "selling a thing for more than was paid for it", i.e., the traders and merchants.[2] The motives of the merchant are different from those of the small independent producer: he is the harbinger of a new type of economy, although he does not at first regard himself as a revolutionary.[3] It would hardly have been possible for the Canonists to condemn this highly useful form of social activity outright. Aquinas introduces his discussion of this awkward problem by recalling Aristotle's distinction between the "natural" kind of exchange by means of which "one thing is exchanged for another, or things for money to meet the needs of life", and that other kind of exchange by means of which things are exchanged for money "not to meet the needs of life, but to acquire gain". The second kind of exchange, trading, is regarded as being in itself "somewhat dishonourable". But there are at least two ways in which a man who sells a thing for more than he paid for it may escape moral condemnation. First, he may direct his gain to some necessary or honourable end—"as when a man uses moderate gains acquired in trade for the support of his household, or even to help the needy." Second, he may lawfully sell a thing for more than he paid for it if, after having originally bought it without any intention of selling it, he later wishes to sell it, provided that in the meantime "he has improved the thing in some way", or if "the price has changed with a change of place or time", or if risk has been involved in transporting

---

[1] Cf. W. Cunningham, *The Growth of English Industry and Commerce* (5th edn.), Vol. II, p. 461; R. H. Tawney, *Religion and the Rise of Capitalism* (Penguin edn.), p. 49; Rudolf Kaulla, *Theory of the Just Price*, chapter 1; and H. R. Sewall, *The Theory of Value before Adam Smith* (Publications of the American Economic Assn., 3rd Series, Vol. II, No. 3), *passim*. See also below, pp. 295-6.

[2] Cf. H. R. Sewall, *op. cit.*, p. 18.

[3] "Into this world there entered the merchant with whom its revolution was to start. But not as a conscious revolutionary; on the contrary, as flesh of its flesh, bone of its bone. The merchant of the Middle Ages was by no means an individualist; he was essentially a co-operator like all his contemporaries" (*Engels on "Capital"*, pp. 106-7).

the thing from one place to another.[1] In other words, the trader can escape moral condemnation if he behaves as far as possible like a small independent producer. Aquinas's discussion indicates that in his day the trader's activities were already being accepted—even if only reluctantly—as an inevitable feature of economic life. But it also suggests that the gains of the trader had not yet come to be conceived as a completely separate and distinctive category of income, since his receipts could apparently still be plausibly assimilated to those of the peasant and craftsman.

In the last analysis, it was the activities of the trader, hesitantly sanctioned in Aquinas's system, which eventually destroyed that system. The basic economic concepts of the *Summa Theologica* could not hope to survive the great development of internal and external commerce in the later Middle Ages. The just price of a commodity could not be rationally assessed according to Aquinas's principles if its seller came from afar and the cost of producing it was therefore unknown.[2] The story of the gradual decline of the economic theory of early Scholasticism is too familiar to require repetition, and one point alone seems to need emphasis here. The mediaeval concept of the just price gradually lost its power over men's minds as the impersonal and unconscious market took over the task of regulating prices. But the habit of thinking of "value" in terms of producers' cost remained firmly rooted in the consciousness of the direct producers themselves, and was later to prove itself one of the most influential of all the economic legacies left by the Schoolmen.

2. *The Mercantilist Theory of Value*

In the days of the decline of Scholasticism, those who were anxious to develop the just price doctrines so as to take account of the needs of expanding trade and commerce (and in particular the need for the gains of the merchants and traders to be recognised as just) found it necessary to retreat from the producers' cost approach to value towards what may be called the "conventional price" approach. Cases in which it was impossible to reconcile the gains of traders with Aquinas's original formulae must have become more and more common, and under these circumstances it became advisable to demonstrate that the price customarily paid and received—i.e., the conventional price—was just. This could be done, without too much

[1] Quotations from A. E. Monroe, *Early Economic Thought*, pp. 62-4.
[2] Cf. H. R. Sewall, *op. cit.*, p. 122.

damage to Aquinas's basic premises, by arguing that the "value" of a commodity was dependent to some extent upon its utility to the purchaser. If the purchasers of a particular commodity were willing to buy it at a price higher than its producers' cost, this price could then be taken to represent the commodity's worth or "real value" *to them*. A certain amount of attention therefore began to be paid to the subjective valuations of the individual consumer, and the concept of "normal need" upon which the older theory had largely relied began to go out of fashion.[1] Thus the transition to the value theory characteristic of the earlier years of Mercantilism was relatively easy. The later ecclesiastical writers themselves laid the foundations of the structure of ideas which the secular publicists of the Mercantilist era were eventually to erect.

It is difficult, however, to make any useful generalisations about the ideas on value which were compounded in the great crucible of the sixteenth and early seventeenth centuries, following on the swift increase in the "extent of the market" after 1492. Any such generalisations would have to be wide enough to cover not only a great number of writers (few of whom were directly concerned to elaborate a theory of value), but also a number of different countries at varying stages of social and economic development. It does seem possible, however, to distinguish three important notions regarding price and value which began to grow in popularity about this time. In the first place, the "value" (or, sometimes, "natural value") of a commodity came to be widely identified with its actual market price. Second, the level of this "value" was regarded as being determined by the forces of the market—i.e., by supply and demand. Third, the concept of "intrinsic value", or utility, as distinct from "value", or market price, began to emerge, and something like a causal connection between the two was often postulated. Consider the following sets of quotations from Nicholas Barbon's pamphlet, *A Discourse of Trade*:

1. "The Price of Wares is the present Value. . . . The Market is the best Judge of Value; for by the Concourse of Buyers and Sellers, the Quantity of Wares, and the Occasion for them are Best known: Things are just worth so much, as they can be sold for, according to the Old Rule, *Valet Quantum Vendi potest*."

2. "The Price of Wares is the present Value, And ariseth by

[1] Kaulla (*op. cit.*, p. 64) remarks that "the austere views of the Scholastics must have caused them to regard leanings towards subjectivism as a sign of decadence".

Computing the occasions or use for them, with the Quantity to serve that Occasion. . . . It is impossible for the Merchant when he has Bought his Goods, To know what he shall Sell them for: The Value of them, depends upon the Difference betwixt the Occasion and the Quantity; tho' that be the Chiefest of the Merchants Care to observe, yet it Depends upon so many Circumstances, that it's impossible to know it. Therefore if the plenty of the Goods, has brought down the Price; the Merchant layeth them up, till the Quantity is consumed, and the Price riseth."

3. "The Value of all Wares arise from their Use; Things of no Use, have no Value, as the *English* Phrase is, *They are good for nothing.* The Use of Things, are to supply the Wants and Necessities of Man: There are Two General Wants that Mankind is born with; the Wants of the Body, and the Wants of the Mind; To supply these two Necessities, all things under the Sun become useful, and therefore have a Value. . . . The Value of all Wares, arriveth from their Use; and the Dearness and Cheapness of them, from their Plenty and Scarcity."

The three ideas which I have distinguished appear to be fairly clearly implied in these three statements.[1]

Barbon's *Discourse* was published in 1690, at a time when the Mercantilist approach to value was already beginning to give way to the Classical approach. The pamphlet is obviously transitional: Barbon looks forward towards Adam Smith almost as often as he looks backward towards the earlier Mercantilists. His comments on value, however, which a number of modern critics have praised because of their emphasis upon utility, must have appeared to many contemporaries to be conservative rather than revolutionary, since they are so obviously based on the traditional Mercantilist outlook. "The excellency of a Merchant", as Petty had put it, lay in "the judicious foresight and computation" of market prices;[2] and it was only natural (particularly in the century of the price revolution) that the merchant should think of the "value" of a commodity in terms of its market price rather than in terms of its producers' cost. It was natural, too, that emphasis should be laid on the influence of demand (and thus of utility) upon the "value" of the commodity. The merchant still had comparatively little control over the process of production and production costs, and accordingly tended to regard the level of his profits as being largely dependent upon the degree to

[1] The quotations from Barbon in this section are taken from the reprint of the *Discourse* edited by J. H. Hollander, pp. 13-16, 39 and 41.
[2] Petty, *Economic Writings* (Hull edn.), Vol. I, p. 90.

which the commodities in which he dealt were suited to the requirements of their purchaser.

It is important to note not only that the profits of the merchant were customarily *regarded* as being paid by the consumer, but also that in the earlier Mercantilist period they actually *were* so paid. The crucial point here is that the means of production, generally speaking, were still in the hands of the direct producers. Profit could be secured by the "exploitation" of the consumer, but only rarely as yet by the exploitation of the direct producer. As Engels put it,

"Production was still predominantly in the hands of workers owning their own means of production, whose work therefore yielded no surplus value to any capital. If they had to surrender a part of the product to third parties without compensation, it was in the form of tribute to feudal lords. Merchant capital, therefore, could only make its profit, at least at the beginning, out of the foreign buyers of domestic products, or the domestic buyers of foreign products; only toward the end of this period . . . were foreign competition and the difficulty of marketing able to compel the handicraft producers of export commodities to sell the commodity under its value to the exporting merchant."[1]

In other words, industrial capital (as distinct from merchant capital) was not yet a really significant factor in economic life, and the only form of profit to attract any great degree of attention was the "profit upon alienation" secured in commerce. The example of Barbon shows how difficult it must have been, even as late as 1690 and even for those who interested themselves in the process of production as well as the process of exchange, to visualise "profit on capital" as an element in the income of the "artificers". Barbon, significantly enough, defined "trade" as not only the selling but also the making of goods, and occasionally used the word "profit" as a blanket term to cover the net gains of both artificer and merchant. But Barbon's artificers, as he himself makes quite clear, are assumed to "cast up Profit, and Loss" with reference solely to *time*. It is only the merchants who "cast up Profit, and Loss" with reference to *interest*.[2] Industrial capital, and the phenomenon of a rate of profit on industrial capital, are still sufficiently inconspicuous to be abstracted from. The

[1] *Engels on "Capital"*, pp. 110-11. Cf. M. H. Dobb, *Studies in the Development of Capitalism*, pp. 199-200.

[2] "Interest is the Rule that the Merchant Trades by; And Time, the Artificer, By which they cast up Profit, and Loss; for if the Price of their Wares, so alter either by Plenty, or by Change of the Use, that they do not pay the Merchant Interest, nor the Artificer for his Time, they both reckon they lose by their Trade."

impending growth of industrial capital (the rudiments of which, as Engels went on to remark, had been formed as early as the Middle Ages) was destined to bring about a tremendous transformation not only in economic reality but also in the theoretical reflection of that reality in the minds of economists. Much of the remainder of the present chapter is in effect an attempt to describe the influence of this development on the form and content of political economy, and in particular on the shape of the theory of value.

3. The Transition to Classical Value Theory

In the late seventeenth century, particularly in Britain, the old producers' cost approach to value begins to show distinct signs of revival. More and more emphasis gradually comes to be laid on production costs, particularly in manufacture. Sometimes, as occasionally with Cary (and, much later, with Steuart), we even find an inclination to reserve the word "value" (used in conjunction with adjectives like "true" or "real") to describe these costs. The "true" or "real" value of a commodity, according to this conception, is less than the price yielded upon its sale by an amount equal to profit. "Artificers", wrote Cary, "by Tools and Laves fitted for different Uses, make such things, as would puzzle a stander by to set a Price on, according to the worth of Mens Labour." Manufactured goods, he maintained, "yield a Price, not only according to the true Value of the Materials and Labour, but an Overplus according to the Necessity and Humour of the Buyers."[1] The majority of economic writers, however, still continued to think of "value" in terms of market price, but an increasing number began to display an interest in the relation between market price and production costs.

This revolution in economic thinking reflected a revolution in economic practice. The writers of the time, broadly speaking, were the spokesmen of the merchant-manufacturers and *parvenu* industrial capitalists of the towns, whose increasing concern with production costs was indicative of far-reaching changes which were taking place in the organisation of production. The existing mode of production was being transformed, both from within and from without. The encroachment from without was carried out by certain sections of the merchant classes which began to exercise direct control over production. The growth of competition (in the sphere of internal

---

[1] John Cary, *An Essay towards Regulating the Trade and Employing the Poor in this Kingdom* (2nd edn., 1719), pp. 98-9 and 11-12.

if not yet so much of external trade) was making it more and more difficult for merchants to gain an adequate profit by the traditional method of exploiting price differences. Some form of control over production itself was gradually found necessary. The forms adopted varied from "putting out" systems—which were usually accompanied by a greater or lesser degree of pressure upon the direct producers— to more radical alterations in the organisation of production designed to increase productivity by taking advantage of the economies made possible through the division of labour and (to a much lesser extent) through new technical discoveries. The latter forms of encroachment, however, were more often carried out from within than from without —by what Mr. Dobb has described as "the rise from the ranks of the producers themselves of a capitalist element, half-manufacturer, half-merchant, which began to subordinate and to organise those very ranks from which it had so recently risen".[1] These various measures of encroachment often involved a considerable advance towards the establishment of capitalist relations of production[2] as the norm in the particular fields of industry where they took place.

The most important precondition of any such advance is, of course, the "freeing" of an abundant supply of wage-labour. Large numbers of direct producers have to be dispossessed of their means of production before their labour can be organised on a capitalist basis. It is fairly clear from the content of the economic literature of the last quarter of the seventeenth century, if not that this process was already appreciably under way, at least that its significance and necessity had been widely appreciated. The literature abounds with suggestions for attracting foreigners to the country by encouraging immigration and permitting naturalisation, for "setting the poor to work", abolishing the death penalty for all but the most serious offences, and so on. "Traffike" gradually ceases to appear in treatises as the most valuable

[1] Dobb, *op. cit.*, pp. 128-9, and chapter 4, *passim.*
[2] The term "relations of production" is generally used in Marxist literature to refer to those relations between men and men in production of which the *property relations* specific to a particular epoch are the legal expression. It is in this sense that we use the term when we are contrasting capitalist "relations of production", say, with feudal "relations of production" or socialist "relations of production". The term was also used by Marx and Engels, however, to include (or to refer exclusively to) those broad relations between men as producers which are characteristic of all societies in which different individuals (or groups) are directly or indirectly assigned to different jobs. It is in this sense that we use the term when we speak, say, of the "relations of production" characteristic of societies based on the production of commodities. (For the Marxist definition of a "commodity", see pp. 37-8 below.) The term is used in both senses in the present work, but the context should indicate in which sense it is being used in any particular place. The matter is dealt with in greater detail on pp. 151-2 below.

form of economic activity. "*People* are . . . in truth the chiefest, most fundamental, and pretious commodity", wrote the author of *Britannia Languens*, "out of which may be derived all sorts of Manufactures, Navigation, Riches, Conquests, and solid Dominion."[1]

It is from this epoch-making discovery of the great productive potentialities of "free" wage-labour organised on a capitalist basis that Classical political economy, and with it the Classical theory of value, really date. Classical political economy takes as its point of departure the idea which Adam Smith stated in the very first sentence of the *Wealth of Nations*—the idea that "the annual labour of every nation is the fund which originally supplies it with all the necessaries and conveniences of life which it annually consumes". Note that Smith speaks, not of the labour of the merchant, or the agriculturist, or the artificer, but of labour in general. The attitude underlying this new concept began to be moulded in the period we are now considering. A precious new commodity, labour power, is thrown upon the market —a commodity which when properly organised, particularly in manufacture, is capable of yielding not only an abundance of material goods to the nation, but also handsome profits to its purchaser. Those who are interested in tapping this new source of riches begin to think of "labour" as a relatively homogeneous, undifferentiated commodity. "The labours of the people bestowed in this way" (upon manufactures), wrote the author of *Britannia Languens*, "must necessarily glomerate the riches of the world and make any nation a prodigy of wealth." "Our moveable riches", said Pollexfen in 1700, "had their original and must have their increase from the labour and industry of our people."[2] General, abstract, human labour slowly begins to be recognised as the primary and universal cost-element in production, the basic cause of that value-difference between output and input upon which national prosperity (and individual profits) ultimately depend. Economists begin to visualise the productive activity of the nation as a whole in terms of the disposition of its labour force. And the foundations are laid for a fundamental distinction which will later play a central part in economic thinking—the distinction between productive and unproductive labour.

To say that the economic spokesmen of the time afforded labour this unique place, however, is not to say that they yet adhered to a "labour theory of value". The Classical labour theory, as we shall see,

[1] *Britannia Languens* (1680), p. 238.
[2] Cited, together with a number of other examples, by E. S. Furniss, *The Position of the Labourer in a System of Nationalism*, chapter 2, pp. 17-19, and *passim*.

was something much more profound and far-reaching than the rather vague formulations of even the most acute of the seventeenth-century writers—few of whom, after all, were directly concerned to formulate a *theory* of economic activity. There were, it is true, plenty of statements made at about this time to the effect that labour "makes the far greatest part of the value of things we enjoy in this world",[1] that labour is "the cause of wealth", "the source of value", and so on. But with one or two prominent exceptions which will be considered later in this chapter, the authors of such statements as these did not intend to put forward a theory of the determination of the value of commodities by labour time. Sometimes they meant simply that "free" labour organised on a capitalist basis, particularly in manufacture, could "glomerate the riches of the world". When their statements implied something deeper than this, they generally meant either one or both of two quite different things, between which it is important to distinguish.

They sometimes meant, in the first place, that the *use value* or *utility* of commodities was largely the creation of labour. Locke's famous discussion of the manner in which labour "puts the difference of value on everything" probably comes into this category. "I think", he said, "it will be but a very modest computation to say, that of the products of the earth useful to the life of man, nine-tenths are the effects of labour. Nay, if we will rightly estimate things as they come to our use, and cast up the several expenses about them—what in them is purely owing to Nature and what to labour—we shall find that in most of them ninety-nine hundredths are wholly to be put to the account of labour." Locke is probably thinking here, not of the capacity of labour in general to confer upon a commodity the power of commanding other commodities in exchange, but rather of the power of specific types of labour (what Marx was later to call concrete as distinct from abstract or undifferentiated labour) to create use values of various kinds. If you examine any common commodity, Locke is telling us, and take away the effects of the labour that has been bestowed upon it, the residuum consists only of raw materials which are almost useless in themselves. "For whatever bread is more worth than acorns, wine than water, and cloth or silk than leaves, skins or moss, that is wholly owing to labour and industry."[2] It is not easy, of

[1] Locke, *Of Civil Government* (Everyman edn.), p. 137.
[2] Locke, *op. cit.*, pp. 136-7. Locke's influence upon the early Classical economists was probably more political than economic. The *Treatises* reflect the essential basis of the Restoration settlement—the unexpressed agreement that the revival of the monarchy

course, to draw a clear dividing line between statements ascribing to labour the creation of use value and those ascribing to it the creation of exchange value, since the expenditure of labour in the production of a commodity normally creates both. But in statements of the type I am now considering, the creation of exchange value, when it is impliedly referred to, is really almost invariably being ascribed, not to the capacity of abstract labour to create exchange value directly, but rather to the capacity of concrete labour to increase the use value of commodities and thereby indirectly to increase their exchange value.[1] It is worth noting that when Locke came to write his *Some Considerations of the Consequences of the Lowering of Interest*, very shortly after the publication of the *Treatises*, he gave an account of the determination of price which differed little from contemporary Mercantilist accounts. "The price of any Commodity", he wrote, "rises or falls, by the proportion of the number of *Buyers* and *Sellers*. . . . The Vent of any thing depends upon its Necessity or Usefulness, as Convenience, or Opinion guided by Phancy or Fashion shall determine."[2]

In the second place, those who then described labour as the source of value and wealth were often meaning to say only that *wage-costs* were usually the most important element in the cost of production of manufactured commodities. The labourers added an amount of value equal at least to the "value of their labour"—i.e., their wages—to the raw materials which they worked up, and this added value was usually very large relative to that of the raw materials themselves. "Most materials of Manufacture are of small value whilst raw and unwrought", wrote the author of *Britannia Languens*, "at least in Comparison of the Manufacture, since by Manufacture they may be made of five, ten or twenty times their first value, according to the *Workmanship*."[3] So important was labour's contribution assumed to be that there was often a tendency to conceive of the "value" of the finished commodity as consisting almost entirely of the "value of the labour"

should not entail the revival of feudal restrictions. The chapter on Property, from which the quotations in the text are taken, was intended to supply a set of moral title-deeds to the property of the farmers, master-craftsmen and merchant-manufacturers who then formed the nucleus of the British bourgeoisie. These classes, Locke was implicitly asserting, had a right to the undisturbed enjoyment of the fruits of their "labour"—a right which was just as well if not better founded than that of those classes whose property had formerly been protected by feudal regulations.

[1] For the Marxian distinction between "abstract" and "concrete" labour, see below, pp. 165-7.

[2] Locke, *Considerations* (1691), in *Works* (1714 edn.), Vol. II, p. 16.

[3] *Britannia Languens*, pp. 23-4.

used to produce it. It is not quite correct, however, to describe this as a "widely accepted wages-cost theory of value".[1] The primary concern of most contemporary writers was not to formulate a theory of value, but to emphasise the importance of securing an abundant supply of cheap labour. Their efforts were largely directed towards the reduction of wage-costs. The advocates of an increased population, of poverty as a spur to industry, and of increased disciplinary measures against the labourers, obviously had this consideration at the back of their minds, and were often honest enough to admit it. But the contemporary tendency to regard the value of a finished commodity as being virtually dependent upon its wages-cost does require some explanation. It is difficult to understand at first sight how such a view could ever have appeared plausible. To the modern economist it seems axiomatic that the commodity would have to sell at a price sufficient to include profits as well as wages if its production were to be continued. But to the seventeenth-century merchant who "put out" raw materials to be worked up by more or less independent direct producers, the *cost* price of the commodity at least would appear to consist almost entirely of wages. And the actual price at which the commodity was finally sold, whether at home or abroad, although it obviously could not have been equal to the wages-cost, must often have borne a fairly regular proportion to it, the more nearly so as profits on mercantile capital were reduced to a common level by competition. To the master-craftsman who had risen from the ranks and taken to trade, again, the selling price of the commodity probably appeared to be resolvable almost entirely into wages-cost, since he would very likely regard his "profit" merely as a sort of superior wage for his own labour. And in any case, it is obvious that in a society where the major economies were still being secured by the extension of the division of labour rather than by the increased introduction of machinery, the level of the wages-bill would have a decisive effect on the selling price.

To sum up, then, the great economic changes which took place in the period we are considering began to divert the attention of economists from the sphere of exchange to that of production, and encouraged the growth of the idea that labour was in some way the "source" or "cause" of wealth and value. But there were as yet only a few traces of a "labour theory of value" in the true Classical sense. When economists spoke of labour as the "source" or "cause"

[1] Furniss, *op. cit.*, p. 159.

of value, they usually meant no more than that exchange value was largely dependent upon wages-cost (including the "wages" of the master-craftsman), or that labour created exchange value by reason of its effect in increasing the use value of commodities. Neither of these ideas really constitutes a "labour theory of value". Their emergence indicates merely that economists are beginning to look *in the direction* of a labour theory of value.

4. *The Classical Concept of "Natural Price"*

The main key to the development of the Classical theory of value in the eighteenth century is to be found in the gradual emergence and recognition of *profit on capital* as a general category of class income which accrued to all who used "stock" in the employment of "productive" wage-labour, and which was qualitatively distinct from the interest on money, the rent of land and the wages of labour.

It had long been recognised, of course, that those who employed "stock" in mercantile pursuits generally received a net reward which was proportioned not to the effort, if any, which they expended, but rather to the value of the "stock" employed. During the eighteenth century, as capitalism developed and extended its field of influence, it gradually came to be recognised that net gains similar in this respect to mercantile profit were now also earned on capital employed in other economic pursuits, such as agriculture and manufacture. These net gains, it was seen, bore a more or less regular proportion to the amount of capital, in whatever sphere it happened to be employed. And, even more important, it also came to be recognised that the *origin* of these net gains was now very different from what it had formerly been. In earlier centuries, generally speaking, profit had appeared as "profit upon alienation" —i.e., as the gain from buying things cheap and selling them dear. In the eighteenth century, on the other hand, profit eventually began to appear as an income uniquely associated with the use of capital in the employment of wage-labour.

The emergence of profit on capital in the Classical sense as a new category of class income was not merely a conceptual but also a historical phenomenon. As Engels once remarked in a similar connection, "we are dealing here not only with a purely logical process, but with a historical process and its explanatory reflection in thought, the logical pursuance of its inner connections".[1] Profit on capital, and the social classes which came to receive incomes of this type, were

[1] *Engels on "Capital"*, p. 100.

of course the ultimate products of several centuries of economic development. But it was apparently not until the latter half of the eighteenth century that profit on capital, as a new generic type of class income, became so clearly differentiated from other types of income that economists were able to grasp its full significance and delineate its basic characteristics. There were a number of obstacles which had to be overcome before this could be done.

In the first place, there were certain difficulties connected with the differentiation of profit from interest on money and rent of land. Profit formally resembled these other types of income in so far as they all appeared to stand in a more or less regular proportion to a capital sum—rent to a sum of money invested in the purchase of land, interest to a sum of money lent out to a borrower, and profit to a sum of money used directly in the employment of wage-labour. During the century prior to the appearance of the *Wealth of Nations*, the vital distinction between *money* (i.e., money as a hoard) and *capital* (i.e., money utilised in order to secure a revenue) began to be recognised by a number of economists. "No Man is richer for having his Estate all in Money, Plate, &c. lying by him", wrote North in 1691, "but on the contrary, he is for that reason the poorer. That man is richest, whose Estate is in a growing condition, either in Land at Farm, Money at Interest, or Goods in Trade."[1] And at about the same time a further important distinction came to be made between capital which was more or less passively utilised (as in the case of "Land at Farm" or "Money at Interest") and capital which was actively utilised (as in the case of "Goods in Trade"). It had become evident that whereas those who utilised capital passively would normally receive as revenue only the ordinary rate of interest or its equivalent, those who utilised it actively in "trade" would normally make a net gain, or "profit", over and above the ordinary rate of interest. The way was then laid open for the development of the Classical concept of interest as a derivative form of income which was paid out of gross profit and ultimately regulated by it. Smith, like Locke and Cantillon and Hume before him, emphasised the fact "that wherever a great deal can be made by the use of money, a great deal will commonly be given for the use of it; and that wherever little can be made by it, less will commonly be given for it".[2] And just as the differentiation of profit from interest in the sphere of "trade" was possible only with the emergence of a

[1] *Discourses upon Trade, etc.*, p. 11. Cf. Marx, *Theories of Surplus Value* (English edn.), p. 32.
[2] *Wealth of Nations* (Cannan edn.), Vol. I, p. 90.

separate class of "traders", so the clear differentiation of profit from rent in the sphere of agriculture was possible only with the emergence of a separate class of agricultural capitalists. An adequate distinction between rent-earning capital invested in the purchase of land and profit-earning capital invested in the actual farming of the land could not be made (unless by way of analogy with other spheres of production) prior to the fairly wide-spread development of capitalist methods of organisation in agriculture.

In the second place, there were certain difficulties connected with the differentiation of profit from wages. As capitalism developed in industry and agriculture, the objective conditions were gradually established for the recognition of the fact that the essential common feature of all active uses of capital was the employment of wage-labour, and thus for the postulation of profit as a new type of class income born of the capital-labour relationship. But it very often happened at this time that the employers of labour had risen from the ranks of the direct producers and still participated more or less actively in the actual process of production. Therefore they naturally persisted in regarding the difference between their paid-out costs and the price they received for their commodities as a sort of superior "wage" for their own personal efforts rather than as a "profit" on the capital, often very meagre, which they had supplied. Even when such employers came to confine themselves to merely supervisory functions, it might still seem plausible to speak of their net reward, as so many economists at this time actually did speak of it, as the "wages of superintendence". How difficult it was, even as late as the 1770's, to appreciate the nature of the difference between wages and profits is shown clearly enough by the emphasis which Smith himself evidently felt obliged to place upon the point. Obviously aware that he was to some extent breaking new ground, Smith went out of his way to insist that the profits of stock are not in fact "the wages of a particular sort of labour, the labour of inspection and direction", but are "altogether different", being "regulated by quite different principles". The owner of capital, said Smith, even though he is "discharged of almost all labour", still expects that "his profits should bear a regular proportion to his capital".[1]

Finally, there were certain obstacles standing in the way of the introduction of the concept of an *average rate* of profit. Before the profits of stock could come to be regarded as bearing a regular proportion

[1] *Wealth of Nations*, Vol. I, pp. 50-1.

to the amount of capital, in whatever sphere it happened to be employed, it was clearly necessary that the field covered by capitalist methods of organisation should be considerably enlarged, that competition in both internal and external trade should be reasonably free, and that capital should be relatively mobile between different places and occupations. Only then was it possible to say, as Smith did, that a commodity whose price exceeds paid-out costs by an amount equal to profit at the normal rate—

> "is then sold precisely for what it is worth, or for what it really costs the person who brings it to market; for though in common language what is called the prime cost of any commodity does not comprehend the profit of the person who is to sell it again, yet if he sells it at a price which does not allow him the ordinary rate of profit in his neighbourhood, he is evidently a loser by the trade; since by employing his stock in some other way he might have made that profit."[1]

It was the emergence of profit on capital as a new category of class income, then, sharply differentiated from other types of income, which cleared the way for the full development of Classical political economy. As the conditions I have described were gradually fulfilled in the real world, the older accounts of "profit" necessarily began to seem more and more inadequate. "Profit" could no longer be treated under the heading of rent, where Petty had implicitly placed it. It could no longer be identified with wages, as with Cantillon and Hutcheson. And it could no longer be regarded simply as a "profit upon alienation" originating in exchange whose level fluctuated "according to circumstances", which was essentially Steuart's view. It became more and more clear that under competitive conditions profit at a reasonably regular rate would be earned on capital in whatever sphere it happened to be employed, and that this profit must be regarded as originating in production rather than in exchange.

The first major theoretical product of these new conditions of which I wish to speak was the Classical concept of a "natural price". It gradually came to be recognised that under competitive conditions commodities tended in the long run to sell at "natural" prices which included profit at the normal or "natural" rate. But full recognition of this fact came very slowly. Indeed, Adam Smith was probably the first, if not to discern it, at least to appreciate and emphasise its significance. Of the contributions of his predecessors, only three seem to be

[1] *Wealth of Nations*, Vol. I, p. 57.

worth describing in this connection—those of Richard Cantillon, Joseph Harris and William Temple.

Petty, with his distinction between the "natural" and the "political" price, had to some extent prepared the way for the Classical concept; but Cantillon, writing about 1730, approached somewhat closer to it than Petty had been able to do. Cantillon distinguishes between the market price of a commodity and what he calls its "intrinsic value". The latter, he says, is "the measure of the quantity of Land and of Labour entering into its production, having regard to the fertility or produce of the Land and to the quality of the Labour". The constituents of the "intrinsic value" of commodities, according to Cantillon, are the "value of the land" and the "value of the labour" used to make them. But "it often happens that many things which have actually this intrinsic value are not sold in the Market according to that value: that will depend on the Humours and Fancies of men and on their consumption". For example, "if a gentleman cuts Canals and erects Terraces in his Garden, their intrinsic value will be proportionable to the Land and Labour; but the Price in reality will not always follow this proportion". The market price may be much greater or much less than "the value of the Land and the expense he has incurred". "Too great an abundance" of a commodity may cause its market price to fall below its "intrinsic value", and in a period of scarcity the reverse may happen. But "in well organised Societies", Cantillon maintains, "the Market Prices of articles whose consumption is tolerably constant and uniform do not vary much from the intrinsic value."[1]

In these passages, of course, Cantillon is saying little more than that market prices often tend to equal costs. He says nothing at this stage about the mechanism by which the market price is *made* equal to the "intrinsic value"; and profit on capital is not specifically included as a separate constituent of the "intrinsic value". In other places, however, Cantillon comes rather closer to the Classical idea of a "natural" equilibrium price which includes profit at the normal rate as a constituent—as for example in the following passage where he speaks of the manner in which entrepreneurs "proportion themselves in a State to the Customers or consumption":

"If there are too many Hatters in a City or in a street for the number of people who buy hats there, some who are least patronised must become bankrupt: if they be too few it will be a profitable

[1] *Essai sur la Nature du Commerce en Général* (Royal Economic Society edn.), pp. 29-31.

Undertaking which will encourage new Hatters to open shops there and so it is that the Undertakers of all kinds adjust themselves to risks in a State."[1]

Cantillon's "intrinsic value", as we have seen, does not expressly include profit on capital as a constituent element, but he may have envisaged "profit"—or what he elsewhere calls the "value of the Labour or Superintendence" of the entrepreneurs—as being included under the heading "value of the labour". "All the Undertakers", he says, "are as it were on unfixed wages."[2] But the idea of profit on capital as a distinct category of income, bearing a regular proportion to the value of the capital employed and representing a clear surplus accruing to the entrepreneur after loan interest and "wages of management" have been paid, is as yet only very hazily expressed, if at all. The capitalist, it appears, is not yet clearly distinguishable from the independent labourer, and for that reason the rewards accruing to each of these two classes still tend to be regarded as being qualitatively similar. "Undertakers", according to Cantillon's use of the term, include not only those who "set up with a capital to conduct their enterprise" but also those who are "Undertakers of their own labour without capital."[3]

Harris, probably basing himself on Cantillon, argued that:

"Things in general are valued, not according to their real uses in supplying the necessities of men; but rather in proportion to the land, labour and skill that are requisite to produce them: It is according to this proportion nearly, that things or commodities are exchanged one for another; and it is by the said scale, that the intrinsic values of most things are chiefly estimated. . . . Men's various necessities and appetites, oblige them to part with their own commodities, at a rate proportionable to the labour and skill that had been bestowed upon those things, which they want in exchange: If they will not comply with the market, their goods will remain on their hands; and if at first, one trade be more profitable than another, skill as well as labour and risques of all sorts, being taken into the account; more men will enter into that business, and in their outvying will undersell one another, till at length the great profit of it is brought down to a *par* with the rest."[4]

[1] *Essai sur la Nature du Commerce en Général*, p. 53. Cf. pp. 117-21.
[2] *Ibid.*, p. 55.   [3] *Ibid.*
[4] *An Essay upon Money and Coins* (1757), pp. 5 and 9. Cf. p. 8: "One great mystery of trade, is to keep off new adventurers, by concealing its profits; and whilst that may be done, the gains will be large."

Harris's account certainly represents a closer approximation to the developed Classical concept than that of Cantillon, although it is properly subject to the same basic criticism. But Harris's treatment of the effects of demand shows that some distance had yet to be travelled. "A quicker or slower demand for a particular commodity", he wrote, "will frequently raise or lower its price, though no alteration hath happened in its intrinsic value or prime cost; men being always ready to take the advantage of one another's fancies, whims or necessities; and the proportion of buyers to sellers, or the demand for any particular commodity in respect to its quantity, will always have an influence on the market."[1] This influence will necessarily be stronger in the case of "natural" products than in that of "artificial" products, so that the former will be "subject to a greater variation in their value" than the latter.[2] Although Harris obviously had the idea of a "natural" equilibrium price at the back of his mind, he does not seem to have clearly visualised this "natural price" as the central point around which the market price fluctuated and towards which it constantly gravitated. Rather, "prime cost" and "the proportion of buyers to sellers" are given almost equal status as determinants, standing side by side with one another. It was not until capitalist competition had developed further, and the proportion of commodities which were freely reproducible had increased, that the Classical theory of value could be properly emancipated from this dualism.

In William Temple's pamphlet *A Vindication of Commerce and the Arts*, which was published in 1758, there is another interesting anticipation of the Classical concept. "I can most clearly perceive", Temple writes, "that the value of all commodities or the price, is a compound of the value of the land necessary to raise them, the value of the labour exerted in producing and manufacturing them, and of the value of the brokerage which provides and circulates them."[3] By "brokerage," as the ensuing passage shows, Temple clearly meant something very like "profit" in Smith's sense of the word. "If the broker's gains do not please him", Temple proceeded, "he will withhold his sales. The farmer will not sow, the manufacturers will leave off their trades, if their employments and occupations produce a loss instead of a profit." And in an appendix to the pamphlet, "brokerage" appears as an important item in a calculation of the national income of Britain

---

[1] *An Essay upon Money and Coins*, pp. 5-6.   [2] *Ibid.*, p. 7.
[3] *A Select Collection of Scarce and Valuable Tracts on Commerce* (1859), p. 522. The appendix referred to below is not included in this reprint. I owe my reference to this pamphlet to Patten, *The Development of English Thought*, pp. 237-8.

in 1600 and 1757. By assuming that the "gains of trade" stand in a certain relationship to the current rate of interest,[1] Temple is able to deduce the "value of the brokerage" in "foreign trade" and "home consumption" from estimates of the annual turnover in each of these fields.[2]

The main significance of the inclusion of profit at the normal rate in the constituents of the long-run competitive price lay in the fact that it enabled the Classical economists to demonstrate that the level of this price was not dependent upon "arbitrary" factors but was rather "subject to law". So long as there was no very marked tendency for the amount of profit earned to bear a reasonably regular relationship to the amount of capital employed, it was difficult to make any general statement about the level of the market price of a commodity other than that it would usually exceed what Smith called "prime cost" by an increment ("profit" or "gain") which varied in each individual case according to the state of supply and demand. Clearly such a statement was of very limited use: it was scarcely capable of serving as the basis for forecasts of any great degree of generality. Once the phenomenon of a normal or "natural" rate of profit had begun to manifest itself on a sufficiently wide scale, however, it became possible to make a much more useful general statement concerning the level of commodity prices. Commodities, it could now be said, tended under competitive conditions to sell at prices equal to "prime cost" plus profit at the "natural" rate. A situation in which the "natural" rate of profit was being earned, so that there was no tendency for firms to enter or leave the industry, could be defined as a situation of equilibrium, in which supply "balanced" or "equalled" demand, and the price at which commodities sold in this situation could be conceived as their "natural" price. The actual market price, although it might differ at any given time from this "natural" price (either because of the existence of monopoly or because of a temporary discrepancy between supply and demand), could then be regarded as "continually gravitating" or "constantly tending" towards it.[3] This advance was sufficiently substantial to make it appear that the

[1] Cf. Smith, *Wealth of Nations*, Vol. I, p. 99: "Double interest is in Great Britain reckoned, what the merchants call, a good, moderate, reasonable profit; terms which I apprehend mean no more than a common and usual profit."

[2] Temple's pamphlet was known, if not to Smith, at least to certain members of Smith's circle. It was dedicated to Charles Townshend's father; and it was brought to the notice of Lord Kames by Josiah Tucker (see Lord Woodhouselee's *Memoirs of the Hon. H. Home of Kames*, p. 6 of appendix, Vol. II).

[3] *Wealth of Nations*, Vol. I, p. 60.

earlier "supply and demand" principle had left the determination of prices to arbitrary factors whereas the new "cost of production" principle made prices subject to law.

5. *The Classical Concept of Labour Cost*

Why, it may be asked, did the Classical economists not rest content with a "cost of production" theory of value? Having shown that the long-run competitive price was equal to the cost of production, including profit at the normal rate, why did they then go on to seek for a determinant of the cost of production itself?

The answer, I think, lies fundamentally in the fact that a cost of production theory must necessarily assume that the constituents of the "natural price"—in particular the level of wages and the rate of profit—are given, independent factors. And when one is dealing with economic problems of the broad, global type, such as those with which the Classical economists increasingly concerned themselves, this assumption is clearly illegitimate. Whether or not one can treat any particular factor as an independent variable naturally depends upon the nature of the problem which one is trying to solve.[1] To the merchant of the sixteenth and seventeenth centuries, interested mainly in the day-to-day prices of a very limited range of goods, a simple "supply and demand" theory of value would suffice, since supply-and demand could reasonably be regarded, in the context of this particular problem, as independent factors. To the economist of the early eighteenth century, interested mainly in the average prices of the relatively small group of goods produced on a capitalist basis and sold under competitive conditions, a cost of production theory of value might suffice, since the constituents of the "natural price" could plausibly be conceived as independent factors. But as the sphere of operation of capitalist commodity production extends, and the prices of more and more goods are revealed as being "subject to law", the constituents of the "natural price" can no longer legitimately be treated as independent determinants of the values of such goods, since they will themselves evidently be partly dependent upon these values. Economists who are interested in dealing with broad fundamental problems such as that of "the nature and causes of the wealth of nations" must then begin to seek for a new value-principle which will be capable of determining not only the values of commodities but also the

[1] See the suggestive treatment of this point by M. H. Dobb, *Political Economy and Capitalism*, pp. 8-10.

values of the productive agents whose rewards make up the "natural price" of these commodities. The Classical economists gradually came to believe—or at least to recognise instinctively—that a value-principle of this type was required before political economy could be transformed into a real science. And, of course, they were perfectly correct in thinking so.

There was another reason, of a rather more special character, why the Classical economists became unwilling to treat the constituents of the "natural price" as independent factors. One of the most important of these constituents, capitalist profit, as we have already seen, had begun to appear, not as a wage which rewarded productive effort, but rather as a surplus related to the size of the capital which happened to be employed. And it had also begun to appear, not as an increment which was somehow "added" to costs in the process of exchange, but rather as something which actually originated in the process of production and was merely *realised* in exchange. Profit, then, was a surplus over cost which originated in the course of production. Generally speaking, at least in its "pure" or "net" form, it was not a compensation for anything which had been physically used up or sacrificed in order to produce the commodity. After all such sacrifices had been compensated for out of the "natural price", profit remained as a clear surplus, which could safely be disposed of in whatever way its recipient pleased without prejudice to the maintenance of the nation's productive activity at its existing level. The Classical economists were particularly interested in this characteristic of profit, because they regarded profit as an extremely important source of capital, and the accumulation of capital as the key to the growth of wealth and abundance. The theory of value, therefore, had to be capable of explaining how the level of profit was determined. The level of profit could not itself be regarded as one of the determinants of value: rather, a new value-principle had to be evolved which would be capable of explaining the origin and persistence of that quantitative value-difference between output and input in production which manifested itself as profit. To the modern economist this problem is likely to appear a little unreal, since the present-day fashion of dealing with the problem·of distribution in terms of undifferentiated "factors of production", whose rewards under competitive conditions are all imputed in precisely the same way from the value of the finished product, has tended to wipe the question of surplus (at least in the Classical sense of the word) off the agenda of economic discussion.

To the Classical economists, however, the problem was a very real one.

It would not have been possible for Adam Smith to proceed as far as he did towards the solution of these new problems if he had inherited only those rudimentary pieces of theoretical apparatus bequeathed by the economists of the seventeenth century. As we have seen, this century had evolved the general idea that labour was in some significant sense the "source" or "cause" of wealth and value. But in most contexts statements of this type were intended only to express approval of the capitalist form of productive organisation and its attendant economies; and even those economists who had meant something more had done little to clarify the concepts involved. There had been no serious attempts to distinguish "wealth" from "value", and no one had been able to explain very clearly just *how* labour created or contributed value to commodities. Some economists had tried to explain the role of labour by arguing that value was largely dependent upon wages-cost. This explanation would no longer do, partly because it necessarily became circular as more and more labour was transformed into wage-labour, and partly because the equilibrium prices of commodities, the level of which the theory of value was required to explain, now included as a constituent element an important item—profit—which could not properly be reduced to wages. Then again, other economists had suggested that labour contributed exchange value to commodities by adding to the use value of the raw materials, thereby increasing the quantity of other commodities which purchasers were willing to give in exchange for them. But an explanation of exchange value in terms of use value, it seemed, would not do either. It had gradually become apparent that although commodities could not be sold unless they possessed utility, the "natural prices" at which they tended to sell bore little relationship to their utility. "Prices or values in commerce", wrote Hutcheson, "do not at all follow the real use or importance of goods for the support, or natural pleasure of life."[1] The concept of utility adopted here by Hutcheson, with its implied reference to a general scale of "normal need", was of course later replaced by the more familiar concept which relates utility to the subjective estimates of individual consumers. But even then the actual prices at which commodities tended to sell under competitive conditions seemed to bear little relation to their "utility". This was sufficiently shown, the Classical

[1] Francis Hutcheson, *A System of Moral Philosophy* (1755), Vol. II, p. 53.

economists believed, by the fact that the equilibrium prices of commodities would not alter (or at least would not permanently alter) merely because the purchasers' estimates of their worth, and therefore their demand for them, happened to increase or diminish. Given conditions of more or less constant returns to scale for the industry as a whole, it was only a change in the cost of production which could possibly bring about a change in the equilibrium price.

Fortunately, however, Smith inherited much more than this. Smith's eighteenth-century predecessors, dissatisfied with the existing accounts of the determination of value, gradually built up a set of new ideas which insensibly became part of the intellectual climate in which Smith worked. As so often happens in the history of thought, the emergence of a new theoretical problem was accompanied by the emergence of a new set of principles and concepts capable of solving it. Side by side with the development of the idea of the "natural price", there grew up the idea that in the last analysis it was *the expenditure of social effort* which conferred value upon a commodity. This concept of social effort as the determinant of value, with labour time as its appropriate measure, is a peculiarly subtle and elusive one, as the following sketch of the history of its development may help to show.

Petty, whose brilliant *obiter dicta* on the subject of value formed the starting-point for so much subsequent work, came remarkably close to the idea that the exchange value of a commodity is determined by the quantity of labour required to produce it. "If a man can bring to *London* an ounce of Silver out of the Earth in *Peru*", he wrote, "in the same time that he can produce a bushel of Corn, then one is the natural price of the other; now if by reason of new and more easie Mines a man can get two ounces of Silver as easily as formerly he did one, then Corn will be as cheap at ten shillings the bushel, as it was before at five shillings *cæteris paribus*." Petty even sought, in another well-known passage, to apply this theory to the problem of the emergence of a value-difference between output and input in the productive process:

"Suppose a man could with his own hands plant a certain scope of Land with Corn, that is, could Digg, or Plough, Harrow, Weed, Reap, Carry home, Thresh, and Winnow so much as the Husbandry of this Land requires; and had withal Seed wherewith to sowe the same. I say, that when this man hath subducted his seed out of the proceed of his Harvest, and also, what himself hath both eaten and given to others in exchange for Clothes, and other Natural necessaries; that the remainder of Corn is the natural and true Rent of the Land for that year; and the *medium* of seven years, or rather of so many years as makes up the Cycle, within which Dearths and Plenties make their revolution, doth give the ordinary Rent of the Land in Corn."[1]

How much English money is this "Corn or Rent" worth, Petty then goes on to ask. "I answer, so much as the money, which another single man can save, within the same time, over and above his expence, if he imployed himself wholly to produce and make it." Petty is here virtually resolving the value-difference between output and input into surplus labour, much in the manner of the later Classical economists. But Petty's account, taken as a whole, differs from theirs in at least two important respects. First, it will be noted that in Petty's example the surplus assumes the form of rent alone, and no mention is made of profit. Presumably, for Petty, "profit" in the Classical sense of the word has not yet emerged as a distinct category of income, and can therefore still plausibly be subsumed under the category rent. Second, there seems to be a certain lack of clarity in Petty's mind concerning the role of labour in the process of value creation. For example, in a discussion of "natural Standards and Measures" of value which follows almost immediately after the striking passages just quoted, Petty makes the following remarks:

"All things ought to be valued by two natural Denominations, which is Land and Labour; that is, we ought to say, a Ship or garment is worth such a measure of Land, with such another measure of Labour; forasmuch as both Ships and Garments were the creatures of Lands and mens Labours thereupon: This being true, we should be glad to finde out a natural Par between Land and Labour, so as we might express the value by either of them alone as well or better than by both, and reduce one into the other as easily and certainly as we reduce pence into pounds."[2]

Here the role of labour is probably being conceived in rather a different light—and, indeed, the whole problem of value determination is being looked at from another point of view.[3]

The nature of one of the main difficulties which the early Classical value theorists had to face is made abundantly clear in these passages from Petty. At the back of their minds was the notion that in some

---

[1] Quotations from *Economic Writings*, Vol. I, pp. 50-51 and 43.
[2] *Ibid.*, pp. 44-5.
[3] On the other hand, it could possibly be argued that Petty's procedure here was the logical ancestor of Ricardo's device for "getting rid of rent".

fundamental and significant sense it was the expenditure of labour which conferred exchange value upon commodities. At the same time, however, it was obvious that the price at which a commodity customarily sold was sufficient not only to reward the labour which had been used to make it, but also to pay "the value of the land". How could one say, therefore, that it was labour alone which determined the value of commodities? Petty, and following him, Cantillon, tried to get out of this difficulty by finding a "natural Par between Land and Labour". Others, notably Locke and Harris, did their best to magnify the *quantitative* importance of labour relative to that of land in this respect. But these efforts to solve the problem, historically speaking, were of significance only in so far as they assisted in laying the foundations of a *qualitative* distinction between the use of land and the expenditure of labour as productive costs. The concept of cost upon which the mature labour theory was based necessarily excluded land as a determinant of value, except to the extent that its maintenance required the expenditure of social effort.

The seventeenth-century idea that "labour is the source of value", as we have seen, was usually just another way of saying that the capitalist form of economic organisation, by virtue of the fact that it was able to carry the division of labour further, was more productive than earlier forms. The idea, in other words, was originally associated with a recognition of the potentialities of the division of labour in capitalist "manufacture" (in Marx's sense).[1] As the eighteenth century progressed, however, the idea that "labour is the source of value" came to be associated with what Marx called the division of labour in *society* rather than with the division of labour in manufacture,[2] and it was largely from this association that the Classical labour theory eventually arose. This is a point of some importance which requires elaboration.

If the division of labour in manufacture is a phenomenon specially associated with capitalism, the division of labour in society is of course as old as society itself. In all types of society, individuals and groups of individuals have specialised in the performance of different productive tasks, and have in some way "exchanged" their activities with one another. But it is only in relatively recent times that this mutual "exchange" of activities has taken the form of the exchange of goods produced *for a market* by individuals or groups who carry on

[1] See *Capital*, Vol. I, chapter 14.
[2] For a discussion of this distinction see *ibid.*, section 4.

their productive activities more or less separately from one another.[1] And it is only under capitalism that this latter form of production and exchange has come to dominate the whole economic scene. With the development of capitalism, it became more and more difficult for any single individual to supply his own wants except by supplying those of others, and the great majority of people became obliged willynilly to work for one another by engaging in the production of goods for the market. The social division of labour became overwhelmingly a division between separate producers of goods for the market.

The two types of division of labour, of course, reciprocally react upon one another in the course of their development. The establishment of the manufacturing division of labour presupposes that a certain stage in the development of the social division of labour has already been reached; and, conversely, the manufacturing division of labour "reacts upon and develops and multiplies" the social division of labour.[2] It is this latter effect which is especially important in the present connection. Marx describes the process as follows:

> "If the manufacturing system seize upon an industry, which, previously, was carried on in connexion with others, either as a chief or as a subordinate industry, and by one producer, these industries immediately separate their connexion, and become independent. If it seize upon a particular stage in the production of a commodity, the other stages of its production become converted into so many independent industries. . . . The territorial division of labour, which confines special branches of production to special districts of a country, acquires fresh stimulus from the manufacturing system, which exploits every special advantage. The Colonial system and the opening out of the markets of the world, both of which are included in the general conditions of existence of the manufacturing period, furnish rich material for developing the division of labour in society."[3]

In a society in which these processes are proceeding rapidly, and in which the old feudal ties have been forcibly dissolved, the paramount importance of the economic tie which binds people to one another as producers of different commodities for the market is bound to impress itself upon men's minds. The idea begins to arise that this tie is in fact, as one writer put it, the "chief cement" which binds people

---

[1] In the Marxian terminology, such goods are called "commodities". Most non-Marxian economists use this word in its ordinary dictionary sense.

[2] Marx, *Capital*, Vol. I (Allen & Unwin edn.), p. 346.

[3] *Ibid.*, pp. 346-7.

together.[1] And the times become ripe for the emergence of one of the most influential abstractions of the modern age—the notion that the relations between men as mutually interdependent producers of commodities somehow lie at the basis of all their other social relations. The Classical labour theory of value was closely associated with this notion. If we regard society as consisting in essence of an association of separate producers who live by mutually exchanging the products of their different labours, we are likely to come to think of the exchange of these products as being in essence the exchange of *quantities of social labour*. And if we begin thinking in these terms, we may well eventually conclude that the *value* of a commodity—i.e., its power of purchasing or commanding other commodities in exchange—is a quality conferred upon it by virtue of the fact that a certain portion of the labour force of society has been allocated to its production.

The beginnings of the Classical emphasis on the interdependence of producers are to be found, appropriately enough, in Petty's writings. Petty was well aware of the great importance of the division of labour; and in one passage some remarks on the manufacturing division of labour lead him directly to a consideration of the social (in this case territorial) division of labour.[2] And there are other works, written round about the turn of the century, in which the idea of the social division of labour can be found in close association with the idea that trade consists essentially in the exchange of labour for labour.[3] But the first really suggestive British treatment of the connection between the division of labour in society and the phenomenon of value[4] is to be found in Mandeville. "By Society", said Mandeville, "I understand a Body Politick, in which Man . . . is become a Disciplin'd Creature, that can find his own Ends in Labouring for others, and where under one Head or other Form of Government each

[1] Harris, *op. cit.*, p. 15, footnote: "The mutual conveniencies accruing to individuals, from their betaking themselves to particular occupations, is perhaps the chief cement that connects them together; the main source of commerce, and of large political communities."

[2] *Economic Writings*, Vol. II, pp. 473-4. Cf. Vol. I, p. 260.

[3] See, e.g., Simon Clement, *A Discourse of the General Notions of Money, Trade, and Exchanges* (1695), pp. 3-4; and *Considerations on the East-India Trade* (1701), reprinted in *Early English Tracts on Commerce* (1856), pp. 591-3.

[4] For a significant French treatment of the subject see the works of Boisguillebert, which are reprinted in *Économistes Financiers du XVIIIe Siècle* (1843), ed. E. Daire. Boisguillebert's *Dissertation sur la Nature des Richesses* is particularly important in this connection. See Marx's interesting comments on Boisguillebert in *Critique of Political Economy*, pp. 59-62.

Member is render'd Subservient to the Whole. . . ."[1] In society, therefore, the institution of money becomes a necessity. It is impossible to name anything else, Mandeville wrote,

> "that is so absolutely necessary to the Order, Oeconomy, and the very Existence of the Civil Society; for as this is entirely built upon the Variety of our Wants, so the whole Superstructure is made up of the reciprocal Services, which Men do to each other. How to get these Services perform'd by others, when we have Occasion for them, is the grand and almost constant Sollicitude in Life of every individual Person. To expect, that others should serve us for nothing, is unreasonable; therefore all Commerce, that Men can have together, must be a continual bartering of one thing for another . . . Which way shall I persuade a Man to serve me, when the Service, I can repay him in, is such as he does not want or care for? . . . Money obviates and takes away all those Difficulties, by being an acceptable Reward for all the Services Men can do to one another. . . . There are great blessings that arise from Necessity; and that every Body is obliged to eat and drink, is the Cement of civil Society. Let Men set what high Value they please upon themselves, that Labour, which most People are capable of doing, will ever be the cheapest. Nothing can be dear, of which there is great Plenty, how beneficial soever it may be to Man; and Scarcity inhances the Price of Things much oftener than the Usefulness of them. . . ."[2]

The second part of *The Fable of the Bees*, in which this passage appears, was published in 1729, and in the same year Benjamin Franklin's *Modest Inquiry into the Nature and Necessity of a Paper Currency* appeared in Philadelphia. In this pamphlet the interdependence of producers in society and the consequent necessity of money are explained very much as Mandeville explained them, but out of the

[1] *The Fable of the Bees* (ed. F. B. Kaye), Vol. I, p. 347. Cf. the references to the division of labour in Vol. I, pp. 356-8; Vol. II, p. 284; and elsewhere.

[2] *Ibid.*, Vol. II, pp. 349-50. Adam Smith, in his famous *Letter to the Authors of the Edinburgh Review*, written in 1755, affirmed that the second volume of *The Fable of the Bees* had "given occasion to the system of Mr. Rousseau". And, as if to give point to this remark, Smith included the following among the passages from Rousseau which he translated in order to give readers of the *Review* "a specimen of his eloquence":

"Thus man, from being free and independent, became by a multitude of new necessities subjected in a manner, to all nature, and above all to his fellow creatures, whose slave he is in one sense even while he becomes their master; rich, he has occasion for their services; poor, he stands in need of their assistance; and even mediocrity does not enable him to live without them. He is obliged therefore to endeavour to interest them in his situation, and to make them find, either in reality or in appearance, their advantage in labouring for his." (*The Edinburgh Review for 1755*, 2nd edn., 1818, pp. 130-3).

analysis there springs, quite naturally, a significant formulation of the labour theory of value:

> "As Providence has so ordered it, that not only different countries, but even different parts of the same country, have their peculiar most suitable productions; and likewise that different men have geniuses adapted to a variety of different arts and manufactures; therefore *commerce*, or the exchange of one commodity or manufacture for another, is highly convenient and beneficial to mankind. . . . To facilitate exchange, men have invented MONEY, properly called a *medium of exchange*, because through or by its means labor is exchanged for labor, or one commodity for another. . . . Trade in general being nothing else but the exchange of labor for labor, the value of all things is . . . most justly measured by labor."[1]

The suggestion that labour is "more proper [than money] to be made a *measure of values*" is supported by an argument borrowed (without acknowledgment) from Petty. "The riches of a country", Franklin concludes, "are to be valued by the quantity of labor its inhabitants are able to purchase"[2]—an interesting anticipation of Smith's "commandable labour" concept.

The notion that the exchange of commodities is in essence the exchange of the labour of the men who produce them became something of a commonplace as the century progressed. Writers like Hume, Gervaise and Tucker popularised the idea that commodities produced for exchange consisted essentially of a mass of congealed or crystallised social effort.[3] Others, like Francis Hutcheson, developed the concept of the social division of labour,[4] and some, like Harris, developed it in close association with a theory of value which laid considerable emphasis on labour. It gradually came to be postulated that a commodity possessed exchange value simply because a part of the *labour of society* had been allocated to its production. It was not enough that *labour* should have been expended upon it: it was also necessary that this labour, as Marx was later to put it, should be "subordinate to the division of labour within society".[5] The expenditure of social labour was slowly recognised as a unique form of cost which was alone

---

[1] Franklin, *Works* (1836 edn.), Vol. II, pp. 263-4 and 267.

[2] *Ibid.*, p. 265. Cf. the letter from Franklin to Lord Kames reproduced in *Memoirs of the Hon. H. Home of Kames*, Vol. II, at p. 85.

[3] Hume, *Essays* (1889 edn.), Vol. I, pp. 293-4, 315, etc.; Gervaise, *The System or Theory of the Trade of the World* (1720), *passim*; R. L. Schuyler, *Josiah Tucker*, p. 146.

[4] W. R. Scott, *Francis Hutcheson*, pp. 235-7.

[5] *Value, Price and Profit*, in *Selected Works*, Vol. I, p. 305.

capable of conferring exchange value upon commodities. Value relations between commodities were revealed as reflections of social relations between men.

But this did not by itself dispose of the old objection that land, as well as labour, contributed something to the value of a commodity. It was not until the vital distinction between *wealth* and *value* had been properly established that it was possible to clarify the problem of the role of land. It had, of course, been appreciated from a fairly early date that the use value of a commodity was something different from its exchange value: the famous water-and-diamonds illustration[1] had been used by several writers before Smith, and there had been economists before Hutcheson who had pointed out that the exchange values of commodities often bore little relation to their utility. But it was some time before the distinction which Ricardo always emphasised between *wealth* (a sum of use values to the creation of which both land and labour contributed) and *value* (which was determined by labour alone) was accurately formulated, although several early economists had employed the distinction without being fully aware of what they were doing. Once land had been got rid of in this way as a determinant of value, it remained only to make it clear that labour contributed value to commodities, not per medium of the reward paid to it but per medium of the expenditure of the labour itself.

The most advanced statement of the labour theory of value prior to the publication of the *Wealth of Nations* was contained in a remarkable pamphlet published anonymously about 1738—*Some Thoughts on the Interest of Money in General*. This pamphlet, to which Marx referred on a number of occasions, has been curiously neglected by later historians of economic thought. It is not entirely free from the confusion just mentioned between the reward of labour and the labour itself as determinants of value, but on the whole it represents a considerable achievement. Consider, for example, the following extract:

"The true and real Value of the Necessaries of Life, is in Proportion to that Part which they contribute to the Maintenance of Mankind; and the Value of them when they are exchanged the one for the other, is regulated by the Quantity of Labour necessarily required, and commonly taken in producing them; and the Value or Price of them when they are bought and sold, and compared to a common Medium, will be govern'd by the Quantity of Labour employ'd,

[1] See below, p. 72.

and the greater or less Plenty of the Medium or common Measure. Water is as necessary for Life as Bread or Wine; but the Hand of God has poured out that upon Mankind in such Plenty, that every Man may have enough of that without any Trouble, so that generally 'tis of no Price; but when and where any Labour must be used, to apply it to particular Persons, there the Labour in making the Application must be paid for, tho' the Water be not: And on that Account, at some Times and in some Places, a Ton of Water may be as dear as a Ton of Wine."[1]

In this short passage, we are presented in swift succession with (a) a definition of the use value of a commodity; (b) a statement of the manner in which the exchange value of a commodity is determined which substantially anticipates Marx's concept of "socially-necessary labour"; (c) a statement of the manner in which the money price, as distinct from the exchange value, of a commodity is determined; and (d) an illustration of the fact that a commodity possessing use value does not usually possess exchange value unless labour has been bestowed upon it. And there is a later passage which is of at least equal importance, since it hardly seems possible that Adam Smith should not have been acquainted with it:

"In the more antient Times, when Commerce was carried on merely by bartering one Commodity for another, I apprehend no other Rule could be made Use of in exchanging one Thing for another, but the Quantity of Labour severally imployed in producing them. One Man has imployed himself a Week in providing this necessary of Life, and for his Pains deserves just as much as will Maintain him for a Week; and he that gives him some other in exchange cannot make a better Estimate of what is a proper Equivalent, than by computing what cost him just as much Labour and Time; which in Effect is no more than exchanging one Man's Labour in one Thing for a Time certain, for another Man's Labour in another Thing for the like Time. In bartering one Commodity for another, 'tis always supposed that he who gives a Thing in exchange, has more than enough to supply his own present Use, and that he who takes it in exchange wants it. A greater Quantity of that Thing in one Hand, or a greater Want of it on the other, at one Time more than another, will make a Variance in such exchange, but this is only *pro hoc & nunc*; and such Variance supposes some common Rule to govern such exchange, when Dealers are upon an equal Foot."[2]

[1] *Some Thoughts*, pp. 36-7.   [2] *Ibid.*, p. 39.

Here we have what appears to be the earliest clear statement of that "rule" which Adam Smith believed to govern the exchange of commodities in earlier forms of society.[1] And we have not only this, but also a clear recognition of the fact that this "rule" applies to the determination of exchange ratios only "when Dealers are upon an equal Foot."[2]

The theory of value towards which the Classical economists gradually felt their way, then, was based on the idea that labour contributed value to commodities *per medium of the expenditure of the labour itself*— i.e., per medium of the proportion of the total *social effort* which it was necessary to expend in order to produce the commodities. When a part of the organised effort of society (directed in accordance with demand) was expended in the production of a commodity, that commodity became, as it were, impregnated with the power of commanding others in exchange. Nature, although she afforded valuable assistance to man, afforded it freely, without any *cost* to him.[3] The only true cost of production, from the point of view of society as a whole, was the expenditure of human labour. In the creation of *wealth*, certainly, labour co-operated with land, although even here labour was regarded as the "father" or "active principle" of wealth, whereas land was visualised as the passive "mother". But the creation of *value* was the prerogative of labour alone. A labour theory of value based on these ideas, besides possessing certain technical advantages over other varieties of cost theory, eventually proved capable of illuminating in a particularly striking fashion the problem of the origin and persistence of that value-difference between output and input upon which, as we have seen, the Classical economists placed so much stress.

[1] *Wealth of Nations*, Vol. I, p. 49.

[2] It is perhaps also worth noting that the idea that "such Variance supposes some common Rule to govern such exchange" was emphasised again and again by Marx.

[3] Cf. *Some Thoughts*, pp. 37-8: "The Labour required to plow and to sow an Acre of Ground, and to gather the Fruits of it, is much the same whether it yields two or four Quarters of Wheat; and if the ordinary Produce is two Quarters and the common Price 5s. *per* Bushel, the two supernumerary Quarters are of the Nature of Water, the Gift of God and of a plentiful Season, and they should be sold for nothing, or the whole Quantity be sold for 2s. 6d. the Bushel."

CHAPTER TWO

ADAM SMITH AND THE DEVELOPMENT
OF THE LABOUR THEORY

1. *The Theory of Value in the "Glasgow Lectures"*

THE system of moral philosophy which Adam Smith most admired was that which proposed to investigate "wherein consisted the happiness and perfection of a man, considered not only as an individual, but as the member of a family, of a state, and of the great society of mankind".[1] And it was precisely this deliberate emphasis on the social relations between man and man which set Smith's own work—not only in moral philosophy but also in political economy—apart from and above that of so many of his predecessors and contemporaries. His primary interest, and that of the brilliant circle of thinkers who gathered around him, was in the nature and development of "civil society"; and political economy for Smith was the main field in which what Marx called the "anatomy" of this civil society was to be sought.[2] The study of civil society was essentially a new one, and Smith seems to have realised that it could not be effectively pursued without a substantial reorientation of philosophical and economic thinking. New tasks required new tools. One of the most important of these new tools, developed quite consciously to assist in the analysis of the new socio-economic relations which were then developing, was the theory of value propounded in Book One of the *Wealth of Nations*.

The present chapter begins with the account of value contained in what are known as the *Glasgow Lectures*,[3] rather than with the more mature theory put forward in the *Wealth of Nations*, because the latter can only be seen in its proper perspective if a genetical approach is adopted. A study of the evolution of Smith's thought on the subject of value, I believe, can help to make the final version of his theory rather more consistent and intelligible than has generally been assumed to be possible.

---

[1] *Wealth of Nations*, Vol. II, p. 259.
[2] Marx, *Critique of Political Economy* (Kerr edn.), p. 11.
[3] The course of lectures on "Justice, Police, Revenue and Arms" which Smith gave while a professor at Glasgow University. A student's notes of these lectures, taken down in 1763, were discovered over a century later, and published by Edwin Cannan in 1896.

There are two important features of the *Glasgow Lectures*, marking them off to some extent from the *Wealth of Nations*, which it seems desirable to stress at the outset. The first of these relates to Smith's treatment of accumulation. In the *Lectures*, the accumulation of capital did not yet play the central role which it was destined to do in the *Wealth of Nations*. It is true that even in the *Lectures* there was a fairly clear recognition of the fact that accumulation is the key to abundance: before society can reap the great advantages of the division of labour, Smith said, "some accumulation of stock is necessary".[1] And Smith also recognised in the *Lectures* that certain political obstacles had to be removed before the "accumulation of stock", and therefore the division of labour, could be carried out on a wide scale:

> "Under the feudal constitution there could be very little accumulation of stock, which will appear from considering the situation of those three orders of men, which made up the whole body of the people: the peasants, the landlords, and the merchants. The peasants had leases which depended upon the caprice of their masters; they could never increase in wealth, because the landlord was ready to squeeze it all from them, and therefore they had no motive to acquire it. As little could the landlords increase their wealth, as they lived so indolent a life, and were involved in perpetual wars. The merchants again were oppressed by all ranks, and were not able to secure the produce of their industry from rapine and violence. Thus there could be little accumulation of wealth at all; but after the fall of the feudal government these obstacles to industry were removed, and the stock of commodities began gradually to increase."[2]

But looking at the *Glasgow Lectures* as a whole, the role of accumulation seems to have been conceived as a relatively subordinate one. Although Smith's treatment of accumulation was even then much in advance of that of his contemporaries, he did not yet visualise the drive to accumulate as the mainspring and motive force of economic development. The economic motive force, as will shortly appear, was viewed in a rather different way.

Related to this is the second feature of the *Glasgow Lectures* to which I want to draw attention—the fact that they contain no trace of the concept of a natural rate of profit. Certain types of "profit" do occasionally appear in the *Lectures*—for example, the "profit" expected

[1] *Lectures* (ed. Cannan), p. 222.   [2] *Ibid.*, p. 220.

by the subscribers to Law's scheme,[1] the "profit" payable to the banker in an exchange transaction,[2] and the "profits" received by certain West Indian sugar planters.[3] And in that early revision of part of the *Lectures* which its discoverer called "an early draft of the *Wealth of Nations*" we read of the "profits" of the traffic of the opulent merchant,[4] the "profits and expences" of the master of the famous pin factory,[5] and the "profite of the merchant" which has to be included in the price of a pin.[6] But nowhere, so far as I can see, is there any definite indication that these "profits" are regarded as bearing any regular relationship to the quantity of stock employed by their recipients. "Profit" simply means "gain". The amount of "profit" received is variously visualised as being dependent upon the degree of risk involved, the amount of good luck experienced, the strength of the monopoly position enjoyed, or the quantity and quality of labour performed—but nowhere is it clearly visualised as varying according to the amount of stock employed. The basic distinction made in the *Wealth of Nations* between the "profits of stock" accruing to the capitalist employer and the "wages of labour" accruing to his employees is not emphasised in the *Glasgow Lectures*. Indeed, the general impression we receive from the *Lectures* as a whole (especially from the sections in which price and value are dealt with) is that Smith then still considered it useful, at least as a first approximation, to regard production as being carried on by more or less independent craftsmen and labourers who still owned their own means of production— the blacksmiths, weavers, tailors, watchmakers, carpenters and their like who so often figure in the *Lectures* as typical producers. Productive units where several individuals are employed seem to be looked upon rather as co-operative establishments consisting of workmen who still retain a certain measure of independence and a "master" who is virtually one of themselves. If one conceives the economic organisation of industry in this manner, it is unlikely that the net reward of the "master" will be regarded as bearing any sort of regular relationship to the quantity of stock which he happens to employ. There are, of course, numerous passages in the *Lectures* (notably those dealing with accumulation) which indicate that Smith was already aware of the importance, if not the precise significance, of the changes in economic organisation which were taking place at this time. But

---

[1] *Lectures*, p. 215.   [2] *Ibid.*, p. 221.   [3] *Ibid.*, p. 225.
[4] W. R. Scott, *Adam Smith as Student and Professor*, p. 327.
[5] *Ibid.*, p. 331.   [6] *Ibid.*, p. 328.

generally speaking the model of the economy which Smith used in the *Lectures* was closer to those employed by Hutcheson, Hume and Cantillon than to that which Smith himself was later to use in the *Wealth of Nations*.

Smith seems to have realised, rather more clearly than most of his predecessors, that the extension of the social division of labour under modern conditions necessarily implied that the market was taking over a number of economic functions which had formerly been performed by other institutions. In the new market economy, where the basic social nexus between individuals was reflected in the fact that the commodities which they produced exchanged for one another on the market at certain *prices*, an understanding of the problem of "What Circumstances regulate the Price of Commodities"[1] began to appear of paramount importance. In approaching this question, Smith, like several of his contemporaries, was evidently impressed by the fact that the prices of many commodities, although they varied from day to day or from season to season in accordance with fluctuations in supply and demand, seemed to revolve around a sort of average or central price. If the actual market price was at any time either above or below this central price, it would tend automatically to return towards it. It was this central price which Smith postulated as the "natural" price whose level it was the primary task of a theory of value to explain. The question of "What Circumstances regulate the Price of Commodities", therefore, seemed to Smith (in the *Lectures*) to resolve itself into two other questions—first, what are the constituents of the natural price, and second, how does it come about that the market price tends to be made equal to the natural price?

So far as the first question is concerned, it will be remembered that Cantillon had already made a distinction between the "market price" of a commodity and its "intrinsic value", the constituents of the latter being described as "the value of the land" plus "the value of the labour" employed in production. Smith's account in the *Lectures* of the constituents of the natural price differed from Cantillon's account of "intrinsic value" in at least one very important respect, relating to "the value of the labour". Smith linked the natural price of a commodity, not to the *actual* price of the labour employed to make it (i.e., not to the actual reward paid to the direct producer, whatever this might happen to be in any particular instance), but to what he called the *natural* price of labour. "A man then has the

---

[1] *Lectures*, p. 173.

natural price of his labour", said Smith, "when it is sufficient to maintain him during the time of labour, to defray the expense of education, and to compensate the risk of not living long enough, and of not succeeding in the business. When a man has this, there is sufficient encouragement to the labourer, and the commodity will be cultivated in proportion to the demand."[1] Smith did not mean by this, as might at first sight appear, that the natural price of a commodity was *equivalent* to the natural price of the labour which produced it. What he meant was simply that the price of the commodity must be sufficiently high to "encourage the labourer"—i.e., to yield to the direct producer, after all his paid-out costs had been met, a reward at least equivalent to the natural price of his labour as so defined. When the commodity is sold at a price sufficiently high to do this and no more, said Smith, it is then sold at its natural price. Smith said very little in the *Lectures* about the other constituents of the natural price, which he possibly then regarded as given. Once the level of the natural price of the labour of the direct producer was determined, the level of the natural price of his product was also determined. The limitations of this analysis—and the reason for these limitations—are obvious enough. Smith has tacitly assumed that the direction of production is in the hands not of capitalist employers who expect to receive the natural rate of profit on their capital, but of more or less independent workmen who expect to receive the natural price of their labour. Profit on capital has not yet emerged—or at least has not yet been recognised by Smith as having emerged—as a general category of income separate and distinct from the wages of labour. Or, what amounts to much the same thing, the socio-economic distinctions which exist in the real world between the capitalist and the direct producer are not yet regarded as relevant to the problem of the determination of commodity prices and incomes. Both classes are simply lumped together as "labourers", and it is assumed that the price which will "sufficiently encourage" the first is determined according to the same principles as that which will "sufficiently encourage" the second. A natural rate of profit, therefore, does not yet appear as a separate constituent of the natural price.

Smith's answer to the second question—how does it come about that the market price tends to be made equal to the natural price—begins with a discussion of the circumstances which regulate market prices. The market price of a commodity, Smith argues, is regulated

[1] *Lectures*, p. 176. Cf. Hutcheson, *A System of Moral Philosophy* (1755), Vol. II, pp. 63-4.

by three circumstances. First, there is "the demand, or need for the commodity". Second, there is "the abundance or scarcity of the commodity in proportion to the need of it". And third, there is "the riches or poverty of those who demand". The market price, in other words, is determined by the relationship between the available supply and the effective demand. And the market price and the natural price, although they are determined according to quite different principles, are "necessarily connected", in the following way:

> "If the market price of any commodity is very great, and the labour very highly rewarded, the market is prodigiously crowded with it, greater quantities of it are produced, and it can be sold to the inferior ranks of people. If for every ten diamonds there were ten thousand, they would become the purchase of everybody, because they would become very cheap, and would sink to their natural price. Again, when the market is over-stocked, and there is not enough got for the labour of the manufacture, nobody will bind to it, they cannot have a subsistence by it, because the market price falls then below the natural price."

It is what Smith called "the concurrence of different labourers", then, which makes the market price tend towards the natural price.[1] Once again, the limitations of this analysis are fairly obvious. Smith had observed that in the real world the efforts and resources of individual producers naturally tended to move towards those occupations which promised the highest rewards, and that it was as a result of this continual movement that prices under competition tended to be adjusted to a level which cut out "abnormal" gains or losses. What he did not at this stage fully appreciate, however, was the real nature of the mechanism which brought about this movement and the consequential price adjustment. In the *Lectures*, he visualised the mainspring of the mechanism in terms of the desire of each individual "labourer" to secure the highest possible return for his labour. It was not until rather later that he realised that this approach was far too broad to be useful. The real mainspring, he eventually saw, was the desire of each individual capitalist to secure the highest possible rate of profit on his capital.

There are two other features of Smith's treatment of these problems in the *Lectures* which must be commented upon before we pass to the *Wealth of Nations*. First, immediately after having examined "What

[1] Quotations in this paragraph from *Lectures*, pp. 176-9.

Circumstances regulate the *Price* of Commodities", Smith proceeded to consider "Money as the Measure of *Value* and Medium of Exchange".[1] Now when we speak of a "measure" of value, we may mean either (or perhaps both) of two things. We may be using the word "measure" in the sense in which a foot rule is a measure of length or a spring balance a measure of weight. Or we may mean by "measure of value" a sort of inherent "measure" which not only measures but also in a sense *embodies* the very stuff or substance of value.[2] In the section of the *Lectures* dealing with "Money as the Measure of Value", Smith considered money as a measure in the first of these two senses. At the beginning of the following section, however, he said: "We have shown what rendered money the measure of value, but it is to be observed that labour, not money, is the true measure of value."[3] It has sometimes been suggested that Smith was here using the word "measure" in the second of the two senses just distinguished, and that the germ of the "labour theory" of the *Wealth of Nations* is to be found in this remark. It is possible that there is an element of truth in this suggestion, but there does not appear to be any real evidence that Smith, at the time he delivered the *Lectures*, regarded this idea of labour as the "true measure" of value—an idea quite frequently to be met with in the work of eighteenth-century writers—as anything very much more than a convenient weapon to use against the Mercantilist notion that opulence consisted in money.[4] In the *Lectures* Smith went a long way towards delineating that "natural price" of a commodity which he eventually came to regard as the monetary expression of its value. But at this stage he had not yet penetrated sufficiently far beneath the surface of the external phenomena of the market to establish contact with the deep underlying forces which ultimately determined the "natural price".

The other point is this. In the *Lectures*, Smith prefaced his discussion of "Cheapness or Plenty" with two sections containing what really amounts to a theory of consumption. "All the Arts", he said in the second section, "are subservient to the Natural Wants of Mankind"; and in the course of his discussion of this theme the following statement occurs:

[1] *Lectures*, pp. 182 ff. (My italics.)
[2] Cf. Marx, *Theories of Surplus Value* (English edn.), p. 116. Cf. also below, p. 63, and p. 64, footnote.
[3] *Lectures*, p. 190.
[4] The fact that the idea could be used for this purpose was no doubt one of the reasons—although I think a subsidiary reason—for its increasing popularity in the eighteenth century.

"To improve and multiply the materials, which are the principal objects of our necessities, gives occasion to all the variety of the arts ... By these again other subsidiary [arts] are occasioned. Writing, to record the multitude of transactions, and geometry, which serves many useful purposes. Law and government, too, seem to propose no other object but this; they secure the individual who has enlarged his property, that he may peaceably enjoy the fruits of it. By law and government all the different arts flourish, and that inequality of fortune to which they give occasion is sufficiently preserved. By law and government domestic peace is enjoyed and security from the foreign invader. Wisdom and virtue too derive their lustre from supplying these necessities. For as the establishment of law and government is the highest effort of human prudence and wisdom, the causes cannot have a different influence from what the effects have."[1]

What Smith is virtually saying in this noteworthy passage is that the way in which a society gets its living determines in large part the nature both of its social institutions and of its ethical norms. Smith, in common with the other members of the so-called "Scottish Historical School",[2] frequently adopted the type of materialist approach to the study of society which is reflected in this passage. To understand the general configuration of society at any given time, the members of the School believed, one must look first to what they called "the mode of subsistence"; and, in particular, to understand the forms of law and government one must look first to "the state of property". The adoption of this approach by men like Adam Smith and John Millar was an extremely important factor in the development of the labour theory of value. For the labour theory of value represents in essence an application, to the study of the special field of exchange relations, of the fundamental idea which lies behind this materialist approach. In order to understand these exchange relations, the labour theory in effect maintains, one must look first to the basic production relations which men enter into with one another in the process of gaining their subsistence. In its formulation in the eighteenth century by Smith, as well as in its development in the nineteenth century

[1] *Lectures*, p. 160.
[2] See Roy Pascal, "Property and Society: The Scottish Historical School of the Eighteenth Century", in *The Modern Quarterly*, Vol. I, No. 2, March 1938; and W. C. Lehmann, "John Millar, Historical Sociologist," in *The British Journal of Sociology*, Vol. III, No. 1, March 1952.

by Marx, the labour theory of value was intimately associated with a materialist conception of history.[1]

2. The Transition to the "Wealth of Nations"

We are all familiar with those curious diagrams depicting several blocks placed on top of one another, the number of which we are invited to count. We count them, and find that there appear to be, say, six. Then, while we are looking at the diagram, its whole pattern and perspective seem to change magically before our eyes, and counting the blocks again we find that there are now no longer six, but seven. A somewhat similar sort of metamorphosis, of a qualitative rather than a quantitative character, occasionally occurs in the field of social science. An observer, looking at the society around him at a given time, sees there a particular pattern of relationships and categories—possibly that pattern which he has been led to expect that he will see. Then, often quite suddenly, the old pattern appears to dissolve and a new and different one takes its place. The observer finds that he has hitherto, at least up to a point, been looking at the wrong things. But this analogy is misleading in one important respect. In the case of the blocks, the transformation takes place entirely in the mind of the beholder. The diagram remains exactly the same: there has merely been a sort of mental reshuffle of the elements of which it is composed. In the case of society, however, the entity which is being observed does not remain the same, but is changing and developing all the time. What often happens, although the observer may not be consciously aware of it, is that he notices that a new set of social relationships is in actual fact emerging from the old, and, anticipating their eventual ascendancy, places them at the basis of a new theoretical system.

In the *Glasgow Lectures*, as we have seen, Smith had employed a traditional model of economic organisation which visualised the chief equilibrating movements of efforts and resources as being initiated by more or less "independent" labourers desiring to maximise the return for their labour. In the *Wealth of Nations*, on the other hand, although there are still many significant traces of this earlier view, these equilibrating movements are mainly visualised as being initiated by owners of capital desiring to maximise their profit. In every

---

[1] I have developed this theme in an article entitled "The Scottish Contribution to Marxist Sociology," which appears in *Democracy and the Labour Movement* (ed. John Saville), London, 1954.

civilised society, said Smith, the landlords, labourers and capitalists form the "three great, original and constituent orders", whose respective revenues—"the rent of land, the wages of labour, and the profits of stock"[1]—together make up the national income. And the real mainspring of economic development in such a society, Smith maintained, is the drive by the third of these "orders" to maximise their profit and accumulate capital. If we are to understand the anatomy of our society, Smith was in effect saying, we must certainly start from the simple relations which exist between men as separate but mutually interdependent producers of different commodities, but we must also recognise that in each stage of social development men engaged in production enter into certain important *class* relations with one another, in the light of which the basic economic processes of that stage must always be analysed. And in Britain in the latter half of the eighteenth century, Smith assumes, the main class relationships are those which exist between the landlords, the labourers and the capitalists.

There is little doubt that it was his study of what was happening in cities like Glasgow which was primarily responsible for Smith's acute analysis of the capital-labour relationship and the phenomenon of accumulation—an analysis far ahead of any other at the time.[2] In Glasgow in the 1750's and '60's, the rate at which economic techniques and relationships were developing and changing was extremely rapid (owing largely to the impact of the tobacco trade), and the new forms of economic organisation which were emerging could be fairly easily contrasted with the older forms which still existed, say, in the Scottish Highlands, or in feudal France, or among the Indian tribes of North America. It was probably at some stage in the course of Smith's contemplation of these phenomena that the model used in the *Glasgow Lectures* began to dissolve, and the outlines of a new system of economic organisation, driven by a new mechanism, began to form in his mind. Certain distinctions, previously unnoticed or abstracted from, began to assume central significance—notably the distinctions between stock and capital, between profits and wages, and between the two social classes who lived by profits and wages. The fact that "in every part of Europe, twenty workmen serve under a master for one that is independent"[3] was seen to be of crucial im-

[1] *Wealth of Nations*, Vol. I, p. 248.
[2] See my article "Adam Smith and the Classical Concept of Profit," in *The Scottish Journal of Political Economy*, Vol. I, No. 2.
[3] *Ibid.*, Vol. I, p. 68. Cf. the remarks on "independence" in the *Glasgow Lectures*, pp. 9 and 155-6.

portance. The elements of the basic pattern of relationships between the three "constituent orders" which is described in the *Wealth of Nations* began to emerge. And, as a consequence, the natural or average rate of profit on capital came to be regarded as a separate constituent of the natural price of commodities.

Dugald Stewart, in the course of a discussion of Smith's analysis of the component parts of the price of commodities into rent, wages and profits, mentioned that "it appears from a manuscript of Mr. Smith's, now in my possession, that the foregoing analysis or division was suggested to him by Mr. Oswald of Dunnikier".[1] This may well be true; although it may also be true that Oswald himself got the idea from Hume, with whom he corresponded on economic problems.[2] But the only question of any real interest in this connection is whether Smith had arrived at the idea (independently or otherwise) prior to his visit to France in 1764.[3] Professor Scott claimed that the "early draft", the date of which he tentatively placed at 1763, contained a "quite explicit" statement of the distributive division into rent, wages and profits.[4] It is true that the manuscript of the "early draft" contains one passage dealing with distributive questions—but as far as I can see only one—of which there is no trace in the student's notes of the *Lectures*, and that in this passage a division of the produce between the "profit" of the master and the wages of the artisans whom he employs is fairly clearly envisaged.[5] But it is fairly clear from the manuscript as a whole that Smith, at the time of its compilation, was not yet thinking in terms of the basic pattern of the *Wealth of Nations*. This seems a reasonable inference from Smith's sketch of the

[1] Dugald Stewart, *Collected Works*, Vol. IX, p. 6. Cf. Vol. X, p. 81.

[2] See *Memorials of James Oswald* (1825), pp. 65-71 and 122-3; and *The Letters of David Hume* (ed. J. Y. T. Greig), Vol. II, p. 94.

[3] The point here, which may not be clear to non-specialists in the history of economic thought, is that there are certain important parallels between some of Smith's doctrines and those put forward by the so-called Physiocrats, who flourished in France during the third quarter of the eighteenth century. Since Smith had contact with the Physiocrats during his visit to France, some ten years before the publication of the *Wealth of Nations*, there has been considerable controversy over the question of the extent of their influence upon him. The best short account of the Physiocratic system is still that given by Marx in the first section of his *Theories of Surplus Value* and in the chapter entitled "From the Critical History" which he contributed to Engels's *Anti-Dühring*. For more detailed information about them the reader is referred to the monumental work by G. Weulersse, *Le Mouvement Physiocratique en France de 756 à 1770* (Paris, 1910).

[4] *Adam Smith as Student and Professor*, pp. 117-18 and 319-20.

[5] The passage appears on p. 331 of Professor Scott's book. Even here, it might be argued that the last four lines on p. 164 of the *Lectures* were intended by the student as a summary of the passage which appears in the first thirteen lines on p. 331 of Professor Scott's book, and that the student simply omitted to copy down the arithmetical illustration.

section dealing with the circumstances which regulate the prices of commodities, which follows more or less exactly the scheme of the *Lectures*. The natural price reappears there as "that price which is sufficient to encourage the labourer",[1] and there is no trace in the manuscript of any suggestion that profit at the average rate should be regarded as one of the constituents of the natural price.

This does not mean that we must revert entirely to the old exaggerated beliefs about the degree of Smith's dependence on the French Physiocrats. On many matters he did not require any instruction from them: for example, his own basic ideas on the virtues of laissez-faire and free trade had apparently been formed at least as early as 1749.[2] And if he learned a certain amount from Physiocrats like Mercier de la Rivière and Nicolas Baudeau, either as a result of personal discussion with them during his stay in Paris or through the books which they subsequently published, it is quite likely that they learned just as much from him.[3] From Turgot, however, whose *Reflections* were probably being composed about the time of Smith's stay in Paris, he may have learned rather more. The central theme of the second half of Turgot's *Reflections* is the idea that "the cultivation of land, manufactures of all kinds, and all branches of commerce depend upon a mass of capitals, or of movable accumulated riches, which having been at first advanced by the Undertakers in each of these different classes of labours, must return to them every year with a steady profit".[4] Smith, as we have seen, had already been impressed by the importance of the "accumulation of stock" before

[1] Scott, *op. cit.*, p. 346.

[2] *Ibid.*, pp. 53-4.

[3] Smith was in Paris during most of 1766. Mercier de la Rivière must then have been writing his *L'Ordre Naturel et Essentiel des Sociétés Politiques*, which was published in the following year. Nicolas Baudeau was converted to Physiocracy under somewhat spectacular circumstances in 1766, and must have begun almost immediately to write his *Première Introduction à la Philosophie Économique*, which was also published in 1767. It is not difficult to detect a significant change of emphasis in these two works, marking them off to some extent from the earlier productions of Quesnay and Mirabeau. The later writers, it is true, still move within the same formal Physiocratic framework, but they lay much greater stress on the distinction between the capitalist and the wage-labourers whom he employs, and they are rather more ready to make concessions to the view that the income of the capitalist normally contains a "net" or "disposable" element. These changes might well have suggested themselves to the French writers in the course of personal debates with Smith, who would undoubtedly have criticised the official Physiocratic doctrine (as Hume did) because of its denial or neglect of these points.

[4] Turgot, *Reflections on the Formation and the Distribution of Riches* (English edn., 1898), pp. 62-3. Turgot proceeds to emphasise that "it is this advance and this continual return of capitals which constitute . . . that useful and fruitful circulation which gives life to all the labours of the society, which maintains movement and life in the body politic."

he went to France, but had probably not yet fully appreciated the extent to which the attainment of what he had called in the *Lectures* the "natural balance of industry"[1] was dependent upon the action of capitalists who, desiring to maximise their rate of accumulation, constantly directed their capitals into those avenues where it was expected that they would yield the highest rate of profit. His discussions with Turgot in Paris in 1766 may have assisted him to develop his own views on this point. In particular, the Physiocratic concept of capital as "advances", upon which Turgot laid such emphasis, may have helped Smith to see more clearly both the new role of accumulation and the significance of the contrast between the capitalist who made the "advances" and the labourer to whom wages were "advanced". But he must have been struck at least as much with the limitations of Physiocratic thought as with its positive features. Was it in fact true, as most of the Physiocrats were then still maintaining, that there was no "disposable" element in the rewards normally received by the master-manufacturer, the capitalist farmer and the merchant? Certainly, at any rate in and around cities like Glasgow, a substantial portion of these rewards did appear to be "disposable" in the Physiocratic sense. This seemed evident from the fact that the classes mentioned appeared to be already accumulating capital at a far greater rate than would be possible according to the Physiocratic "privations" theory.[2] The Physiocrats' attitude on this point, which must have seemed to Smith quite arbitrary and dogmatic, may well have assisted substantially in persuading him of the importance of the phenomenon whose existence they sought to deny. The economic theory of Physiocracy seemed to be inconsistent with the fact of capitalist accumulation, and an alternative theory had to be found.

The accumulation of capital, then, became the great axis around which the argument of the *Wealth of Nations* revolves. The accumulation of capital is presented in that work as the essential precondition and basic cause of the growth of opulence. "The annual produce of the land and labour of any nation", Smith says,

"can be increased in its value by no other means, but by increasing either the number of its productive labourers, or the productive powers of those labourers who had before been employed. The number of its productive labourers, it is evident, can never be much increased, but in consequence of an increase of capital, or of the

[1] *Lectures*, p. 180.
[2] For an account of this theory see, e.g., Turgot, *op. cit.*, p. 44.

funds destined for maintaining them. The productive powers of the same number of labourers cannot be increased, but in consequence either of some addition and improvement to those machines and instruments which facilitate and abridge labour; or of a more proper division and distribution of employment. In either case an additional capital is almost always required."[1]

And the drive to accumulate is both mainspring and regulator of the mechanism of the economic process: it is in fact the principal medium through which the famous "invisible hand" transmits its beneficent power to human society. It operates in three main ways. First and foremost, it leads to a substantial increase in real income over time. The annual produce of England's land and labour, Smith writes, is much greater now than it was either at the Restoration or the Revolution.[2] *Therefore*, he says, the capital annually employed in cultivating the land and maintaining the labour must likewise be much greater. "In the midst of all the exactions of government", Smith writes,

"this capital has been silently and gradually accumulated by the private frugality and good conduct of individuals, by their universal, continual, and uninterrupted effort to better their own condition. It is this effort, protected by law and allowed by liberty to exert itself in the manner that is most advantageous, which has maintained the progress of England towards opulence and improvement in almost all former times, and which, it is to be hoped, will do so in all future times."[3]

Second, it leads to the optimum allocation of capital (from the point of view of society) between different employments:

"Every individual is continually exerting himself to find out the most advantageous employment for whatever capital he can command. It is his own advantage, indeed, and not that of the society, which he has in view. But the study of his own advantage naturally or rather necessarily leads him to prefer that employment which is most advantageous to the society."[4]

And third, it leads to the optimum allocation of resources within the particular employment so selected:

[1] *Wealth of Nations*, Vol. I, p. 325. Cf. *ibid.*, Vol. I, pp. 2 and 259.
[2] Smith refers to the period which had passed since the Restoration as "the happiest and most fortunate period of them all" (p. 327).
[3] *Wealth of Nations*, Vol. I, pp. 327-8.
[4] *Ibid.*, p. 419, Cf. Vol. II, pp. 127-9.

"The person who employs his stock in maintaining labour, necessarily wishes to employ it in such a manner as to produce as great a quantity of work as possible. He endeavours, therefore, both to make among his workmen the most proper distribution of employment, and to furnish them with the best machines which he can either invent or afford to purchase. His abilities in both these respects are generally in proportion to the extent of his stock, or to the number of people whom it can employ."[1]

But the process of accumulation, of course, could not be considered in isolation. What was accumulated had first to be produced and distributed. The basic economic processes of production, distribution and accumulation are analysed by Smith with specific reference to the new pattern of class relationships which he had come to detect in the society of his day. The three "great, original and constituent orders" stand in certain definite relations to the economic resources of society and therefore to one another, and the basic economic processes can be adequately explained only if full account is taken of the nature of these social relations. Consider, for example, the question of the distribution of the national income among the land-lords, the capitalists and the labourers. The landlords' income, rent, "is not at all proportioned to what the landlord may have laid out upon the improvement of the land", and it costs him "neither labour nor care". Rent is "naturally a monopoly price", which the landlords are able to exact because they enjoy a protected monopoly of the available supply of land. Their tenants, the capitalist farmers, are obliged to pay this rent for the use of the land; and they are able to pay it because the selling price of their product is generally sufficient to cover their paid-out costs and "the ordinary profits of farming stock in the neighbourhood".[2] The capitalists' income, profit, is not proportioned to the amount of "labour" which they may happen to perform. It is born, in the last analysis, of the capital-labour relationship. It owes its origin to the fact that the labour of the workmen whom the capitalists hire is capable of adding sufficient value to the raw materials to pay not only the wages of the workmen but also "the profits of their employer upon the whole stock of materials and wages which he advanced".[3] The capitalists are able to appropriate this sur-plus because the labourers generally "stand in need of a master to advance them the materials of their work, and their wages and

[1] *Wealth of Nations*, Vol. I, p. 259.   [2] *Ibid.*, Vol. I, pp. 145–6 and 248.
[3] *Ibid.*, Vol. I, p. 50.

maintenance till it be compleated".[1] And the labourers' income, wages, is less than the value of the whole produce of their labour precisely because of the fact that they own neither capital nor land and therefore "stand in need of a master", etc.[2] It was only natural that Smith should have laid this emphasis upon the relations of production in his account of the basic economic processes, since one of his main purposes was to analyse the effects of the changes which were visibly occurring in these relations in the society in which he lived. I stress this point here because the basic feature of orthodox economics in the post-Classical period, as we shall see later, was its tendency to abstract from these relations and to characterise them as irrelevant to the analytic purpose.

3. The Theory of Value in the "Wealth of Nations"
(a) The "Real Measure" of Value

Smith's discussion of value in the *Wealth of Nations* proceeds naturally from his discussion of the division of labour in society. "When the division of labour has been once thoroughly established", he writes,

> "it is but a very small part of a man's wants which the produce of his own labour can supply. He supplies the far greater part of them by exchanging that surplus part of the produce of his own labour, which is over and above his own consumption, for such parts of the produce of other men's labour as he has occasion for. Every man thus lives by exchanging, or becomes in some measure a merchant, and the society itself grows to be what is properly a commercial society."[3]

[1] *Wealth of Nations*, Vol. I, p. 67.

[2] Smith also emphasised the fact that "in disputes with their workmen, masters must generally have the advantage". Masters, he wrote, "are always and everywhere in a sort of tacit, but constant and uniform combination, not to raise the wages of labour above their actual rate" (*ibid.*, pp. 68–9).

[3] *Ibid.*, Vol. I, p. 24. Cf. the following passage from *The Theory of Moral Sentiments* (Stewart's edn. of the *Works*, Vol. I, pp. 145-6): "All the members of human society stand in need of each others assistance, and are likewise exposed to mutual injuries. Where the necessary assistance is reciprocally afforded from love, from gratitude, from friendship, and esteem, the society flourishes and is happy. All the different members of it are bound together by the agreeable bands of love and affection, and are, as it were, drawn to one common centre of mutual good offices. But though the necessary assistance should not be afforded from such generous and disinterested motives, though among the different members of the society there should be no mutual love and affection, the society, though less happy and agreeable, will not necessarily be dissolved. Society may subsist among different men, as among different merchants, from a sense of its utility, without any mutual love or affection; and though no man in it should owe any obligation, or be bound in gratitude to any other, it may still be upheld by a mercenary exchange of good offices according to an agreed valuation."

It is with this passage that Smith introduces his chapter "Of the Origin and Use of Money", and there is a similar reference to the social division of labour in the first paragraph of the chapter which follows—the famous chapter entitled "Of the Real and Nominal Price of Commodities, or of their Price in Labour, and their Price in Money".

The question of the division of labour had engaged Smith's attention from a very early date. It forms the main subject both of the so-called "early draft" and of two of the still earlier manuscripts discovered by Professor Scott.[1] Smith generally uses the phrase "division of labour" as a blanket term which will cover both the social division of labour and the division of labour in industry, although in some places he does make a distinction between them—as, for example, where he remarks that "the nature of agriculture, indeed, does not admit of so many subdivisions of labour, nor of such an entire seperation of one business from another, as commonly takes place in manufactures".[2] In the *Wealth of Nations*, he sets out in the first chapter to illustrate the effects of what he calls "the division of labour, in the general business of society" by considering the manner in which it operates "in some particular manufactures". It is commonly supposed, he proceeds, that the division of labour is carried furthest in some "very trifling" manufactures (such as that carried on in the famous pin manufactory). This supposition, however, according to Smith, is simply the result of an optical illusion. In certain "great manufactures", where the work may really be "divided into a much greater number of parts, than in those of a more trifling nature", there are so many workmen employed that it is "impossible to collect them all into the same workhouse", and therefore the division of labour has been "much less observed".[3] As Marx pointed out, Adam Smith is here virtually assuming that "the difference between the . . . social division of labour, and the division in manufacture, is merely subjective". In reality, although there are certainly numerous analogies and connections between them, the two are essentially different. Whereas the tie which binds together the independent labours of, say, the dyer, the spinner and the weaver is "the fact that their respective products are commodities", the division of labour in manufacture is characterised by "the fact that the detail labourer produces no

[1] Scott, *op. cit.*, pp. 379-85. [2] *Ibid.*, pp. 329-30.

[3] *Wealth of Nations*, Vol. I, pp. 5-6. Mandeville, too, illustrated the effects of the division of labour in general by the example of a particular manufacture—in this case watch-making (*op. cit.*, Vol. II, p. 284).

commodities".[1] In the second and third chapters of the *Wealth of Nations*, however, dealing respectively with "the principle which gives occasion to the division of labour" and the connection of the division of labour with "the extent of the market", Smith concerns himself almost exclusively with the division of labour in society, and it is out of this analysis that his discussion of value springs. In every civilised society each labourer works for and is dependent upon every other labourer. As Smith puts it, "he supplies them abundantly with what they have occasion for, and they accommodate him as amply with what he has occasion for".[2] Under these circumstances, the possession of a useful object upon the production of which labour has been expended customarily conveys to its possessor "the power of purchasing other goods": or, in other words, the object acquires exchange value. It acquires this exchange value, Smith's argument implies, by virtue of the fact that it is the product of the labour of an individual or group of individuals in a society which is characterised by and dependent upon the mutual interchange of the products of the separate labours of individuals. The exchange of commodities is in essence the exchange of social activities. The value relationship between commodities which manifests itself in the act of exchange is in essence the reflection of a relationship between men as producers. Value, as Marx was later to put it, is a social relation.

It is easy enough, of course, to see all this in the *Wealth of Nations* if one starts from the vantage-point of Marx's *Capital*. But that is not to say that it is not really there. It is true, I think, that Smith did in fact tend to conceive of value as an attribute which was conferred upon a commodity by virtue of the fact that it was a product of social labour. It was in this sense, indeed, and only in this sense, that Smith regarded labour as the "source" or "cause" of value.

Now it is of the essence of a value-principle that it should be *quantitative* in character—in other words, that it should enable us to explain not only why it is that a commodity possesses "the power of purchasing other goods", but also why it is that it possesses this power *to the extent* that it does.[3] If we merely say that a commodity possesses value because it is a product of social labour, we have not yet

---

[1] *Capital*, Vol. I, pp. 347-8. For the Marxian concept of a "commodity", see above, pp. 37-8.

[2] *Wealth of Nations*, Vol. I, p. 13.

[3] Schumpeter (*History of Economic Analysis*, p. 590) is one of the few historians of economic thought who have recognised that these two things are "not strictly the same". He does not seem to have realised, however, how important this is in relation to the interpretation of Smith's theory of value.

arrived at a quantitative value-principle capable of performing all the tasks which lie ahead of it. We have simply defined the *source* of the commodity's power of attracting other commodities in exchange; we have yet to explain how the *extent* to which it possesses this power is regulated or determined.

Of course, if we decide to regard the labour used to produce a commodity not only as the source of its value but also as constituting the very *substance* of its value, so that the commodity is looked upon as a sort of mass of "congealed" or "crystallised" attractive power,[1] we are much nearer a solution. We may then conclude that a commodity acquires value not only because but also to the extent that it is a product of social labour. The extent of its attractive power, we may say, varies directly with the quantity of social labour used to produce it. In other words, we can find the *determinant* of its attractive power without seeking any further than the conditions of production of the commodity itself.

But Smith did not normally look at the matter quite in this way. It was certainly true, he believed, that a commodity came to possess value because social labour had been expended upon its production. But he did not regard this labour as constituting the substance of its value. According to his way of looking at it, a commodity acquired value because, *but not necessarily to the extent that*, it was a product of social labour. In order to find out how the extent of its value was regulated, Smith believed, one must first find out how its value ought properly to be *measured*. And the measure of its value, in Smith's opinion, could not be ascertained by looking at the conditions of its production. The measure of value must be sought not in the conditions of production of the commodity, but rather in the conditions of its exchange, just as we might decide to measure the lifting power of a magnet not by investigating the amount of magnetisation it had received but by weighing the articles it actually proved capable of lifting. The "real measure" of the exchange value of a commodity, said Smith, must be ascertained by referring to the actual "power of purchasing other goods" which it normally manifested on the market. Having ascertained the "real measure" of its value in this manner, one could then—and only then—proceed to consider the final problem of what regulated or determined its value.

In a society characterised by the division of labour, the exchange of commodities is in essence the exchange of social labour. This was

[1] Cf. above, p. 51.

the simple abstraction from which Smith started. It might have been thought, therefore, that he would have concluded that the "real measure" of the value of a commodity was *the quantity of labour embodied in the other goods* for which it would exchange on the market. But in actual fact he concluded that the "real measure" of the value of a commodity was *the quantity of labour* for which it would exchange on the market.[1] It was in this decision to make commandable labour rather than the labour embodied in commandable commodities the "real measure" of value that most of the difficulties associated with Smith's theory of value had their origin.

What Smith was looking for, of course, was an abstract general-isation concerning the "real measure" of value which would be applicable to all commodity exchanges in all types of society. The highly developed and differentiated society whose outlines Smith delineated was peculiarly capable, as Marx noted, of giving birth to abstract categories which not only served as the expression of its own conditions of production, but also at the same time enabled it "to gain an insight into the organization and the conditions of production which had prevailed under all the past forms of society".[2] The concept of the social division of labour is a good example of this. But even the most abstract categories, as Marx emphasised, "in spite of their applica-bility to all epochs . . . are by the very definiteness of the abstraction a product of historical conditions as well, and are fully applicable only to and under those conditions".[3] And some abstractions, it may be added, while appearing on the surface to be safely applicable to all epochs, are in fact so much the peculiar product of the particular

---

[1] The essential point here is this: Whenever you sell a commodity on the market and use the proceeds to buy something else, you are in effect exchanging labour for labour, and it can plausibly be said that the "real worth" or "real value" of your commo-dity to you is measurable by the quantity of "labour" which it can enable you to command in such an exchange. But the "something else" which you buy with the proceeds of the sale of your commodity may be either the present services of a certain quantity of labour, or another commodity upon which a certain quantity of labour has been expended in the past. And these two quantities of labour, as Smith well knew, need not necessarily be the same: in fact they will only be the same in a society based on production by small indepen-dent producers owning their own means of production. If, then, you want to measure the "real value" of your commodity—i.e., the quantity of "labour" which it can enable you to command—are you to do so with reference to the quantity of present labour which you can hire with the proceeds of its sale, or with reference to the quantity of past labour embodied in the other commodity which you can buy with these proceeds? It seems to me that if you start your analysis of value, as Smith did, from the idea that the exchange of commodities is in essence the exchange of the different labours which men have embodied in them, your choice ought logically to swing towards the second of these two alternatives. Smith, however, for reasons which I make an attempt to guess at in the text below, adopted the first alternative.

[2] Marx, *Critique of Political Economy*, p. 300.   [3] *Ibid.*

society which generated them that any attempt to apply them to earlier social formations is bound to lead to error and confusion. The category "profit" is perhaps an example. And the idea of commandable labour as the "real measure" of value seems to me to be another. It bears very distinct marks of the society in which it was born —a capitalist society in which labour power has become a commodity. It is only in such a society that men are likely to associate the "real worth" of a commodity with its power of purchasing *labour itself*, as distinct from its power of purchasing the *products* of labour.

Smith probably began by considering the problem of value in relation to the basic economic processes peculiar to a fairly developed capitalist economy. He was concerned in particular, as we have seen, with the analysis of the process of capitalist accumulation. This process, he believed, could be properly understood only if it were conceived in terms of the employment of "productive" wage-labour by capitalists in successive periods of production. In the first period, a capitalist hired a certain number of labourers in order to produce commodities which he believed were likely to be in demand. These commodities were eventually produced and put on the market, and the price at which they were sold was usually sufficient not only to cover the wages bill and the cost of raw materials, etc., but also to provide profit and rent at the "natural" rates. Thus, assuming that no hitch occurred in the process of realising this "natural" price, and assuming also that there was no substantial increase in the wage-rate, it would be possible for the capitalist in the next period of production to command the services of a greater number of "productive" labourers than in the period immediately past. The extent of this potential addition to his labour force could be regarded as a measure of the accumulation which it was possible for him (and his landlord) to carry out in the new period. And what was true in the case of each individual capitalist was also true for the nation as a whole.

Now it must have been obvious to Smith that a proper analysis of this process required the use of a value-principle which would reduce the various physical products involved to a common factor and thus enable quantitative significance to be attached to the successive differences between input and output. And to one who looked at the process of accumulation in this way, and at the general problem of value in the way I have described above, a possible "real measure" of value must have suggested itself almost immediately. From the point of view of a capitalist employer, who organises the production of commodities not because he wishes to consume them himself or to exchange them for subsistence goods but because he wishes to sell them at a profit and accumulate capital,[1] the most appropriate measure of the "real value" of these commodities may well appear to be the amount of wage-labour which the proceeds of their sale enable him to command in the next period of production. The larger the quantity of wage-labour which the commodities will command, the larger will be the addition he is able to make to his labour force, and the larger, therefore, will be the amount which can be accumulated. To the capitalist, then, it may well appear that "labour" is the "real measure" of the value of the commodities—provided we mean by "labour" the quantity of wage-labour which the receipts from the sale of the commodities will hire on the market.[2]

With the aid of such a measure of value, Smith believed, it was possible to reduce both input and output to a common factor ("labour") in such a way that a quantitative value-difference between them was revealed—a difference which could plausibly be regarded as a measure of the surplus or "net revenue" yielded in the capitalist productive process. The quantity of labour which the national product would purchase or command (i.e., the *value* of that product) was generally greater than the quantity of labour required to produce it (i.e., than the *cost* of the product), and the difference between these two quantities of labour was a measure of the amount of accumulation which it was possible for the community to carry out in the next period of production.[3]

In its origins, then, Smith's concept of commandable labour as the "real measure" of value may have been in large part a product of his concern with the analysis of the particular problem of accumulation under capitalism. But in the *Wealth of Nations* the concept is expressed in a general form intended to be applicable to all types of society in

[1] That is, to use the familiar Marxist symbols, it is an M-C-M′ process and not a C-M-C one.

[2] Such a concept would clearly increase in plausibility as the proportion of commodities which were in fact exchanged for labour rather than for other commodities increased— i.e., roughly, as commodity production by independent producers was replaced by *capitalist* commodity production and labour power was increasingly transformed into a commodity. This is not to say, of course, that Smith was correct in using this concept as the basis of his "real measure". Indeed, his use of it is properly subject to the same sort of criticism as that which Marx made of Ricardo—that "at a point when he [is] only as yet concerned in explaining value, and [is] therefore as yet only dealing with the *commodity*, he suddenly bursts in with . . . conditions which arise from the higher development of capitalist productive relations" (*Theories of Surplus Value*, p. 251). See below, pp. 119-20.

[3] Cf. *Wealth of Nations*, Vol. I, p. 56.

which the social division of labour has "thoroughly taken place". Smith's theory of value, I believe, cannot be properly understood unless it is appreciated that his argument concerning the "real measure" consisted essentially of an attempt to generalise the basic concept in this way. There are two main steps in this process of generalisation. First, abstracting from all particular forms of economic organisation, Smith tries to show that in every society characterised by the division of labour (and not merely in a capitalist society) the "real worth" or "real value" of a commodity to its possessor depends upon the amount of other people's labour which it enables him to command:

"Every man is rich or poor according to the degree in which he can afford to enjoy the necessaries, conveniencies, and amusements of human life. But after the division of labour has once thoroughly taken place, it is but a very small part of these with which a man's own labour can supply him. The far greater part of them he must derive from the labour of other people, and he must be rich or poor according to the quantity of that labour which he can command, or which he can afford to purchase. The value of any commodity, therefore, to the person who possesses it, and who means not to use or consume it himself, but to exchange it for other commodities, is equal to the quantity of labour which it enables him to purchase or command. Labour, therefore, is the real measure of the exchangeable value of all commodities."[1]

Second, he tries to frame the basic distinction mentioned above between the *cost* of a commodity and its "real worth" or "real value" in general terms, so that it applies to commodities produced in any (and not only in a capitalist) society:

"The real price of every thing, what every thing *really costs* to the man who *wants to* acquire it, is the toil and trouble of acquiring it. What every thing is *really worth* to the man who *has* acquired it, and who wants to dispose of it or exchange it for something else, is the toil and trouble which it can save to himself, and which it can impose upon other people."[2]

[1] *Wealth of Nations*, Vol. I, p. 32.

[2] *Ibid.*, Vol. I, p. 32. The italics, which are of course mine, sufficiently indicate what I believe to be the correct interpretation of this much-disputed passage. It is perhaps worth while clarifying the assumption which lies behind Smith's rather confusing identification of the quantity of labour which "it can save to himself" with that which "it can impose upon other people", since the point has been the subject of a certain amount of comment (see, e.g., Cannan, *A Review of Economic Theory*, p. 165). If the possessor of a commodity decides to sell it, he may be able to hire, say, 20 days' labour with the proceeds. This is the amount of labour which his commodity can "impose upon other people". In that time the labourers whom he hires may be able to make him, say, 50 pairs of shoes. Smith

Smith then goes on to argue that his measure is in fact a *real* measure, in the sense that it penetrates through the veil of money to certain fundamental social relationships lying beneath the external phenomena of exchange:

> "What is bought with money or with goods is purchased by labour, as much as what we acquire by the toil of our own body. That money or those goods indeed save us this toil. They contain the value of a certain quantity of labour which we exchange for what is supposed at the time to contain the value of an equal quantity. Labour was the first price, the original purchase-money that was paid for all things. It was not by gold or by silver, but by labour, that all the wealth of the world was originally purchased; and its value, to those who possess it, and who want to exchange it for some new productions, is precisely equal to the quantity of labour which it can enable them to purchase or command."[1]

Finally, since it is obvious that "a commodity which is itself continually varying in its own value, can never be an accurate measure of the value of other commodities", Smith endeavours to show that "labour" possesses the quality of invariability. To show this he is obliged to argue that when the quantity of goods currently paid to the labourer for a given quantity of labour happens to vary, it is actually the value of these goods and not that of the labour which varies. "Equal quantities of labour", he writes,

> "at all times and places, may be said to be of equal value to the labourer. In his ordinary state of health, strength and spirits; in the ordinary degree of his skill and dexterity, he must always lay down the same portion of his ease, his liberty, and his happiness. The price which he pays must always be the same, whatever may be the quantity of goods which he receives in return for it. Of these, indeed, it may sometimes purchase a greater and sometimes a smaller quantity; but it is their value which varies, not that of the labour which purchases them . . . Labour alone, therefore, never varying in its own value, is alone the ultimate and real standard by which the value of all commodities can at all times and places be estimated and compared. It is their real price; money is their nominal price only."[2]

simply assumes that if he had had to make the 50 pairs of shoes himself, it would have taken him 20 days—the same time as it takes the labourers. Thus his commodity can "impose upon other people", and therefore "save to himself", 20 days' labour.

[1] *Wealth of Nations*, Vol. I, pp. 32-3. Cf. Hume, *Essays* (1889 edn.), Vol. I, p. 293.
[2] *Wealth of Nations*, Vol. I, p. 35.

(b) The "Regulator" of Value

Having selected commandable labour as his "real measure" of exchangeable value, Smith turned in the next chapter to the problem of what he called the "regulation" of value. A commodity's "real value" was *measured* by the quantity of labour which it would command. But how was this "real value" *regulated*? What, in other words, determined that the commodity would command just that quantity of labour, and no more or less?

Smith believed, as I have already said, that a commodity possessed value by virtue of the fact that it was a product of social labour. How far, then, was the quantity of social labour employed in producing it instrumental in regulating the amount of labour which it would purchase or command? This was the first question which Smith asked. It was certainly true, as he insisted again and again, that the amount of labour which a commodity would purchase or command (and therefore its value) was *greater or less* according as the amount of labour required to produce it was greater or less. For example:

"As it cost less labour to bring those metals from the mine to the market, so when they were brought thither they could purchase or command less labour."[1]

"In a country naturally fertile, but of which the far greater part is altogether uncultivated, cattle, poultry, game of all kinds, &c. as they can be acquired with a very small quantity of labour, so they will purchase or command but a very small quantity. The low money price for which they may be sold, is no proof that the real value of silver is there very high, but that the real value of those commodities is very low."[2]

"The consideration of these circumstances may, perhaps, in some measure explain to us why the real price both of the coarse and of the fine manufacture, was so much higher in those ancient, than it is in the present times. It cost a greater quantity of labour to bring the goods to market. When they were brought thither, therefore, they must have purchased or exchanged for the price of a greater quantity."[3]

But according to Smith this was not enough to constitute embodied labour the "regulator" of value. What he was looking for in his search for a "regulator" was a "circumstance which can afford [a] rule for exchanging [commodities] for one another".[4] If the quantity

---

[1] *Wealth of Nations*, Vol. I, p. 34. [2] *Ibid.*, Vol. I. pp. 186-7.
[3] *Ibid.*, Vol. I, p. 246. [4] *Ibid.*, Vol. I, p. 49.

of embodied labour was to be accepted as a "regulator" of exchangeable value in this strict sense, it would have to be shown not only that the quantity of commandable labour varied with and in the same direction as the quantity of embodied labour, but also that these two quantities of labour were always precisely equal. Smith therefore proceeded to ask whether this could in fact be shown, dealing first with "that early and rude state of society which precedes both the accumulation of stock and the appropriation of land" and in which "the whole produce of labour belongs to the labourer".[1] In this state of things the quantity of embodied labour would indeed tend to be equal to the quantity of commandable labour. "The quantity of labour commonly employed in acquiring or producing any commodity", therefore, would then be "the only circumstance which can regulate the quantity of labour which it ought commonly to purchase, command, or exchange for." In such a society,

"the proportion between the quantities of labour necessary for acquiring different objects seems to be the only circumstance which can afford any rule for exchanging them for one another. If among a nation of hunters, for example, it usually costs twice the labour to kill a beaver which it does to kill a deer, one beaver should naturally exchange for or be worth two deer. It is natural that what is usually the produce of two days or two hours labour should be worth double of what is usually the produce of one day's or one hour's labour."[2]

Suppose, for example, that one day's labour is required to kill a deer, and that the current rate of exchange on the market is one beaver for two deer. If under these circumstances it takes more than two days to kill a beaver, an exchange of beaver for deer at the ruling prices would represent a bad bargain from the point of view of the beaver hunter. Presumably in such a case there would be a tendency for beaver hunters to shift over to deer hunting, and this shift would continue until the price ratios were roughly equal to the embodied labour ratios.

But today, Smith proceeds, we are concerned with a society in which production is ordinarily carried on, not by small independent producers like the deer and beaver hunters, but by dependent labourers under the direction of a capitalist master. Here the whole produce of labour does not belong to the labourer. "As soon as stock has accumulated in the hands of particular persons, some of them will

[1] *Wealth of Nations*, Vol. I, p. 49.   [2] *Ibid.*, Vol. I, pp. 49-50.

naturally employ it in setting to work industrious people, whom they will supply with materials and subsistence, in order to make a profit by the sale of their work, or by what their labour adds to the value of the materials."[1] Under these circumstances, the selling price of a commodity must obviously be sufficient to cover not only the labourers' wages and the cost of the materials, but also the profits of the capitalist. And once the labourer is forced to give up this portion of the produce of his labour to the capitalist, the amount of labour required to produce a commodity is no longer equal to the amount of labour which it can purchase or command:

> "In this state of things, the whole produce of labour does not always belong to the labourer. He must in most cases share it with the owner of the stock which employs him. Neither is the quantity of labour commonly employed in acquiring or producing any commodity, the only circumstance which can regulate the quantity which it ought commonly to purchase, command, or exchange for. An additional quantity, it is evident, must be due for the profits of the stock which advanced the wages and furnished the materials of that labour."[2]

Similarly, "as soon as the land of any country has all become private property", the landlords "demand a rent even for its natural produce", so that a further portion of the produce of labour must be given up by the labourer. "This portion, or, what comes to the same thing, the price of this portion, constitutes the rent of land, and in the price of the greater part of commodities makes a third component part."[3] In modern times, therefore, Smith believed, the "regulator" of value was no longer the quantity of embodied labour: it should rather be sought by enquiring into the manner in which the equilibrium levels of wages, profit and rent which make up the "natural price" were determined. And his own enquiries into this problem seem to have been conducted on the assumption that the constituents of the natural price could legitimately be regarded as *independent* determinants of value. Such, at any rate, appears to be the only possible interpretation of his statement that wages, profit and rent are "the three original sources . . . of all exchangeable value".[4]

---

[1] *Wealth of Nations*, Vol. I, p. 50.   [2] *Ibid.*, Vol. I, p. 51.   [3] *Ibid.*

[4] *Ibid.*, Vol. I, p. 54. From what has been said above it should be clear that it is incorrect to suggest, as a number of commentators have done, that Smith intended the "commandable labour" measure as a *substitute* for the embodied labour regulator. All that Smith said was that in ancient times the quantity of embodied labour regulated the quantity of commandable labour (and therefore value); and that in modern times the constituents

(c) The Role of Utility and Demand

The foundations of the basic Classical distinction between use value and exchange value were laid by Smith in the following well-known passage:

"The word VALUE, it is to be observed, has two different meanings, and sometimes expresses the utility of some particular object, and sometimes the power of purchasing other goods which the possession of that object conveys. The one may be called 'value in use'; the other, 'value in exchange'. The things which have the greatest value in use have frequently little or no value in exchange; and, on the contrary, those which have the greatest value in exchange have frequently little or no value in use. Nothing is more useful than water: but it will purchase scarce any thing; scarce any thing can be had in exchange for it. A diamond, on the contrary, has scarce any value in use; but a very great quantity of other goods may frequently be had in exchange for it."[1]

The concept of "value in use" implied in the water-diamond illustration is essentially the same as that implied in Hutcheson's remark that "prices or values in commerce do not at all follow the real use or importance of goods for the support, or natural pleasure of life".[2] The usefulness of commodities is measured with reference to an abstract scale of "normal need" upon which expensive goods like diamonds are given a very low rating and free goods like water a very high one. "Value in use" in this sense is evidently not even a necessary condition of value in exchange, let alone its determinant.

The concept of "value in use" with which we are more familiar today measures the usefulness of commodities with reference to their power to satisfy any human want or need, whether normal or abnormal. Value in use in this sense *is* a necessary condition of value in exchange: in order to possess the "power of purchasing other goods" a commodity must clearly possess the power to satisfy someone's want. In addition, of course, the person or persons for whom it possesses utility must be able and willing to pay something for it. Smith explained this fairly obvious point as follows:

"The market price of every particular commodity is regulated by the proportion between the quantity which is actually brought to market, and the demand of those who are willing to pay the

of the natural price regulated the quantity of commandable labour. The "commandable labour" measure was clearly intended to be applicable both to ancient and to modern times.

[1] *Wealth of Nations*, Vol. I, p. 30.   [2] See above, p. 34.

natural price of the commodity, or the whole value of the rent, labour, and profit, which must be paid in order to bring it thither. Such people may be called the effectual demanders, and their demand the effectual demand; since it may be sufficient to effectuate the bringing of the commodity to market. It is different from the absolute demand. A very poor man may be said in some sense to have a demand for a coach and six; he might like to have it; but his demand is not an effectual demand, as the commodity can never be brought to market in order to satisfy it."[1]

Having made the point, Smith left it at that. His lectures at Glasgow on "Cheapness or Plenty" had begun with what was virtually a theory of consumption, but upon more mature consideration he seems to have come to the conclusion that a detailed examination of men's mental attitudes towards the things they purchased belonged more appropriately to the theory of moral sentiments than to the theory of the nature and causes of the wealth of nations.

It is sometimes suggested that if Smith's attention could have been drawn to the marginal utility theory of value he would have welcomed it as affording the basis for a solution of the so-called "paradox of value" which was exemplified in the water-diamond illustration. But quite apart from the fact that there is no evidence that Smith ever looked upon the apparent discrepancy between "value in use" and "value in exchange" as if it were a paradox requiring solution, it cannot be too strongly emphasised that any approach to the problem of the determination of value from the side of utility and demand (as opposed to that of cost and supply) would have been regarded by him as quite alien to the general outlook of the *Wealth of Nations*. Smith makes it perfectly clear that in his opinion demand has nothing directly to do with the determination of exchange value. He agrees, of course, that demand does exercise a considerable influence in economic life, and carefully describes at least three ways in which it does so. First, the extent of demand limits the extent of the division of labour.[2] Second, consumers' demand regulates the *amount* of each commodity which is produced—i.e., the total quantity of social effort which is allocated from time to time to each different sector of production.[3] And third, the effective demand (in conjunction with

---

[1] *Wealth of Nations*, Vol. I, p. 58.   [2] *Ibid.*, Vol. I, pp. 19-23.

[3] See, e.g., *ibid.*, Vol. I, p. 402: "The quantity of every commodity which human industry can either purchase or produce, naturally regulates itself in every country according to the effectual demand, or according to the demand of those who are willing to pay the whole rent, labour and profits which must be paid in order to prepare and bring it to market." Cf. *ibid.*, pp. 60 and 117.

the available supply) regulates the market price of every commodity[1] and thus the extent of any divergence which may exist between market and natural price. But Smith insisted that the level of the natural price (as distinct from that of the market price) was independent of fluctuations in effective demand. If the effective demand for a particular commodity increased, then its market price would tend to rise above its natural price. But in the absence of monopoly or state interference this rise in price, by virtue chiefly of its effect on profits, would attract new resources into the field, and the resulting increase in output would eventually cause the market price to sink back again to the level of the natural price. The original increase in effective demand would certainly have brought about an increase in the *amount* of the commodity produced, but no change would have taken place (other things remaining equal, and given the usual Classical assumption of constant returns to scale for the industry as a whole)[2] in the natural price of the commodity. And since demand has nothing directly to do with the determination of the natural price, which is the monetary expression of value, it has therefore nothing directly to do with the determination of value itself.[3] It would be wrong to suggest that Smith gave clear expression to the idea that *output* is dependent upon the allocation of labour (and thus upon demand) and *value* upon the productivity of labour. But enough has been said to suggest that Smith can and should be regarded at least as one of the most important heralds of this idea.

(d) The Reduction of Skilled to Unskilled Labour

The idea that different types or grades of labour have to be appropriately weighted before labour time can properly be used as a guide to relative "values" was, of course, much older than the *Wealth of Nations*. In the Canonist systems, for example, the social status of the direct producer, his skill, and the intensity of his labour, were frequently held to play an important part in the determination of the "just price" of his product. The question of his status, however, gradually assumed less and less importance as capitalism developed,

---

[1] See, e.g., the passage quoted in the text on pp. 72-3 above.

[2] This assumption, which was discredited by the work of Marshall, Pigou, and other neo-Classical economists, has to some extent been rehabilitated in our own times. See, e.g., the famous article by P. Sraffa in the *Economic Journal* of December 1926, and cf. Chamberlin, *The Theory of Monopolistic Competition*, pp. 85-7.

[3] Smith did argue, however, that the demand for labour, land and capital played an important part in the determination of the equilibrium levels of wages, rent and profit which constituted the natural price.

although even in the eighteenth century some of Smith's predecessors were still to be found suggesting that the price of a commodity often varied to some extent with the status of its direct producer. Hutcheson, for example, said that the value of commodities—

"is also raised, by the dignity of station in which, according to the custom of a country, the men must live who provide us with certain goods, or works of art. Fewer can be supported in such stations than in the meaner; and the dignity and expence of their stations must be supported by the higher prices of their goods or services."[1]

Once the basic distinction between those who live by profits and those who live by wages has been established, however, differences in "status" within the latter class, except in so far as they merely reflect differences in skill, become more or less irrelevant to the question of the determination of price.

Most of the other differences in "status" which formerly existed within the broad class of those concerned in production come to be resolved, as it were, into the basic social division between the class of capitalists and the class of wage-labourers. Broadly speaking, then, once labour power has become a commodity, and is sold under reasonably competitive conditions, the only differences in the *quality* of labour of which it is really necessary to take account in connection with the problem of value are those which are due to differences in skill and intensity.

Even so, the problem of estimating the relative values of different commodities in terms of labour, in cases where labour of different degrees of skill or intensity is involved, remains difficult enough. Smith first discussed this problem near the beginning of his chapter on the measure of value:

" It is often difficult to ascertain the proportion between two different quantities of labour. The time spent in two different sorts of work will not always alone determine this proportion. The different degrees of hardship endured, and of ingenuity exercised, must likewise be taken into account. There may be more labour in an hour's hard work than in two hours easy business; or in an hour's application to a trade which it cost ten years labour to learn, than in a month's industry at an ordinary and obvious employment. But it is not easy to find any accurate measure either of hardship or ingenuity. In exchanging indeed the different productions of

[1] *A System of Moral Philosophy* (1755), Vol. II, p. 55.

different sorts of labour for one another, some allowance is commonly made for both. It is adjusted, however, not by any accurate measure, but by the higgling and bargaining of the market, according to that sort of rough equality which, though not exact, is sufficient for carrying on the business of common life."[1]

He returned to the problem again in the following chapter, in the course of his discussion of the determination of value in the "early and rude state of society":

" If the one species of labour should be more severe than the other, some allowance will naturally be made for this superior hardship; and the produce of one hour's labour in the one way may frequently exchange for that of two hours labour in the other.

"Or if the one species of labour requires an uncommon degree of dexterity and ingenuity, the esteem which men have for such talents, will naturally give a value to their produce, superior to what would be due to the time employed about it. Such talents can seldom be acquired but in consequence of long application, and the superior value of their produce may frequently be no more than a reasonable compensation for the time and labour which must be spent in acquiring them. In the advanced state of society, allowances of this kind, for superior hardship and superior skill, are commonly made in the wages of labour; and something of the same kind must probably have taken place in its earliest and rudest period."[2]

Smith's phraseology in these passages is no doubt a little unsatisfactory in places, but his argument as a whole does not really seem to be open to the accusation of circularity which is sometimes made against it. Smith does not suggest that the theoretical reduction of skilled to unskilled labour, or of more intensive to less intensive labour, should be carried out by referring to the rewards actually received in the market by the labourers concerned. All he says is (a) that *in theory* an adjustment must be made, and (b) that *in practice* an adjustment is made, "not by any accurate measure, but by the higgling and bargaining of the market". Smith does not enlarge upon the manner in which the theoretical adjustment should be made, but he gives a number of indications of the line which he might have followed (at least in the case of the reduction of skilled to unskilled labour)[3] had he thought this matter of sufficient

---

[1] *Wealth of Nations*, Vol. I, p. 33.   [2] *Ibid.*, Vol. I, p. 49.

[3] This was the problem in which Smith was more particularly interested: The reduction of more intensive to less intensive labour does not present the same degree of difficulty as the reduction of skilled to unskilled labour. For one thing, differences in the *average* intensity of labour in the various industries within a single country are not likely to be

importance to require further elaboration. He would probably have emphasised that in the great majority of cases differences in skill were due almost entirely to differences in education and training. Most talents and skills, he believed, were acquired rather than inborn:

"The difference of natural talents in different men is, in reality, much less than we are aware of; and the very different genius which appears to distinguish men of different professions, when grown up to maturity, is not upon many occasions so much the cause, as the effect of the division of labour. The difference between the most dissimilar characters, between a philosopher and a common street porter, for example, seems to arise not so much from nature, as from habit, custom, and education."[1]

This being so, the comparatively rare cases where superior skill was due to innate ability might be abstracted from and the adjustment of skilled to unskilled labour made simply by referring back to the labour costs of training. This seems to be what Smith has in mind when he suggests in one of the above-quoted passages that the superior value of the produce of those possessing superior talents "may frequently be no more than a reasonable compensation for the time and labour which must be spent in acquiring them".[2]

4. The Place of Smith in the History of Value Theory

If the above interpretation of Smith's value theory is correct, it follows that his theory has very little in common with those modern theories which attack the problem primarily from the side of demand. It is therefore as a *cost* theory[3] that its place in the history of value

nearly as great as differences in the average degree of skill; and where they do exist they are likely to be compensated for to some extent by a number of the circumstances which Smith considered in his treatment of wage-differences in chapter 10 of the *Wealth of Nations*. Such differences in intensity as remain might perhaps be dealt with (if this degree of refinement were thought to be necessary) by transferring an average worker from his own industry to another and instructing him to work there with his usual intensity. The reduction of the more intensive labour to the less intensive could then be carried out on the basis of a simple comparison of relative physical productivities. The problem is obviously more important when we are considering differences in the normal degree of intensity *in different countries*. Cf. Marx, *Capital*, Vol. I (Allen & Unwin edn.), pp. 407-17 (particularly p. 409, footnote), 533-5 and 571.

[1] *Wealth of Nations*, Vol. I, p. 17. Cf. the discussion of the talents of opera-singers, etc., on pp. 108-9; and see also pp. 124-5.

[2] Cf. the passage on p. 103, *ibid.*, where Smith compares investment in an expensive machine with investment in education.

[3] I use the term "cost theory" to include any theory which approaches the problem of the price of a commodity from the angle of the "costs" (including profits) which have to be covered if it is to be worth a producer's while to carry on producing it. Some "cost theories" say no more than that the equilibrium price is determined by the cost of production; others go further and seek for an ultimate determinant of the cost of production itself.

theory must be estimated. And as a theory of this type, it will be obvious that it has certain important defects. These defects all owe their origin to Smith's selection of commandable labour as the "real measure" of value.

In the first place, Smith's "real measure" involved the introduction of an unnecessary dichotomy into value theory. One method was used to value output and another to value input. The value of output was estimated in terms of the amount of labour which it would purchase or command. The value of input, on the other hand, was in effect estimated in terms of the amount of labour required to produce the output. It was the difference between these two quantities of labour, as we have seen, which Smith regarded as an appropriate measure of potential accumulation. But there is, in fact, another and much more satisfactory method of reducing input and output to "labour" in such a way as to allow the emergence of a value-difference in the productive process to reveal itself. This alternative method, that of Marx (and to some extent of Ricardo), values output in terms of the total quantity of labour required to produce it, and input in terms of the quantity of labour required to produce the capital goods, raw materials, and human energy used up in the production of the output. It is only fair to point out, however, that Marx might not have been able to arrive at this alternative method if he had not been able to make use of Smith's (and Ricardo's) work and to learn from their mistakes.

In the second place, as we have seen, Smith's theory requires us to say that the value of labour is somehow invariable, so that a change in the quantity of labour which a commodity will command may always be taken to indicate a change in the value of that commodity, even when nothing at all has happened to the conditions of production of the commodity and the only change has been in the current wage-rate. And this is something which few people would really want to say. As Ricardo pointed out, it is unusual, to say the least of it, to suggest that labour "never varies in its own value". The value of labour does in fact vary, "being not only affected, as all other things are, by the proportion between the supply and demand, which uniformly varies with every change in the condition of the community, but also by the varying price of food and other necessaries, on which the wages of labour are expended".[1]

In the third place, and related to this, Smith's theory requires us to

[1] Ricardo, *Works* (Sraffa's edn.), Vol. I, p. 15.

say that the value of a product varies with variations in the division of that product between wages on the one hand and profits and rent on the other, irrespective of changes in the conditions of its production. This, as we now know, was Ricardo's chief objection to Smith's theory.[1] Suppose that a particular commodity takes ten hours' labour to produce in Smith's "early and rude state of society", before labour has become wage-labour. The amount of labour which it will purchase or command will then also be ten hours. Now suppose that capital is accumulated and land appropriated, but that the commodity still requires ten hours' labour to produce. Owing to the fact that profit and rent have now to be paid to the new classes which have become entitled to share in the produce of labour, the amount of labour which the commodity will purchase or command will now be greater than ten hours. Although the technical conditions of production of the commodity have remained the same, its "value" in Smith's sense must be said to have increased. Ricardo insisted that it was quite wrong to speak, as Smith tended to do, "as if, when profits and rent were to be paid, they would have some influence on the relative value of commodities, independent of the mere quantity of labour that was necessary to their production".[2]

The place which we afford to Smith's analysis in the history of value theory will largely depend upon the extent to which we believe that these characteristics of his theory constituted a "rejection" of the labour theory of value. Many historians of economic thought, noting in particular Smith's conclusion that the quantity of labour embodied in a commodity no longer regulated the quantity which it would purchase or command under modern conditions, have decided— usually, one suspects, with some relief—that Smith did in fact "reject" the labour theory. To argue thus, I believe, is not only to misunderstand the labour theory, but also to underestimate the importance of Smith's contribution.

The labour theory is in essence an expression of the idea that the fundamental relationships into which men enter with one another in the field of production ultimately determine the relationships into which they enter in the field of exchange.[3] As Marx put it in one of his early works: "In principle, there is no exchange of products—

[1] Ricardo, *Works*, Vol. I, pp. xxxv–xxxvii.
[2] *Ibid.*, Vol. I, p. 23, footnote.
[3] Cf. M. H. Dobb, *Political Economy and Capitalism*, p. 39. See also below, pp. 151 ff., where this point is elaborated.

but there is the exchange of the labour which co-operated in production. The mode of exchange of products depends upon the mode of exchange of the productive forces."[1] When Marx came to expound and develop the labour theory, he considered it his primary task to demonstrate the *effects* of this dependence in the real world. He endeavoured, in other words, to show "how the law of value operates"— i.e., how the fundamental relationships between man and man in the field of production are reflected in their relationships in the field of exchange in different historical periods. Under certain circumstances and in certain historical periods, he argued, the "law of value" operates immediately and directly, so that embodied labour ratios tend to be *equal* to equilibrium price ratios. Under other circumstances and in other periods it operates indirectly (in a manner analysed in Volume III of *Capital*), so that the relative quantities of labour embodied in different commodities, although they may not be precisely *equal* to their relative equilibrium prices, may nevertheless be said ultimately to *determine* them.

Smith could hardly have been expected to look at the problem in precisely these terms. Smith's historical task, as Marx himself appreciated, was in fact a twofold one. First, he had to attempt "to penetrate to the inner physiology of bourgeois society". Second, he had to "describe the living forms in which this inner physiology manifests itself outwardly, to show its relations as they appear on the surface, and partly also to find a nomenclature and the corresponding abstract ideas for these phenomena".[2] The completion of the first task could not very well precede that of the second, and the wonder is not that Smith failed to formulate the value problem in the same way as Marx, but that he managed to proceed as far as he actually did in the direction of Marx's formulation.

The labour theory of value in fact owes so much to Smith that it is absurd to suggest, at least without serious qualification, that he "rejected" it. He began correctly and logically by associating the phenomenon of value with the fact that in every modern society characterised by the division of labour individuals are related to one another in their capacity as separate producers of commodities, mutually exchanging the products of their labour on some sort of market. He went on from this position to search for a "real measure" of value. Unfortunately he chose a measure which turned out to be

[1] *Poverty of Philosophy*, pp. 65-6. (Quoted also by Dobb, *loc. cit.*)
[2] Marx, *Theories of Surplus Value* (English edn.), pp. 202-3.

unsuited to the task which it was required to perform; but at least he should be given the credit for recognising the necessity of invariability in a measure, and for posing (and in part solving) the problem of the reduction of skilled to unskilled labour. Then, as the next step in his analysis, he asked himself to what extent, if at all, the quantity of labour used to produce a commodity was instrumental in regulating its value (as estimated in the "real measure"). Smith seems to have been the first to ask the question in this way, and the fact that he asked it is much more important than the fact that he failed to answer it satisfactorily. He came to the conclusion, which was later accepted in essence by Ricardo and Marx, that the quantity of embodied labour directly regulated the value of commodities in pre-capitalist society, and that a change in the quantity of embodied labour would bring about a change in the value of commodities in all forms of society. In modern times, however, since the quantity of commandable labour was necessarily greater than the quantity of embodied labour, Smith decided that value was no longer regulated by the latter,[1] but rather by the wages, profit and rent which constituted the "natural" price of the commodity. If the fact that Smith was the first to ask the question to which this was his final answer illustrates his great perceptiveness, the fact that he was content with this answer, and went straight on to enquire into the determinants of the "natural" levels of wages, profit and rent without suspecting that he was in effect thereby giving up the search for a value-principle which he had so brilliantly begun, illustrates that naïvety which in Marx's opinion constituted the "great charm" of the Wealth of Nations.[2]

[1] See, however, Wealth of Nations, Vol. I, pp. 311-12, where embodied labour ratios are clearly visualised as governing "the proportion between the value of gold and silver and that of goods of any other kind" in modern times.

[2] Theories of Surplus Value, pp. 263-4.

CHAPTER THREE

DAVID RICARDO AND THE DEVELOPMENT OF THE LABOUR THEORY

1. *Some General Considerations*

THE embryo labour theory of value put forward in the *Wealth of Nations*, as we have seen, was in its origins the product of a capitalist society in which the social division of labour was being considerably developed and extended.[1] Once the theory had been formulated, however, its further evolution necessarily became to a certain extent independent of this society. In other words, like all theories of this type, it became the subject of a process which is commonly known as "internal development".

But the "independence" which such a theory acquires in the course of its "internal development" must usually be to quite a large extent relative and limited. The particular lines along which the labour theory was developed after the publication of the *Wealth of Nations* can hardly be explained purely in terms of the intellectual contemplation and logical analysis of the original theory by subsequent economists. It is true that development of this sort cannot occur *without* intellectual contemplation and logical analysis—but one does not and cannot contemplate and analyse in a vacuum. However much the thinker may imagine that he is operating exclusively in an inner world of pure thought and logic, the outer world necessarily intrudes, wearing a number of different and often unexpected disguises.

For example, the "internal development" of an embryo theory is frequently marked by amendments designed to make it appear self-consistent. These amendments often appear to the investigator who introduces them simply as the end-products of a process of logical analysis with which external reality has very little to do. But in many cases what the investigator is in actual fact doing is to strip

---

[1] Naturally I mean by this no more than that the emergence of such a society was a *precondition* of the formulation of the labour theory and a potent influence on the *manner* in which it was formulated and developed. As should have been made clear in the first chapter, the labour theory was not just "another" theory of value, exuded, as it were, by a new form of society. It arose as the result of attempts to provide a more useful explanation of economic reality than the older theories had been able to do, and did in fact represent a considerable scientific advance.

away from the theory certain survivals of outmoded concepts, reflecting former states of reality, which are still entangled in it. No new theory is ever entirely new: it is necessarily constructed to some extent from ideological material bequeathed by earlier generations, and in its embryo form it is therefore quite likely to embody the remnants of concepts more appropriate to earlier social conditions, whose presence may make the theory appear logically inconsistent or self-contradictory to later thinkers. The analytical process whereby these inconsistencies or contradictions are removed may seem to these thinkers to be purely logical in character, but in actual fact it may mark an important step in the direction of making the theory a more faithful expression and reflection of contemporary reality. Thus when Ricardo accused Smith of erecting two inconsistent "standard measures of value",[1] and discarded one of them, he no doubt believed that he was merely correcting a logical error, whereas in actual fact he was also purging the Classical theory of value of the outmoded idea—a product of earlier centuries—that value is dependent upon wages-cost.

Then again, the development of an embryo theory such as that which we are now considering is obviously dependent to a very large extent upon the nature of the main problems with which the investigator chooses to concern himself. The very fact that this theory rather than another is selected for development and refinement, while the choice may possibly appear to the investigator to be purely a matter of abstract logic or common sense, may actually reflect a recognition (intuitive or otherwise) that this theory, when further developed, is likely to be useful in connection with the particular problems upon which he has decided to concentrate. The actual lines along which the theory is developed, too, while again possibly appearing purely as the result of a logical process, may in fact be greatly influenced by the nature of the problems in connection with which it is to be used. The way in which the tool is fashioned will naturally depend upon the tasks it is meant to perform. And, of course, the range of possible choices of problem at any given time (if not the actual choice itself) is in the last analysis presented to the investigator by the social environment in which he works.

Classical political economy was primarily concerned to assist those policy-makers who aimed to increase the wealth of nations.[2]

[1] See below, pp. 98 ff.
[2] Cf. Smith, *Wealth of Nations* (Cannan edn.), Vol. I, p. 395; and cf. Vol. II, p. 177. Cf. also Ricardo, *Works* (Sraffa's edn.), Vol.IV, p. 41.

Its main task was to discover the relevant laws relating to the origin and increase of wealth and to propound them in such a way as to define the "areas of decision" open to the policy-makers.[1] In the late eighteenth and early nineteenth centuries, as was only natural, the majority of economists regarded the accumulation of capital as the basic cause of the increase of wealth, and their theoretical systems were therefore primarily designed to illuminate the nature and effects of the accumulation process. The main problem, however, presented itself to Smith and Ricardo respectively in two rather different ways. Smith wished above all to attack certain social institutions which still hindered accumulation, and certain social attitudes (such as the old idea that spending is good for trade) which still discouraged it. For this purpose, all that was really required was a general theoretical analysis of the accumulation process and an account of the manner in which accumulation and the increase of wealth were related. The question of the effect of accumulation upon the distributive shares could be regarded as a secondary and subordinate one. To Ricardo, on the other hand, the question of the effect of accumulation upon the distributive shares—and in particular upon the proportions in which the social surplus was distributed between the landlords and the capitalists—came to assume much greater importance. For in Ricardo's time, as Professor Hollander has pointed out, there was a widespread recognition of the fact "that England's resisting power depended upon the flourishing condition of her manufactures and upon the maintenance, undiminished, of industrial profits". This sentiment, which "pervaded business and financial circles and became the veritable milieu of economic thought",[2] was based on the assumption that profits constituted by far the most important source of capital accumulation.[3] Other things being equal, then, it was better that the social surplus should consist of profit rather than of rent. To define the appropriate "areas of decision", therefore, it was necessary to work out, in much more detail than Smith had done, the laws which showed how rent and profit would behave in "the natural course of things"[4] as capital accumulated and society progressed in wealth and prosperity. This was a problem with important political implications at the time, since the struggle between the landlords and the industrial capitalists over such vital issues as the Corn Laws

---

[1] Cf. B. S. Keirstead, *The Theory of Economic Change*, p. 32, and Ricardo, *Works*, I, p. 106, footnote.

[2] J. H. Hollander, *David Ricardo: A Centenary Estimate*, p. 16.

[3] Cf. Ricardo, *Works*, IV, pp. 37 and 234.   [4] Ricardo, *Works*, IV, p. 21.

and parliamentary reform was growing in intensity. To solve this problem a theory of value was evidently required; and the sequel will show how closely the development of Ricardo's ideas on value theory was associated with his attempts to find an adequate solution of it.

Finally, the development of such a theory is often marked by amendments deliberately designed to bring it into closer correspondence with the facts. Not only must the logical inconsistencies be dealt with; not only must the theory be developed with specific reference to the particular problems which it is desired to solve with its aid; but it is also necessary to remove any inconsistencies which may emerge between the theory and the facts. And here again the external world necessarily intrudes, simply because the facts themselves are apt to change. When the facts change the theory must, if possible, be adapted to fit them. At certain stages of development, therefore, it may become necessary to attempt to disentangle the essence of the theory from the particular context of problems and facts in which it has previously appeared and to reapply it to a new situation.[1] I am speaking here, of course, of *real* inconsistencies which emerge between an old theory and new facts. The process whereby *apparent* inconsistencies between a theory and the facts which it is being used to explain are removed is very different. Ricardo, for example, observing that in the real world the equilibrium price ratios of the majority of commodities were not in fact precisely equal to their embodied labour ratios, characterised this as a "contradiction",[2] and attempted—unsuccessfully—to resolve it. Marx, however, building on Ricardo's work, was able to deal satisfactorily with this particular problem; and it would be wrong to suggest that developments in the external world since Ricardo's time were directly or primarily responsible for his ability to do so.

There is one other general point, also of importance in the consideration of Ricardo's development of the labour theory, which may conveniently be mentioned here. The development of the labour theory in the Classical period was intimately associated with the development of a new *method* of political economy. Most of the economists of the seventeenth century had begun their investigations by considering what Marx called the "living aggregate"—e.g., "population, nation, state, several states, etc." By breaking down this aggregate into "less and less complex abstractions", they usually

[1] See the Preface to the present work.   [2] See below, pp. 112 ff.

arrived in the end at "certain leading, abstract general principles, such as division of labour, money, value, etc." Then, as Marx put it,

"as soon as these separate elements had been more or less established by abstract reasoning, there arose the systems of political economy which start from simple conceptions, such as labour, division of labour, demand, exchange value, and conclude with state, international exchange and world market."[1]

In the early chapters of the *Wealth of Nations*, for example, we find a deliberate attempt to work upwards from "simple conceptions, such as labour, division of labour, demand, exchange value" towards the "living aggregate". And Smith's Classical successors—in particular Ricardo—followed in his footsteps in this respect. As might be expected, the development of the new concept of value—"the most general and therefore the most comprehensive expression of the economic conditions of commodity production", as Engels once called it[2]—greatly encouraged and was in turn encouraged by the development of this new method of political economy.

2. *Ricardo's Treatment of Value Prior to 1817*

During the first few years in which he wrote on economic questions, Ricardo seems to have concerned himself primarily with currency problems and only incidentally with matters of general theory. In particular, of course, he was interested in the analysis of the currency and exchange phenomena which followed the suspension of specie payments by the Bank of England in 1797. Concentrating as he did on problems of this type, he could hardly have been expected to give more than passing attention to the question of the general causes of changes in the *relative* values of commodities. Nevertheless it is possible to reconstruct some of his early views on the latter question from the material which he wrote in this period.

On the first page of his pamphlet, *The High Price of Bullion* (1810), Ricardo puts forward a crude theory of value:

"Gold and silver, like other commodities, have an intrinsic value, which is not arbitrary, but is dependent on their scarcity, the quantity of labour bestowed in procuring them, and the value of the capital employed in the mines which produce them."[3]

---

[1] Marx, *Critique of Political Economy* (Kerr edn.), pp. 292-3.
[2] *Anti-Dühring* (English edn.), p. 340.   [3] *Works*, III, p. 52.

But naturally it is not this "intrinsic value" which primarily interests him at the present stage of his researches. He is concerned at the moment to discuss the causes of the depreciation of the paper currency. The paper currency, however, is (or ought to be) the representative of a "standard measure of value", and "it can only be by a comparison to this standard that its regularity, or its depreciation, may be estimated". Here, then, in a rather special context, we are first introduced to the vexed question of the "invariable measure of value". "A measure of value", says Ricardo in a footnote,

> " should itself be invariable; but this is not the case with either gold or silver, they being subject to fluctuations as well as other commodities. Experience has indeed taught us, that though the variations in the *value* of gold or silver may be considerable, on a comparison of distant periods, yet for short spaces of time their value is tolerably fixed. It is this property, among their other excellencies, which fits them better than any other commodity for the uses of money. Either gold or silver may therefore, in the point of view in which we are considering them, be called a measure of value."[1]

Here certain implicit assumptions are made which were later to prove of some importance in connection with Ricardo's development of the theory of value. If the exchange value of a commodity be defined, with Smith, as the power of purchasing other goods which it conveys to its owner, what does it mean, exactly, to say that the value of a commodity used as a measure of this exchange value is "tolerably fixed"? All it can mean is that, if there is an alteration in the rate at which the commodity whose exchange value is being measured exchanges on the market for the commodity being used as a measure, then this alteration can be said to be due to some cause operating solely on the commodity being measured. To say this, we must be able to assume that "value" is not merely a relation (as Bailey was later to suggest), but that it is a quality which somehow inheres in or is attached to each individual commodity and which can therefore alter quite independently of changes in the value of other commodities. Thus when two commodities alter in relative (or "exchangeable") value, we must be able to assume that the alteration is the net resultant of changes which have taken place in the *individual* "values" of one or both of the commodities, each considered in isolation.

The nature of Ricardo's main enquiries at this time did not call

1 *Works*, III, p. 65. Cf. p. 391.

for any very profound researches in this field, and there is no indication in his writings that he then considered that anything was really lacking in Smith's account of value. In a few places, however, Ricardo's early statements foreshadow the lines which his subsequent enquiries were to follow. In his *Notes on Bentham* (1810-11), for example, at a point where Bentham expresses the opinion that all value is founded on utility, Ricardo comments:

> "I like the distinction which Adam Smith makes between value in use and value in exchange. According to that opinion utility is not the measure of value."[1]

And in other places we find the beginnings of the important distinction which Ricardo was later to make between wealth and value. "The rise of prices and the increase of riches", he says, "have no necessary connection. Machinery adds to the real riches of a community at the same time that prices fall."[2] But Ricardo still accepts without question Adam Smith's doctrine that a rise in wages will lead to a rise in prices,[3] just as he still accepts Smith's view that profits are lowered by the competition of capitals.[4] When considered in the light of subsequent events, the years before 1815 were notable rather for the emergence of the basic problem of distributional shares to prominence in Ricardo's mind, than for the development of the theory of value which was destined to play such an important part in the solution of this problem.

Ricardo's *Reply to Bosanquet* was published in January 1811, and his next published work, the *Essay on the Profits of Stock*, did not appear until February 1815. Apart from the first four or five months of 1811, during which Ricardo apparently wrote the appendix to the fourth edition of his *High Price of Bullion* and a number of manuscript notes on monetary problems, the gap has to be filled by referring to Ricardo's correspondence—in particular, his correspondence with Malthus, which dates from June 1811. For more than two years this correspondence was concerned almost exclusively with matters arising directly out of a criticism by Malthus (in the *Edinburgh Review* of February 1811) of Ricardo's two currency pamphlets. The main question at issue was whether anything other than the "redundant" or "deficient" state of the currency could influence the rate of exchange. Ricardo argued that a "relatively redundant currency" is the

---

[1] *Works*, III, p. 284. In the manuscript, "measure" replaces "source".
[2] *Ibid.*, III, p. 334. Cf. p. 308.   [3] *Ibid.*, III, p. 270.   [4] *Ibid.*, III, p. 92.

"invariable cause" of an unfavourable balance of trade.[1] Malthus agreed that "the effects of a redundancy of currency upon the exchange are *sure*", but maintained that "they are slow compared with the effects of those mercantile or politi[cal] transactions, not connected with the question of currency".[2] Eventually, however, the correspondence (and no doubt the personal conversations) between the two men took a different turn, and an important new problem emerged. Unfortunately two key letters from Malthus written at this crucial point in the discussions are among those which are still missing,[3] but judging from Ricardo's replies it seems that Malthus probably raised a new point—that since 1793 there had been both an increase in capital and an increase in the rate of profit, whereas according to the orthodox Smithian theory, which was still accepted by Ricardo as well as by Malthus, an increase in capital should have been acccompanied by a fall in the rate of profit. This fact could only be explained, Malthus may have argued, by recognising that there had been an increase in the demand (particularly from overseas) for British commodities, and that this had raised the value of these commodities. In that case, the concurrent increase in the quantity of money— and thus the "relatively redundant currency"—might well have been not the cause of the increase in value (as Ricardo had in effect been maintaining) but rather the effect of it.[4] At any rate, Ricardo apparently felt himself obliged at this stage to provide an alternative explanation of the fact that an increase in capital had been accompanied by an increase in profits. "I have little doubt", he wrote,

> "that for a long period, during the interval you mention, there has been an increased rate of profits, but it has been accompanied with such decided improvements of agriculture both here and abroad,— for the French revolution was exceedingly favorable to the increased production of food, that it is perfectly reconcileable to my theory. My conclusion is that there has been a rapid increase of Capital which has been prevented from shewing itself in a low rate of interest by new facilities in the production of food."[5]

Here the Smithian idea that the rate of profit tends to be lowered by the competition of capitals is married with the current idea, then

---

[1] *Works*, VI, p. 26.   [2] *Ibid.*, VI, p. 82.

[3] Those to which Ricardo's letters of 10 August and 17 August 1813 are replies. See *ibid.*, pp. 92-5.

[4] Cf. the interpretation given by G. S. L. Tucker in his article "The Origin of Ricardo's Theory of Profits" (*Economica*, November 1954). This article appeared after the present chapter was written.

[5] *Works*, VI, pp. 94-5.

very prevalent in business circles, that a decrease in the price of corn (per medium of its effect on wages) means higher profits.[1] From this time onwards, the question of the effect of an increase in capital on the rate of profit was destined to be one of Ricardo's primary concerns.

Ricardo's personal discussions with Malthus on this topic continued (although their correspondence directly relating to it was not resumed until June 1814), and by February 1814 his views had developed to the point where he was able to set them down on paper. The manuscript of these "papers on the profits of Capital"[2] has not been found, but it is evident, from a description which Ricardo gave to Trower of the "subject in dispute" between himself and Malthus, that they must have contained the essential elements of the theory of profit which Ricardo was later to put forward in the first part of his *Essay on Profits*. "I contend", wrote Ricardo on 8 March 1814,

> "that the arena for the employment of new Capital cannot increase in any country in the same or greater proportion than the Capital itself, unless Capital be withdrawn from the land[,] unless there be improvements in husbandry,—or new facilities be offered for the introduction of food from foreign countries;—that in short it is the profits of the farmer which regulate the profits of all other trades,—and as the profits of the farmer must necessarily decrease with every augmentation of Capital employed on the land, provided no improvements be at the same time made in husbandry, all other profits must diminish and therefore the rate of interest must fall. . . . Nothing, I say, can increase the profits permanently on trade, with the same or an increased Capital, but a really cheaper mode of obtaining food."[3]

Here, for the first time, Ricardo substitutes a new explanation of the tendency of the rate of profit to fall, based on the law of diminishing returns in agriculture,[4] for that of Adam Smith, which he had hitherto accepted without serious question.

At this time, then, Ricardo was arguing that the diminishing returns in agriculture which normally accompanied accumulation (in the absence of "improvements in husbandry") would necessarily

---

[1] If this interpretation is correct, it follows that Ricardo had not yet arrived at his own theory of profit—although the train of thought which soon resulted in that theory had definitely been started.

[2] *Works*, IV, p. 3.   [3] *Ibid.*, VI, pp. 103-4.

[4] Ricardo had long been familiar with the concept of diminishing returns: cf. *Works*, III, p. 287.

operate to reduce the profits of the capitalist farmer, and that they would therefore also operate to reduce the *general* rate of profit on capital, since "it is the profits of the farmer which regulate the profits of all other trades". Mr. Sraffa has suggested that the "rational foundation" of this principle of the determining role of agricultural profits is to be found in Ricardo's assumption that in agriculture the same commodity, corn, constitutes both input and output, so that the rate of agricultural profit is independent of price changes. Thus if the rate of profit is to be equal in all trades, "it is the exchangeable values of the products of *other* trades relatively to their own capitals (*i.e.*, relatively to corn) that must be adjusted so as to yield the same rate of profit as has been established in the growing of corn".[1] It does seem quite possible that Ricardo then had something like this in mind. If one starts off with this "corn-ratio" theory of agricultural profits, there will undoubtedly be a temptation, when one is discussing the causes of a secular decline in the general rate of profit, to speak of agricultural profits as leading or regulating this decline.[2]

The arena for the employment of a theory of profit was greatly increased about this time by the growth of public interest in the Corn Law question, and when the correspondence between Ricardo and Malthus was resumed in June 1814 it was this question which was uppermost in their minds. When Malthus argued, in a letter which is still missing, that it was by no means certain that restrictions on the importation of corn would tend to lower the rate of profit, Ricardo replied by putting forward (*inter alia*) the following general proposition:

"The rate of profits and of interest must depend on the proportion of production to the consumption necessary to such production,— this again essentially depends upon the cheapness of provisions, which is after all, whatever intervals we may be willing to allow, the great regulator of the wages of labour."[3]

Malthus argued in reply that "this rate of production, or more definitely speaking, the proportion of production to the consumption necessary to such production, seems to be determined by the quantity of accumulated capital compared with the demand for the products of capital, and not by the mere difficulty and expence of producing

[1] *Works*, I, p. xxxi.

[2] This proposition is dependent for its plausibility upon the further assumption that the corn-margin is fixed by the level of the population and its subsistence needs at any given time. Cf. *Works*, IV, p. 24, footnote.

[3] *Ibid.*, VI, p. 108.

corn".[1] Therefore, since restrictions on importation (as Malthus believed) "must necessarily be attended with a diminution of capital"[2] it seemed to follow that there would be a tendency for these restrictions to cause profits to rise. Ricardo replied, first, that effective demand "cannot augment or long continue stationary with a diminishing capital"[3] (thus initiating a well-known debate on "Say's Law"[4]); and second, that a diminution of capital would in fact operate on profits by way of its effect upon "the state of the cultivation of the land",[5] rather than by way of the mechanism which Malthus had postulated. This phase of the controversy (which ended in February 1815 with the publication of Malthus's two pamphlets on rent and the Corn Laws and Ricardo's *Essay on Profits*) culminated in the following statement by Ricardo of his views on the manner in which accumulation and diminishing returns operated on profits:

" Accumulation of capital has a tendency to lower profits. Why? because every accumulation is attended with increased difficulty in obtaining food, unless it is accompanied with improvements in agriculture; in which case it has no tendency to diminish profits. If there were no increased difficulty, profits would never fall, because there are no other limits to the profitable production of manufactures but the rise of wages. If with every accumulation of capital we could tack a piece of fresh fertile land to our Island, profits would never fall."[6]

And in the same letter Ricardo recognised, significantly enough, that "the consideration of money value" might be the foundation of the difference between himself and Malthus on the Say's Law question.[7]

Up to this point, Ricardo had used the law of diminishing returns in agriculture only in connection with the theory of profit, and as far as we know had not yet attempted to apply it to the theory of rent.[8] The extant correspondence between Ricardo and Malthus up to January 1815 contains no specific reference to rent, although in a letter of 30 August 1814 Ricardo remarked that the report of the Lords committee on the corn question, which had just appeared, "discloses some important facts",[9] and there is a reference in a letter of 6 February 1815 which shows that at least one aspect of the subject

[1] *Works*, VI, p. 111.   [2] *Ibid.*, VI, p. 116.   [3] *Ibid.*, VI, p. 114.
[4] Roughly, the idea that "supply creates its own demand".
[5] *Works*, VI, p. 133. Cf. p. 119.   [6] *Ibid.*, VI, p. 162.   [7] *Ibid.*, VI, p. 164.
[8] See Sraffa's account in *ibid.*, IV, pp. 7-8.   [9] *Ibid.*, VI, p. 130.

had already been discussed between them.[1] In any event, upon reading Malthus's *Inquiry into Rent* Ricardo was able to put his own ideas down on paper in a very short time, and his *Essay on Profits*, in which his own theory of profits was combined with a variant of Malthus's theory of rent, appeared only three weeks after the *Inquiry*.

The main theoretical argument of the *Essay*, which is designed to explain the effect of the accumulation of capital upon the proportions in which the social surplus is distributed between rent and profit, is developed in two stages. In the first, the analysis is conducted on the assumption that the price of corn and the wages of labour remain stationary. As capital accumulates and population increases, it is necessary to resort to less fertile or less well-situated land (or to employ additional capital on the land already being cultivated) in order to provide more food. The law of diminishing returns comes into operation, and as the margin extends the amount of resources required to produce a unit of raw produce on the marginal land gradually increases. By a familiar argument it is shown that rent will then arise (and gradually increase) on the non-marginal land, and that the rate of profit in agriculture will decline. And since "it is the profits of the farmer which regulate the profits of all other trades", this will cause a decline in the *general* rate of profit on capital. In the second stage of the argument, the assumption that the price of corn and the wages of labour remain stationary is dropped, and the manner in which accumulation and diminishing returns operate on profit by way of their effect upon wages is considered. Ricardo argues that "the sole effect . . . of the progress of wealth on prices, independently of all improvements, either in agriculture or manufactures, appears to be to raise the price of raw produce and of labour, leaving all other commodities at their original prices, and to lower general profits in consequence of the general rise of wages".[2] The effects worked out on the assumption of stationary prices and wages, therefore, are reinforced when the variations in prices and wages which must actually accompany accumulation are taken into account.

As an integral part of the second stage of his argument, Ricardo put forward a rudimentary theory of exchange value which directly associates the value of a commodity with the difficulty or facility of its production:

"The exchangeable value of all commodities, rises as the difficulties of their production increase. If then new difficulties occur in the

[1] *Works*, VI, p. 173.   [2] *Ibid.*, IV, p. 20.

production of corn, from more labour being necessary, whilst no more labour is required to produce gold, silver, cloth, linen, &c. the exchangeable value of corn will necessarily rise, as compared with those things. On the contrary, facilities in the production of corn, or of any other commodity of whatever kind, which shall afford the same produce with less labour, will lower its exchangeable value. Thus we see that improvements in agriculture, or in the implements of husbandry, lower the exchangeable value of corn; improvements in the machinery connected with the manufacture of cotton, lower the exchangeable value of cotton goods; and improvements in mining, or the discovery of new and more abundant mines of the precious metals, lower the value of gold and silver, or which is the same thing, raises the price of all other commodities. Wherever competition can have its full effect, and the production of the commodity be not limited by nature, as in the case with some wines, the difficulty or facility of their production will ultimately regulate their exchangeable value."[1]

Here for the first time in Ricardo's work the basic idea lying behind the mature theory of value which he was to develop in the *Principles* is set forth. Its formulation in the *Essay* is not unambiguous; but at any rate Ricardo had sufficient confidence in it to reject his earlier view—which he had held at least as late as July 1814[2]—that "the price of corn regulates the prices of all other things".[3] And Ricardo's rejection of this view was of course a cornerstone of the argument of the *Essay*, since if the price of corn in fact regulated the prices of all other things profits might *not* fall with a general rise in wages.

In the *Principles*, the argument that "it is the profits of the farmer which regulate the profits of all other trades" is dropped, although, as Mr. Sraffa puts it, "the more general proposition that the productivity of labour on land which pays no rent is fundamental in determining general profits continues to occupy a central position".[4] Accumulation and diminishing returns are assumed to act on profits through the medium of their effect on the general level of wages. "In all countries, and all times," says Ricardo, "profits depend on the quantity of labour requisite to provide necessaries for the labourers, on that land or with that capital which yields no rent."[5] Or, as he states it earlier, profits depend upon the "proportion of the annual

---

[1] *Works*, IV, pp. 19-20. Cf. *Wealth of Nations*, Vol. I, p. 35: "At all times and places that is dear which it is difficult to come at, or which it costs much labour to acquire; and that cheap which is to be had easily, or with very little labour."

[2] *Works*, VI, p. 114.   [3] *Ibid.*, IV, p. 21, footnote.   [4] *Ibid.*, I, p. xxxiii.
[5] *Ibid.*, I, p. 126.

labour of the country [which] is devoted to the support of the labour-ers".[1] Here Ricardo's old proposition concerning the dependence of profit upon "the proportion of production to the consumption necessary to such production"[2] has been in effect re-cast in terms of the labour theory of value, consumption being valued in terms of the quantity of labour required to produce the "necessaries for the labourers", and production in terms of the quantity of labour required to produce the total national product.[3]

Between February 1815 and the time, at the end of that year, when he began serious work on the *Principles*, Ricardo's theory of value underwent a certain amount of further development. Various aspects of the value problem began to present themselves with in-creasing frequency in his correspondence with Malthus, and in August-September there was an interesting exchange of opinions with Say on the question of the relation between value and utility.[4] In August and September, too, he wrote his *Proposals for an Economical and Secure Currency*, in which he gave rather more detailed consideration to the value problem than he had done in his earlier monetary writings. He incorporated the idea of the dependence of value upon "difficulty or facility of production"; he made a clear distinction between price and value, specifically rejecting utility as a measure of the latter; and he emphasised the difficulties involved in detecting, when two com-modities varied in relative value, in which of the two the variation had its origin.[5]

But the developments which occurred when Ricardo began work on the *Principles*, under the schoolmasterly eye of James Mill, were, of course, very much more important. At the end of December he is writing to Mill saying:

> "I know I shall be soon stopped by the word price, and then I must apply to you for advice and assistance. Before my readers can understand the proof I mean to offer, they must understand the theory of currency and of price. They must know that the prices of commodities are affected two ways one by the alteration in the relative value of money, which affects all commodities nearly at the same time,—the other by an alteration in the value of the particular commodity, and which affects the value of no other thing, excepting it ent[er] into its composition.—This invariability

[1] *Works*, I, p. 49, Cf. II, pp. 61-2.   [2] *Ibid.*, VI, p. 108. See above, p. 91.
[3] See Sraffa, in *ibid.*, I, p. xxxii.   [4] *Ibid.*, VI, pp. 245-9 and 270-3.
[5] *Ibid.*, IV, pp. 59-62.

of the value of the precious metals, but from particular causes relating to themselves only, such as supply and demand, is the sheet anchor on which all my propositions are built; for those who maintain that an alteration in the value of corn will alter the value of all other things, independently of its effects on the value of the raw material of which they are made, do in fact deny this doctrine of the cause of the variation in the value of gold and silver."[1]

Mill, however, does not seem to have given a great deal of "advice and assistance" to Ricardo on questions of theory such as this, his role being mainly confined to that of adviser on matters of style and arrangement[2]—and even on hours of work and the length of social visits.[3] Having agreed with Ricardo that "the problem to be solved" was indeed "to tell how the events in question operate upon the relative proportions of exchangeable commodities",[4] Mill appears to have left him more or less to his own devices. In April 1816 Ricardo writes to Malthus that "obstacles almost invincible oppose themselves to my progress";[5] and Malthus encouragingly replies that the reason for this is that Ricardo has "got a little into a wrong track". "On the subject of determining all prices by labour", Malthus explains, "and excluding capital from the operation of the great principle of supply and demand, I think you must have swerved a little from the right course."[6] Notwithstanding this fairly broad hint, Ricardo continued working along the same lines, and it was not long before he came face to face with "the curious effect which the rise of wages produces on the prices of those commodities which are chiefly obtained by the aid of machinery and fixed capital"[7]—a problem which for a time "very much impeded" his investigations into "the question of price and value".[8] In November, however, Mill expressed himself as satisfied with the results of Ricardo's work on the "general principle". Ricardo was at last equipped with one of the basic tools necessary to deal adequately with what he had come to regard as "the most difficult, and perhaps the most important topic of Political Economy, namely the progress of a country in wealth and the laws by which the increasing produce is distributed".[9]

---

[1] *Works*, VI, pp. 348–9. Cf. VII, p. 3.
[2] See Sraffa's account in *ibid.*, I, pp. xix–xxii.   [3] *Ibid.*, VI, p. 340.
[4] *Ibid.*, VII, p. 7.   [5] *Ibid.*, VII, p. 28.   [6] *Ibid.*, VII, p. 30.
[7] *Ibid.*, VII, p. 82. See below, pp. 103 ff.   [8] *Ibid.*, VII, p. 71.
[9] *Ibid.*, VII, p. 24.

3. The Theory of Value in the First Edition of the "Principles"[1]

It is useful, I think, to consider the chapter on value in the first edition of Ricardo's *Principles* from the point of view of the critique of Adam Smith of which it largely in effect consists. Prior to the publication of the *Principles* Ricardo had never had occasion to express publicly his disagreement with any aspect of Smith's theory of value—except to the extent to which such disagreement was implicit in his opposition (in the *Essay*) to the idea that "the price of corn regulates the prices of all other things". But it seems probable that he had come to appreciate the nature of what he called Smith's "original error respecting value" at a fairly early stage in his more mature consideration of the value problem. Certainly, at any rate, he was able by the end of 1816 to recognise the extent to which Smith's "faulty" opinions on such subjects as bounties and the colonial trade were founded on this "original error".[2] And it is evident from the structure of the first chapter of the *Principles* that the development and refinement of Ricardo's theory of value proceeded more or less hand in hand with his critical analysis of Smith's account.

The first stage of Ricardo's critique is summed up in the section-heading with which (in the second and third editions) the first chapter of the *Principles* begins:

> "The value of a commodity, or the quantity of any other commodity for which it will exchange, depends on the relative quantity of labour which is necessary for its production, and not on the greater or less compensation which is paid for that labour."[3]

Ricardo commences his argument under this heading by quoting Smith's famous paragraph concerning the distinction between value in use and value in exchange. "Utility", says Ricardo, " . . . is not the measure of exchangeable value, although it is absolutely essential to it."[4]

[1] The 1st edn. appeared in 1817, the 2nd in 1819 and the 3rd in 1821.

[2] *Works*, VII, p. 100. Cf. chapters XXII and XXV of the *Principles*.

[3] *Ibid.*, I, p. 11. This section-heading is not found in edn. 1 (which does not divide the first chapter into sections), but it accurately summarises the main content of the first part of this chapter in edn. 1 (up to p. 17 in the *Works*).

[4] *Ibid.*, I, p. 11. It is interesting to note that Ricardo's conclusion that utility is essential to exchange value is based on a definition of utility which relates it to the capacity of a commodity to contribute in some way to our "gratification". His rejection of utility as "the measure of exchangeable value", however, is based on Smith's paragraph which impliedly relates utility to a scale of "normal need". Cf. the fuller treatment in chapter XX of the *Principles*; and see above, pp. 72-3.

He then goes on to make it clear that the law of value which he is going to expound applies only to "such commodities . . . as can be increased in quantity by the exertion of human industry, and on the production of which competition operates without restraint."[1] All other commodities—those "the value of which is determined by their scarcity alone" and which "form a very small part of the mass of commodities daily exchanged on the market"[2]—are relegated to the position of lesser breeds without the law. How, then, are the values of the relevant commodities determined?[3] Ricardo quotes a number of passages from the *Wealth of Nations* which are claimed to support the view that, at least in "the early stages of society", it is "the quantity of labour realized in commodities" which regulates their exchangeable value.[4] Abstracting for the moment from the question of whether this "rule" does in fact operate (as Smith believed) only in "the early stages of society", Ricardo embarks immediately upon his polemic against Smith's "commandable labour" measure. "Adam Smith", says Ricardo,

> "who so accurately defined the original source of exchangeable value, and who was bound in consistency to maintain, that all things became more or less valuable in proportion as more or less labour was bestowed on their production, has himself erected another standard measure of value, and speaks of things being more or less valuable, in proportion as they will exchange for more or less of this standard measure. Sometimes he speaks of corn, at other times of labour, as a standard measure; not the quantity of labour bestowed on the production of any object, but the quantity which it can command in the market: as if these were two equivalent expressions, and as if because a man's labour had become doubly efficient, and he could therefore produce twice the quantity of a commodity,

[1] *Works*, I, p. 12.   [2] *Ibid.*

[3] The reader should perhaps be reminded here that Ricardo accepted the traditional Classical idea that when commodities were sold at their "natural prices" (i.e., at their cost of production, including profit at the normal or "natural" rate) they were being sold "at their values". The "natural prices" at which freely reproducible commodities tended to sell under conditions of competition were conceived as the monetary expression of their "values". According to Ricardo's (and Marx's) view, it was the primary function of a theory of value to explain what ultimately determined or regulated these "natural prices".

[4] *Works*, I, pp. 12-13. In a subsequent section Ricardo makes it clear that "not only the labour applied immediately to commodities affect their value, but the labour also which is bestowed on the implements, tools, and buildings, with which such labour is assisted". The past labour embodied in these "implements, tools, and buildings" (and also in the raw materials used) contributes to the total value of the final product in so far as they are used up in its production. See *ibid.*, I, pp. 22-5.

he would necessarily receive twice the former quantity in exchange for it."[1]

This statement is hardly fair to Smith, who never really spoke of embodied labour and commandable labour "as if these were two equivalent expressions". But Ricardo's main objection to the commandable labour measure is not affected by this exaggeration. What Ricardo really wanted to attack was Smith's assumption that the quantity of commandable labour can be usefully regarded as an "invariable" measure of value, when in fact labour is palpably "subject to as many fluctuations as the commodities compared with it".[2] Gold and silver and corn, says Ricardo, are subject to fluctuations from many different causes. And, he asks,

"is not the value of labour equally variable; being not only affected, as all other things are, by the proportion between the supply and demand, which uniformly varies with every change in the condition of the community, but also by the varying price of food and other necessaries, on which the wages of labour are expended?"[3]

If, then, Smith was wrong in talking about labour "never varying in its own value",[4] commandable labour could not be said to constitute a reliable "standard measure of value". The value of a commodity estimated in such a measure would have to be regarded as changing with every change in the compensation paid to the labourer, even though nothing at all had happened to the difficulty or facility of its production. This was a position, Ricardo's argument implied, which few people would really wish to adopt. And, what was more, if a change did occur in the difficulty or facility of its production, the commandable labour measure would not fully reflect it unless—which was very unlikely—the real wage of the labourer happened at the same time to change *pari passu* with his productivity.

---

[1] *Works*, I, pp. 13-14. The point that Ricardo is making at the end of this passage is simply this—that in measuring changes in the value of commodities different results will be obtained from the use of the embodied labour measure and the commandable labour measure *unless* the real wage rate (in terms of the commodity whose value is being measured) always varies *pari passu* with productivity. And this, of course, would happen only rarely, since (as Ricardo put it in a letter to Malthus of August 1816) "it is very seldom that the whole additional produce obtained with the same quantity of labour falls to the lot of the labourers who produce it" (*Works*, VII, p. 57). Cf. *Wealth of Nations*, Vol. I, pp. 66-7.

[2] *Works*, I, p. 14. Cf. above, p. 78.   [3] *Ibid.*, I, p. 15.

[4] *Wealth of Nations*, Vol. I, p. 35.

The second stage of Ricardo's critique of Smith is summed up in the following passage:

"Though Adam Smith fully recognized the principle, that the proportion between the quantities of labour necessary for acquiring different objects, is the only circumstance which can afford any rule for our exchanging them for one another, yet he limits its application to 'that early and rude state of society, which precedes both the accumulation of stock and the appropriation of land'; as if, when profits and rent were to be paid, they would have some influence on the relative value of commodities, independent of the mere quantity of labour that was necessary to their production."[1]

It was certainly true, as we have seen, that Smith often spoke as if the value of a commodity in modern times, as distinct from its value in the "early and rude state of society", were determined by adding up the wages, profit and rent into which the natural price seemed to him ultimately to resolve itself. We now know that this was the source of Ricardo's main objection to Smith's theory of value. "Adam Smith thought", wrote Ricardo to Mill in December 1818,

"that as in the early stages of society, all the produce of labour belonged to the labourer, and as after stock was accumulated, a part went to profits, that accumulation, necessarily, without any regard to the different degrees of durability of capital, or any other circumstance whatever, raised the prices or exchangeable value of commodities, and consequently that their value was no longer regulated by the quantity of labour necessary to their production."[2]

Ricardo, who was seeking for a theory of value which would be capable of application to the problem of the progressive redistribution of the national product as capital accumulation increased, could hardly have been expected to look with favour on a theory which, apart from anything else, appeared to suggest that the value of the national product might change appreciably merely as the result of a change in its distribution.[3] The manner in which the proceeds from the sale of a commodity were divided up from time to time between the main social classes, Ricardo believed, made no difference to the *value* of the commodity, which, in modern as well as in ancient times, varied

---

[1] *Works*, I, 22-3, footnote. On this passage, and in particular on the question of the reasons for its omission in edn. 3, see Sraffa's account in *Works*, I, pp. xxxv-xxxix.

[2] *Ibid.*, VII, p. 377.   [3] See below, p. 112.

only when there was a change in the quantity of labour required to produce it.[1]

The development of Ricardo's thought along these lines dictated to a large extent the form which the earlier chapters of the *Principles* were to assume. Since Smith had suggested that the payment of profit and rent prevented the "rule" which regulated value in ancient times from regulating it also in modern times, it was necessary for Ricardo to show clearly that profit and rent did not in fact have this effect. Adam Smith, said Ricardo,

> "has no where analyzed the effects of the accumulation of capital, and the appropriation of land, on relative value. It is of importance, therefore, to determine how far the effects which are avowedly produced on the exchangeable value of commodities, by the comparative quantity of labour bestowed on their production, are modified or altered by the accumulation of capital and the payment of rent."[2]

Ricardo, therefore, accepting the determination of value by labour time as his foundation, proceeded systematically to enquire to what extent this foundation was consistent with the payment of profit to the owners of capital and the payment of rent to the owners of land.[3] In the first draft of the *Principles*, which Ricardo sent to Mill in October 1816, the logical pattern of the argument as a whole must have been rather more obvious than it was in the version finally published, since Mill commented as follows on Ricardo's treatment:

> "Your explanation of the general principle that quantity of labour is the cause and measure of exchangeable value, excepting in the cases which you except, is both satisfactory, and clear.
>
> "Your exposition and argumentation to shew, in opposition to A. Smith, that profits of stock do not disturb that law, are luminous. So are the exposition and argumentation to shew that rent also operates no such disturbance."[4]

[1] Subject, of course, to the "modifications" which he later introduced and which will be discussed below.

[2] *Works*, I, p. 23, footnote.

[3] Cf. Marx, *Theories of Surplus Value* (English edn.), p. 203. The essence of Ricardo's argument on the question of the payment of profit is contained in the passage quoted on p. 102 below.

[4] *Works*, VII, p. 98. The "exceptions" referred to in the first paragraph are, presumably, those commodities (such as "rare statues and pictures, scarce books and coins", etc.), the value of which, according to Ricardo, is "determined by their scarcity alone". (See *Works*, I, p. 12.) Mill goes on to remark that "to this extent the disquisition is remarkably free of that sin which most easily besets you, of crowding too many points into one place; and summoning all the parts of the science at once to prove a particular point. The argument thus far is not only convincing, but clear, and easily understood."

Unfortunately, this simple pattern was destined to be blurred by the insertion, between the arguments relating to profit and to rent, of certain material which in the first draft probably appeared in a later section.[1] The third stage of Ricardo's critique of Smith, about which something must now be said, was reflected in this material.

Smith, as I have already noted above, had argued that a rise in the price of corn, by way of its effect on wages, would bring about a rise in the prices of all other commodities. Ricardo had opposed this idea in his *Essay on Profits*, but as his theory of value developed he was able to give his opposition a rather more scientific basis than that which he had given it in the *Essay*. His own idea that a change in the price of corn, while it would indeed alter wages, would not thereby affect the price of any other commodity, was, in fact, as he soon came to realise, a logical corollary of the doctrine that the payment of profits does not disturb the operation of embodied labour as the determinant of value. When profits came to be paid, the produce of labour was divided up between the class which owned the means of production and the class which furnished the labour, but this did not mean that the determinant of value which used formerly to operate in the primitive community of the deer and beaver hunters now automatically ceased to operate:

"All the implements necessary to kill the beaver and deer might belong to one class of men, and the labour employed in their destruction might be furnished by another class; still, their comparative prices would be in proportion to the actual labour bestowed, both on the formation of the capital, and on the destruction of the animals. Under different circumstances . . . those who furnished an equal value of capital for either one employment or for the other, might have a half, a fourth, or an eighth of the produce obtained, the remainder being paid as wages to those who furnished the labour; yet this division could not affect the relative value of these commodities, since whether the profits of capital were greater or less, whether they were 50, 20, or 10 per cent. or whether the wages of labour were high or low, they would operate equally on both employments."[2]

According to this analysis, then, it appeared that a change in the proportions in which the produce was divided up between profits

---

[1] Cf. Sraffa, in *Works*, I, pp. xvi-xviii, and particularly p. xvii, footnote 2.
[2] *Ibid.*, I, p. 24. Cf. pp. 26-9.

and wages would not affect the relative values of commodities
(including the monetary commodity). Thus a change in the price
of corn, while it would almost certainly bring about a change
in wages, would not thereby affect the prices of any other commodity.[1]

But Ricardo soon found that he was wrong in saying that a change
in wages (and therefore in profits) would necessarily and in all cases
"operate equally on both employments". In a case where the capitals
required to produce two commodities were differently constituted
—for example, where one of the commodities was produced with a
relatively large amount of fixed and a relatively small amount of
circulating capital, while the other was produced with a relatively
small amount of fixed and a relatively large amount of circulating
capital—it was possible to show that a rise in wages which brought
about a reduction in the rate of profit (or vice versa) would in fact
affect the relative values of the commodities.[2] This did not mean,
however, according to Ricardo, that Smith was correct in saying
that a rise in wages would bring about a rise in the prices of commodities in general. In actual fact, he argued, a rise in wages would
cause no commodities whatever to rise in price, but would on the
contrary cause an absolute *fall* in the prices of all commodities in the
production of which any fixed capital at all was employed, this fall
being greater as the proportion of fixed to circulating capital was
greater.[3]

The gist of Ricardo's argument can be illustrated by a simple
arithmetical example. Suppose that we have three commodities,
A, B and C, in the production of each of which a total capital of 100
is employed. In the case of A, this 100 consists entirely of circulating
capital; in the case of B it is divided equally between fixed and circulating; and in the case of C 80 is fixed and 20 circulating. We assume
that all the fixed capital is used up in the particular period of production we are considering; that the circulating capital consists entirely
of wages; and that the average rate of profit on capital is 20 per cent.
The equilibrium price of the output of each of the three commodities—

[1] Except in so far as "raw material from the land" entered into its composition. See
Works, I, p. 117, and cf. IV, p. 20, footnote.

[2] Ricardo also showed that a similar effect would be produced if the fixed capitals
were of different "durabilities". In edn. 2, as a result of a criticism by Torrens, he added
the further case of a difference in the "durabilities" of the *circulating* capitals (see *Works*,
I, pp. xlii and 60-1, footnote).

[3] See *Works*, I, pp. 62-3.

equal to its cost of production, including profits at the average rate—will then be 120, as in the following table:

		Capital		Profit (20%)	Equilibrium Price
		Fixed	Circulating		
A.	..	0	100	20	120
B.	..	50	50	20	120
C.	..	80	20	20	120

Suppose now that wages increase by 10 per cent., and that there is a consequential fall in the rate of profit from 20 per cent. to $9\frac{1}{11}$ per cent.[1] The situation will then be as follows:

		Capital		Profit ($9\frac{1}{11}$%)	Equilibrium Price
		Fixed	Circulating		
A.	..	0	110	10	120
B.	..	50	55	9·5	114·5
C.	..	80	22	9·3	111.3

It will be seen that none of the three commodities has risen in price; that each of the two commodities in the production of which fixed capital has been employed (B and C) has fallen in price; and that this fall is greater in the case of commodity C, where the proportion of fixed to circulating capital is greater.

The main moral which Ricardo drew from this analysis, in the first edition of the *Principles*, was that Adam Smith and the other

---

[1] The figure of $9\frac{1}{11}$ per cent. has been selected so as to make the new equilibrium price of commodity A, in the production of which no fixed capital is employed, exactly the same as the old. This is in effect what Ricardo does in his own rather more ponderous examples (see, e.g., I, p. 59). The procedure is not quite so arbitrary as it may appear at first sight. For Ricardo, in edns. 1 and 2 of the *Principles*, proceeded by "supposing money . . . to be always the produce of the same quantity of unassisted labour"—with the additional tacit assumption, as Mr. Sraffa puts it, that the period taken to produce and bring to market the monetary commodity (and all other commodities) was a year (I, p. xlii). On this assumption, the prices of that class of commodities "where the advances consist solely in the payment of labour, and the returns come in exactly in the year" would not in fact change with a rise in wages; capital in the case of this class of commodities would necessarily lose precisely what labour gained; and the fall in the rate of profit in this branch of production would determine the fall in the *general* rate of profit. The main conclusion which Ricardo draws from his examples—that a rise in wages will cause a fall in the prices of all commodities in the production of which any fixed capital is employed—is obviously dependent upon this assumption. But the proposition that a rise in wages will cause the prices of commodities produced with a high proportion of fixed to circulating capital to fall *relatively* to the prices of those produced with a low proportion remains true whatever assumption is made about the conditions of production of the monetary commodity.

"writers of distinguished and deserved reputation"[1] who had maintained that a rise in wages must necessarily be followed by a rise in
the prices of all commodities were quite mistaken. So far from the
prices of all commodities rising as a result of a rise in wages, none
would in fact rise and the great majority would actually fall. The
paradoxical character of this conclusion seems to have appealed to
Ricardo, and in the first edition of the *Principles* he went out of his
way to emphasise it. It was of course true that in order to reach this
conclusion it had to be conceded that a change in wages might cause
commodities to vary in relative value even though nothing at all
had happened to the quantities of labour required to produce them.
The relative values of commodities produced with the aid of differently constituted capitals, it now appeared, might vary not only when
the *productivity* of labour varied but also when the *wages* of labour
varied. Thus the accumulation of capital did after all seem to disturb
the law of value. But the point which was important for Ricardo
was that it did not disturb it *in the way that Adam Smith had postulated*.
The mere fact of the division of the product between wages and profit,
consequent upon accumulation, did not affect it. In opposition to
Smith, Ricardo maintained that "it is not because of this division
into profits and wages,—it is not because capital accumulates, that
exchangeable value varies, but it is in all stages of society, owing
only to 2 causes: one the more or less quantity of labour required,
the other the greater or less durability of capital:—that the former is
never superseded by the latter, but is only modified by it."[2] Thus
accumulation, in so far as it occasioned "different proportions of fixed
and circulating capital to be employed in different trades" and gave
"different degrees of durability to such fixed capital", certainly
introduced "a considerable modification to the rule, which is of
universal application in the early stages of society".[3] But it introduced
no more than a *modification* to that rule. Adam Smith's view that the
labour theory applied only to primitive times, and that it had to be
replaced by some sort of "cost of production" theory when capital
accumulated, was decisively rejected.

4. *The Theory of Value in the Third Edition of the "Principles"*
    Prior to the publication of Mr. Sraffa's edition of the *Works and
Correspondence*, it was widely believed that Ricardo eventually came

[1] *Works*, I, p. 63.   [2] *Ibid.*, VII, p. 377.
[3] *Ibid.*, I, p. 66. Cf. Marx's treatment of this problem in *Capital*, Vol. III, chapter 11.

to realise that the labour theory of value was too shaky and unreliable to serve as a foundation for the imposing structure of distribution theory which he had erected upon it. His famous letter to McCulloch of 13 June 1820, in which he expressed some dissatisfaction with the theory,[1] was almost invariably given prominence in histories of economic thought; and certain of the changes made in the second and third editions of the *Principles* were frequently adduced as evidence of a gradual "retreat" from the theory presented in the first edition. Mr. Sraffa, however, in his introduction to the *Principles*, comes to the conclusion that "an examination of the changes in the text in the light of the new evidence lends no support" to "the view of a retreat in Ricardo's position over successive editions". "The theory of edition 3", he writes, "appears to be the same, in essence and in emphasis, as that of edition 1."[2] It is difficult not to be persuaded by the impressive evidence which Mr. Sraffa brings forward.[3] There seems to be no doubt that, apart from the one lapse in his letter to McCulloch, Ricardo persisted to the end in his belief that "in fixing on the quantity of labour realised in commodities as the rule which governs their relative value we are in the right course".[4] Economists may still argue, if they wish, that Ricardo was misled into false enquiries on the question of value. But what has always been one of the chief props of this argument—the notion that Ricardo himself eventually recognised that he had been misled—has been irretrievably knocked away.

The main alterations to the chapter on value in the third edition were connected with Ricardo's increasing preoccupation with the problem of defining an "invariable" measure of value. This was a problem to which Ricardo had already given some attention—although not a great deal—in the first and second editions. "If any one commodity could be found", he had there said,

---

[1] *Works*, VIII, pp. 191-7. See particularly p. 194.   [2] *Ibid.*, I, p. xxxviii.

[3] In only one place does Mr. Sraffa's argument seem unconvincing. A statement in edns. 1 and 2 to the effect that "in the early stages of society" the exchangeable value of freely reproducible commodities "depends solely" upon the quantity of embodied labour was amended in edn. 3 by the replacement of "depends solely" with "depends almost exclusively". Mr. Sraffa's explanation, which relates the amendment to the change in the choice of standard from edn. 1 to edn. 3, seems to me to be a shade too ingenious. Should not the amendment rather be related to Ricardo's recognition in 1820 (under the stimulus of a criticism by Malthus in the latter's *Principles*) that the cause which brings about the "considerable modification" to the law of value actually "operates in every stage of society"—i.e., not only in capitalist society, but also in those "early stages of society" to which Ricardo's statement specifically refers? See *Works*, I, pp. xxxix and 12, and II, p. 59.

[4] *Works*, VIII, p. 344.

"which now and at all times required precisely the same quantity of labour to produce it, that commodity would be of an unvarying value, and would be eminently useful as a standard by which the variations of other things might be measured. Of such a commodity we have no knowledge, and consequently are unable to fix on any standard of value."[1]

If a commodity possessing this quality could in fact be found, Ricardo had said, we should be able to use it to ascertain, when two commodities *which were produced with similarly constituted capitals* varied in relative value, how much of the variation was to be attributed to a cause which affected the value of one and how much to a cause which affected the value of the other.[2] In the case of these commodities, we should find that "the utmost limit to which they could permanently rise", when measured in terms of the "invariable" standard, would be "proportioned to the additional quantity of labour required for their production; and that unless more labour were required for their production, they could not rise in any degree whatever".[3] But if the commodities were produced with capitals of different "proportions" and "durabilities", this would no longer be the case, and "the relative value of the commodities produced, would be altered in consequence of a rise in wages",[4] even though this were unaccompanied by any change in the difficulty or facility of production. That was really as far as Ricardo specifically pursued the matter in the first and second editions of the *Principles*.

Malthus, in his own *Principles* (1820), criticised Ricardo for maintaining that a rise in wages would lower the prices of the great majority of commodities. It was true, Malthus agreed, that in cases where commodities were produced with a large quantity of fixed capital and where a long time elapsed before the returns came in, it was natural to suppose

"that the fall of price arising from a fall of profits should, in various degrees, more than counterbalance the rise of price which would naturally be occasioned by a rise in the price of labour; and consequently on the supposition of a rise in the money price of labour and a fall in the rate of profits, all these commodities will, in various degrees, naturally fall in price."[5]

[1] *Works*, I, p. 17, footnote. [2] *Ibid.*, I, pp. 27-8 and 54.
[3] *Ibid.*, I, pp. 29-30 and 56.
[4] *Ibid.*, I, p. 56. The paragraph from which this statement is quoted does not appear in edn. 2, but a paragraph of similar import is substituted for it.
[5] *Ibid.*, II, p. 62.

But in the case of that other "large class of commodities" where there was little or no fixed capital employed and the returns came in rapidly, it was by no means natural to suppose this, since the tendency for the price to fall would *not* "more than counterbalance" the tendency for it to rise. The prices of this class of commodities, therefore, would in fact rise with a rise in wages. On the borderline between these two classes there would be a third class, where "a rise or fall of wages is exactly compensated by a fall or rise of profits"—a line which Ricardo had placed, "at a venture, among those commodities where the advances consist solely in the payment of labour, and the returns come in exactly in the year".[1] This third class, Malthus added, wherever the line be placed, "can embrace but a very small class of objects", and "upon a rise in the price of labour, all the rest will either fall or rise in price, although exactly the same quantity of labour continues to be employed upon them."[2]

Ricardo was not impressed by the sting in the tail of Malthus's analysis. "Mr. Malthus", he said,

"shews that in fact the exchangeable value of commodities is not *exactly* proportioned to the labour which has been employed on them, which I not only admit now, but have never denied."[3]

But he was quite prepared to agree that Malthus was correct in saying that with a rise in wages some commodities would in fact rise in price. "I inadvertently admitted", he confessed, "to consider the converse of my first proposition."[4] And the idea that a class of commodities produced under certain conditions could be conceived as constituting a sort of borderline between commodities which would fall and commodities which would rise in price with a change in wages excited his interest. It was not long before he saw more clearly its relevance to the problem of the "invariable" measure of value. Soon after reading Malthus's book it became apparent to Ricardo that his presentation of this problem in the first and second editions had been to some extent deficient, in that he had failed to take full and specific account of the "variety of circumstances" under which the "invariable" monetary medium might be supposed to be produced. "I have not been sufficiently explicit", he wrote to McCulloch, in a letter discussing Malthus's critique,

---

[1] *Works*, II, pp. 62–5. Cf. above, p. 104, footnote.   [2] *Works*, II, p. 65.
[3] *Ibid.*, II, p. 66.   [4] *Ibid.*, II, p. 64.

"for I ought to have said that if the medium is produced under certain circumstances, there are many commodities which may rise in consequence of a rise in labour, altho' there are many others which would fall, while a numerous portion would vary very little."[1]

From here it is only a short step to the idea that the degree of imperfection of an "invariable" measure of value can be reduced if we postulate not only that it should always require the same quantity of labour to produce it but also that it should be produced under circumstances which represent a sort of mean between the two extremes of high and low "proportions" and "durabilities" of capital.[2]

Most of the major alterations in the third edition of the *Principles* are the result of Ricardo's development of this idea. In the first place, there is a restatement of the doctrine relating to the effect upon relative prices of a change in wages:

"It appears, too, that in proportion to the durability of capital employed in any kind of production, the relative prices of those commodities on which such durable capital is employed, will vary inversely as wages; they will fall as wages rise, and rise as wages fall; and, on the contrary, those which are produced chiefly by labour with less fixed capital, or with fixed capital of a less durable character than the medium in which price is estimated, will rise as wages rise, and fall as wages fall."[3]

In spite of this amendment, of course, it still remained true that those who maintained that "a rise in the price of labour would be uniformly followed by a rise in the price of all commodities" were wrong, since in fact only *some* commodities would rise;[4] and it also remained true—a point which Ricardo seemed especially concerned to emphasise in the third edition—that "this cause of the variation of commodities is comparatively slight in its effects" when seen in relation to "the other great cause", namely, "the increase or diminution in the quantity of labour necessary to produce them".[5]

In the second place, in the new section headed "On an invariable measure of value", Ricardo makes an attempt to define the proper mean between the two extremes of high and low "proportions" and "durabilities" of capital. No measure can possibly be perfect,

[1] *Works*, VIII, p. 180. Ricardo insisted, however, that "this is all implied in my book".
[2] *Ibid.*, VIII, pp. 191-3. Cf. pp. 343-4.
[3] *Ibid.*, I, p. 43. There are a number of minor consequential amendments which it is not necessary to specify.
[4] *Ibid.*, I, p. 46.   [5] *Ibid.*, I, p. 36.

he argues, for even if we could find one which always required the same quantity of labour to produce it, it would still be "subject to relative variations from a rise or fall of wages, on account of the different proportions of fixed capital which might be necessary to produce it, and to produce those other commodities whose alteration of value we wished to ascertain".[1] And, of course, differences in the durabilities, as well as the proportions, of capital might similarly affect the reliability of the measure. Thus a commodity always requiring the same quantity of labour to produce it "would be a perfect measure of value for all things produced under the same circumstances precisely as itself, but for no others".[2] The best we can do, therefore, is to strike some sort of mean between the two extremes. Ricardo selects gold as his measure, suggesting that it may be considered as a commodity "produced with such proportions of the two kinds of capital as approach nearest to the average quantity employed in the production of most commodities". "May not these proportions", he asks, "be so nearly equally distant from the two extremes, the one where little fixed capital is used, the other where little labour is employed, as to form a just mean between them?"[3] Some of the further implications of this analysis, and its development in Ricardo's thought after the publication of the third edition of the *Principles*, will be considered in the next section.

5. *The Final Stage*: *The Development of the Concept of Absolute Value*

The discovery of the papers on *Absolute Value and Exchangeable Value*, upon which Ricardo was working during the last weeks of his life, has given a new interest and importance to the question of the development of his ideas on value after the appearance of the third edition of the *Principles*. In particular, it has become possible to detect the emergence of a new trend in his thought—a trend which developed out of his increasing concern with the problem of the relationship between "relative" (or "exchangeable") value and "absolute" value.

"The inquiry to which I wish to draw the reader's attention", said Ricardo in the *Principles*, "relates to the effect of the variations in the relative value of commodities, and not in their absolute value."[4]

---

[1] *Works*, I, p. 44.   [2] *Ibid.*, I, pp. 44-5.   [3] *Ibid.*, I, pp. 45-6.

[4] *Ibid.*, I, p. 21. Cf. VIII, p. 279: "The doctrine is less liable to objections when employed not to measure the whole absolute value of the commodities compared, but the variations which from time to time take place in relative value."

The formal rationale of the concept of absolute value, as we have seen, lies in the assumption that a change in the relative values of two commodities can be usefully regarded as the net resultant of a change which has taken place in the "absolute" (or "real") value of one or both of them considered individually. The "absolute" value of a commodity, in the broad sense, is in fact its value as measured by an "invariable" standard.

The difficulties inherent in the problem of measuring absolute value begin to become evident only when we recognise that commodities (including the commodity used as a standard) are actually subject to fluctuations in relative value, not only from a change in the quantity of labour required to produce them, but also from "a rise of wages, and consequent fall of profits, if the fixed capitals employed be either of unequal value, or of unequal duration".[1] Under these circumstances, how can the absolute value of a commodity be measured? Or, to put the same question in another way, what qualities must a measure possess in order to be "perfect" or "invariable"? I have already noted the solution to this problem which Ricardo propounded in the third edition of the *Principles*. In his final paper, following up a suggestion he had made to McCulloch to the effect that all the exceptions to the general rule that the value of a commodity depended upon embodied labour could be conceived of in terms of differences in the *time* taken to produce the commodity and to bring it to market,[2] Ricardo decided that the "just mean" was represented by "a commodity produced by labour employed for a year".[3] This, he asserted, was "a mean between the extremes of commodities produced on one side by labour and advances for much more a year, and on the other by labour employed for a day only without any advances". The fact that this measure was "produced in the same length of time as corn and most other vegetable food which forms by far the most valuable article of daily consumption", said Ricardo, would decide him "in giving it a preference".[4]

According to Ricardo's way of looking at the problem, as we have seen, a measure of absolute value was only *perfect*—i.e., perfectly invariable—if it always required the same quantity of labour to produce it *and* if the constitution and durability of the capital required to produce it were the same as that of the capital required to produce

---

[1] *Works*, I, p. 53.   [2] *Ibid.*, VIII, pp. 180 and 191-3.
[3] *Ibid.*, IV, p. 405. See Sraffa's account in I, pp. xliv-xlv.
[4] *Ibid.*, IV, pp. 405-6.

the commodity being measured. The measure which Ricardo finally arrived at was selected precisely because it appeared to deviate from this standard of perfection less than any other possible measure. Now, if the measure were perfect in this sense, it is evident that no commodity estimated in it could possibly vary in value unless there were a change in the quantity of labour required to produce it. *The measure would not reflect the effect of a change in wages at all.* This concept of a perfect measure of absolute value which would act as a sort of sieve, allowing through the mesh the effects produced by a change in wages and retaining only those produced by a change in the quantity of embodied labour, appealed strongly to Ricardo, and remained the pivot of his thought on the value problem until the end of his life.

Why should Ricardo have selected and so stubbornly defended this particular criterion of the perfection of a measure of absolute value? One reason which weighed with him, perhaps, was the *convenience* (in relation to the central problem of distribution) of a measure which did not reflect the effect of changes in wages, since, as Mr. Sraffa says, "if a rise or fall of wages by itself brought about a change in the magnitude of the social product, it would be hard to determine accurately the effect on profits".[1] But rather more important than this, I think, was the fact that at the back of Ricardo's mind there always lurked the idea that there was something unique and fundamental about the role which human labour played in the process of value-creation—so unique and fundamental, indeed, that it simply made no sense to speak of a commodity as "varying in absolute value" if no more or no less labour was required to produce it. In his final paper on value this idea was given classic expression. "To me it appears a contradiction", Ricardo wrote, "to say a thing has increased in natural value while it continues to be produced under precisely the same circumstances as before."[2]

It is Ricardo's increasing tendency to *identify* the absolute value of a commodity with the quantity of labour embodied in it which represents that new trend in his thought of which I spoke at the beginning of this section. Even in the new material incorporated in the third edition of the *Principles* there are signs of this trend, particularly in the chapter on *Value and Riches*. Take, for example, the following passage:

---

[1] *Works.*, I, p. xlviii. Cf. above, p. 100.
[2] *Ibid.*, IV, p. 375. "Natural" is obviously used here as a synonym for "absolute".

"A franc is not a measure of value for any thing, but for a quantity of the same metal of which francs are made, unless francs, and the thing to be measured, can be referred to some other measure which is common to both. This, I think, they can be, for they are both the result of labour; and, therefore, labour is a common measure, by which their real as well as their relative value may be estimated. This also, I am happy to say, appears to be M. Destutt de Tracy's opinion. He says, 'as it is certain that our physical and moral faculties are alone our original riches, the employment of those faculties, labour of some kind, is our only original treasure, and that it is always from this employment, that all those things are created which we call riches, those which are the most necessary, as well as those which are the most purely agreeable. It is certain too, that all those things only represent the labour which has created them, and if they have a value, or even two distinct values, they can only derive them from that labour from which they emanate.' "[1]

A month or two after the appearance of the third edition, we find Ricardo explaining to Trower:

"I do not, I think, say that the labour expended on a commodity is a measure of its exchangeable value, but of its positive value. I then add that exchangeable value is regulated by positive value, and therefore is regulated by the quantity of labour expended.

"You say if there were no exchange of commodities they could have no value, and I agree with you, if you mean exchangeable value, but if I am obliged to devote one month's labour to make me a coat, and only one weeks labour to make a hat, although I should never exchange either of them, the coat would be four times the value of the hat; and if a robber were to break into my house and take part of my property, I would rather that he took three hats than one coat."[2]

In his next letter to Trower he writes similarly:

"In speaking of exchangeable value you have not any idea of real value in your mind—I invariably have. . . . The fault lies not in the doctrine itself, but in my faulty manner of explaining it. The exchangeable value of a commodity cannot alter, I say, unless either its real value, or the real value of the things it is exchanged for alter. This cannot be disputed. If a coat would purchase 4 hats and will afterwards purchase 5, I admit that both the coat and the hats have varied in exchangeable value, but they have done so in consequence of one or other of them varying in real value."[3]

[1] *Works*, I, pp. 284-5. [2] *Ibid.*, IX, p. 2. [3] *Ibid.*, IX, p. 38.

And another interesting formulation of the same idea appears in a letter to Malthus written about a month later:

> "Nothing is to me so little important as the fall and rise of commodities in money, the great enquiries on which to fix our attention are the rise or fall of corn, labour, and commodities in real value, that is to say the increase or diminution of the quantity of labour necessary to raise corn, and to manufacture commodities. It may be curious to develop the effect of an alteration of real value on money price, but mankind are only really interested in making labour productive, in the enjoyment of abundance, and in a good distribution of the produce obtained by capital and industry. I cannot help thinking that in your speculations you suppose these much too closely connected with money price."[1]

Here are two further passages in which the quantity of labour worked up in a commodity is virtually identified with its absolute value. The first is from the pamphlet *On Protection to Agriculture*, which appeared in April 1822, and the second from a letter to Malthus of August 1823:

> "When I use the term—a low value of corn, I wish to be clearly understood. I consider the value of corn to be low, when a large quantity is the result of a moderate quantity of labour. In proportion, as for a given quantity of labour a smaller quantity of corn is obtained, corn will rise in value."[2]

> "I estimate value by the quantity of labour worked up in a commodity.... The difference between us is this, you say a commodity is dear because it will command a great quantity of labour, I say it is only dear when a great quantity has been bestowed on its production."[3]

And Ricardo's increasing concern with this aspect of the problem was accompanied by a growing sharpness in his opposition to the views of those who put forward different theories of value—notably Say with his utility theory, and Malthus with his commandable labour measure and his superficial "supply and demand" approach—and also by a growing impatience with the highly scholastic attempts of his own disciples to explain away the difficulties associated with the labour theory.[4] In the final papers on *Absolute Value and Exchangeable Value* all these different strands of thought are gathered together.

The idea I have been describing underlies a great deal of the argument

---

[1] *Works*, IX, p. 83. Cf. p. 100: "Too much importance is attached to money—facility of production is the great and interesting point."

[2] *Ibid.*, IV, p. 235.   [3] *Ibid.*, IX, p. 348.   [4] *Ibid.*, IX, *passim*.

of these final papers. It underlies, for example, the following criticism by Ricardo of Malthus's commandable labour measure:

"In Mr. Malthus's measure provided the labourer were always paid the same quantity of corn for his labour the value would always be the same although to obtain this same quantity double the expenditure of labour and capital might be necessary at one time to what was necessary at another. If by improvements in husbandry corn could be produced with half the expenditure of labour and capital it would by Mr. M be said to be unaltered in value provided the same quantity and no more was given to the labourer as wages. It is indeed acknowledged by Mr. Malthus, (and how could it be denied?) that under such circumstances corn would fall very considerably in money price—it would fall also in the same degree in exchangeable value with all other things, but still Mr. M says it would not fall in absolute value, because it did not vary in his measure of value. On the contrary all these things as well as money would under the circumstances supposed vary in this measure and therefore he would say they had all risen considerably in value. He would say so altho' with respect to any one or more of them great improvements may have been made in the means of producing them by the application of machinery, or from any other cause which should render it cheap in price and lower in exchangeable value with regard to all things corn and labour excepted. In Mr. Ricardo's measure every thing to which such improvements were applied would fall in value[,] and price and value would be synonymous while gold the standard of money cost the same expenditure of capital and labour to produce it."[1]

It underlies, too, Ricardo's main criticism of Torrens's idea that in modern times value is determined by the quantity of capital required to produce commodities rather than by the quantity of labour:

"A yard of cloth may be worth 5 loaves of sugar. The difficulty of producing cloth and sugar may be increased two fold, or it may be doubly easy to produce them both, in neither of these cases will the relative value of these two commodities alter, a yard of cloth will be still worth 5 loaves of sugar, and because their relative value has not altered Col. Torrens would lead you to infer that their real value has not altered—I say their real value has certainly altered, in one case they have both, the yard of cloth and the 5 loaves of sugar, become less valuable, in the other they have both become more valuable."[2]

[1] *Works*, IV, pp. 372-3; and cf. pp. 407-8. Cf. also I, pp. 15-16.
[2] *Ibid.*, IV, p. 394. Cf. pp. 374-5.

And in one place the idea is stated specifically, with greater clarity than ever before in Ricardo's writings:

> "I may be asked what I mean by the word value, and by what criterion I would judge whether a commodity had or had not changed its value. I answer, I know no other criterion of a thing being dear or cheap but by the sacrifices of labour made to obtain it. Every thing is originally purchased by labour—nothing that has value can be produced without it, and therefore if a commodity such as cloth required the labour of ten men for a year to produce it at one time, and only requires the labour of five for the same time to produce it at another it will be twice as cheap. Or if the labour of ten men should be still required to produce the same quantity of cloth but for 6 months instead of twelve cloth would fall in value.
>
> "That the greater or less quantity of labour worked up in commodities can be the only cause of their alteration in value is completely made out as soon as we are agreed that all commodities are the produce of labour and would have no value but for the labour expended upon them."[1]

6. The Place of Ricardo in the History of the Labour Theory

Ricardo, as we have seen, began his researches into the value problem on the basis of the familiar Classical idea that when a commodity was sold at its cost of production (including profit on capital at the average rate) it was being sold "at its value". Its cost of production, or "natural price", was conceived as the monetary expression of its value.[2] Ricardo argued that "the relative cost of production of two commodities"—i.e., the ratio in which they would normally exchange for one another on the market—was "nearly in proportion to the quantity of labour from first to last respectively bestowed upon them".[3] It was "nearly", and not exactly, in proportion, of course, because there would necessarily be a difference between cost of production ratios and embodied labour ratios in the case of commodities produced with differently constituted capitals.[4]

In the *Principles*, Ricardo was primarily concerned, as he put it

---

[1] *Works*, IV, p. 397.   [2] See, e.g., *ibid.*, I, p. 47, footnote.
[3] *Ibid.*, II, p. 35.

[4] Ricardo more often considered this proposition in its "dynamic" form—i.e., that in the case of such commodities a rise or fall in wages would cause a *change* in their cost of production ratios without anything having happened to the quantities of labour required to produce them. Cf. Sraffa in *ibid.*, I, p. xlvii.

himself, with "the effect of the variations in the relative value of commodities, and not in their absolute value".[1] But it is difficult to make statements about the one without at the same time implicitly making statements about the other. It is especially difficult when the problem of a theory of value and that of an "invariable" measure or standard of value are as closely related in one's mind as they were in Ricardo's. "It is . . . of considerable use towards attaining a correct theory", wrote Ricardo, "to ascertain what the essential qualities of a standard are, that we may know the causes of the variation in the relative value of commodities, and that we may be enabled to calculate the degree in which they are likely to operate."[2] The problem of defining the qualities of an "invariable" measure of value, which occupied so much of his attention after the publication of the second edition of the *Principles*, was not really a new problem: in essence, Ricardo was still concerning himself with the question of the validity of the simple theory of value which he had announced in the first section of the first edition of the *Principles* in 1817.

Nevertheless, the concept of absolute value was much more fully developed in the later period; and, as I have shown above, the tendency to identify absolute value with embodied labour became more and more apparent. No doubt it was always present to some extent: one can scarcely talk about embodied labour as the "source" and "foundation" of value, and as being "realised" in commodities,[3] without at the same time tending to regard value as virtually *consisting* of embodied labour. But it was only in the last phase that this idea was clearly and consciously stated and emphasised. In emphasising it, Ricardo was no doubt trying to give coherent expression to his more or less instinctive feeling that "in fixing on the quantity of labour realised in commodities as the rule which governs their relative value we are in the right course".[4] If "the power of producing value" were really attributable to "the labour of man alone";[5] if it were true that "all commodities are the produce of labour and would have no value but for the labour expended upon them";[6] and if therefore the labour embodied in commodities constituted the very *substance* of their value—then it could hardly be doubted that we were "in the right course" in seeking to link exchange ratios to embodied labour ratios. Embodied labour ratios, it appeared, *ought* to be the

[1] *Works*, I, p. 21.   [2] *Ibid.*, I, p. 17.
[3] See, e.g., *ibid.*, I, p. 13, where all these three expressions are used.
[4] *Ibid.*, VIII, p. 344.   [5] *Ibid.*, I, p. 285.   [6] *Ibid.*, IV, p. 397.

sole regulators of exchange ratios;[1] and if they proved upon examination not to be so, then this was a "contradiction" which had somehow to be solved. And if the "contradiction" turned out to be very
difficult to solve, this was not to be taken as an indication of the
inadequacy of the basic doctrine, but rather as an indication of "the
inadequacy of him who has attempted to explain it".[2]

The question of Ricardo's place in the history of the labour theory
may perhaps be considered, first, in relation to the advance which he
made beyond Smith's version of the theory, and, second, in relation
to the extent to which he cleared the path for Marx. Ricardo, as we
have seen, begins in the *Principles* with the assumption that the determination of value by labour time is the necessary starting-point for a
proper understanding of the anatomy of capitalist society, and then
proceeds to enquire "whether the other economic relations or categories
conflict with this definition of value, or how far they modify it".[3]
This mode of approach represented a considerable advance over that
of Smith, whose accounts of what Marx called "the hidden structure
of the bourgeois economic system" on the one hand, and of "the
living forms in which this inner physiology manifests itself outwardly",[4] had proceeded more or less independently, often contra-
dicting one another and not being causally connected in anything like
a satisfactory manner. "At last, however", as Marx puts it,

"Ricardo comes on the stage, and calls to science: Halt!—The
foundation, the starting point for the physiology of the bourgeois
system—for the understanding of its internal organic coherence
and life process—is the determination of *value by labour time*.
Ricardo starts with this, and compels science to leave its old beaten
track and render an account of how far the rest of the categories
it has developed and described—the relations of production and
commerce—correspond to or conflict with this foundation, with the
starting point; how far in general the science that merely reflects
and reproduces the phenomenal forms of the process—how far
therefore also these phenomena themselves—correspond to the
foundation on which the inner connections, the real physiology of
bourgeois society, rests, or which forms its starting point; and what
in general is the position with regard to this contradiction between
the apparent and the actual movement of the system. This is therefore

[1] "Ought", of course, only in the sense that this conclusion seemed to follow logically
from the premises.
[2] *Works*, VIII, p. 142.   [3] Marx, *Theories of Surplus Value*, p. 201.
[4] *Ibid.*, p. 202.

the great historical significance of Ricardo for the science."[1]

But Ricardo's mode of approach in the *Principles*, according to Marx, although historically justified, was still scientifically inadequate, because "it skips necessary intermediate links and tries to establish *direct* proof of the consistency of economic categories with each other".[2] In particular, by his initial identification of "value" with cost of production, Ricardo in effect postulates the existence not only of commodities as such ("and nothing else has to be postulated", says Marx, "in considering value as such"), but also of "wages, capital, profit, and even the general rate of profit itself".[3] Thus Ricardo really begins by taking it for granted that in the case of commodities produced with the aid of differently constituted capitals "value" ratios will diverge from embodied labour ratios in a quantitatively indeterminate manner. Since they must necessarily diverge in this manner, there is in Ricardo's opinion little that can be done about it, except to admit that the original law requires a certain amount of "modification", and to seek for an "invariable" measure of value which will as far as possible show commodities as varying in value only when there is a change in the quantity of labour required to produce them.

Ricardo's criterion of the "perfection" of an "invariable" measure, as I have tried to point out above, was in large part a reflection of his deep-rooted feeling that in spite of all appearances to the contrary embodied labour did in some significant sense constitute and regulate the "value" of a commodity. The fact that embodied labour ratios were not in normal cases strictly proportionate to exchange ratios appeared to Ricardo as a "contradiction"—a contradiction which he himself was unable to solve. Fundamentally, his failure to solve it was due to the fact (already indicated above) that "at a point when he was only as yet concerned in explaining value, and was therefore as yet only dealing with the *commodity*, he suddenly bursts in with the *general rate of profit* and all the conditions which arise from the higher development of capitalist productive relations".[4] Instead of assuming the general rate of profit in advance, Marx argues,

"Ricardo should rather have investigated how far its existence is in any way consistent with the determination of value by labour time; and he would then have found that instead of being consistent

---

[1] *Theories of Surplus Value*, p. 203.   [2] *Ibid.*, p. 202.

[3] *Ibid.*, p. 205.   [4] *Ibid.*, p. 251.

with it, *prima facie* it contradicts it, and its existence has therefore to be explained through a number of intermediary stages—an explanation which is something very different from merely including it under the law of value."[1]

In Marx's opinion, then, it is only if the problem of the "contradiction" is posed in terms of the *derivation* of equilibrium prices from labour-determined "values" that it can be adequately solved. Ricardo, "instead of deriving the difference between production prices [i.e., equilibrium prices] and values from the determination of value itself, admits that values are themselves determined by influences independent of labour time". Here, Marx adds, "would have been the place for him to define the concept of 'absolute' or 'real' value, or 'value' as such".[2] Marx was not of course aware of the increasing emphasis which Ricardo in fact laid on "the concept of 'absolute' or 'real' value" in the last years of his life, nor of his increasing tendency to identify absolute value with embodied labour. Had Marx known of this he would probably have regarded it as an important step in the direction of the correct solution of the "contradiction". Certainly most of the essential ingredients of the Marxian solution—including the quite indispensable idea that profits depend upon the "proportion of the annual labour of the country [which] is devoted to the support of the labourers"[3,4]—were ready to hand in Ricardo's work by the time he died. The important quality which was lacking in Ricardo, but abundantly present in Marx, was a proper appreciation of the fact that problems of economic theory, even in such abstruse spheres as that of value, were not only problems of logic but also problems of history.

[1] *Theory of Surplus Value*, p. 212.   [2] *Ibid.*, p. 232.

[3] Ricardo, *Works*, I, p. 49.

[4] And even including—in a deleted passage (IV, p. 312)—a distinction very close in substance to that later made by Marx between constant and variable capital.

CHAPTER FOUR

KARL MARX'S THEORY OF VALUE (1)

1. *The Development of Value Theory from Ricardo to Marx*

THE two decades between 1823, when Ricardo died, and 1844, when Marx wrote his *Ökonomisch-philosophische Manuskripte*, saw a number of important developments in the field of value theory. On the one hand, the labour theory which Ricardo had put forward was increasingly attenuated and vulgarised by several of his supporters, and rejected outright by many of his opponents who developed new theories in place of it. On the other hand, the idea that all value was attributable to the expenditure of human labour was enthusiastically adopted by a number of radical economists who used it to support their demand that the working class should receive the whole (or at least a greater share) of the produce of its labour. These two decades, in fact, witnessed the first stage of that fascinating historical process whereby the labour theory of value was in effect rejected by the orthodox economists and taken over by representatives of the working-class movement. The second—and incomparably more important—stage of this process was ushered in by Karl Marx.

Ricardo, as a contemporary critic pointed out, had believed that "the idea of value in commodities *cannot even be conceived* without being mingled with the idea of their relation to mankind and to human labour, of which *some portion* must always be employed in procuring them originally".[1] After Ricardo's death, the retreat of the more respectable economists from this basic idea was quite remarkably rapid. After 1826, when the third edition of James Mill's *Elements of Political Economy* was published, practically the only reputable economist to continue to defend Ricardo's theory of value (apart from a few relatively unimportant popularisers who did little more than expound it) was J. R. McCulloch, and his defence contained a number of rather bizarre elements which afforded an easy target for the critics. By 1829 Samuel Read could refer, not too unfairly, to "the almost universal rejection of labour as the standard";[2] and by

---

[1] Samuel Read, *An Inquiry into the Natural Grounds of Right, etc.* (1829), p. viii, footnote.
[2] *Op. cit.*, p. 203.

1831 Cotterill could state that he felt himself obliged to repeat the usual arguments against the labour theory only because he suspected that "there are some Ricardians still remaining".[1] In place of the labour theory, the critics of Ricardo began to erect new theories of value, the lineal descendants of which are the various theories regarded as orthodox in the West today.

The reaction against Ricardo's theory of value took a number of different forms. In the first place, his concept of real or absolute value was criticised by men like Torrens, Bailey, and the anonymous author of *Observations on Certain Verbal Disputes in Political Economy*, on the grounds that exchange value was something essentially relative. In the second place, his opinion that explanations of value in terms of "supply and demand" *alone* were quite worthless was disputed by the followers of Lauderdale and Malthus (and, of course, by Malthus himself).[2] In the third place, his contention (as against Say) that a commodity is not in fact "valuable in proportion to its utility"[3] was attacked by a number of writers who laid increasing emphasis on the role played by utility in the determination of value. For the most part, these writers held some sort of supply and demand theory, and their emphasis on utility signified little more than that greater attention was being paid to the "demand side" of the so-called value equation; but in a few fairly well-known cases economists were to be found putting forward what was in effect a utility theory of value. This new emphasis on utility was often associated with one or another variant (usually fairly rudimentary) of the "productivity" theory of distribution. The value of the "productive services" of the agents of production, some writers began to urge, must be derived from the utility to consumers of the goods which the agents contributed to produce; and the moral was occasionally drawn (as, e.g., by Read

[1] C. F. Cotterill, *An Examination of the Doctrine of Value, etc.*, p. 8.

[2] Schumpeter, *History of Economic Analysis*, p. 601, says that Ricardo "was completely blind to the nature, and the logical place in economic theory, of the supply-and-demand apparatus and . . . took it to represent a theory of value distinct from and opposed to his own". But the point is, surely, that it was then *in fact being put forward* as "a theory of value distinct from and opposed to his own"—as, e.g., by Malthus (cf. the latter's *Principles*, chapter 2, secs. 2 and 3). To suggest, as Schumpeter does, that Ricardo was unaware of the fact that "the concepts of supply and demand apply to a mechanism that is compatible with any theory of value and indeed is required by all" (p. 601) seems to me to be quite mistaken, in view of such explicit statements as those in *Works*, Vol. II, pp. 38-53; VII, 250-1; VIII, 276-7, 279; etc. All that Ricardo maintained was that it was not enough to say *only* that supply and demand regulated value. That was simply "saying nothing" (VIII, 279). A theory of value, in his opinion, had to make some determinate statement about the *level* at which the forces of supply and demand fixed prices in the "normal" case.

[3] *Works*, Vol. VIII, p. 276.

and Simon Gray) that each "factor" normally received as a reward precisely what it contributed to the value of the final product. In the fourth place, and finally, Ricardo's contention that the cost of production of a commodity (which "determines supply at a particular price"[1] and therefore regulates the price itself) must be reduced to terms of *labour* cost, was contradicted by a number of economists. Some of them thought it sufficient to say that *money* costs of production determined long-period equilibrium prices, or, like Torrens, that relative values were determined by the relative quantities of *capital* employed,[2] thus impliedly suggesting that it was unnecessary to seek for any "real" cost underlying the cost in money or commodities. Others, like Scrope and Senior, did endeavour to discover the "real" cost which lay behind supply, finding it not in labour alone but in labour plus abstinence—thus implicitly suggesting that a theory of value could legitimately be framed in terms of two or more determinants without any obligation to reduce them to a common factor.[3]

Ricardo and his disciples were of course themselves partly responsible for this rapid retreat from the labour theory. Ricardo's formulation of the theory, as we have seen, was by no means beyond reproach, and the well-meaning but often unfortunate defences put up by men like Mill and McCulloch tended only to make matters worse. In particular, Ricardo's admission that his original law of value required "considerable modification" in the case of commodities produced with the aid of differently constituted capitals gave the critics an obvious handle.[4] The case of the wine in the cellar increasing in value year by year without any human labour being expended upon it, which had so worried Ricardo,[5] proved a stumbling-block for his disciples also. When Mill suggested that in such cases as this the "hoarded labour" (i.e., the capital) employed created additional value in proportion to the quantity of it applied, just as the "immediate labour" did in other cases,[6] and when McCulloch argued that the

---

[1] Ricardo, *Works*, Vol. II, p. 45.

[2] For Ricardo's comments on this view, see *Works*, Vol. IV, pp. 393 ff.

[3] Cf. M. H. Dobb, *Political Economy and Capitalism*, pp. 10–12.

[4] Malthus set the tone here by emphasising, with some justification, that differences in the constitution of capitals tend to increase as civilisation advances, becoming "prodigious" in modern times (*Principles of Political Economy*, 2nd edn., 1836, p. 88).

[5] See, e.g., *Works*, Vol. IX, pp. 330–1.

[6] See, e.g., *Elements* (2nd edn.), pp. 98–9. What Mill is really trying to say here, I think, is that both immediate labour and hoarded labour produce not only value but surplus value, each in proportion to the quantity applied.

"labour" *of nature* was responsible for the increase in the wine's value,[1] the critics naturally seized upon these extremely scholastic explanations (which Ricardo himself always recognised as mere verbal evasions of the issue) in order to pour scorn upon the labour theory itself. None of them made any real attempt to put forward an alternative solution to the "contradiction" which Ricardo's analysis had revealed. Other weaknesses in Ricardo's presentation of the theory which came under fire from the critics were his failure to explain how the apparently unequal exchange between capital and labour could be reconciled with the labour theory; his lack of clarity (at least in his published work) in distinguishing between *relative* and *absolute* value and between a *cause* and a *measure* of value; and the obscurity which occasionally surrounded some of his remarks on the determination of the value of labour.

But there is a more important reason for the persistent rejection or dilution of the labour theory which is characteristic of so many writers during this period. The labour theory—or, rather, the notion which came to be associated with it that "labour produces all"— had begun to be used by a number of radical writers, and by the working-class organisations with which they were often associated, to support their claims for various measures of economic and social reform. If labour in fact "produced all", these writers were asking, why should it not also receive all—or at least considerably more than it did at present? Naturally these claims were bitterly opposed: Thomas Hodgskin was a name to frighten children with in the days following the repeal of the Combination Laws in 1824. It was probably inevitable, therefore, that many of the more conservative economists should come to regard Ricardo's theory of value not only as logically incorrect but also as socially dangerous. "That labour is the sole source of wealth", wrote John Cazenove in 1832, "seems to be a doctrine as dangerous as it is false, as it unhappily affords a handle to those who would represent all property as belonging to the working classes, and the share which is received by others as a robbery or fraud upon *them*."[2] There is little doubt that this use (or misuse) of Classical value theory by the British radical writers was a potent factor in intensifying the reaction against Ricardo. Some of Ricardo's opponents (Scrope, Read and Longfield, for example) seem to have been fairly well aware of what they were doing: it was the *dangerous* character of

---

[1] See, e.g., *Principles of Political Economy* (1st edn.), p. 313. It is only fair to note that this doctrine was dropped in the second and subsequent editions of the *Principles*.

[2] *Outlines of Political Economy*, p. 22, footnote.

Ricardo's doctrines, rather than what they believed to be their falsity, with which they were primarily concerned, and they gave remarkably frank expression to the idea that political economy would have to be re-written from a new angle to make it suitable for consumption by the labouring classes. Most of the critics of Ricardo were no doubt more innocent, but the objective effect of their attacks on Ricardo was the same—to cut the ground from under the feet of Hodgskin and his fellow-radicals by exorcising or amending those parts of Ricardian doctrine upon which the latter relied. It is surely not merely fanciful to see much of this reaction against Ricardo as a reflection of the general shift by the British bourgeoisie at about this time from an offensive position as against the landlords to a defensive position as against the rising working-class movement.[1]

The majority of the radical writers—men like Hodgskin, Gray, Ravenstone, Thompson, Edmonds and others—were more or less agreed that "labour" was in some significant sense the only source of wealth and value (between which they seldom took proper care to distinguish), and that the net revenues received by the non-labouring classes were essentially deductions from the "whole produce" of this labour. The necessity for some kind of social reform seemed to them to follow, as a sort of logical corollary, from these premises. The labour theory of value, in the somewhat obscure and ambiguous form in which they often stated it, was invested with an ethical and political significance which has clung to it in the popular consciousness ever since, and from which it is sometimes claimed that it cannot possibly be dissociated. This is a question of some importance, which can perhaps be most conveniently introduced at this juncture.

Those who suggest that the labour theory of value necessarily embodies a particular ethical or political viewpoint often emphasise the part played in its early development by Locke. It is certainly true that Locke tended to regard the expenditure of labour on the production of a commodity, not only as conferring "value" upon it (leaving aside here the question of what kind of value), but also as conferring a right of property in the commodity upon the individual who had expended his labour in its production. No one would wish to deny, either, that the Lockean theory of property rights contributed largely to the building up of the political atmosphere in which the

[1] Cf. my article "The Decline of Ricardian Economics in England", *Economica*, February 1950. Cf. also von Thünen, *Der Isolierte Staat* (Rostock, 1842-63), Vol. I, part 2, pp. 36-48 and 62.

Classical labour theory of value was eventually able to flourish, or that many of the radicals did in fact look at the labour theory through Lockean spectacles.[1] But that is by no means the same as saying that the theory itself necessarily embodies a particular ethical or political viewpoint.[2] The Classical labour theory, as I have tried to show above, grew up in direct association not so much with the Lockean theory of property rights as with the concept of the social division of labour. In essence, it was another way of saying that the relations between things which manifested themselves in the sphere of commodity exchange were dependent upon the relations between men which manifested themselves in the sphere of commodity production. And this idea in itself does not seem to me to involve any very definite ethical or political presuppositions. Certainly there is no evidence at all that Smith or Ricardo, or Marx for that matter, ever looked upon the labour theory as anything other than a scientific tool to be used in the search for the objective laws of economic movement.[3]

One of the main sources of the confusion which still remains on this question is the fact that the labour theory of value is often to be found in close association with some sort of theory of *surplus* value. It is frequently suggested by critics that in such cases the existence of surplus value is actually "derived" from the labour theory itself, rather than from an objective study of the facts concerning the distribution of income. If "surplus value" does not in fact exist, but is merely a sort of logical derivative of the labour theory, then the suggestion that a particular ethical or political attitude is inherent in the labour theory certainly becomes rather more plausible. But historically at any rate, so far from the existence of surplus value being derived from the labour theory, the labour theory was in fact evolved precisely in order to explain the manifest existence of surplus value in the real world. The emergence of a value-difference between input and output,

[1] Cf. the following early statement from Charles Hall's *The Effects of Civilization* (1805), p. 68: "Whatever things a man makes with his own hands, out of such materials as his proportionate share of land yields, must be allowed to be his own; and these may be accumulated, if they are not consumed by the maker of them; or they may be exchanged for other things, made by and belonging to other people, of an equal value; to be strictly estimated by the quantity of labour employed in making the things exchanged."

[2] Cf. on this whole point M. H. Dobb, in a review in *Economica*, Vol. XIX, No. 73, pp. 94–5.

[3] Cf. Dobb, *op. cit.*, p. 95: "Every economic theory has, inevitably, its moral implications, and the positivist attempt to divorce the two may well have gone too far. But to say that certain implications of a theory rest on a particular moral postulate remains distinct from the proposition that the theory itself is so derived."

which eventually resolved itself into rent and profit and which was not significantly attributable to any expenditure of productive effort on the part of its recipients, was regarded by the Classical economists as a simple fact.[1] One of the main tasks which the labour theory was asked to perform was that of accounting for the origin and persistence of this surplus value and measuring its extent. The labour theory, it is true, when applied to the analysis of the economic process, allowed the phenomenon of surplus value to reveal itself, and, indeed, tended to bring it into relief—unlike certain modern theories of value which tend to mask it completely.[2] But surplus value cannot be said to be "derived" from the labour theory in any less rarefied sense than this.

Ethics and politics may indeed come into the picture if we decide to *pass judgment* on this phenomenon. But the labour theory does not in itself involve any particular ethical or political attitude towards it. It certainly cannot be taken to imply, for example, that the surplus value ought to accrue to the labourers rather than to the landlords and capitalists. This is in fact a question upon which upholders of the labour theory have often been sharply divided. Both Adam Smith and William Thompson, for instance, accepted some sort of labour theory of value, and both of them saw the origin of profit in the surplus value which the labourers employed by the capitalist added to the raw materials upon which they worked.[3] But the respective judgments which they passed on this state of affairs were of course very different indeed. Smith, by and large, regarded an economic system based on the appropriation of surplus value by landlords and capitalists as the best of all *possible* systems. Thompson, on the other hand, roundly condemned such a system. In actual fact, it was only when the working-class movement began to grow in strength and articulateness, and alternative modes of economic organisation began to be mooted, that the appropriation of surplus value came to be at all

---

[1] When Keynes said that "interest to-day rewards no genuine sacrifice, any more than does the rent of land" (*General Theory*, p. 376), he was in effect saying of interest and rent what the Classical economists tended to say not only of these two classes of income but also of profit.

[2] Cf. M. H. Dobb, *Political Economy and Capitalism*, pp. 22 and 30-3.

[3] See, e.g., *Wealth of Nations*, Vol. I, p. 67: "In all arts and manufactures the greater part of the workmen stand in need of a master to advance them the materials of their work, and their wages and maintenance till it be compleated. He shares in the produce of their labour, or in the value which it adds to the materials upon which it is bestowed; and in this share consists his profit." Cf. Ricardo, IV, pp. 379-80; and Thompson, *Inquiry into the Principles of the Distribution of Wealth*, p. 166.

widely condemned.[1] And it was only then that it began to be suggested, by both friends and enemies of the working-class movement, that the labour theory embodied a particular ethical and political viewpoint.

In so far as writers like Thompson, Proudhon and Rodbertus adopted this attitude towards the labour theory, their work came in for strong criticism from Marx. It was quite wrong, Marx argued in effect, to suggest that it followed from the labour theory itself that the whole produce of labour ought to accrue to the labourers and that therefore a socialist system ought to be instituted. This was mere utopianism, and the negation of science. It was quite true, of course, that when the labour theory was applied to the study of capitalist reality the fact that certain classes received "unearned" incomes was brought into relief. But, as Engels put it, "If we now say: that is unjust, that ought not to be so, then that has nothing immediately to do with economics. We are merely saying that this economic fact is in contradiction to our moral sentiment."[2] The labour theory was a scientific tool for the analysis of capitalist reality, and to suggest that it embodied a particular ethical or political viewpoint was simply to mix up economics and morality. The necessity for socialism certainly followed from the laws of capitalist development which the labour theory helped to reveal; but it definitely did not follow, as a sort of logical corollary, from the labour theory itself.

One point, however, remains to be added. While it is true that the

[1] The earlier attitude to the appropriation of surplus value is well illustrated by a passage in Mrs. Marcet's immortal *Conversations on Political Economy*. The inimitable Mrs. B. has just given her pupil Caroline an explanation, along the traditional Smithian lines, of the origin of profits. The tender-hearted Caroline says that she has "some scruple as to the mode of obtaining this income". If the labourer can in fact produce more than the value of his wages, why should he not be allowed to keep the whole of his earnings? "It is surely a great discouragement to his industry", Caroline opines, "to be obliged to yield part of them to his employer." The burden of Mrs. B.'s reply to this sentimental heresy is simply that if the capitalist were compelled to "allow the labourer the whole of the profit arising from his work", nobody would be prepared to give the labourer any work, and "industry would be paralysed". "So far from considering the profits which the capitalist derives from his labourers as an evil", she concludes, "I have always thought it one of the most beneficent ordinations of Providence, that the employment of the poor should be a necessary step to the increase of the wealth of the rich." (Quotations from 6th edn., 1827, pp. 95-8.)

[2] From Engels's preface to the first German edn. of Marx's *Poverty of Philosophy*, reprinted in the English edn. (Lawrence and Wishart), at p. 11. Engels qualifies this remark by adding the following: "But what formally may be economically incorrect, may all the same be correct from the point of view of world history. If the moral consciousness of the mass declares an economic fact to be unjust, as it has done in the case of slavery or serf labour, that is a proof that the fact itself has been outlived, that other economic facts have made their appearance, owing to which the former has become unbearable and untenable. Therefore, a very true economic content may be concealed behind the formal economic incorrectness."

labour theory of value in itself does not *embody* any particular ethical or political viewpoint, it is also true that in the case of Marx (and to some extent in the case of Smith) it was *associated with* a very definite ethical and political viewpoint. When an economist sets out to analyse the economic process he generally starts with a kind of "vision" (as Schumpeter calls it)[1] of that process. This "vision" normally includes some sort of basic *principle of causation* which the economist decides will be useful in the explanation of the process, and this principle of causation tends to find expression in the theory of value with which his subsequent analysis begins. The theory of value, in other words, expresses in a generalised way the *angle* from which the economist believes the process should be analysed. The labour theory, for example, says in effect that the process should be analysed in terms of the social relations between men and men in the production of commodities. In the case of Marx, the particular principle of causation expressed in this theory was identical with that applied by him to the other (non-economic) aspects of the social process as a whole; and this principle was of course intimately bound up with the particular philosophy which he extended to his study of social life. Thus Marx's labour theory of value, being so closely associated with the materialist conception of history and philosophical materialism, was naturally also associated with the ethical and political conclusions involved in the world outlook of Marxism. But it will be clear that this association was entirely different in character from what it is often supposed to have been, and that it by no means impugns the scientific quality of the labour theory.

2. *The Early Development of Marx's Economic Thought*

I have suggested above that the labour theory of value, in its formulation in the eighteenth century by Adam Smith, was closely associated with a rudimentary materialist conception of history. Smith, like Marx, was a whole man, whose aim was to combine a theory of political economy and a theory of history—and, of course, a theory of moral philosophy—into one great general system. After Smith's death, however, a divorce occurred almost immediately between the Classical theory of history and the Classical theory of political economy. The former was developed by John Millar, who was not particularly competent in matters of economic theory; and the latter was developed

[1] *History of Economic Analysis*, p. 41.

by Ricardo, who, in spite of the efforts of James Mill,[1] was never able to work up much enthusiasm over sociological questions. In the work of some of the post-Ricardian radicals, notably Bray, Proudhon and Rodbertus, there are vague signs of a *rapprochement*, but it was left to Marx to bring about the decisive reunion, at a very much higher level. The first really definite intimation of this reunion was made by Marx in *The Poverty of Philosophy* (1847). And the outward and visible sign of it was once again, as it had been in the beginning, a close association between the labour theory of value and a materialist conception of history.

The labour theory of value was not, of course, Marx's starting-point. Indeed, if we limit ourselves to that early period (from 1836 to 1847, say) in which he developed and gradually co-ordinated the leading ideas which were to serve him as a basis for his future work, his adoption of the labour theory of value appears rather as a culmination, a sort of condensed summing-up of his main conclusions, than as a starting-point. The story of how Marx came to the labour theory must be told as an integral part of the story of how he became a Marxist.

When Marx went to Berlin University as a student in 1836, it was almost inevitable that he should soon have been attracted towards Hegelianism. But the doctrine of Hegel taken as a whole, as Engels was later to remark, "left plenty of room for giving shelter to the most diverse practical party views. And in the theoretical Germany of that time, two things above all were practical: religion and politics. Whoever placed the chief emphasis on the Hegelian *system* could be fairly conservative in both spheres; whoever regarded the dialectical *method* as the main thing could belong to the most extreme opposition, both in politics and religion."[2] Marx attached himself to the Hegelian left wing—the so-called "Young Hegelians", who were at that time mainly concerned with the struggle against religion. His doctoral dissertation of 1841, however, at least in the opinion of some authorities, shows that the process of his emancipation from Hegel's idealism (or, as he and Engels liked to call it, his turning of Hegel right side up)[3] was by that time already beginning. In particular, the "Absolute Spirit", of which Hegel had regarded history as the unfolding, was beginning to give place in Marx's thought (as it had just done in

---

[1] See, e.g., Ricardo's *Works*, Vol. VII, pp. 195-7. See also *ibid.*, p. 382, where Ricardo reports to Mill that he has "read Millar with great pleasure".

[2] Engels, *Ludwig Feuerbach*, English edn. (Lawrence and Wishart), pp. 25-6.

[3] See, e.g., *Ludwig Feuerbach*, pp. 34 and 97.

Bruno Bauer's) to the concept of "the self-consciousness of man-kind".[1]

The main body of the most determined Young Hegelians, Engels tells us,

"was, by the practical necessities of its fight against positive religion, driven back to Anglo-French materialism. This brought it into conflict with its school system. While materialism conceives nature as the sole reality, nature in the Hegelian system represents merely the 'alienation' of the absolute idea, so to say, a degradation of the idea. In all circumstances thinking and its thought-product, the idea, is here the primary, nature the derived element, which only exists at all by the condescension of the idea. And in this contradiction they floundered as well or as ill as they could."[2]

This contradiction, Engels proceeds, was "dissolved" with the publication in 1841 of Feuerbach's *Essence of Christianity*, which "without circumlocutions . . . placed materialism on the throne again". "Nature", said Feuerbach (according to Engels's account),

"exists independently of all philosophy. It is the foundation upon which we human beings, ourselves products of nature, have grown up. Nothing exists outside nature and man, and the higher beings our religious fantasies have created are only the fantastic reflection of our own essence."[3]

With Feuerbach, then, "the self-consciousness of mankind" gave place simply to the human being, to "man" in his whole self.[4]

While Marx apparently shared to the full in the "liberating effect" of Feuerbach's book,[5] this effect does not seem to have shown itself at all decisively in his work until his *Critique of the Hegelian Philosophy of Law*, which he probably wrote between March and August 1843.[6] For much of the period between April 1841 (when he was awarded

---

[1] See H. P. Adams, *Karl Marx in his Earlier Writings*, chapter 3. Cf. also J. D. Bernal, *Marx and Science*, pp. 11-12; and Franz Mehring, *Karl Marx*, pp. 25-31. See also the appendix in the 1948 edn. of the latter work, pp. 540-2.

[2] *Ludwig Feuerbach*, pp. 27-8.   [3] *Ibid.*, p. 28.

[4] Cf. H. P. Adams, *op. cit.*, p. 84.   [5] *Ludwig Feuerbach*, p. 28.

[6] There has been some dispute over the date of composition of this work. Riazanov, the editor of the *Collected Works* of Marx and Engels in which it was first published, argued that it was unlikely to have been written prior to March 1843. Landshut and Mayer, the editors of a later German edition, on the other hand, maintained that the most probable time of composition was between April 1841 and April 1842. From a remark in Marx's *Critique of Political Economy* (pp. 10-11 of the Kerr edn.) it seems probable that at least the major part of the work was written between the dates mentioned in the text above, but it may well be that he had actually begun it some time earlier.

his doctorate) and March 1843 he engaged himself in political journalism. In the course of his activities in this sphere, he came face to face with a number of social and economic problems, the examination of which was destined to exert an important influence on the development of his thought. For example, he wrote an article, which appeared in Arnold Ruge's *Anecdota*, on the censorship instruction issued in January 1842 by Frederick William IV; and as contributor to and later editor of the *Rhenish Gazette* he published a number of pieces dealing with such subjects as the freedom of the press, communism, the penal laws against wood-pilfering in forests, and the situation of the vine-growers in the Moselle district.[1] During this period he was by no means a communist: he was still what might perhaps be called a liberal in politics. But in his various struggles against social injustice he was evidently coming to experience at first hand the restrictive effects of feudal bureaucracy, and was beginning to sense the character of the underlying economic forces which were largely responsible for the conflicts he was investigating.[2] When the *Rhenish Gazette* was suppressed in March 1843, Marx retired once again to his study, and embarked (as it appears) on his *Critique of the Hegelian Philosophy of Law*. On March 13, a few days before he resigned his editorship of the *Rhenish Gazette*, he had commented in a letter to Ruge that "Feuerbach's aphorisms [in his *Preliminary Theses on the Reform of Philosophy*, which appeared in *Anecdota*] are not to my liking in one point only, namely, that they concern themselves too much with nature and too little with politics, although an alliance with politics is the only way in which contemporary philosophy can become truth".[3] His *Critique of the Hegelian Philosophy of Law* took Marx some little way further along the road towards this alliance. Like Feuerbach, Marx now "insists on the human being as the fundamental reality", in opposition to Hegel, whose "method of treating concepts as the fundamental realities makes the relations of human beings a consequence of the relations of concepts".[4] And in some passages, particularly those where Marx discusses the relations between state and society, there are glimpses of the next stage in Marx's journey along this road—the substitution of *man in society* for Feuerbach's abstract "human being".[5]

---

[1] These important articles are described by H. P. Adams, *op. cit.*, chapters 4 and 5, *passim*.

[2] Cf. Bernal, *op. cit.*, p. 14.   [3] Mehring, *op. cit.*, p. 53.

[4] Adams, *op. cit.*, p. 83.

[5] I should emphasise here that although I am telling the story of Marx's early intellectual development in terms of his progress through a series of specific "stages", I am doing so mainly in order to highlight the *general direction* of this development. Naturally

This next stage, however, was not really reached until the writing of the two important essays which Marx contributed to the *Deutsch-Französische Jahrbücher*. Marx left Germany for Paris, where he and Ruge were to edit this journal, in November 1843; but the two essays which he wrote for the first (and only) issue—*On the Jewish Question* and *Introduction to a Critique of the Hegelian Philosophy of Law*— were probably drafted before he left Germany.[1] Their basic theme is announced right at the outset of the *Introduction*:

> "As far as Germany is concerned the criticism of religion is virtually completed and the criticism of religion is the premise of all criticism. . . .
>
> "The foundation of profane criticism is: man makes religion, religion does not make man. Religion, indeed, is the self-awareness and self-assurance of man when he has either not yet come to himself or has lost himself again. *But 'man' is no abstract being, drifting about outside the world. 'Man' is the world of man, the state, society.* These—the state, society,—produce religion, a false, 'upside-down' consciousness of the world, because they are a world where everything is upside-down. Religion is the general theory of this world. . . . The struggle against religion is thus indirectly the struggle against the world whose spiritual aroma is religion. . . .
>
> "The transcendence of religion, as the illusory happiness of the people, is the demand for their real happiness. The demand that they abandon illusions about their condition is the demand to abandon a condition which requires the illusions. The criticism of religion is therefore in embryo the criticism of the vale of tears whose halo is religion."[2]

Here, then, Feuerbach's abstract "human being" at last gives place to man in society, man in his social relations.

Basing himself on this concept, Marx approaches in these two remarkable essays very much closer to that alliance of philosophy with politics which he was now quite consciously striving to bring about. In the *Introduction*, we have what is to all intents and purposes a preliminary sketch of the Marxian theory of the proletarian revolution, and, in the *Jewish Question*, an early draft of the Marxian theory

---

the "stages" were by no means as definite and precise as might perhaps appear from the text. In particular, some scholars would want to argue that Marx in effect skipped the Feuerbachian "stage" altogether.

[1] Mehring, *op. cit.*, pp. 73-4.

[2] The basis of this translation is that contained in Bernal, *op. cit.*, pp. 13-14. (My italics.) But it has been amended in several places on the advice of Mr. M. Milligan, whose assistance here and elsewhere in this section I gratefully acknowledge.

of socialism, with a clear rejection of utopianism.[1] But the analysis is still clothed in "philosophic" dress: Marx cannot yet be said to have become a Marxist. Hegel's dialectics are there, and Feuerbach's materialism, and both are developed further. There are frequent hints of the great all-embracing theoretical system which is soon to emerge.[2] But it is evident that an element of considerable importance —what we might call the "economic" element—is still missing. During the next two years the missing link was supplied and the whole system welded together.[3] The completion of the foundations of the Marxian theory was above all made possible by Marx's realisation of the fact that "the anatomy of . . . civil society is to be sought in political economy".[4]

Three influences operating on Marx during his stay in Paris in 1844 may be said to have largely contributed towards this realisation. First, there was Paris itself. Marx's shift from Germany, where industry was relatively primitive and the working-class movement relatively undeveloped, to France, where the working-class movement was not only much more powerful but also visibly moving towards socialist ideas, evidently exercised a considerable influence on the development of his thought. I have already suggested, when dealing with the evolution of Adam Smith's thought, that the facility with which the situation of different countries at different stages of socio-economic development can be contrasted may affect the extent to which the attention of social scientists is directed to the importance of "economic" factors in the historical process; and there seems to me to be an interesting parallel in this respect between the evolution of Smith's thought and that of Marx. It was surely no accident that Marx's main subjects of study during 1844 should have been the French Revolution and political economy.

The second influence was that of Engels. Engels's opportunities to contrast a relatively undeveloped economy with a relatively

[1] The two essays have been translated into English (not very satisfactorily) by H. J. Stenning in a volume entitled *Selected Essays*. Cf. the accounts in Mehring, *op. cit.*, pp. 64 ff., and Adams, *op. cit.*, chapter 7.

[2] Particularly important in this connection are the glimpses of the materialist conception of history in the essay *On the Jewish Question*.

[3] Cf. Adams, *op. cit.*, p. 92: "The Marxian doctrine of 1844 does not combine the two elements, dialectic and materialism, in a single system. Three or even two years later the system is there. Intensive study of economics and above all of economic history filled the interval. . . ." Mention should also be made in this connection of Marx's intensified study of the French Revolution and his development of the concept of the class struggle.

[4] Marx, *Critique of Political Economy* (Kerr edn.), p. 11. I have substituted "civil" for "civic".

developed one were even greater than Marx's, for in 1842 he left Germany for England, to take up a position in a spinning firm in which his father was a partner. In England at this time, of course, it was even more evident than in France that "the anatomy of civil society" was to be sought in political economy. Prior to his departure for England, Engels's intellectual development had been somewhat similar to Marx's; and Engels too, after his arrival in the new country, began to study political economy. His influence on Marx really dates from the publication in the *Deutsch-Französische Jahrbücher* of his remarkable article *Outlines of a Critique of Political Economy*, which was in fact the starting-point of Marx's economic research; but it was not until September 1844 that the partnership between the two men was, as it were, formally constituted. In the beginning, it was Engels rather than Marx who was the economist of the partnership, and the importance of his influence on Marx at this time lay not only in the fact that his own economic studies were then more advanced, but also in the fact that Marx was able to obtain, from a man who had come to think very much in the same terms as he himself had, up-to-date information concerning the development of British industry and the British working-class movement.

The third influence was that of the Classical economists, notably Smith and Ricardo. Marx's note-books of this period have been preserved.[1] They contain lengthy extracts not only from Smith and Ricardo, but also from Say, James Mill, McCulloch, and others, together with Marx's own comments on certain passages. And as well as the note-books, we also have the manuscripts on political economy and philosophy which Marx wrote in the summer of 1844. These manuscripts require further discussion, since they sum up an extremely important stage in the development of Marx's thought.

The manuscripts are by no means in a finished state, and it is perhaps rash, especially for one who is not a philosopher, to try to summarise their main themes. But broadly speaking, Marx appears in this work (which was intended as the first of a series in which a systematic theory of society would be developed) to be attempting to draw certain important parallels and differences between Hegelian philosophy and Classical political economy—parallels and differences which seem to have been revealed to him largely as a result of his study of Classical political economy, and in particular of the Classical concept of labour. Both systems of thought, he argues in effect, possess the virtue that

[1] *Marx-Engels Gesamtausgabe*, Abt. 1, Bd. 3.

they regard *labour* as being in a certain sense the "essence" of man: but whereas "the only labour which Hegel knows and recognises is *abstract mental* [*geistig*] labour",[1] the Classical economists conceive of labour in a much more important sense. In particular, as distinct from their predecessors the Mercantilists and the Physiocrats, the Classical economists recognise that labour constitutes "the unique *essence of wealth*",[2] thus doing away with the old idea that wealth, or private property, is something as it were *exterior* to man, and insisting instead that it is really something of which man is the very substance. Then again, both systems of thought possess the defect that they treat certain abstractions as if they were ultimate realities, without recognising that it is necessary to bring them down to earth. Hegel regards concepts as the ultimate realities, so that with him the relations of human beings (which according to Marx actually constitute the real "subject") are seen as a consequence of the relations of concepts (which actually constitute the real "predicate"). And Classical political economy, while there is little fault to be found with the actual laws which it propounds, is nevertheless guilty of starting out from the assumption of private property without criticising it, without showing how the laws which it propounds proceed from the very essence of private property itself.

Marx's own critique of private property in the manuscripts is expressed in terms of the interesting Hegelian (and Feuerbachian) concept of "estrangement". At the end of what is called the "first manuscript", after an extended survey and criticism of the facts and laws regarding wages, profit and rent disclosed by the economists (mainly Smith),[3] there is a section entitled "Estranged

---

[1] *Gesamtausgabe*, Abt. 1, Bd. 3, p. 157.   [2] *Ibid.*, p. 108.

[3] One passage from the section on wages may perhaps be quoted here, since it illustrates both the general character of Marx's critique and the essential part which the concept of labour played in it. The political economist, Marx says, "tells us that originally and according to the very concept the *whole product* of labour belongs to the labourer. But at the same time he tells us that in reality the labourer receives no more than the necessary minimum of the product—only so much as is necessary for him to exist not as man but as labourer, to reproduce not humanity but the slave class of labourers. The political economist tells us that everything is purchased with labour, and that capital is nothing else but accumulated labour, but at the same time he tells us that the labourer, far from being able to purchase everything, is forced to sell himself and his humanity. The rent of the idle landowner usually amounts to a third of the produce of the earth, and the profit of the active capitalist amounts even to as much as double the interest on money, but the gain which the labourer makes at best is such that two of his four children must starve to death. According to the political economist it is only through labour that man increases the value of the products of nature, labour being his active property, but according to that same political economy the landowner and capitalist, who *qua* landowner and capitalist are merely privileged and idle gods, are everywhere in a superior position to the labourer and lay down laws for him. According to the political economist labour

Labour"[1] in which Marx's version of the concept of estrangement is explained. Political economy, Marx argues, does not properly understand the laws which it puts forward; it does not understand how these laws originate from the nature of private property itself. The starting-point ought rather to be the objective economic fact that the more wealth the worker produces the poorer he grows. A portion of the worker's labour, of his life, is embodied in his product, and becomes "estranged" from him. The product of the worker's labour stands opposed to him as something alien, as a power independent of him. And the estrangement of labour shows itself not only in the result of production, but also in the very act of production. Man's own productive activity becomes something alien to him, belonging not to him but to another. He works only when he is physically compelled to do so, and he feels really free only when performing his animal, as opposed to his human, functions. In addition, the estrangement of labour estranges man from his own species, for it is in production that man confirms himself as a conscious member of his species.[2] The product of labour is the objectivisation of the life of man as a species, and the estrangement of labour in effect deprives him of his life as a species. The real importance of all this lies in the fact that by creating a product which does not belong to him, the producer also creates the power of the non-producer over production and the product. The consequence of the estrangement of labour is private property, and political economy, in propounding the laws of private property, has in fact done no more than give expression to the laws of estranged labour.

Marx does not deny, however, that political economy has on the whole expressed these laws accurately. His main ground of complaint, in effect, is that political economy has not delved sufficiently far into the question of the origin and nature of the capital-labour relationship. "The relationship of *private property*", Marx writes,

is the only invariable price of things, but there is nothing more exposed to chance than the price of labour, nothing exposed to greater fluctuations. The division of labour increases the productive power of labour, and the wealth and refinement of society, but it reduces the worker to a machine. Labour brings about the accumulation of capital, and with it the increasing prosperity of society, but it makes the labourer increasingly dependent upon the capitalist, places him in a position in which competition is greater, and drives him into the wild race of over-production, which is followed by a correspondingly slack period. According to the political economist the interest of the labourer never stands opposed to the interest of society, but society always and necessarily stands opposed to the interest of the labourer."

1 *Gesamtausgabe*, Abt. 1, Bd. 3, pp. 81 ff.

2 "The practical creation of an *objective world*, the *act of working upon* inorganic nature, is the confirmation of man as a conscious member of the species [*Gattungswesen*]" (p. 88). Cf. *The German Ideology* (English edn.), p. 7.

"is labour, capital and the interconnection between the two";[1] and he asserts that the manner in which labour and capital "come to confront one another as two persons is for the economist an *accidental* event which can therefore only have an external explanation."[2] The main problem with which Marx was concerned in these sections of the manuscripts was essentially the same as that with which he was later to concern himself in *Capital*. His method of treatment in *Capital* was of course very different indeed—we hear little more of the concept of estrangement after *The German Ideology*—but the gap between the two approaches is not quite as wide as may appear at first sight. The idea of the product of labour standing opposed to the producer as an alien entity survives in the vital concept of the fetishism of commodities. The notion of productive activity as the confirmation of man as a species also survives, although in a rather less fanciful form: Marx and Engels always thought of the essential distinction between man and other animals in terms of man's capacity to *produce*.[3] And the idea of social labour as "the *unique* principle of political economy",[4] of course, remained with Marx to the end. "It is only when *labour* is regarded as the essence of private property", wrote Marx in the manuscripts, "that economic movement as such can be fully understood in its real exactitude."[5]

In another important section of the manuscripts, Marx discusses the question of the division of labour in society. The study of the division of labour and exchange, he says,

> "is of great interest, because they are the *perceptible externalised* expressions of human *activity* and *inherent* power [*wesenskraft*] as *generic* activity and inherent power.
> "The assertion that the *division of labour* and *exchange* are based on *private property* is nothing other than the assertion that *labour* is the essence of private property, an assertion which the economist cannot prove and which we want to prove for him. It is precisely in the fact that *division of labour* and *exchange* are formations of private property, precisely in this fact that there lies the double proof both that *human* life needed *private property* for its realisation and on the other hand that it now needs the elimination of private property.
> "*Division of labour* and *exchange* are the two *phenomena* in relation to which the economist touches upon the social nature of his science, and unconsciously expresses at the same time the contradiction

[1] *Gesamtausgabe*, Abt. 1, Bd. 3, p. 103.   [2] *Ibid.*, p. 133.
[3] See, e.g., Engels's *Dialectics of Nature* (English edn.), p. 291.
[4] *Gesamtausgabe*, Abt. I, Bd. 3, p. 98.   [5] *Ibid.*, p. 138.

of his science, the basing of society on non-social separate interests."[1]

The division of labour, he says again, is "the economic expression of the *social nature of labour* within the alienation".[2] In this section, Marx comes very close to the important notion that the really fundamental tie which unites men to one another in societies based on private property in the means of production is their relationship as producers (and therefore as exchangers) of commodities. The way is now clearly laid open for the substitution of *man in his economic relations* for "man in society".

Marx's study of the Classical concept of labour, then, can be said to have been the final and perhaps the most decisive of the several influences contributing to the synthesis of his general system. Certainly, at any rate, the formulations of the materialist conception of history in these manuscripts are considerably in advance of the anticipations contained in Marx's earlier work. Take, for example, the following passage:

> "This *material*, directly *perceptible* private property is the material, perceptible expression of *estranged human* life. Its movement—production and consumption—is the perceptible manifestation of the movement of all production hitherto, i.e., the realisation or reality of man. Religion, family, state, law, morality, science, art, etc., are merely *particular* ways of production and are subject to its general law. The positive transcendence of *private property* as the appropriation of *human* life *is therefore the positive* transcendence of all estrangement, that is, the return of man from religion, family, state, etc., to his *human*, i.e., *social* existence."[3]

And in some of the passages dealing with the transition from feudalism to capitalism—which read on occasion like a first draft of parts of *The German Ideology*—the principle is even more clearly implied. Physiocracy is recognised as being directly "the *economic* dissolution of feudal property",[4] and Classical political economy as "a product of modern *industry*",[5] in accordance with the basic idea that "as

---

[1] *Gesamtausgabe*, Abt. 1, Bd. 3, pp. 143-4.   [2] *Ibid.*, p. 139.   [3] *Ibid.*, pp. 114-15.

[4] *Ibid.*, p. 109. Marx adds that it is "therefore just as directly the *economic transformation*, the restoration, of this feudal property, except that its language is now no longer feudal, but becomes economic".

[5] *Ibid.*, p. 107. The whole passage in which this phrase occurs is worth quoting, since it illustrates very well the importance which Marx ascribed to the Classical concept of labour. "*The subjective essence* of private property", he writes, "of *private property* as an activity in itself, as *subject*, as *person*, is labour. It therefore goes without saying that political economy, which recognised *labour* as its principle—*Adam Smith*—that is, which no longer knew private property merely as a *condition* outside man, that this political economy

generic consciousness, man confirms his real *social life* and merely repeats his real existence in thought".[1] Then in another place there is an interesting description of the different ideologies of the landed proprietor and the capitalist, in which the economic basis of the conflict between them is clearly visualised.[2] And the two following passages will serve to illustrate the extent to which Marx had by this time come to understand the nature of the motive forces lying behind the transition from one mode of production to another:

> "With the transformation of the slave into a *free* labourer, i.e., into a *recipient of wages*, the landlord is himself transformed into an industrial lord, a capitalist, a transformation which comes about first of all through the intermediacy of the *tenant-farmer*."[3]
> "The *difference* between capital and land, between profit and rent, and the difference between both of these and wages, *industry*, *agriculture*, and *immoveable* and *moveable* property, is still a *historical* difference, not founded in the nature of the thing, a *fixed* element in the formation and genesis of the opposition between capital and labour."[4]

It is clear that the distance is not very great between the manuscripts of 1844 and *The Poverty of Philosophy* of 1847, in which the materialist conception of history and the labour theory of value once more appear in close association.

Between 1844 and 1847, Marx's intellectual development was inseparably bound up with that of Engels. As mentioned above, Engels's influence had already exerted itself on Marx through the medium of the *Outlines of a Critique of Political Economy*, in which the germs of a surprising number of distinctively "Marxian" economic theories are to be found. But as from September 1844, when Engels spent some time with Marx in Paris, the influence became more personal. While in Paris, Engels wrote his contribution to *The Holy Family*, the first work in which he and Marx collaborated. This somewhat turgid "Critique of Critical Criticism" contains an interesting section of Proudhon, in which a number of the leading ideas of Engels's *Outlines* and Marx's *Ökonomisch-philosophische Manuskripte* are co-ordinated and further developed.

---

should be regarded as a product of the real *energy* and *movement* of private property, as a product of modern *industry*, and, on the other hand, as having speeded up the energy and development of this *industry*, as having glorified it and made it into a force of *consciousness*."

[1] *Gesamtausgabe*, Abt. 1, Bd. 3, p. 117.   [2]*Ibid.*, pp. 100-103.   [3] *Ibid.*, p. 100.
[4] *Ibid.*, pp. 99-100.

When Marx was expelled from France at the beginning of 1845, and went to Brussels to live, Engels joined him there a month or two later. It was at this second meeting, apparently, that Marx first put before Engels, in fairly precise terms, the basic proposition of the materialist conception of history. This proposition, Engels later remarked, "we both of us had been gradually approaching for some years before 1845. How far I had independently progressed towards it is best shown by my *Condition of the Working Class in England in 1844*. But when I again met Marx at Brussels, in spring, 1845, he had it already worked out, and put it before me in terms almost as clear as those in which I have stated it here."[1]

In the summer of 1845, Marx and Engels travelled together to England, mainly in order to establish new contacts with the British working-class movement and to further their economic research. They stayed there for about six weeks. Marx apparently studied a number of "books and extracts" which were in Engels's possession, and "such books as were procurable in Manchester".[2] Upon their return to Brussels, they decided, as Marx put it, "to work out together the contrast between our view and the idealism of the German philosophy, in fact to settle our accounts with our former philosophic conscience. The plan was carried out in the form of a criticism of the post-Hegelian philosophy."[3] This work, *The German Ideology*, contains the first detailed account of the Marxian materialist conception of history. Although Engels was later to say of it, perhaps over-modestly, that the section dealing with Feuerbach (the first and most important section) "proves only how incomplete our knowledge of economic history was at the time",[4] and although it does occasionally "lay more stress on the economic side than is due to it",[5] it sets out quite unambiguously from the basic idea lying behind the materialist conception—the idea that

> "men, developing their material production and their material intercourse, alter, along with this, their real existence, their thinking and the products of their thinking. Life is not determined by consciousness, but consciousness by life."[6]

There is no direct development of the labour theory of value in *The German Ideology*, but a number of indications can be found of the

[1] Preface to the English edn. of 1888 of *The Communist Manifesto*. Cf. *Selected Works* of Marx, Vol. I, pp. 192-3, and *Ludwig Feuerbach*, pp. 52-3, footnote.
[2] *The Poverty of Philosophy*, p. 9.   [3] *Critique of Political Economy*, p. 13.
[4] *Ludwig Feuerbach*, p. 16.   [5] *Selected Works*, Vol. I, p. 383.
[6] *The German Ideology*, pp. 14-15.

form which that theory was eventually to assume in Marx's hands. In particular, great emphasis is laid on the division of labour in society—"one of the chief forces of history up till now", as Marx and Engels call it in one place.[1] The core of the analysis in the Feuerbach section is in fact to be found in the account which Marx and Engels give of the contradictions which are implicit in the division of labour as such,[2] and of the various historical extensions of the division of labour—between town and country, production and commerce, etc.[3] Division of labour and private property, Marx and Engels argue, are identical expressions: "in the one the same thing is affirmed with reference to activity as is affirmed in the other with reference to the product of the activity."[4] And the major historical extensions of the division of labour reflect changes in property relationships: for example, "the separation of town and country can also be understood as the separation of capital and landed property, as the beginning of the existence and development of capital independent of landed property".[5] Noteworthy also in *The German Ideology* are a passage in which the essential features of what Marx and Engels later came to describe as "commodity production" are delineated;[6] a number of hints of the concept of "fetishism of commodities" which was destined to play such an important part in the development of the labour theory;[7] and, finally, the following significant remarks regarding the *method* of political economy:

> "If you proceed from production, you necessarily concern yourself with the real conditions of production and with the productive activity of men. But if you proceed from consumption, you merely declare that consumption is not at present 'human', that it is necessary to cultivate true consumption, and so on. Content with this, you can afford to ignore the real living conditions and the activity of men."[8]

The German Ideology was not published in the lifetime of Marx and Engels. Left by its authors to "the gnawing criticism of the mice", after they had failed to find a publisher for it, it did not appear in full until 1932. Thus it happened that the leading points of the new theory were "first presented scientifically, though in a polemic form" in Marx's *The Poverty of Philosophy*, written in the winter of 1846-7.[9] This work, the last which properly comes within the period of early

---

[1] *The German Ideology*, p. 39.   [2] *Ibid.*, pp. 20 ff.   [3] *Ibid.*, pp. 43 ff.
[4] *Ibid.*, p. 22.   [5] *Ibid.*, p. 44.   [6] *Ibid.*, pp. 63-4.
[7] E.g., *ibid.*, pp. 22-3.   [8] *Ibid.*, p. 164.
[9] *Critique of Political Economy*, pp. 13-14.

development being considered in the present section, is of some importance from the point of view of the history of the labour theory, since it contains Marx's first direct attempt to analyse the economic category exchange value from the viewpoint of the materialist conception of history.

Proudhon's *What is Property?*, which appeared in 1840, had received a favourable reception from Marx and Engels, who described it in *The Holy Family* as having "achieved everything that the criticism of political economy from the standpoint of political economy can achieve".[1] Their attitude towards Proudhon's *System of Economic Contradictions* (1846), subtitled *Philosophy of Poverty*, however, was extremely critical, and when Marx received the book in December 1846 he set to work almost immediately on a reply to it, which he called *The Poverty of Philosophy*. In a letter to Annenkov, written shortly after receipt of Proudhon's book, Marx sets out clearly the main grounds of his disagreement:

". . . M. Proudhon, mainly because he lacks the historical knowledge, has not perceived that as men develop their productive forces, that is, as they live, they develop certain relations with one another and that the nature of these relations must necessarily change with the change and growth of the productive forces. He has not perceived that *economic categories* are only the *abstract expressions* of these actual relations and only remain true while these relations exist. He therefore falls into the error of the bourgeois economists who regard these economic categories as eternal and not as historic laws which are only laws for a particular historical development, a development determined by the productive forces. Instead therefore, of regarding the political-economic categories as abstract expressions of the real, transitory, historic, social relations, Monsieur Proudhon only sees, thanks to a mystic transposition, the real relations as embodiments of these abstractions. These abstractions themselves are formulæ which have been slumbering in the heart of God the Father since the beginning of the world."[2]

In *The Poverty of Philosophy* this leading thesis of the materialist conception of history is consistently maintained, and, in particular, Marx shows (to quote his own words, written some time later) "how confused, wrong and superficial Proudhon remains with regard to *exchange value*, the basis of the whole thing, and how he

[1] *Gesamtausgabe*, Abt. 1, Bd. 3, p. 203.
[2] *Selected Correspondence* of Marx and Engels (Lawrence and Wishart edn.), p. 12.

even mistakes the utopian interpretation of *Ricardo's* theory of value
for the basis of a new science".[1]

At first sight, the economics of chapter 1 of *The Poverty of Philosophy* (the section dealing with the theory of value) seems to be almost
wholly Ricardian. Again and again, both here and elsewhere in the
book, Marx quotes from Ricardo in order to refute Proudhon or to
dispute the latter's claims to originality. After an interesting discussion
at the beginning of the work on demand and utility, based mainly
on the traditional Classical analysis, Marx proceeds to give an acute
summary of Ricardo's theory of value, arguing that whereas Ricardo's
theory is "the scientific interpretation of actual economic life",
Proudhon's is merely "the utopian interpretation of Ricardo's
theory".[2] Marx insists that Proudhon "confounds the value of commodities measured by the quantity of labour embodied in them with
the value of commodities measured by 'the value of labour' ", thereby
(according to Marx) falling into much the same error as that of which
Ricardo accused Adam Smith.[3] Ricardo is quoted extensively on the
effects of competition,[4] on money,[5] on inventions,[6] and (indirectly)
on the effects upon prices of a rise in wages.[7] Marx accepts Ricardo's
"subsistence theory" of wages without even mentioning that "social
element" in wages which was destined to play an important part
in Marx's later economic work and upon which Ricardo himself
laid a certain amount of emphasis.[8] Similarly, the Ricardian theory
of rent is accepted without serious question,[9] although here there
are definite hints of things to come.[10] There is no distinction between
"labour" and "labour power", and no serious analysis of surplus
value;[11] and Marx's consideration of the "modifications" to the
labour theory does not take him very far beyond Ricardo.[12]

Nevertheless, even in *The Poverty of Philosophy* Marx wears his
Ricardianism with a difference. It is in this very work, where more

---

[1] *Selected Correspondence* of Marx and Engels, p. 172.

[2] *The Poverty of Philosophy*, p. 43. "Ricardo establishes the truth of his formula", Marx
proceeds, "by deriving it from all economic relations, and by explaining in this way all
phenomena, even those like ground rent, accumulation of capital and the relation of wages
to profits, which at first sight seem to contradict it; it is precisely that which makes his
doctrine a scientific system." Cf. above, pp. 101 and 118-9.

[3] *Ibid.*, pp. 47-9.   [4] *Ibid.*, pp. 55-6.   [5] *Ibid.*, p. 74.

[6] *Ibid.*, p. 81.   [7] *Ibid.*, p. 140.   [8] *Ibid.*, pp. 44-5. Cf. pp. 85-6.

[9] *Ibid.*, pp. 129 ff.   [10] See particularly pp. 136-7.

[11] The section on "Surplus Labour" (pp. 76 ff.) does not directly discuss the question
of the emergence and appropriation of surplus *value*.

[12] Marx's comments on the reduction of skilled to unskilled labour, however (pp.
46-7), represent an advance over Ricardo's.

than anywhere else Marx appears on the surface to be purely and
simply a Ricardian in his economics, that the Copernican step which
enabled him to move above and beyond Ricardo is decisively taken.
The central theme of *The Poverty of Philosophy* is that the economic
categories—rent, profit, wages, exchange, value, division of labour,
competition, money, etc.—are not absolute and eternal, but merely
the abstract expressions of concrete, historical and transitory production-relations between men. And Marx makes it quite clear that in
his opinion Ricardo as well as Proudhon was guilty of "represent[ing]
the bourgeois relations of production as eternal categories".[1]

How, then, looked at from the viewpoint of the materialist conception of history, does the category exchange value appear? In the
first place, value appears as a *historical* phenomenon. It presupposes
exchange and the division of labour,[2] each of which has a history
of its own. Exchange, Marx points out, has developed from the
days when "only the superfluity, the excess of production over
consumption, was exchanged", to the present time, when almost
all products are exchanged.[3] And the division of labour, too, has
assumed different forms in the course of its history, all of them
"originally born of the conditions of production" and becoming
"so many bases of material production".[4] The category value, therefore, is applicable only in a society based on one or another form
of the division of labour, and on one or another form of what Marx
here calls "individual exchange".

In the second place, value appears as the expression of a *production-
relation between men* in such a society. The relationship which manifests itself on the market between goods which are the subject of
"individual exchange" is in essence an expression of the relationship
between the separate producers of these goods. The following passage
from *The Poverty of Philosophy*, which occurs near the end of the
chapter on value and in a sense sums it up, shows how closely Marx
had then approached to this fundamental idea, which was his starting-
point in *Capital*:

> "In principle, there is no exchange of products—but there is the
> exchange of the labour which co-operated in production. The mode
> of exchange of products depends upon the mode of exchange of
> the productive forces. In general, the form of exchange of products
> corresponds to the form of production. Change the latter, and the

[1] *The Poverty of Philosophy*, p. 135. Cf. pp. 102-3.
[2] *Ibid.*, pp. 28-9.   [3] *Ibid.*, p. 30.   [4] *Ibid.*, p. 114. Cf. pp. 154-5.

former will change in consequence. Thus in the history of society we see that the mode of exchanging products is regulated by the mode of producing them. Individual exchange corresponds also to a definite mode of production which itself corresponds to class antagonism. There is thus no individual exchange without the antagonism of classes."[1]

It is fairly evident, I think, that Marx had by now arrived at the notion that the labour theory of value is in essence another way of stating the proposition that "the mode of exchange of products depends upon the mode of exchange of the productive forces". Once this point has been reached, the period of early development of Marx's thought comes to an end, and the period of mature development, refinement and application begins.

3. Marx's Economic Method

The materialist conception of history, then, was the starting-point of Marx's subsequent economic researches, and dictated to a large extent the *economic method* which he adopted. It would be quite wrong to imagine, however, that Marx regarded the materialist conception as a sort of fixed and predetermined scheme to which the economic facts had willynilly to conform. Rather, he regarded it as a hypothesis which had to be tested by applying it to the economic facts, and his various economic works—notably the *Critique of Political Economy* and *Capital*—can perhaps most conveniently be looked upon as steps in this long and arduous testing process. Lenin puts this point well when he says that Marx,

"having expressed this hypothesis in the 'forties, set out to study the factual (*nota bene*) material. He took one of the economic formations of society—the system of commodity production—and on the basis of a vast mass of data (which he studied for not less than twenty-five years) gave a most detailed analysis of the laws governing the functioning of this formation and its development. This analysis is strictly confined to the relations of production between the members of society: without ever resorting to factors other than relations of production to explain the matter, Marx makes it possible to discern how the commodity organisation of social economy develops, how it becomes transformed into capitalist economy, creating the antagonistic (within the bounds now of relations of production) classes, the bourgeoisie and the proletariat, how it develops the productivity of social labour and how it thereby

[1] *The Poverty of Philosophy*, pp. 65-6.

introduces an element which comes into irreconcilable contradiction to the very foundations of this capitalist organisation itself. . . . Now—since the appearance of *Capital*—the materialist conception of history is no longer an hypothesis, but a scientifically demonstrated proposition."[1]

One may or may not agree with the judgment which Lenin delivers at the conclusion of this passage, but it cannot be doubted that his account of the *character* of Marx's economic researches is essentially correct.

Marx and Engels emphasised again and again that their primary source-material was the concrete facts of social life and development. "We set out", they wrote in *The German Ideology*,

> "from real, active men, and on the basis of their real life-process we demonstrate the development of the ideological reflexes and echoes of this life-process. . . . This method of approach is not devoid of premises. It starts out from the real premises and does not abandon them for a moment. Its premises are men, not in any fantastic isolation or abstract definition, but in their actual, empirically perceptible process of development under definite conditions."[2]

This is an approach which is evidently opposed not only to that of the idealists (to whom, according to Marx and Engels, history is "an imagined activity of imagined subjects"), but also to that of the empiricists (to whom history is "a collection of dead facts").[3] One must necessarily begin with certain general abstractions, but these must always "arise from the observation of the historical development of men". And too much should not be expected of them. In particular, it should be remembered that "they can only serve to facilitate the arrangement of historical material, to indicate the sequence of its separate strata. But they by no means afford a recipe or schema, as does philosophy, for neatly trimming the epochs of history."[4]

These general abstractions—the leading propositions of the materialist conception of history—constituted the hypothesis which Marx set out to test in the field of economics. Given this basic purpose, the first task as Marx saw it was to define and investigate the simplest and most elementary of the relevant economic categories, "without ever

---

[1] Lenin, *Selected Works* (English edn.), Vol. XI, pp. 420-2.

[2] *The German Ideology*, pp. 14-15. Cf. Venable, *Human Nature: the Marxian View*, pp. 7 ff.

[3] *The German Ideology*, p. 15.   [4] *Ibid.*

resorting to factors other than relations of production to explain the matter". Having done this, one must then proceed gradually from the simple to the complex, building up the concrete whole from the separate abstract parts. And at every stage in the analysis, of course, the categories must be considered in their interdependence and in the process of their development, and the conclusions must be tested against the facts.

As I have so far described it, Marx's method does not appear to differ appreciably from that adopted by any responsible social scientist in arriving at and testing a hypothesis. But there is rather more to Marx's methodology than this—so much more, indeed, that Engels went so far as to say that "the working out of the method which forms the foundation of Marx's *Critique of Political Economy* [and, of course, of *Capital*—R.L.M.] we consider a result of hardly less importance than the basic materialistic outlook itself".[1] Within the framework of the broad methodological approach outlined above, Marx adopted what might be called the "logical-historical method", one of the most interesting and significant of the fruits of his Hegelian studies. The description which Engels gave of this method in a review of the *Critique* in 1859 has not been bettered, and it can be reproduced almost in its entirety without apology:

"Marx was, and is, the only one who could undertake the work of extracting from the Hegelian logic the kernel which comprised Hegel's real discoveries in this sphere, and to construct the dialectical method divested of its idealistic trappings, in the simple shape in which it becomes the only true form of development of thought. . . .

"The criticism of economics, even according to the method secured, could still be exercised in two ways: historically or logically. Since in history, as in its literary reflection, development as a whole proceeds from the most simple to the most complex relations, the historical development of the literature of political economy provided a natural guiding thread with which criticism could link up and the economic categories as a whole would thereby appear in the same sequence as in the logical development. This form apparently has the advantage of greater clearness, since indeed it is the *actual* development that is followed, but as a matter of fact it would thereby at most become more popular. History often proceeds by jumps and zigzags and it would in this way have to be followed everywhere, whereby not only would much material of minor importance have to be incorporated but there would be

[1] *Ludwig Feuerbach*, p. 98.

much interruption of the chain of thought; furthermore, the history of economics could not be written without that of bourgeois society and this would make the task endless, since all preliminary work is lacking. The logical method of treatment was, therefore, the only appropriate one. But this, as a matter of fact, is nothing else than the historical method, only divested of its historical form and disturbing fortuities. The chain of thought must begin with the same thing that this history begins with and its further course will be nothing but the mirror-image of the historical course in abstract and theoretically consistent form, a corrected mirror-image but corrected according to laws furnished by the real course of history itself, in that each factor can be considered at its ripest point of development, in its classic form.

"In this method we proceed from the first and simplest relation that historically and in fact confronts us, therefore, here, from the first economic relation to be found [the relation between the producers of commodities—R.L.M.] We analyse this relation. Being a *relation* already implies that it has two sides *related to each other*. Each of these sides is considered by itself, which brings us to the way they behave to each other, their reciprocal interaction. Contradictions will result which demand a solution. But as we are not considering an abstract process of thought taking place solely in our heads, but a real happening which has actually taken place at some particular time, or is still taking place, these contradictions, too, will have developed in practice and will probably have found their solution. We shall trace the nature of this solution, and shall discover that it has been brought about by the establishment of a new relation whose two opposite sides we now have to develop, and so on."[1]

This, then, was the method of the *Critique*, as it was also the method of *Capital*. No doubt it was occasionally carried to excess (for reasons which Marx partly explained in his preface to the second edition of *Capital*)[2] but in Marx's hands it proved on the whole to be extraordinarily fruitful. And it had one characteristic which was of some importance in view of the fact that it was being used in connection with the testing of a hypothesis—it required, as Engels remarked, "historical illustrations, continual contact with reality".[3]

Although the field covered by *Capital* extends as far as (and sometimes even further than) the historical boundaries of the system of commodity production, Marx was of course particularly interested

[1] *Ludwig Feuerbach*, pp. 98-9. Cf. *Capital*, Vol. III (Kerr edn.), p. 24.
[2] See *Capital*, Vol. I, p. xxx. Cf. *Selected Correspondence*, pp. 220-1.
[3] *Ludwig Feuerbach*, p. 101.

in the analysis of one specific form of commodity production—
the capitalist form. "In this work", Marx wrote in the preface to the
first edition of *Capital*, "I have to examine the capitalist mode of
production, and the conditions of production and exchange corresponding to that mode. . . . It is the ultimate aim of this work, to lay
bare the economic law of motion of modern society."[1] It was true,
of course, as Engels noted, that in order to carry out this task "an
acquaintance with the capitalist form of production, exchange and
distribution did not suffice. The forms which had preceded it or those
which still exist alongside it in less developed countries had also, at
least in their main features, to be examined and compared."[2] But
even so, *Capital* was far from being a treatise on what Engels called
"political economy in the widest sense"—that is, "the science of
the conditions and forms under which *the various human societies*
have produced and exchanged and on this basis have distributed their
products".[3] *Capital* was primarily concerned with one particular
human society: it dealt in the main with the origin, development
and decline of *capitalist* commodity production.

Related to this was a further feature of Marx's economic method
which deserves mention here. The use of the logical-historical method
in the study of any particular social formation does not necessarily
mean that "the economic categories [ought to be arranged] in the
order in which they were determining factors in the course of history".[4]
Rather, their order of sequence ought to be settled by the relation
which they bear to one another in the particular social formation
under review. The point is, as Marx emphasised, that "under all
forms of society there is a certain industry which predominates
over all the rest and whose condition therefore determines the rank
and influence of all the rest. It is the universal light with which all
the other colours are tinged and are modified through its peculiarity."[5]
In modern bourgeois society, it has to be recognised that "capital
is the all dominating economic power".[6] The capital-labour relationship is the dominant, determining relationship, and must therefore
be put in the forefront of the investigation. The natural temptation
to "start with rent", a category historically prior to capital, must
therefore be resisted, since in bourgeois society "agriculture comes

[1] *Capital*, Vol. I, pp. xvii and xix.
[2] *Anti-Dühring* (Lawrence & Wishart edn.), p. 169.
[3] *Ibid.*, pp. 165 and 168. (My italics.) See below, pp. 264 and 269-70.
[4] *Critique of Political Economy*, p. 304.
[5] *Ibid.*, p. 302.   [6] *Ibid.*, p. 303.

to be more and more merely a branch of industry and is completely dominated by capital".[1]

It remains to give some preliminary indication of the manner in which Marx's methodology was related to his treatment of the labour theory of value. The main task which Marx set himself in *Capital*, as we have seen, was to explain the origin and development of the capitalist economic formation in terms of the developing relationships between men as producers. It had to be shown, in the case both of commodity production in general and of capitalist commodity production in particular, that "a definite [form of] production . . . determines the [forms of] consumption, distribution, exchange, and also the mutual relations between these various elements".[2] In this demonstration the labour theory of value evidently played a key role, since it is in effect "a particular way of stating that social relations of production determine relations of exchange".[3] This whole question requires special consideration.

A useful starting-point, I think, is the following statement made by Marx in *Wage-Labour and Capital*:

> "In production, men not only act on nature but also on one another. They produce only by co-operating in a certain way and mutually exchanging their activities. In order to produce, they enter into definite connections and relations with one another and only within these social connections and relations does their action on nature, does production, take place."[4]

These "social connections and relations" which men enter into with one another in production are evidently extremely complex, and one may look at them from at least two different angles.

First, one may begin by drawing attention to the fact that in any society based on the social division of labour different individuals (or groups) are directly or indirectly assigned to different jobs, so that the activities of these separate individuals (or groups) must somehow be mutually "exchanged" for one another. A basic distinction which is likely to impress itself on our minds if we begin by emphasising this aspect of men's production-relations is that between "exchanges" of activities which take the form of the *exchange of commodities*, and

[1] *Critique of Political Economy*, pp. 302-3.

[2] *Ibid.*, p. 291. In the original the last eight words are italicised.

[3] M. H. Dobb, in *The Modern Quarterly*, Vol. III. No. 2, Spring 1948, p. 67. Cf. *Capital*, Vol. I, p. 74: "Magnitude of value expresses a relation of social production."

[4] *Selected Works*, Vol. I. p. 264.

"exchanges" of activities which take other forms. The exchange of commodities—i.e., of goods produced for some sort of market by "private producers more or less separate from each other"[1]—is a relatively recent phenomenon. Although it began (according to Marx's account) on the boundaries of primitive communities,[2] and although it existed in systems based on slavery and increased in extent under feudalism, it was only under capitalism that the relation between men as producers *of commodities* came to dominate the whole economic scene.[3]

Second, one may begin by drawing attention to the fact that societies can usefully be distinguished from one another on the basis of differences in those relations between men as producers of which the *property relations* specific to a particular epoch are the legal expression.[4] Depending on the character and mode of distribution of the means of production, men may organise themselves—or be organised—in many different ways in order to produce the things they require. Their "mutual exchange of activities" in any given period may be based upon relations of subordination, or of co-operation, or of a transitional and mixed character. It is these relations, according to Marx, which lend their character to the whole complex of production-relations in existence at any given time, and which therefore afford the proper basis for distinguishing one economic system from another and for dividing the history of mankind into stages.

In *Capital* Marx was concerned not with the whole history of mankind, but rather with the development of the broad system of commodity production up to and including the stage of capitalist commodity production. And it was this capitalist stage, as we have seen, which was Marx's *main* object of concern. Now the period during which this development of commodity production took place was, of course, characterised by a succession of different economic systems, which can be differentiated from one another on the basis just described. But according to Marx's method, the starting-point of research must be the study of the fundamental relation between men as producers of commodities, in its general and abstract form, as it persists throughout the whole period. The first task must be to

---

[1] *Anti-Dühring*, p. 336. Cf. the definitions in *ibid.*, p. 221, and *Capital*, Vol. I, pp. 9 and 43.

[2] See, e.g., *Capital*, Vol. I, pp. 59–60.   [3] Cf. above, pp. 37–8.

[4] Cf. *Critique of Political Economy*, p. 12. It is in this sense that the term "relations of production" is usually employed in Marxist literature. Cf. above, p. 19, footnote.

analyse the nature of this basic production-relation, and to show in broad general terms how it "determines the [forms of] consumption, distribution, exchange" in *all* commodity-producing societies. The second and main task, as Marx saw it, was to analyse the manner in which this broad and simplified picture of the way in which production-relations determine other economic relations is altered and modified when the capitalist system of commodity production replaces the earlier systems.

Once it has been understood that this is essentially what Marx was trying to do in his economic work, the question of the place of the labour theory of value in his system is virtually answered. The nearest that Marx came to answering this question himself was in his famous letter to Kugelmann of July 1868:

". . . Even if there were no chapter on 'value' in my book, the analysis of the real relationships which I give would contain the proof and demonstration of the real value relation. The nonsense about the necessity of proving the concept of value arises from complete ignorance both of the subject dealt with and of the method of science.

"Every child knows that a country which ceased to work, I will not say for a year, but for a few weeks, would die. Every child knows, too, that the mass of products corresponding to the different needs require different and quantitatively determined masses of the total labour of society.

"That this necessity of distributing social labour in definite proportions cannot be done away with by the *particular form* of social production, but can only change the *form it assumes*, is self-evident. No natural laws can be done away with. What can change, in changing historical circumstances, is the *form* in which these laws operate.

"And the form in which this proportional division of labour operates, in a state of society where the interconnection of social labour is manifested in the *private exchange* of the individual products of labour, is precisely the *exchange value* of these products.

"The science consists precisely in working out *how* the law of value operates. So that if one wanted at the very beginning to 'explain' all the phenomena which apparently contradict that law, one would have to give the science *before* the science."[1]

In this exceptionally important passage, Marx proceeds as follows: First, he emphasises that an understanding of "the subject dealt

[1] *Letters to Kugelmann* (Lawrence & Wishart edn.), pp. 73-4. I have separated the passage into paragraphs for convenience.

with *and of the method of science*" is required if his theory of value is to be properly understood. He then goes on to point out that the social division of labour necessarily has a *quantitative* aspect—i.e., that it implies not only that the total labour of society must be allocated between the production of different goods, but also that these different goods require "*quantitatively determined*" masses of labour to be allocated to their production. Following on from here, he describes this "necessity of distributing social labour in definite proportions" as a "natural law" which cannot be done away with, but which may operate in different ways according to "changing historical circumstances". The particular form in which it operates in societies where goods are produced as commodities, he then suggests, is precisely the *exchange value* of these goods—meaning by this not only that these goods possess exchange value *because* they are the products of proportionally distributed labour in such societies, but also, evidently, that the *quantity* of exchange value which a unit of each good possesses relatively to a unit of every other is dependent upon the relative quantities of the labour of society which it is necessary to allocate to their production. Finally, having thus made it clear that exchange value is a historical category associated with systems of commodity production and with systems of commodity production alone, he points out that the main task of the political economy of commodity production must be to work out "*how* the law of value operates". One must not try right "at the very beginning" to " 'explain' all the phenomena which apparently contradict that law" (as Ricardo had done): rather, one should try to explain the phenomena which apparently contradict the law *in terms of the operation of the law itself.*

To Marx, then, the task of showing how relations of production "determine the [forms of] consumption, distribution, exchange" reduced itself, in its essentials, to the task of showing "how the law of value operates" as commodity production develops. The particular way in which he went about fulfilling this task was largely dictated by the general methodological approach which he adopted, and, more especially, by the broad aims which he had primarily in view when writing *Capital.* He was not concerned to distinguish the way in which the law of value operated under capitalism from the way in which it operated under, say, feudalism, or slavery, or primitive communism. Rather, he tended to abstract in this connection from the specific features differentiating one pre-capitalist form of commodity production from another,[1] and to concentrate on distinguishing the way in which the law of value operated under capitalism from the way in which it operated under all these earlier systems taken together *in so far as they were characterised by "simple" commodity production in which the normal exchange was one of "value" for "value"* [2] What he was mainly interested in analysing was the manner in which the introduction of *capitalist* commodity production modified the influence which the basic relation between men as producers could be assumed to have exerted upon exchange relations under simple commodity production. Under both simple and capitalist commodity production, he argued, the basic relation between men as producers of commodities (which persisted throughout the whole period of commodity production) exerted its influence on exchange relations by making the exchange ratios of commodities *a function* of embodied labour ratios.[3] The replacement of simple commodity production, in which the direct producers owned their own means of production, by capitalist commodity production, in which the direct producers owned nothing but their labour power (which had itself now become a commodity), did not mean that exchange ratios ceased to be *a*

[1] Cf. *Capital*, Vol. I, p. 148: "The appearance of products as commodities presupposes such a development of the social division of labour, that the separation of use-value from exchange-value, a separation which first begins with barter, must already have been completed. But such a degree of development is common to many forms of society, which in other respects present the most varying historical features." In other contexts, of course, it was precisely these "varying historical features" which Marx was especially concerned to emphasise.

[2] The "simple" circulation of commodities, according to Marx's account, is characterised by the formula C-M-C (Commodities-Money-Commodities), as distinct from the capitalist form of circulation which is characterised by the formula M-C-M (Money-Commodities-Money). "Simple" commodity production is generally carried on by independent producers who do not employ wage-labour and who "sell in order to buy". The typical case is that of the peasant who sells corn in order to buy clothes, or that of the independent craftsman who sells clothes in order to buy corn. "The circuit C-M-C starts with one commodity, and finishes with another, which falls out of circulation and into consumption. Consumption, the satisfaction of wants, in one word, use-value, is its end and aim. The circuit M-C-M, on the contrary, commences with money and ends with money. Its leading motive, and the goal that attracts it, is therefore mere exchange value" (*Capital*, Vol. I, p. 127). In the simple circulation of commodities, the two extremes of the circuit "are both commodities, and commodities of equal value" (*ibid.*). It is possible, of course, that the two extremes (say, corn and clothes) may in fact represent different quantities of value. "The farmer may sell his corn above its value, or may buy clothes at less than their value. He may, on the other hand, 'be done' by the clothes merchant. Yet, in the form of circulation now under consideration, such differences in value are purely accidental. The fact that the corn and the clothes are equivalents, does not deprive the process of all meaning, as it does in M-C-M. The equivalence of their values is rather a necessary condition to its normal course" (*ibid.*, p. 128).

[3] I use the term "function" here in the sense in which it is used in mathematics. When we say that x is a function of y, we mean that x and y are related to one another in such a way that x depends upon and varies with y. The particular form which this dependence takes is defined by the "shape" of the function.

function of embodied labour ratios. But the introduction of capitalism did mean that the *shape* of the function was altered: exchange ratios were related to embodied labour ratios in a different and more complex way. Whereas under simple commodity production the law of value operated so as to make exchange ratios roughly equivalent to embodied labour ratios, under capitalist commodity production it operated in a different way, so that although ratios were still *ultimately determined* by embodied labour ratios, the two were no longer necessarily (or even normally) equivalent to one another.

I have emphasised this point here partly because it is necessary to grasp it if we are to understand the meaning of Marx's theory of value and the role which it played in his general system, but more particularly because it is of crucial importance if we wish to extract the *essence* of what Marx said from its context and reapply it to the present-day situation. For Marx, as we have seen, the task of showing "how the law of value operates" was virtually identical with the task of showing how relations of production determined relations of exchange. The particular way in which Marx went about this task was largely dictated by the fact that he was primarily concerned to contrast the basic characteristics of commodity production under competitive capitalism with those of simple commodity production. If, however, we are primarily concerned to contrast the basic characteristics of commodity production under, say, monopoly capitalism with those of commodity production under, say, competitive capitalism, the way in which we go about this task will be rather different. This is a problem which will be further discussed in the final section of the present work.

CHAPTER FIVE

KARL MARX'S THEORY OF VALUE (II)

1. *The Concept of Value in Chapter 1 of "Capital"*

"IN bourgeois society", wrote Marx in his preface to the first edition of *Capital* (Vol. I), "the commodity-form of the product of labour—or the value-form of the commodity—is the economic cell-form. To the superficial observer, the analysis of these forms seems to turn upon minutiae. It does in fact deal with minutiae, but they are of the same order as those dealt with in microscopic anatomy."[1] In Part I of *Capital*, under the heading "Commodities and Money", Marx attempts a detailed analysis of this "economic cell-form", using the force of abstraction as his microscope.

Referring specifically to this first Part of *Capital* in his preface, Marx said:

"Every beginning is difficult, holds in all sciences. To understand the first chapter, especially the section that contains the analysis of commodities, will, therefore, present the greatest difficulty. That which concerns more especially the analysis of the substance of value and the magnitude of value, I have, as much as it was possible, popularised. . . .[2] I pre-suppose, of course, a reader who is willing to learn something new, and therefore to think for himself."[3]

Every beginning is difficult, for one reason, because one has to be very careful not to "give the science *before* the science"—i.e., in the case of political economy, not to take as given right at the beginning economic categories which should properly be developed only at a later stage. Having already criticised Ricardo and Proudhon for doing precisely this, Marx had to be specially careful not to fall into the same error himself. Beginnings are difficult, too, if one's methodological approach cannot be stated in detail at the outset without appearing to anticipate results which are still to be

---

[1] *Capital*, Vol. I, p. xvi.

[2] A footnote here reads as follows: "This is the more necessary, as even the section of Ferdinand Lassalle's work against Schulze-Delitzsch, in which he professes to give 'the intellectual quintessence' of my explanations on these subjects, contains important mistakes. . . ."

[3] *Capital*, Vol. I, pp. xv-xvi.

proved.[1] And this particular beginning was difficult for at least two other reasons as well—first because a considerable amount of the ground had already been covered in the *Critique*, and second because some of the passages on value in Marx's earlier economic works had been seriously misunderstood in working-class circles. Thus Marx had to decide which of the points "only hinted at in the earlier book" should be "worked out more fully" in *Capital*, and which of the points worked out fully in the *Critique* should be only "touched upon" in *Capital*;[2] and he had at the same time to decide which parts of the analysis he could afford to "popularise" without risking further misunderstandings.

The analysis begins with a reformulation of the passages in the *Critique* dealing with what Marx had there called the "twofold aspect" of commodities—"that of *use value* and *exchange value*".[3] A commodity, he writes, "is, in the first place, an object outside us, a thing that by its properties satisfies human wants of some sort or another".[4] Use values "constitute the substance of all wealth, whatever may be the social form of that wealth. In the form of society we are about to consider [i.e., commodity-producing society—R.L.M.] they are, in addition, the material depositories of exchange value."[5]

Exchange value, Marx proceeds, "at first sight, presents itself as a quantitative relation, as the proportion in which values in use of one sort are exchanged for those of another sort, a relation constantly changing with time and place". Thus exchange value "appears to be something accidental and purely relative, and consequently an intrinsic value, i.e., an exchange value that is inseparably connected with, inherent in commodities, seems a contradiction in terms". But, he suggests, things will appear otherwise if we "consider the matter a little more closely".[6] The passages in which he goes on to do this have been so seriously and persistently misinterpreted that they must be reproduced in full. The paragraphs are numbered for convenience.

[1] Cf. Marx's preface to the *Critique*, in which he writes: "I omit a general introduction which I had prepared, as on second thought any anticipation of results that are still to be proven, seemed to me objectionable, and the reader who wishes to follow me at all, must make up his mind to pass from the special to the general." However, he adds, "some remarks as to the course of my own politico-economic studies may be in place here", and he goes on to give an account of the materialist conception of history, "which, once reached, continued to serve as the leading thread in my studies".

[2] *Capital*, Vol. I, p. xv.   [3] *Critique*, p. 19.   [4] *Capital*, Vol. I, p. 1.
[5] *Ibid.*, Vol. I, pp. 2-3.   [6] *Ibid.*, Vol. I, p. 3.

(1) "A given commodity, *e.g.*, a quarter of wheat, is exchanged for x blacking, y silk, or z gold, &c.—in short, for other commodities in the most different proportions. Instead of one exchange value, the wheat has, therefore, a great many. But since x blacking, y silk, z gold, &c., each represent the exchange value of one quarter of wheat, x blacking, y silk, z gold, &c., must, as exchange values, be replaceable by each other, or equal to each other. Therefore, first: the valid exchange values of a given commodity express something equal; secondly, exchange value, generally, is only the mode of expression, the phenomenal form, of something contained in it, yet distinguishable from it.

(2) "Let us take two commodities, *e.g.*, corn and iron. The proportions in which they are exchangeable, whatever those proportions may be, can always be represented by an equation in which a given quantity of corn is equated to some quantity of iron: *e.g.*, 1 quarter corn$=$x cwt. iron. What does this equation tell us. It tells us that in two different things—in 1 quarter of corn and x cwt. of iron, there exists in equal quantities something common to both. The two things must therefore be equal to a third, which in itself is neither the one nor the other. Each of them, so far as it is exchange value, must therefore be reducible to this third.

(3) "A simple geometrical illustration will make this clear. In order to calculate and compare the areas of rectilinear figures, we decompose them into triangles. But the area of the triangle itself is expressed by something totally different from its visible figure, namely by half the product of the base into the altitude. In the same way the exchange values of commodities must be capable of being expressed in terms of something common to them all, of which thing they represent a greater or less quantity.

(4) "This common 'something' cannot be either a geometrical, a chemical, or any other natural property of commodities. Such properties claim our attention only in so far as they affect the utility of those commodities, make them use-values. But the exchange of commodities is evidently an act characterised by a total abstraction from use-value. Then one use-value is just as good as another, provided only it be present in sufficient quantity. Or, as old Barbon says, 'one sort of wares are as good as another, if their values be equal. There is no difference or distinction in things of equal value. . . . An hundred pounds' worth of lead or iron, is of as great value as one hundred pounds' worth of silver or gold.' As use-values, commodities are, above all, of different qualities, but as exchange values they are merely different quantities, and consequently do not contain an atom of use-value.

(5) "If then we leave out of consideration the use-value of

commodities, they have only one common property left, that of being products of labour. . . ."[1]

In the first three of these paragraphs, Marx is really laying down the formal requirements of a theory of value. To begin with, he insists in effect that although exchange value necessarily presents itself in a purely relative form, it is not possible to arrive at an adequate *theory* of value unless one assumes that differences (or changes) in relative values are the net resultant of differences (or changes) in the individual values of one or more of the commodities concerned, each taken in isolation.[2] Marx does not state this specifically: in his deliberately "popularised" account he contents himself with showing by a simple illustration that the value-relationships which commodities bear to one another in exchange are capable of expression in an absolute as well as in a relative form.

Such an approach requires that some common quality inhering in or attaching to commodities must be selected as constituting the substance of value. This quality, Marx suggests, must be something which is capable of expression in quantitative terms, and which although "contained in" the commodity is nevertheless "distinguishable from it". Here, as Mr. Dobb has pointed out, Marx is merely stating (again in "popularised" form) one of the familiar formal requirements of a theory of value—that "the determining constants must express a relationship with some quantity which is not itself a value".[3]

In the fourth paragraph, Marx disposes of the idea that the "common 'something' " can be "either a geometrical, a chemical, or any other natural property of commodities". Such properties, Marx says, claim our attention only in so far as they make the commodities use values; but the exchange of commodities is characterised by "a total abstraction from use-value". This argument has often been misunderstood. Böhm-Bawerk, for example, complained that Marx, having demonstrated no more than that "the special forms under which the values in use of the commodities may appear" were abstracted from in exchange, went on to infer from this that *use value as such* was abstracted from. What this in effect amounted to, said Böhm-Bawerk, was a confusion between "abstraction from the genus, and abstraction from the specific forms in which the genus manifests itself".[4] But in actual fact Marx was not concerned at all, in this

[1] *Capital*, Vol. I, pp. 3-4.   [2] Cf. above, p. 87.
[3] *Political Economy and Capitalism*, p. 10.
[4] Böhm-Bawerk, *Karl Marx and the Close of his System* (Sweezy's edn.), p. 74.

particular place, with what Böhm-Bawerk called the "genus"—i.e., use value as such: he was concerned only with "the special forms under which the values in use of the commodities may appear". These forms, he argued, were "abstracted from" in exchange in the simple sense illustrated in the quotation from Barbon—namely (as he put it in the *Critique*) that "entirely apart from their natural forms and without regard to the specific kind of wants for which they serve as use-values, commodities in certain quantities equal each other, take each other's place in exchange, pass as equivalents, and in spite of their variegated appearance, represent the same entity".[1] For this reason, Marx argued, the "common 'something'" cannot be a natural property such as weight, volume, etc.

In the fifth paragraph, Marx says in effect that if we leave out of consideration such natural properties as these, commodities have in fact only one common property left *which fulfils the formal requirements he has just been describing*—the quality of being the products of labour. That this is what Marx meant by this much-disputed statement is, I think, reasonably clear from the context. Marx was hardly so stupid as to fail to recognise that commodities possessed other "common properties" besides those of weight, volume, etc., and of being the products of labour. All commodities possessing exchange value, for example, were obviously appropriated by private individuals, were the products of nature as well as of labour, and were objects of utility. The question was, however, whether any of these other "common properties" were capable of expression in quantitative terms and were "contained in" and yet "distinguishable from" the commodity in the sense described above. It appeared evident to Marx that none of them were in fact capable of fulfilling these requirements, so that if weight, volume, etc., were excluded the quality of being the products of labour was the only *relevant* "common property" left.

If Marx had been writing *Capital* twenty or thirty years later, when the marginal utility theory was becoming fashionable, it is possible that he would at this juncture have elaborated his reasons for believing that the "common property" which commodities had of being objects of utility was not in fact capable of fulfilling the formal requirements. There are two points which he might appropriately have emphasised in the context of the particular argument we have been considering—first, that the utility of a commodity is not a directly measurable quantity, and second, that utility cannot

[1] *Critique*, p. 21.

possibly be regarded as an independent determining factor without a quite illegitimate identification of desire and satisfaction.[1] As it was, he simply accepted the Classical view, with which we are already familiar, that the particular estimates of the utility of a commodity made by the individuals who purchase it do not in fact determine its long-period equilibrium price, as is sufficiently shown by the fact that a change in the estimates made of its utility by the purchasers does not normally alter that price.[2] Marx no doubt took it for granted —perhaps over-optimistically—that the more learned readers of the "popularised" sections would understand that this view was implied in what he said.

Later in Part I Marx makes it clear that his *logical* abstraction from utility at the beginning of the book is a reflection, as it were, of a *historical* abstraction. Exchange value, in Marx's view, is a historical category, appropriate only to the particular period in which goods are produced and exchanged as commodities. It is only when goods come to be produced and exchanged as commodities, in other words, that exchange value comes to develop a "form of its own".[3] When products first begin to be exchanged they confront one another merely as use values,[4] and the ratios in which they are exchanged are up to a point arbitrary and variable, since they largely depend upon the subjective estimates of the utility of the products made by the parties to the exchange. Eventually, however, as a result of the repetition and extension of exchanges, the products are transformed into commodities, whose use values become the "material depositories" of a new quality—exchange value. And when this happens there is a significant change in the manner in which ratios of exchange are determined. Marx describes the process as follows:

"The first step made by an object of utility towards acquiring exchange-value is when it forms a non-use-value for its owner,

[1] See on this point M. H. Dobb, *Political Economy and Capitalism*, pp. 27-8 and 156 ff.
[2] A useful statement of the Classical view was made by Ricardo in a letter to Malthus in which he commented upon Say's opinion that "a commodity is valuable in proportion to its utility". This would be true, Ricardo says, "if buyers only regulated the value of commodities; then indeed we might expect that all men would be willing to give a price for things in proportion to the estimation in which they held them, but the fact appears to me to be that the buyers have the least in the world to do in regulating price—it is all done by the competition of the sellers, and however the buyers might be really willing to give more for iron, than for gold, they could not, because the supply would be regulated by the cost of production, and therefore gold would inevitably be in the proportion which it now is to iron, altho' it probably is by all mankind considered as the less useful metal" (*Works*, VIII, pp. 276-7).
[3] *Critique*, p. 53.
[4] Cf. Hilferding, *Böhm-Bawerk's Criticism of Marx* (Sweezy's edn.), p. 126.

and that happens when it forms a superfluous portion of some article required for his immediate wants. Objects in themselves are external to man, and consequently alienable by him. In order that this alienation may be reciprocal, it is only necessary for men, by a tacit understanding, to treat each other as private owners of those alienable objects, and by implication as independent individuals. But such a state of reciprocal independence has no existence in a primitive society based on property in common, whether such a society takes the form of a patriarchal family, an ancient Indian community, or a Peruvian Inca State. The exchange of commodities, therefore, first begins on the boundaries of such communities, at their points of contact with other similar communities, or with members of the latter. So soon, however, as products once become commodities in the external relations of a community, they also, by reaction, become so in its internal intercourse. The proportions in which they are exchangeable are at first quite a matter of chance. What makes them exchangeable is the mutual desire of their owners to alienate them. Meantime the need for foreign objects of utility gradually establishes itself. The constant repetition of exchange makes it a normal social act. In the course of time, therefore, some proportion at least of the products of labour must be produced with a special view to exchange. From that moment the distinction becomes firmly established between the utility of an object for the purposes of consumption, and its utility for the purposes of exchange. Its use-value becomes distinguished from its exchange-value. On the other hand, the quantitative proportion in which the articles are exchangeable, becomes dependent on their production itself. Custom stamps them as values with definite magnitudes."[1]

It is only when products are fully converted into commodities, then, that they appear stamped as "values with definite magnitudes". The task of determining the exchange ratios of the products is then taken away from the parties to the exchange, who had formerly fixed them on the basis of their own subjective estimates of their utility, and handed over to the relations of production, which henceforth fix them *in abstraction from* purchasers' estimates of their utility. "The quantitative proportion in which the articles are exchangeable", as Marx puts it, "becomes dependent on their production itself."

Many critics of Marx, from Böhm-Bawerk onwards, have discussed the argument contained in the five paragraphs quoted above as if it were (to quote a recent writer) "Marx's proof of the labour

[1] *Capital*, Vol. I, p. 60. Cf. *Critique*, pp. 53 ff.

theory of value".[1] They have then tried to show that the argument, considered as such a proof, is quite unsatisfactory, and have generally concluded by suggesting that Marx used it as a sort of façade to cover a mere *definition* of value which was purely arbitrary and dogmatic. This type of attack seems to me to be misconceived. It is true, of course, that Marx began with a particular *concept* of value which he had arrived at fairly early in his economic studies. Value was conceived as embodied or crystallised labour. But this concept was very far from being arbitrary or dogmatic. As we saw in the last chapter, it was intimately associated with the particular hypothesis which Marx set out to test in *Capital*—the materialist conception of history. If the basic relation between men as commodity-producers in fact determined their exchange relations—i.e., the value-relations between their products—it could only do so per medium of the relative quantities of labour which they bestowed on these products. The concept of value as embodied labour in effect expressed Marx's view that the economic process should be analysed in terms of the social relations between men and men in the production of commodities. The concept in itself could not of course be "proved" by a logical argument of the type used to prove a theorem in geometry.[2] But the *theory* of value erected on the basis of the concept naturally had to be proved. First of all, Marx believed, it was necessary to prove that a theory of value erected on the basis of this particular concept, and this particular concept alone, was capable of fulfilling the formal requirements of a theory of value. This was essentially what Marx set out to do in the five paragraphs we have just been discussing. But this was far from being the whole of "Marx's proof of the labour theory of value", as Böhm-Bawerk and his followers tended to assume. It was also necessary to demonstrate that a theory of value erected on the basis of this particular concept was in fact capable of providing a real solution of the problems which were put before it. The really important part of "Marx's proof of the labour theory of value" was contained in the subsequent sections of *Capital*, in which Marx applied the theory to the analysis of economic reality, and in particular to the problem of distribution.

So far, in dealing with Marx's concept of value as embodied

---

[1] Alexander Gray, *The Development of Economic Doctrine*, p. 310.

[2] Cf. *Letters to Kugelmann*, p. 73, where Marx says that "the nonsense about the necessity of proving the concept of value arises from complete ignorance both of the subject dealt with and of the method of science". But although the concept could not be "proved" in this sense, it was of course necessary to analyse the real social relationships which underlay the concept.

labour, we have ignored his important distinction between "abstract labour" and "useful labour"—a distinction which he regarded as "the pivot on which a clear comprehension of political economy turns".[1] Something must be said about this part of his analysis before we proceed further.

Use value can be considered "objectively as utility of the product", or "subjectively as usefulness of the work".[2] When it is considered "subjectively" in this sense, the concept of useful (or "concrete") labour emerges. Useful labour, defined as "productive activity of a definite kind and exercised with a definite aim",[3] is the creator of *use value*, and is clearly "a necessary condition, independent of all forms of society, for the existence of the human race".[4] But the labour which finds expression in *value*, according to Marx, "does not possess the same characteristics that belong to it as a creator of use-values".[5] The labour which creates *value* (as distinct from use value) is abstract labour—i.e., productive activity as such, from which all differences between the various kinds of activity have been abstracted. Just as, when we are considering commodities as values, we abstract from their different use values, "so it is with the labour represented by those values: we disregard the difference between its useful forms".[6] Labour, according to this view, "possesses the same two-fold nature"[7] as the commodity which it produces.

This concept of abstract labour, or labour in general, Marx pointed out, is "truly realized only as a category of the most modern society", where "individuals pass with ease from one kind of work to another, which makes it immaterial to them what particular kind of work may fall to their share".[8] But the abstraction expresses a relation which in fact dates back to the much earlier time when products first began to be converted into commodities. That was the time when, as Marx put it in the *Critique*, labour began to "acquire its social character from the fact that the labour of the individual [took] on the abstract form of universal labour".[9] Marx's point here is that whereas labour necessarily assumes a *social* character from the moment when men begin in any way to work for one another,[10] the *specific form* in which this social character manifests itself differs from epoch to epoch. Under the patriarchal system of production, for example,

[1] *Capital*, Vol. I, p. 8.   [2] *Selected Correspondence*, p. 106.
[3] *Capital*, Vol. I, p. 9.   [4] *Ibid.*, Vol. I, p. 10.   [5] *Ibid.*, Vol. I, p. 8.
[6] *Ibid.*, Vol. I, p. 12.   [7] *Ibid.*, Vol. I, p. 8.
[8] *Critique*, p. 299. Cf. *Capital*, Vol. I, p. 29.
[9] *Critique*, p. 29.   [10] *Capital*, Vol. I, p. 42.

"when spinner and weaver lived under the same roof, when the female members of the family did the spinning, and the male members did the weaving to supply the wants of their own family[,] then yarn and linen were *social* products, spinning and weaving were *social* labour within the limits of the family. But their social character did not manifest itself in the fact that yarn, as a universal equivalent, could be exchanged for linen as a universal equivalent, or that one was exchanged for the other, as identical and equivalent expressions of the same universal labour-time. It was rather the family organization with its natural division of labour that impressed its peculiar social stamp on the product of labour."[1]

But when commodity production began, the social character of labour began to manifest itself in quite a different form. "When exchange has acquired such an extension that useful articles are produced for the purpose of being exchanged", wrote Marx,

"and their character as values has therefore to be taken into account, beforehand, during production[,] . . . the labour of the individual producer acquires socially a two-fold character. On the one hand, it must, as a definite useful kind of labour, satisfy a definite social want, and thus hold its place as part and parcel of the collective labour of all, as a branch of a social division of labour that has sprung up spontaneously. On the other hand, it can satisfy the manifold wants of the individual producer himself, only in so far as the mutual exchangeability of all kinds of useful private labour is an established social fact, and therefore the private useful labour of each producer ranks on an equality with that of all others. The equalisation of the most different kinds of labour can be the result only of an abstraction from their inequalities, or of reducing them to their common denominator, viz., expenditure of human labour power or human labour in the abstract."[2]

In a commodity-producing society, then, and in a commodity-producing society alone, the social character of each producer's labour manifests itself in the fact that this labour "ranks on an equality with that of all others"—i.e., is reduced to abstract labour. And "the social character that his particular labour has of being the equal of all other particular kinds of labour, takes the form that all the physically different articles that are the products of labour, have one common quality, viz., that of having value."[3] Thus it is in their capacity as the products of *abstract* labour, according to Marx's view,

---

[1] *Critique*, pp. 28–9. Cf. *Capital*, Vol. I, pp. 47–50.
[2] *Capital*, Vol. I, p. 44.   [3] *Ibid.*, Vol. I, p. 45.

that commodities most distinctly "bear . . . marks of the relations of social production"[1] peculiar to commodity-producing societies. The property of being the product of *abstract* labour is the property which above all reveals a commodity as the bearer of these relations of production.[2]

2. *The Refinement and Development of the Concept*

The concept of value which emerges from the analysis described in the preceding section requires a certain amount of refinement and development before it can become capable of serving as the basis for an adequate *theory* of value. In accordance with the concept, all commodities, in so far as they represent values, are visualised as "crystals" of a certain "social substance"[3]—human labour in the abstract; and the magnitude of the value possessed by each commodity is regarded as being most appropriately measured by the quantity of this value-creating substance embodied in it—i.e., by the amount of labour *time* taken to produce it. But if we approach the value problem in this manner, we immediately come face to face with the obvious objection that if values were in fact determined and measured in this way, "the more idle and unskilful the labourer, the more valuable would his commodity be, because more time would be required in its production".[4] To argue thus, however, Marx answers, would be to misunderstand the nature of that abstract labour which constitutes the substance of value. "The labour . . . that forms the substance of value", he writes,

"is homogeneous human labour, expenditure of one uniform labour-power. The total labour-power of society, which is embodied in the sum total of the values of all commodities produced by that society, counts here as one homogeneous mass of human labour-power, composed though it be of innumerable individual units. Each of these units is the same as any other, so far as it has the character of the average labour-power of society, and takes effect as such; that is, so far as it requires for producing a commodity, no more time than is needed on an average, no more than is socially necessary. The labour-time socially necessary is that required to produce an article under the normal conditions of production, and with the average degree of skill and intensity prevalent at the time. The introduction of power looms into England probably reduced by one half the labour required to weave a given quantity

[1] *Critique*, p. 20.   [2] Cf. *Selected Works*, Vol. I, p. 305.
[3] *Capital*, Vol. I, p. 5.   [4] *Ibid*.

of yarn into cloth. The hand-loom weavers, as a matter of fact, continued to require the same time as before; but for all that, the product of one hour of their labour represented after the change only half an hour's social labour, and consequently fell to one-half its former value."[1]

This "averaging" process, Marx's argument implies, takes place in history before it takes place in the minds of economists. It is simply an aspect of that general historical process whereby, as the system of commodity production develops, each individual's labour is reduced to abstract labour. It need hardly be added that the "normal conditions of production" referred to here by Marx are exclusively *technical* conditions, and that it is quite legitimate, in the present context, to regard these conditions as being essentially independent of the values of the commodities concerned.[2]

But another and rather more serious difficulty now arises—the famous problem of "the reduction of skilled to unskilled labour". Marx instructs us to measure the quantity of socially-necessary labour required to produce a given commodity in terms of labour possessing "the average degree of skill . . . prevalent at the time" in the industry producing the commodity. But if we wish to use the Marxian concept of value as the basis for a theory which will explain differences (or changes) in the relative equilibrium prices of two or more different commodities, something more than this is evidently required. It has to be recognised that the "average degree of skill" prevalent in one industry at a given time may differ from that prevalent in another; and that the equilibrium prices of commodities produced by relatively skilled labour are generally higher, in relation to the number of hours of labour time expended in their production, than those of commodities produced by relatively unskilled labour. The values of commodities, therefore, can be said to be determined by the quantity of labour required on the average to produce them only if proper account is taken of the different degrees of labour skill which are required (on the average) in the case of the different commodities. The most convenient method of overcoming this difficulty would of course be to "reduce" skilled labour to unskilled (or "simple") labour, expressing the values of all commodities in terms of the latter. But we cannot legitimately do this unless we also provide a statement

[1] *Capital*, Vol. I, pp. 5-6.

[2] I mention this point merely because some critics have suggested that Marx, by introducing the "normal conditions of production" into his definition of socially-necessary labour, in effect reduced his argument to circularity.

of the laws according to which this reduction is effected. And these laws, naturally, must explain the reduction without reference either to the wages which the skilled and unskilled workers actually receive, or to the ratios at which their products actually exchange on the market. Otherwise we should merely be doing what Marx once described (in another context) as "moving in a vicious circle, . . . determin[ing] relative value by a relative value which itself needs to be determined".[1]

In chapter 1 of *Capital*, Marx does not attempt to resolve this particular difficulty. All he is concerned to do at this early stage in his argument is to demonstrate that the reduction of skilled to unskilled labour does in fact take place in the real world, and that this reduction is essentially an aspect of the general process whereby individual labours are reduced to abstract labour. "The value of a commodity", he says in an oft-quoted passage,

"represents human labour in the abstract, the expenditure of human labour in general. And just as in society, a general or a banker plays a great part, but mere man, on the other hand, a very shabby part, so here with mere human labour. It is the expenditure of simple labour-power, *i.e.*, of the labour-power which, on an average, apart from any special development, exists in the organism of every ordinary individual. Simple average labour, it is true, varies in character in different countries and at different times, but in a particular society it is given. Skilled labour counts only as simple labour intensified, or rather, as multiplied simple labour, a given quantity of skilled being considered equal to a greater quantity of simple labour. Experience shows that this reduction is constantly being made. A commodity may be the product of the most skilled labour, but its value, by equating it to the product of simple unskilled labour, represents a definite quantity of the latter labour alone.[2] The different proportions in which different sorts of labour are reduced to unskilled labour as their standard, are established by a social process that goes on behind the backs of the producers, and, consequently, appear to be fixed by custom. For simplicity's sake we shall henceforth account every kind of labour to be unskilled, simple labour; by this we do no more than save ourselves the trouble of making the reduction."[3]

[1] *Poverty of Philosophy*, p. 48.

[2] An important footnote here reads as follows: "The reader must note that we are not speaking here of the wages or value that the labourer gets for a given labour time, but of the value of the commodity in which that labour time is materialised. Wages is a category that, as yet, has no existence at the present stage of our investigation."

[3] *Capital*, Vol. I, pp. 11-12.

What Marx is saying here is reasonably clear, and it is difficult to understand why the passage should have been so persistently mis-interpreted. All that he says is that in the real world the proportions in which different kinds of skilled labour are reduced to unskilled labour are established by a social process of whose character the producers themselves are generally unaware[1]—which is surely a fairly evident fact. The question of the actual laws according to which the reduction is made is deliberately left over until later, the most appropriate point to introduce it being, in Marx's opinion, that at which the question of wages, or the value of labour power, comes up for consideration. If this were not clear from the quoted passage itself, it should certainly be clear from (a) Engels's statement in *Anti-Dühring* to the effect that "at this point, in the development of the theory of value" the process by which skilled labour is reduced to unskilled "has only to be stated but not as yet explained";[2] (b) Marx's statement in the corresponding passage in the *Critique* that "this is not the place to consider the laws regulating this reduction";[3] and (c) the fact that Marx actually does consider these laws later on in *Capital*.

The matter is reintroduced in the chapter on "The Buying and Selling of Labour-Power" in Part II of *Capital*. "In order to modify the human organism", Marx there says,

> "so that it may acquire skill and handiness in a given branch of industry, and become labour-power of a special kind, a special education or training is requisite, and this, on its part, costs an equivalent in commodities of a greater or less amount. This amount varies according to the more or less complicated character of the labour-power. The expenses of this education (excessively small in the case of ordinary labour-power), enter pro tanto into the total value spent in its production."[4]

Here, then, Marx makes it clear that training costs are a constituent element in the value of labour power. And in the following chapter he explains that labour power which has had these training costs expended upon it is not only itself of a higher value but also *creates* proportionally higher values than unskilled labour power. "In the creation of surplus-value", he writes,

---

[1] Smith, it will be remembered, emphasised that the necessary adjustment is made "by the higgling and bargaining of the market, according to that sort of rough equality which, though not exact, is sufficient for carrying on the business of common life" (*Wealth of Nations*, Vol. I, p. 33). Cf. Ricardo, *Works*, Vol. I, pp. 20-22.

[2] *Anti-Dühring*, p. 222.   [3] *Critique*, p. 25.

[4] *Capital*, Vol. I, pp. 150-1.

"it does not in the least matter, whether the labour appropriated by the capitalist be simple unskilled labour of average quality or more complicated skilled labour. All labour of a higher or more complicated character than average labour is expenditure of labour-power of a more costly kind, labour-power whose production has cost more time and labour, and which therefore has a higher value, than unskilled or simple labour-power. This power being of higher value, its consumption is labour of a higher class, labour that creates in equal times proportionally higher values than un-skilled labour does. Whatever difference in skill there may be between the labour of a spinner and that of a jeweller, the portion of his labour by which the jeweller merely replaces the value of his own labour-power, does not in any way differ in quality from the additional portion by which he creates surplus-value. In the making of jewellery, just as in spinning, the surplus-value results only from a quantitative excess of labour, from a lengthening-out of one and the same labour-process, in the one case, of the process of making jewels, in the other of the process of making yarn.[1]

"But on the other hand, in every process of creating value, the reduction of skilled labour to average social labour, e.g., one day of skilled to six days of unskilled labour, is unavoidable. We there-fore save ourselves a superfluous operation, and simplify our analysis, by the assumption, that the labour of the workman employed by the capitalist is unskilled average labour."[2]

To Marx, then, the problem of the reduction of skilled to unskilled labour did not seem a particularly important one, partly because the distinction between skilled and unskilled labour was to some extent illusory, partly because the number of skilled labourers in his time was relatively small, but more especially because the solution of the problem appeared to him to be so evident. Skilled labour power "being of higher value" (because its production "has cost more time

---

[1] Here there is the following footnote: "The distinction between skilled and unskilled labour rests in part on pure illusion, or, to say the least, on distinctions that have long since ceased to be real, and that survive only by virtue of a traditional convention; in part on the helpless condition of some groups of the working-class, a condition that prevents them from exacting equally with the rest the value of their labour-power. Accidental circumstances here play so great a part, that these two forms of labour sometimes change places. Where, for instance, the physique of the working-class has deteriorated, and is, relatively speaking, exhausted, which is the case in all countries with a well developed capitalist production, the lower forms of labour, which demand great expenditure of muscle, are in general considered as skilled, compared with much more delicate forms of labour; the latter sink down to the level of unskilled labour."

[2] Capital, Vol. I, pp. 179-80. Cf. ibid., Vol. I, pp. 342-3, and Vol. III, p. 168. It should be carefully borne in mind that the main question which Marx is discussing in the quoted passage is how the employer of skilled labour manages to extract surplus value from his employees notwithstanding the fact that their labour is of a higher value, and therefore usually more highly paid, than unskilled labour.

and labour"), "its consumption is labour of a higher class, labour that creates in equal times proportionally higher values than unskilled labour does". This key sentence was misinterpreted (somewhat wilfully, one cannot help feeling) by Bernstein, who argued that Marx was here deducing the higher value of the product of skilled labour from the higher wage paid to that labour.[1] But it is surely clear from the context that Marx was in fact doing nothing of the sort. He was simply saying (a) that the value of the skilled labour power was higher because it had cost more labour to produce; and (b) that *because* it had cost more labour to produce, it was able to create a product of a higher value. Marx evidently regarded the labour expended on training the skilled labourer as being stored up, as it were, in his person, to be manifested when he actually begins to work. The expenditure of skilled labour, therefore, as Hilferding puts it, "signifies the expenditure of all the different unskilled labours which are simultaneously condensed therein".[2]

On the assumption that differences in skill are due entirely to differences in training costs, there is little difficulty (at least in theory) in reducing skilled to unskilled labour. One may simply calculate the amount of simple labour (including his own) which was expended in training the labourer, and then average this out over the whole of his expected productive life. If p hours is his expected productive life, and t hours of simple labour have been expended upon him and by him during the training period, then when he starts work each hour of his labour will count (for the purpose of estimating the value of the commodity he produces) as $1 + \frac{t}{p}$ hours of simple labour.[3] The case where differences in the "average degree of skill" are due entirely to differences in natural ability, or to a combination of natural ability and training costs, however, is a little more difficult. Marx did not deal specifically with this case, possibly because he felt, as Adam Smith had done, that "the difference of natural talents in different men is, in reality, much less than we are aware of".[4] Or possibly he assumed

---

[1] See Hilferding, *op. cit.*, pp. 141 ff. The controversy over Bernstein's statement was complicated by an incautious statement of Hilferding's to the effect that if Bernstein had been correct in his interpretation Marx would have used the word "*daher*" instead of "*aber*" at a crucial point in the key sentence. Unfortunately, in the fourth German edition of *Capital* (published long before Hilferding wrote, but apparently not consulted by him in this connection) Engels did in fact substitute "*daher*" for "*aber*". The whole episode constitutes an amusing comedy of errors—even more so when it is appreciated that the real meaning of the sentence is in fact the same whichever of the two words is used.

[2] Hilferding, *op. cit.*, p. 145.

[3] Cf. Sweezy, *Theory of Capitalist Development*, p. 43.

[4] *Wealth of Nations*, Vol. I, p. 17.

that the *average* level of natural ability was roughly the same in each industry, so that differences in the "average degree of skill" between one industry and another could be safely regarded as being due more or less exclusively to differences in training costs. This would probably be a reasonable enough assumption in the case of the great majority of industries, since there are relatively few "specialist" industries to which men of unusual natural ability are particularly attracted. If one were anxious to leave no loose ends whatever, I see no reason in principle why "specialist" industries of this type should not be grouped together and dealt with in terms of the sort of analysis which Marx (and Ricardo) reserved for agriculture. The labour theory could then be regarded as applying only *at the margin* in the case of industries normally employing persons of unusual and highly special-ised natural ability. But it must be emphasised that such refinements are not really necessary in order to give the labour theory the requisite degree of generality.

The discussion outlined above "started from exchange value, or the exchange relation of commodities, in order to get at the value that lies hidden behind it". Having isolated and examined this "value", Marx now returns to the "form under which value first appeared to us", and subjects it to a searching analysis. The task which he sets himself in this part of his work is well described in the following paragraph:

"Every one knows, if he knows nothing else, that commodities have a value form common to them all, and presenting a marked contrast with the varied bodily forms of their use-values. I mean their money form. Here, however, a task is set us, the performance of which has never yet even been attempted by *bourgeois* economy, the task of tracing the genesis of this money form, of developing the expression of value implied in the value relation of commodities, from its simplest, almost imperceptible outline, to the dazzling money form. By doing this we shall, at the same time, solve the riddle presented by money."[1]

There is no need for us to follow Marx's rather complex analysis of the "elementary", "expanded" and "money" forms of value in any detail. Essentially, what he is trying to do here is to reveal the contradictions which result from the reciprocal interaction of the two sides of the value equation, and to demonstrate the nature of the solutions of these contradictions which logic—and history—demand

[1] *Capital*, Vol. I, p. 15.

and provide. The contradictions, as Engels said, "are not merely of abstract theoretical interest, but . . . at the same time . . . reflect the difficulties which emerge from the nature of the immediate exchange relations, of simple barter, reflect the impossibilities in which this first crude form of exchange necessarily terminates. The solution to these impossibilities is to be found in the fact that the property of representing the exchange value of all other commodities is transferred to a special commodity—*money*."[1]

Marx's interesting discussion of "the fetishism of commodities and the secret thereof", with which chapter 1 concludes, makes explicit a number of the attitudes which underlie the argument of the preceding sections. Marx's thesis, briefly, is that many current errors and confusions over the problem of value—and therefore over the problems of political economy in general—are due to the fact that in commodity-producing societies the basic socio-economic relation between *men* appears disguised, as it were, as a relation between *things*. "As a general rule", Marx writes,

> "articles of utility become commodities, only because they are products of the labour of private individuals or groups of individuals who carry on their work independently of each other. The sum total of the labour of all these private individuals forms the aggregate labour of society. Since the producers do not come into social contact with each other until they exchange their products, the specific social character of each producer's labour does not show itself except in the act of exchange. In other words, the labour of the individual asserts itself as a part of the labour of society, only by means of the relations which the act of exchange establishes directly between the products, and indirectly, through them, between the producers. To the latter, therefore, the relations connecting the labour of one individual with that of the rest appear, not as direct social relations between individuals at work, but as what they really are, material relations between persons and social relations between things."[2]

In other words, as Marx put it in the *Critique*, "the relation of persons in their work appears in the form of a mutual relation between things, and between things and persons".[3] Just as in the religious world "the productions of the human brain appear as independent beings endowed with life, and entering into relation both with one another and the human race", so it is in the world of commodities with the

---

[1] *Ludwig Feuerbach*, pp. 100-101.   [2] *Capital*, Vol. I, pp. 43-4.
[3] *Critique*, pp. 30-1.

products of men's hands. "This", says Marx, "I call the Fetishism which attaches itself to the products of labour, so soon as they are produced as commodities, and which is therefore inseparable from the production of commodities."[1]

The categories of bourgeois political economy, Marx argues, are "forms of thought expressing with social validity the conditions and relations of a definite, historically determined mode of production, viz., the production of commodities". Therefore, he says, "the whole mystery of commodities, all the magic and necromancy that surrounds the products of labour as long as they take the form of commodities, vanishes . . . so soon as we come to other forms of production". Marx reviews in turn the situation of Robinson Crusoe on his island; the European middle ages, with their social relations of production characterised by personal dependence; the patriarchal industries of a peasant family which produces articles for home use; and finally "a community of free individuals, carrying on their work with the means of production in common"—a community in which "the labour-power of all the different individuals is consciously applied as the combined labour-power of the community". He demonstrates that in all these cases "the social relations of the individual producers, with regard both to their labour and to its products, are . . . perfectly simple and intelligible". There is no possibility of the real social relations between the producers being "disguised under the shape of social relations between the products of labour". It is only under the system of commodity production—and even there only in the later stages of its development—that the "mystification" becomes really serious.[2]

As the use of money increases, and more and more articles become commodities, the mystification is heightened, reaching its maximum under capitalism. To the producers of commodities, Marx argues, "their own social action takes the form of the action of objects, which rule the producers instead of being ruled by them".[3] And this has an important effect upon bourgeois political economy, which, according to Marx, although it "has indeed analysed, however incompletely, value and its magnitude, and has discovered what lies beneath these forms", has never asked *why* "labour is represented by the value of its product and labour time by the magnitude of that value". Its formulae, Marx says,

[1] *Capital*, Vol. I, p. 43.   [2] Quotations from *ibid.*, Vol. I, pp. 47-50.
[3] *Ibid.*, Vol. I, p. 46.

"which bear stamped upon them in unmistakeable letters, that they belong to a state of society, in which the process of production has the mastery over man, instead of being controlled by him, such formulae appear to the bourgeois intellect to be as much a self-evident necessity imposed by nature as productive labour itself."[1]

It is true, Marx agrees, that political economy has now outgrown the illusions of the monetary system. But, he asks, "does not its superstition come out as clear as noon-day, whenever it treats of capital?"[2] And in an amusing passage in Volume III of *Capital*, discussing what he calls the "trinitarian formula" of modern political economy in which land, labour and capital are assumed to "produce" the income which accrues to their owners, he says that in this formula

"we have the complete mystification of the capitalist mode of production, the transformation of social conditions into things, the indiscriminate amalgamation of the material conditions of production with their historical and social forms. It is an enchanted, perverted, topsy-turvy world, in which Mister Capital and Mistress Land carry on their goblin tricks as social characters and at the same time as mere things."[3]

In other words the mystification which surrounds commodity production as such necessarily also surrounds the specific *forms* of commodity production—in particular the capitalist form. "The life-process of society", Marx asserts,

"which is based on the process of material production, does not strip off its mystical veil until it is treated as production by freely associated men, and is consciously regulated by them in accordance with a settled plan."[4]

[1] *Capital*, Vol. I, pp. 52-3. Cf. *ibid.*, p. 65.   [2] *Ibid.*, Vol. I, p. 54.

[3] *Ibid.*, Vol. III, p. 966. Marx goes on to say: "It is the great merit of classic economy to have dissolved this false appearance and illusion, this self-isolation and ossification of the different social elements of wealth by themselves, this personification of things and conversion of conditions of production into entities, this religion of everyday life. It did so by reducing interest to a portion of profit, and rent to the surplus above the average profit, so that both of them meet in surplus-value. It represented the process of circulation as a mere metamorphosis of forms, and finally reduced value and surplus-value of commodities to labour in the actual process of production. Nevertheless even the best spokesmen of classic economy remained more or less the prisoners of the world of illusion which they had dissolved critically, and this could not well be otherwise from a bourgeois point of view."

[4] *Ibid.*, Vol. I, p. 51.

3. The Application of the Concept

Marx, then, defined the *value* of a commodity at any given time and place as the amount of socially-necessary simple labour required to produce it (or, rather, to reproduce it)[1] at that time and place, and proceeded in Volume I of *Capital* on the assumption that commodities did in fact tend to sell "at their values"—i.e., that the long-run equilibrium prices of freely reproducible commodities tended under reasonably competitive conditions to be proportionate to the quantities of socially-necessary simple labour required to produce them.[2]

It is important to note at the outset that Marx's theory of value, like those of Smith and Ricardo, did not pretend to explain any prices other than those at which "supply and demand equilibrate each other, and therefore cease to act".[3] The prices in which Marx was primarily interested were those which manifested themselves at the point where supply and demand "balanced" or "equilibrated" one another. The very fact that the forces of supply and demand did actually "balance" at this point was taken by Marx as an indication that the level of the equilibrium price could not be adequately explained merely in terms of the interaction of these forces.[4] The relation of supply and demand could certainly explain *deviations* from the equilibrium price, but it could not explain the level of the equilibrium price itself. It was in fact precisely *through* fluctuations in "supply and demand" that the law of value operated to determine the equilibrium price.[5]

Prices, then, might diverge from values in cases where supply and demand did not "balance". And not only was the price-form "compatible with the possibility of a quantitative incongruity between magnitude of value and price", but it might also "conceal a qualitative inconsistency, so much so, that . . . price ceases altogether to express value". In other words, "an object may have a price without having value".[6] This was particularly important, of course, in the case of land and natural objects. The mystery of the origin of "the exchange value of mere forces of nature"[7] would ultimately have to

[1] *Capital*, Vol. III, p. 166; *Critique*, p. 26.

[2] With Marx, as with Ricardo, the quantity of labour required to produce a commodity was taken to include not only the present labour, but also the past labour required to produce the capital goods and raw materials used up in production.

[3] *Selected Works*, Vol. I, p. 301. Cf. *ibid.*, pp. 310-11.

[4] Cf. *Capital*, Vol. III, p. 223.

[5] Cf. *Selected Works*, p. 261; *Capital*, Vol. I, pp. 46 and 74-5; and *Capital*, Vol. III, pp. 224 ff.

[6] *Capital*, Vol. I, p. 75.   [7] *Critique*, p. 73.

be solved, of course (per medium of the theory of rent), but in a first approximation the problem could be safely ignored—i.e., as Marx put it, "landed property is taken as $=0$".[1]

Just as Marx's concept of value involved an abstraction from utility (in the sense indicated above), so the theory of the determination of equilibrium price based upon it involved a similar abstraction from demand. In common with his Classical predecessors, Marx assumed that changes in demand would not in themselves (on the supposition of constant returns to scale for the industry as a whole) bring about changes in the long-run equilibrium prices of the commodities concerned.[2] But this is not at all to say that Marx *ignored* demand. It remained true, as he emphasised, (a) that a commodity had to be in demand before it could possess exchange value; (b) that changes in demand might cause the actual market price of a commodity to deviate from its equilibrium price; (c) that price under conditions of monopoly was "determined only by the eagerness of the purchasers to buy and by their solvency";[3] and (d) that demand was the main force determining the proportion of the social labour force allocated to any given productive sector at any given time.

This last point was one of particular importance. If a diminution in the demand for, say, linen, brought about a situation in which the total quantity of labour actually allocated to the linen industry was greater than the total quantity which society required to be allocated there under the existing technical conditions, then the effect upon the price of linen, according to Marx, would be the same "as if each individual weaver had expended more labour-time upon his particular product than is socially necessary".[4] Some critics have suggested that Marx, in making this statement, is in effect admitting that the quantity of socially-necessary labour required to produce a yard of linen is partly dependent upon demand conditions. But Marx does not say that the change in demand will cause a change in the quantity of socially-necessary labour: he says only that the effect of the change in demand upon the price of linen will be the same *as if* each weaver had expended more than the quantity of socially-necessary labour on his product, which is of course something very different.

---

[1] *Selected Correspondence*, p. 106. I do not deal directly with the Marxian theory of rent, or with any other aspects of Marx's theory of the distribution of surplus value among the property-owning classes, in the present work.

[2] See, e.g., *Selected Works*, Vol. I, pp. 289-90.

[3] *Capital*, Vol. III, p. 900.

[4] *Capital*, Vol. I, p. 80. Cf. *ibid.*, Vol. III, pp. 226-7.

All he is doing, in fact, is to make it clear that one of the conditions requiring to be fulfilled before a yard of linen will sell "at its value" is that *the total quantity of labour allocated to the linen industry* (and therefore the total supply of linen) should be just sufficient to satisfy the aggregate demand. In other words, supply must be equal to demand— which in Marx's view is just another way of saying that use value is a prerequisite of exchange value not only in the case of each individual commodity, but also in the case of the whole mass of commodities. "Every commodity", writes Marx in Volume III of *Capital*,

> "must contain the necessary quantity of labour, and at the same time only the proportional quantity of the total social labour time must have been spent on the various groups. For the use-value of things remains a prerequisite. The use-value of the individual commodities depends on the particular need which each satisfies. But the use-value of the social mass of products depends on the extent to which it satisfies in quantity a definite social need for every particular kind of product in an adequate manner, so that the labour is proportionately distributed among the different spheres in keeping with these social needs, which are definite in quantity.... The social need, that is the use-value on a social scale, appears here as a determining factor for the amount of social labour which is to be supplied by the various particular spheres. But it is only the same law, which showed itself in the individual commodity, namely that its use-value is the basis of its exchange-value and thus of its surplus-value."[1]

The quantity of socially-necessary labour required to produce a unit of any commodity, then, was by no means dependent upon demand conditions. Demand certainly determined the total quantity of labour to be allocated to the industry producing any commodity under given conditions of labour productivity, but it was this productivity, and not the demand, which determined the value of a unit of the commodity. And Marx often argued, in addition, that demand was by no means autonomous, but largely dependent upon the distribution of income[2] and the actions of the producers themselves[3]— this being another reason why any theory of value which started from the demand side was necessarily doomed to failure.

When Marx embarked upon his preliminary (Volume I) analysis of the laws governing the production of surplus value under capitalism, then, he proceeded on the assumption that commodities tended

[1] *Capital*, Vol. III, p. 745.   [2] *Ibid.*, Vol. III, pp. 214 and 222-3.
[3] *Critique*, p. 280.

to sell "at their values" in the sense defined above. Now it can easily be shown that under developed capitalism, once an average rate of profit has been established to which all individual rates tend more or less automatically to conform, exchange ratios will not in fact tend to be equal to embodied labour ratios unless the capitals concerned are similarly constituted—i.e., in Marx's terminology, unless their organic compositions[1] are equal.[2] If we assume that commodities tend to sell "at their values" (in the Marxian sense) under developed capitalism, then, we implicitly assume either that organic compositions are equal or that rates of profit are unequal. But the actual tendencies under capitalism are towards the inequality of organic compositions and the equality of rates of profit rather than the reverse. Why, then, did Marx conduct his preliminary analysis of surplus value on the assumption that commodities tended to sell "at their values"?

The reasons underlying Marx's procedure here should become fairly clear if we remember what was said above regarding his general economic method and the plan of *Capital*. Marx begins with an analysis of the commodity as such, and then goes on to consider "its ideologically and historically secondary form, a capitalistically modified commodity".[3] His main task is to enquire into the modifications which take place in the general laws of commodity production and exchange when the capitalist system of commodity production replaces the earlier systems. In order to reveal the *essence* of these modifications, Marx seems to have believed, it is useful to assume that capitalism impinges on a system of "simple" commodity production in which the normal exchange is one of "value" for "value", and that in the early stages of the conversion of this "simple" commodity production into capitalist commodity production all commodities

---

[1] The organic composition of capital is represented by the ratio $\frac{c}{v}$, where c ("constant" capital) is the amount spent on machinery and buildings (in so far as they are used up in production) plus raw materials, and v ("variable" capital) is the amount spent on labour power.

[2] The argument upon which this conclusion is based is discussed in every book on Marxian political economy, and need therefore only be briefly summarised here. If commodities are to sell "at their values", they must sell at prices which are sufficient to cover depreciation and raw materials (c), wages (v), and surplus value (s). This surplus value, which according to the Marxian account is the only possible source of profit, is created entirely by the labourers employed by v, and it must be assumed that the amount of it created by the average labourer $\left(\frac{s}{v}\right)$ is the same in all spheres of production. Now under developed capitalism the rate of profit $\left(\frac{s}{c+v}\right)$ must also be the same in all spheres of production. But it is obvious that both these equalities cannot prevail at the same time unless we postulate a third—viz., that the organic composition of capital $\left(\frac{c}{v}\right)$ is also the same in all spheres of production.

[3] *Capital*, Vol. III, p. 24.

continue for some time to exchange "at their values". The capitalists in each sphere of production reduce the reward of the direct producers to the subsistence level and appropriate surplus value; their competition within each sphere tends to establish a single price for the commodity produced in that sphere; but there is as yet no competition between the capitalists in different spheres and therefore no average rate of profit. Thus differences in the organic compositions of capital as between the spheres will be associated with differences in rates of profit rather than with divergences between exchange ratios and embodied labour ratios. In such a state of affairs, the phenomenon of the creation and appropriation of surplus value appears, as it were, in its "pure" form, free from the pall of obscurity which the subsequent formation of an average rate of profit tends to spread over it. This state of affairs, then, which can reasonably be assumed to have been the *historical* starting-point,[1] must be the logical starting-point as well.[2]

But capitalism, having once found a foothold, soon proceeds to modify the way in which the law of value operates. The extension and intensification of capitalist competition leads to the formation of an average rate of profit, which means that equilibrium exchange ratios begin to diverge from embodied labour ratios in all cases where the organic composition of the capitals concerned is different. Commodities now tend to sell in proportion to their "prices of production" (i.e., their "natural prices" in the Classical sense) instead of in proportion to their "values". And as in history, so in logic. In the first approximation, Marx believed, one should assume that commodities sell "at their values", and explain the origin of surplus value on this basis. One should then logically "derive" average profits from surplus value, and "transform" values into prices of production, thus arriving at the second approximation in which the initial assumption is dropped. By adopting this procedure, Marx maintained, it was possible to show that the law of value still operated—i.e., that the basic relations

[1] Cf. *Capital*, Vol. III, p. 212: "Competition first brings about, in a certain individual sphere, the establishment of an equal market-value and market-price by averaging the various individual values of the commodities. The competition of the capitals in the different spheres then results in the price of production which equalises the rates of profit between the different spheres. This last process requires a higher development of capitalist production than the previous process."

[2] The assumption that commodities sold "at their values" under capitalism was of course made quite deliberately and with full consciousness of the fact that it would later have to be removed. See *Selected Correspondence*, pp. 129-33, and *Capital*, Vol. I, pp. 144, footnote, 203, footnote, and 293-4. The whole question of the transformation of values into prices of production is dealt with in some detail in Marx's critique of Ricardo in the *Theories of Surplus Value*, which was written some years before the appearance of Volume I of *Capital*.

between men as producers of commodities still *ultimately* determined relations of exchange—even when simple commodity production became "capitalistically modified" and commodities no longer actually tended to sell "at their values". As will be seen in the following section, Marx believed that any other procedure would leave political economy without a rational basis.

On the basis of his initial assumption, then, Marx goes on to examine the economic aspects of the relation between wage-labour and capital, a relation which, as he puts it, "determines the entire character of the mode of production"[1] in capitalist societies. He leaves aside for future consideration certain other socio-economic relations (e.g., that between landlord and capitalist) which are regarded by him as essentially derivative. He is concerned in particular to disclose the laws which regulate the distribution of income between wage-labour and capital. This is a problem in which the theory of value must necessarily be called upon for assistance, since the economic relation between wage-labour and capital normally takes the form of an exchange relation. And it is a problem, too, which can only be adequately solved "on the supposition that prices are regulated by the average price".[2] Experience shows that the capitalist usually receives a "normal" profit even though he buys his raw materials, labour power, etc., at the equilibrium prices fixed by the market, and sells his finished commodities at the equilibrium prices which are similarly fixed by the market. Explanations of profit couched in terms of "cheating" or "buying cheap and selling dear" are therefore definitely ruled out: if you cannot explain the general nature of profit on the assumption that it is derived from selling commodities at their normal equilibrium prices (i.e., *on the Volume I assumptions*, "at their values"), said Marx, then "you cannot explain it at all".[3] This was a point of much more than merely formal significance. If Marx could show how profit was derived from buying and selling commodities "at their values", then this would be equivalent, he believed, to showing that it was through, rather than in spite of, the much-vaunted "freedom" and "equality" characteristic of a competitive capitalist economy that exploitation was carried on in modern times.[4]

---

[1] *Capital*, Vol. III, p. 1,025.   [2] *Ibid.*, Vol. I, p. 144, footnote.

[3] *Selected Works*, Vol. I, p. 312. Cf. *Anti-Dühring*, p. 227.

[4] Cf. *Capital*, Vol. I, p. 200: "The essential difference between the various economic forms of society, between, for instance, a society based on slave labour, and one based on wage labour, lies only in the mode in which . . . surplus-labour is in each case extracted from the actual producer, the labourer."

Marx's preliminary solution of the problem of profit in Volume I is so familiar that a very short summary of it is all that is required here. If it is a fact of experience that the capitalist usually finishes up with more money than he started with, even when he buys and sells everything at its equilibrium price—i.e., "at its value", on the Volume I assumptions—then it is evident that he "must be so lucky as to find, within the sphere of circulation, in the market, a commodity, whose use value possesses the peculiar property of being a source of value, whose actual consumption, therefore, is itself an embodiment of labour, and consequently, a creation of values".[1] And history in fact does put such a unique commodity on to the market, by "freeing" the direct producer from his means of production and thus transforming his *labour power*—i.e., his capacity to labour—into a commodity. The value of the commodity labour power, like that of all other commodities, can be taken (in this first approximation) to be determined by the quantity of labour required to reproduce it—i.e., roughly, by the amount of labour required to produce the commodities which are regarded as necessary to keep a labourer and his family going for a given time. But "the past labour that is embodied in the labour-power, and the living labour that it can call into action; the daily cost of maintaining it, and its daily expenditure in work, are two totally different things."[2] If the length of the working day is x hours, then the cost in labour of maintaining a worker for that time will generally be less than x hours. Thus even though labour power is bought at its value, its use adds a *surplus* value (i.e., a value over and above its own value) to the value of the raw materials and depreciated machinery and buildings used up in production—a surplus which the capitalist is normally able to realise when he sells the finished commodity, even though he sells it at no more than its value. Thus in the case of each individual branch of production (on the Volume I assumptions) the "distribution of the product" between wage-labour and capital will depend upon the proportion in which the working day is there divided up between what Marx called "necessary" and "surplus" labour; and over the economy as a whole it will depend upon the ratio between the aggregate quantity of labour employed and the quantity employed to produce wage-goods.[3] This means that capital

---

[1] *Capital*, Vol. I, p. 145.   [2] *Ibid.*, Vol. I, p. 174.

[3] Cf. *ibid.*, Vol. I, p. 522: "Just as the individual labourer can do more surplus-labour in proportion as his necessary labour-time is less, so with regard to the working population. The smaller the part of it which is required for the production of the necessary means of subsistence, so much the greater is the part that can be set to do other work." Cf. Dobb, *Political Economy and Capitalism*, pp. 46 and 72; and cf. also above, pp. 94-5.

has in fact "developed into a coercive relation, which compels the working class to do more work than the narrow round of its own life-wants prescribes".[1] This forcible extension of working time for the benefit of an exploiting class is of course no new phenomenon;[2] it is in the method, rather than the fact, of exploitation that capitalism differs from previous forms of class society. In particular, the process of exploitation under capitalism is based not on a violation of the primary laws of commodity production, but, on the contrary, on their operation.[3]

The application of the labour theory of value to the commodity labour power involves two special difficulties. In the first place, in contradistinction to other commodities, "there enters into the determination of the value of labour-power a historical and moral element". The wants of a labourer depend not only upon "the climatic and other physical conditions of his country", but also to a great extent upon "the degree of civilisation of a country, more particularly on the conditions under which, and consequently on the habits and degree of comfort in which, the class of free labourers has been formed". This implies that if the working class can hold the price of its labour power above its value for a long enough period, it may thereby eventually succeed in raising the very *value* of its labour power. But it still remains true, of course, that "in a given country, at a given period, the average quantity of the means of subsistence necessary for the labourer is practically known".[4]

In the second place, it is evident that "if you call labour a commodity, it is not like a commodity which is first produced in order to exchange".[5] The production of labour power, unlike the production of other commodities, is not normally controlled by individuals who constantly adjust the supply to changes in demand in order to

[1] *Capital*, Vol. I, pp. 296-7.

[2] Cf. *ibid.*, Vol. I, p. 218: "Capital has not invented surplus-labour. Wherever a part of society possesses the monopoly of the means of production, the labourer, free or not free, must add to the working time necessary for his own maintenance an extra working time in order to produce the means of subsistence for the owners of the means of production, whether this proprietor be the Athenian καλὸς κἀγαθός, Etruscan theocrat, civis Romanus, Norman baron, American slave owner, Wallachian Boyard, modern landlord or capitalist."

[3] See *ibid.*, Vol. I, pp. 596-8 and 812-8. The main thesis of these important passages is stated on p. 812: "However much . . . the capitalist mode of appropriation may appear to flout the primary laws of commodity production, it nevertheless arises, not from any violation of these laws, but, on the contrary, from their operation."

[4] Quotations from *ibid.*, Vol. I, p. 150. Cf. *Selected Works*, Vol. I, pp. 332-3.

[5] *Capital*, Vol. I, p. 546, footnote. The words are not Marx's, but those of an earlier writer from whom he is quoting.

maximise their net receipts. Thus the usual mechanism whereby prices are brought into conformity with values appears to be lacking in the case of the commodity labour power.[1] What justification had Marx, then, in the earlier part of his Volume I analysis, for assuming that labour power, just like all other commodities, was bought and sold at its value? It is not sufficient to reply that this was in effect merely an *a fortiori* assumption of the "even if . . ." type, designed to buttress Marx's contention that exploitation was carried on through the laws of commodity exchange rather than through "force" or "unequal exchanges". There is no doubt a strong element of truth in this. But it is evident that if the preliminary analysis of surplus value is carried out on the basis of such an assumption, it must subsequently be shown that economic forces exist which are sufficiently powerful, if not to keep the price of labour power constantly in conformity with its value, at least to keep it from rising so far above its value as to absorb the whole of the surplus. This consideration was of course present in Marx's mind from the outset. In a letter to Engels of April 1858, outlining an early plan of his economic work, Marx pointed out that in the whole of the first section "it is assumed [*inter alia*] that the wages of labour are constantly equal to their lowest level", this being, as he put it, "the only possible way to avoid having to deal with everything under each particular relation". "The movement of wages themselves", he added, "and the rise and fall of the minimum come under the consideration of wage labour."[2] Once the assumption of the equality of the value and the price of labour power had been dropped, however, and it had been admitted that under certain circumstances the price of labour power might rise above its value and remain at that level for quite long periods (particularly when the rate of capital accumulation was high),[3] the problem of the limit to the rise of wages had to be fairly and squarely faced. Marx dealt with it in his chapter on *The General Law of Capitalist Accumulation*.

---

[1] Cf. *Capital*, Vol. I, p. 652, where Marx points out that even if a rise in wages did stimulate an increase in population, in the way in which the Classical economists suggested it did, the lag would be so great between the rise in wages and "any positive increase of the population really fit to work", that "the time would have been passed again and again, during which the industrial campaign must have been carried through, the battle fought and won". See also p. 658, where Marx describes as a "law of capitalistic society" the fact that "not only the number of births and deaths, but the absolute size of the families, stand in inverse proportion to the height of wages". Cf., however, p. 657, where Marx speaks of "the premium that the exploitation of children sets on their production".

[2] *Selected Correspondence*, p. 106.

[3] Cf., e.g., *Capital*, Vol. I, pp. 531-2 and 625-35.

Broadly speaking, he argued there that the dynamic development of modern industry usually involved a secular increase in the organic composition of capital, so that the demand for labour (while it might increase absolutely) tended to decline relatively to the accumulation of capital. This relative diminution in the demand for labour, together with the absolute diminution which took place whenever wages happened to rise substantially,[1] was generally successful in keeping the long-run equilibrium price of labour power fairly near to its value. It did this not only directly, but also indirectly through the creation and maintenance of a "reserve army" of labour, which was replenished in times of depression and whose existence naturally militated against the efforts of the working class to increase—and at times even to maintain—the level of wages. "The demand for labour", Marx claimed,

"is not identical with increase of capital, nor supply of labour with increase of the working class. It is not a case of two independent forces working on one another. Les dés sont pipés. Capital works on both sides at the same time. If its accumulation, on the one hand, increases the demand for labour, it increases on the other the supply of labourers by the 'setting free' of them, whilst at the same time the pressure of the unemployed compels those that are employed to furnish more labour, and therefore makes the supply of labour, to a certain extent, independent of the supply of labourers. The action of the law of supply and demand of labour on this basis completes the despotism of capital."[2]

Thus although there was no Lassallean "Iron Law of Wages"[3] to prevent the working class from bettering their position, the general tendency of capitalist production, Marx believed, was to push the price of labour power downwards towards its value.

4. The Analysis in Volume III of "Capital"

At the beginning of Volume III of *Capital*, Marx described as follows the relation between this volume and the two which had preceded it:

[1] A rise in wages could affect the demand for labour in two ways. First, if it were sufficiently substantial the rate of accumulation might be checked. Second, it might induce the capitalist to substitute machinery for labour.

[2] *Capital*, Vol. I, pp. 654-5. Cf. *ibid.*, pp. 653-4: "The industrial reserve army, during the periods of stagnation and average prosperity, weighs down the active labour-army; during the periods of over-production and paroxysm, it holds its pretensions in check. Relative surplus-population is therefore the pivot upon which the law of demand and supply of labour works. It confines the field of action of this law within the limits absolutely convenient to the activity of exploitation and to the domination of capital."

[3] On the "iron law of wages" see Marx, *Critique of the Gotha Programme* (English edn.), pp. 21-5. Cf. the comment by Engels on p. 39.

"In the first volume we analyzed the phenomena presented by the *process of capitalist production*, considered by itself as a mere productive process without regard to any secondary influences of conditions outside of it. But this process of production, in the strict meaning of the term, does not exhaust the life circle of capital. It is supplemented in the actual world by the *process of circulation*, which was the object of our analysis in the second volume. We found in the course of this last-named analysis, especially in part III, in which we studied the intervention of the process of circulation in the process of social reproduction, that the capitalist process of production, considered as a whole, is a combination of the processes of production and circulation. It cannot be the object of this third volume to indulge in general reflections relative to this combination. We are rather interested in locating the concrete forms growing out of the *movements of capitalist production as a whole* and setting them forth. In actual reality the capitals move and meet in such concrete forms that the form of the capital in the process of production and that of the capital in the process of circulation impress one only as special aspects of those concrete forms. The conformations of the capitals evolved in this third volume approach step by step to that form which they assume on the surface of society, in their mutual interactions, in competition, and in the ordinary consciousness of the human agencies in this process."[1]

In conformity with this plan, the first major step which Marx took in Volume III—and the only one which directly concerns us here— was the derivation of profit from surplus value. "The surplus-value and the rate of surplus-value", Marx wrote, "are, relatively, the invisible and unknown essence, while the rate of profit and the resulting appearance of surplus-value in the form of profit are phenomena which show themselves on the surface."[2] Or, as he put it in another place, "profit is . . . that disguise of surplus-value which must be removed before the real nature of surplus-value can be discovered. In the surplus-value, the relation between capital and labour is laid bare."[3] But once this relation has been laid bare, the disguise must be put on again and examined, for it is by no means unrelated to the thing which it disguises. That is essentially the task which Marx undertakes in the first two parts of Volume III.

Surplus value, in accordance with the Volume I analysis, is related to one part of the capital only—the part which is spent on wages. But profit is related to the whole of the capital. Thus, as we have

[1] *Capital*, Vol. III, pp. 37-8.   [2] *Ibid.*, Vol. III, p. 56.
[3] *Ibid.*, Vol. III, p. 62. Cf. above, p. 181.

already seen above, immediately one starts trying to explain the process whereby surplus value is converted into profit one comes face to face with the fact that if the rates of profit received on two capitals of different organic compositions are to be the same, then the amount of profit received by the owner of at least one of the capitals must be greater or less than the amount of surplus value produced with its aid. If one has argued, as Marx has, that the only possible permanent source of profit under competitive conditions is the value produced by the surplus labour of the workers employed by the capitalist,[1] there is clearly only one way of explaining the process of conversion so as to take account of this fact. One must argue that the *aggregate* surplus value produced over the economy as a whole is, as it were, re-allocated among the different capitalists so that they share in it not in accordance with the amount of capital they have spent on wages but in accordance with the *total* amounts of capital which they have severally employed.[2] The only possible alternative would be to reject the whole Volume I analysis and to say that a capital of 100 always produced the same amount of surplus value (and profit) no matter how it was constituted—in which case, Marx believed, "political economy would then be without a rational basis".[3]

This conversion of surplus value into average profit necessarily implies the transformation of values into what Marx called "prices of production". Under capitalism, commodities produced by capitals whose organic composition is different from the social average do *not* tend to sell "at their values", but at "prices of production" which diverge from their values. Marx's "price of production", which includes profit at the average rate, is "the same thing which Adam Smith calls *natural price*, Ricardo *price of production*, or *cost of production*, and the physiocrats *prix nécessaire*, because it is in the long run a prerequisite of supply, of the reproduction of commodities in every individual sphere".[4] These prices of production, Marx insists, have

---

[1] Cf., e.g., *Capital*, Vol. III, p. 176: "The only source of surplus-value is living labour."

[2] "While the capitalists in the various spheres of production recover the value of the capital consumed in the production of their commodities through the sale of these, they do not secure the surplus-value, and consequently the profit, created in their own sphere by the production of these commodities, but only as much surplus-value, and profit, as falls to the share of every aliquot part of the total social capital out of the total social surplus-value, or social profit produced by the total capital of society in all spheres of production. Every 100 of any invested capital, whatever may be its organic composition, draws as much profit during one year, or any other period of time, as falls to the share of every 100 of the total social capital during the same period" (*Ibid.*, Vol. III, pp. 186-7).

[3] *Ibid.*, Vol. III, pp. 176-7.   [4] *Ibid.*, Vol. III, p. 233.

to be derived from the values of commodities as analysed in Volume I, otherwise there is no possibility of demonstrating that they are in any significant sense "subject to law". Prices of production, he says,

"are conditioned on the existence of an average rate of profit, and this, again, rests on the premise that the rates of profit in every sphere of production, considered by itself, have previously been reduced to so many average rates of profit. These special rates of profit are equal to $\frac{s}{C}$ in every sphere of production, and they must be deduced out of the values of the commodities, as shown in volume I. Without such a deduction an average rate of profit (and consequently a price of production of commodities), remains a vague and senseless conception."[1]

Given the feasibility of such deduction, however, it is surely apparent that Marx's Volume III analysis of exchange ratios in terms of prices of production ought properly to be regarded as a modification, rather than as a refutation, of the Volume I analysis in terms of values. The total amount of surplus value available for allocation among the capitalists is determined according to the simple Volume I analysis; the values of the constituent elements of the individual capitals may also be taken (at least for the moment) to be determined according to the Volume I analysis; and it can therefore be said that the level of the average rate of profit, and with it both the individual prices of production and *the degree of divergence of individual prices of production from values*, are also ultimately determined according to the Volume I analysis. The fact that during a particular historical period "commodities are not exchanged simply as commodities, but as products of capitals"[2]—i.e., as "capitalistically modified" commodities—does indeed introduce a "disturbance" into the operation of the law of value as described in Volume I. But it is a *calculable* disturbance, and "in the exact sciences it is not the custom to regard a calculable disturbance as a refutation of a certain law".[3]

---

[1] *Capital*, Vol. III, pp. 185-6. Cf. *Theories of Surplus Value*, p. 231: "The average profit, and therefore also the production prices, would be purely imaginary and without basis if we did not take the determined value as the foundation. The equalisation of the surplus values in different spheres of production makes no difference to the absolute magnitude of this total surplus value but only alters its distribution among the different spheres of production. The determination of the surplus value itself however only arises from the determination of value by labour time. Without this, the average profit is an average of *nothing*, a mere figment of the imagination. And in that case it might just as well be 1,000 per cent. as 10 per cent."

[2] *Capital*, Vol. III, p. 206.

[3] P. Fireman, quoted by Engels in his preface to Volume III of *Capital*, p. 25. Cf. Hilferding, *Böhm-Bawerk's Criticism of Marx* (Sweezy's edn.), p. 161: "The law of value, directly valid for the social product and its parts, enforces itself only inasmuch as certain

Marx illustrated this argument with a set of simple arithmetical formulae which are summarised in the following table.[1]

	1.	2.	3.	4.	5.	6.	7.	8.
Capitals	Used–up c	Cost Price	Surplus Value	Value	Profit	Price of Pro-duction	Devia-tion of Price from Value
I 80c + 20v	50	70	20	90	22	92	+ 2
II 70c + 30v	51	81	30	111	22	103	− 8
III 60c + 40v	51	91	40	131	22	113	−18
IV 85c + 15v	40	55	15	70	22	77	+ 7
V 95c + 5v	10	15	5	20	22	37	+17
			110	422	110	422	

Marx deliberately simplifies the calculation by assuming that none of the five commodities concerned enters into the production of any of the others. Thus capitals I to V can be considered as the component parts of one single capital of 500. Each of the constituent capitals shown in col. 1 totals 100, but the cost price of each of the outputs is less than 100, since it is assumed that only a portion of the value of the constant capital is transferred to the commodity in the period we are considering.[2] The amount so transferred is shown in col. 2, and the cost price, which is the sum of v and used-up c, is shown in col. 3. It is assumed that the working day is everywhere equally divided between necessary and surplus labour, so that surplus value (shown in col. 4) is equal to v. The total *value* of each of the outputs being considered (shown in col. 5) represents the sum of the cost price and the surplus value. Now it is evident that the sale of these commodities at their values would result in very unequal rates of profit on each of the capitals. In actual fact, however, Marx maintains, the total pool of surplus value, amounting to 110, is allotted ("by means of competition")[3] to the individual capitals in accordance

definite modifications, conformable to law, occur in the prices of the individual capital-istically-produced commodities—but these modifications can only be made comprehens-ible by the discovery of the social nexus, and the law of value renders us this service."

[1] This table is an amalgamation of those on pp. 183 and 185 of *Capital*, Vol. III, with some of the figures rearranged.

[2] The turnover periods of v are assumed to be the same in each case.

[3] *Capital*, Vol. III, p. 186.

with the total size of each—in this case uniformly, so that each receives a profit of 22 (col. 6). The "price of production" (col. 7), then, at which each output actually tends to sell, is the sum of the cost price and the profit, and differs in each case from the value. But since the total profit is by definition equal to the total surplus value, it naturally follows that in the present case the sum of the values is equal to the sum of the prices of production, or, to put the same thing in another way, that the deviations of prices from values (col. 8) cancel one another out.[1]

Marx's statement that the sum of the prices is equal to the sum of the values has come in for considerable criticism. From Böhm-Bawerk[2] onwards, critics have questioned whether this statement can be held to be meaningful, whether it embodies a tautology, and so on, and have generally concluded that Marx's statement is quite untenable. Some of the difficulty no doubt arises from the fact that Marx, having illustrated this equality arithmetically in the particular case just described (the case where mutual interdependence is abstracted from), immediately went on to say that "in the same way the sum of all the prices of production of all commodities in society, comprising the totality of all lines of production, is equal to the sum of their values".[3] The implication of this statement, read in its context, might seem to be that when the assumption that none of the commodities concerned entered into the production of any of the others was dropped, so that the values of input as well as those of output had to be transformed into prices of production, a transformation carried out on the basis of a redistribution of the "pool" of surplus value would bring out total prices equal to total values in the arithmetical sense. This is in fact not so. On any plausible set of assumptions regarding the manner in which the different branches of the economy are inter-related, it will soon be found on experimenting with various sets of figures that if the values of input as well as those of output are to be transformed into prices of production, it is normally impossible to effect a simultaneous transformation which will make total profit equal to total surplus value and at the same time make total prices of production equal to total values. In all but very exceptional cases, we may preserve one of these equalities, but not both.[4] If Marx's attention

[1] It is evident that the only case where price and value would coincide would be one in which the constitution of the capital concerned coincided with the "social average."

[2] *Op. cit.*, pp. 32-8.   [3] *Capital*, Vol. III, p. 188.

[4] For an example of one of these exceptional cases, see the transformation exhibited in Tables II and IIIb on pp. 111 and 120 of Sweezy's *Theory of Capitalist Development*.

had been drawn to this fact, he might well have reformulated some of his expressions regarding the equality of total prices and total values, while still insisting on the essential point they were designed to express—*viz.*, that after the transformation of values into prices of production the fundamental ratio between the value of labour power and the value of commodities in general, upon which profit depended,[1] could still be said to be determined in accordance with the Volume I analysis.[2] In the special case where none of the commodities concerned enters into the production of any of the others, he might have said, the ratio remains the same for the simple reason that the relevant quantities remain the same—the denominator remains the same by hypothesis, and the numerator remains the same because *in this case* the sum of the prices necessarily equals the sum of the values. In the more difficult case where the various branches of production are mutually interdependent, he might have added, the sum of the prices does not necessarily "come out" equal to the sum of the values, but the fundamental ratio can still be said to be determined in accordance with the Volume I analysis.

However, it would be wrong to suggest that Marx simply ignored this more difficult case. On the contrary, his examination of it, although by no means detailed, was sufficiently well organised to be said to constitute a second stage in his argument. He begins by dropping the assumption that none of the commodities concerned enters into the production of any of the others. In actual fact, he writes, "the price of production of one line of production passes, with the profit contained in it, over into the cost-price of another line of production". At first sight it might seem as if this would mean that the profit accruing to each capitalist might be counted several times in a calculation such as that which has just been made, but Marx has little difficulty in disposing of this superficial objection. The dropping of the assumption, however, does indeed make one "essential difference", which Marx describes as follows:

"Aside from the fact that the price of a certain product, for instance the product of capital B, differs from its value, because the surplus-value realized in B may be greater or smaller than the profit of others contained in the product of B, the same fact applies also to those commodities which form the constant part of its capital, and which indirectly, as necessities of life for the labourers, form

[1] See above, p. 183.
[2] Cf. M. H. Dobb, *Political Economy and Capitalism*, pp. 72-3.

its variable part. So far as the constant part is concerned, it is itself equal to the cost-price plus surplus-value, which now means cost-price plus profit, and this profit may again be greater or smaller than the surplus-value in whose place it stands. And so far as the variable capital is concerned, it is true that the average daily wage is equal to the values produced by the labourers in the time which they must work in order to produce their necessities of life. But this time is in its turn modified by the deviation of the prices of production of the necessities of life from their values. However, this always amounts in the end to saying that one commodity receives too little of the surplus-value while another receives too much, so that the deviations from the value shown by the prices of production mutually compensate one another. In short, under capitalist production, the general law of value enforces itself merely as the prevailing tendency, in a very complicated and approximate manner, as a never ascertainable average of ceaseless fluctuations."[1]

Marx returned to the same point a few pages later, pointing out that the transformation process involves a modification of the Volume I assumption that "the cost-price of a commodity is equal to the value of the commodities consumed in its production". The price of production of a certain commodity, he writes,

"is its cost-price for the buyer, and this price may pass into other commodities and become an element of their prices. Since the price of production may vary from the value of a commodity, it follows that the cost-price of a commodity containing this price of production may also stand above or below that portion of its total value which is formed by the value of the means of production consumed by it. It is necessary to remember this modified significance of the cost-price, and to bear in mind that there is always the possibility of an error, if we assume that the cost-price of the commodities of any particular sphere is equal to the value of the means of production consumed by it. Our present analysis does not necessitate a closer examination of this point."[2]

And in a later passage, repeating the same point once more, he argued that "this possibility does not alter the correctness of the rules laid down for commodities of average composition".[3]

This is where the so-called "transformation problem" comes into

---

[1] Quotations from *Capital*, Vol. III, pp. 188-90. There is a similar passage at the end of Marx's comments on Bailey in the *Theories of Surplus Value* (not included in the English edn.) which shows that the point had occurred to him several years before the publication of the first volume of *Capital*.

[2] *Capital*, Vol. III, pp. 194-5.   [3] *Ibid.*, Vol. III, pp. 241-3.

the picture.[1] Marx's "method of transforming prices into values", it is said, meaning by this his original calculation outlined in the table above, contains an "error", since it does not take account of the fact that the values of elements of input as well as those of elements of output have to be transformed into prices.[2] It is then claimed that Marx can be rescued from this "error" simply by showing the *formal possibility* of a consistent "derivation of prices from values" in cases where the transformation affects all elements of both input and output. When values are transformed into prices, the ratio of price to value in the case of a given commodity must be the same when the commodity is considered as input as when it is considered as output; and after the transformation the rate of profit must come out equal in the case of each capital concerned. These ratios of price to value, and the rate of profit, are regarded as the unknowns in the problem. The "transformation problem" then reduces itself to this: can the relations between the various branches of production, and the various conditions which are to be fulfilled as a result of the transformation, be expressed in the form of an equational system which is "determinate" in the mathematical sense—i.e., roughly, in which the number of equations is equal to the number of unknowns? The assumption lying behind these investigations is that if the relations and conditions can in fact be so expressed, Marx's method of "deriving prices from values" is itself transformed from an invalid to a valid one.

The best-known solution, that of Bortkiewicz,[3] commences with the particular set of value-relationships postulated by Marx as existing between the three main departments of the economy (I=means of production; II=workers' consumption goods; III=capitalists' consumption goods) under conditions of simple reproduction. Employing the usual notation, these value-relationships can be expressed as follows in the form of three equations:

$$\text{I.} \quad c_1 + v_1 + s_1 = c_1 + c_2 + c_3$$
$$\text{II.} \quad c_2 + v_2 + s_2 = v_1 + v_2 + v_3$$
$$\text{III.} \quad c_3 + v_3 + s_3 = s_1 + s_2 + s_3$$

[1] This is a rather special problem, and the reader may skip to p. 198 below without losing anything of very great importance. I deal with it in detail here only because a considerable amount of attention has recently been paid to it by critics of Marx.

[2] As will be clear from what has been said above, it was not intended to take account of this fact, since mutual interdependence was specifically abstracted from.

[3] *On the Correction of Marx's Fundamental Theoretical Construction in the Third Volume of "Capital"*, reprinted as an appendix to Sweezy's edn. of Böhm-Bawerk and Hilferding.

If we take the ratio of price to value to be x in the case of means of production, y in the case of workers' consumption goods, and z in the case of capitalists' consumption goods; if we further call the average rate of profit r; and if we state as a condition of the problem that the relations appropriate to simple reproduction should continue to obtain after the transformation of values into prices as before it, then the following equalities must hold:

$$\text{I.} \quad c_1 x + v_1 y + r(c_1 x + v_1 y) = (c_1 + c_2 + c_3)x$$
$$\text{II.} \quad c_2 x + v_2 y + r(c_2 x + v_2 y) = (v_1 + v_2 + v_3)y$$
$$\text{III.} \quad c_3 x + v_3 y + r(c_3 x + v_3 y) = (s_1 + s_2 + s_3)z$$

Here there are four unknowns (x, y, z and r), and only three equations. Bortkiewicz reduces the unknowns to three by the ingenious expedient of assuming: (a) that the value scheme was expressed in terms of money, and (b) that gold is the money commodity, and is produced in department III, in which case z may reasonably be taken as $=1$. The equational system thereupon becomes determinate, and solutions for x, y and r can be fairly readily derived. Upon applying these solutions to various sets of figures, it is seen that total profit comes out equal to total surplus value, but that total prices normally diverge from total values. Neither the equality nor the divergence, however, has anything more than formal significance. As Bortkiewicz himself says, in relation to a particular set of figures,

"That the total price exceeds the total value arises from the fact that Department III, from which the good serving as value and price measure is taken, has a relatively low organic composition of capital. But the fact that total profit is numerically identical with total surplus value is a consequence of the fact that the good used as value and price measure belongs to Department III."[1]

It is only in the special case where the organic composition of the capital employed in Department III is equal to the social average that the sum of the prices will come out equal to the sum of the values.

Winternitz, in a note in the *Economic Journal* of June 1948, adopts the same general attitude towards the problem as Bortkiewicz, but clears the Bortkiewicz solution of certain redundancies and unnecessary artificialities. He commences with the usual value schema in the three departments:

[1] Bortkiewicz, *op. cit.*, p. 205.

$$\text{I.}\quad c_1 + v_1 + s_1 = a_1$$
$$\text{II.}\quad c_2 + v_2 + s_2 = a_2$$
$$\text{III.}\quad c_3 + v_3 + s_3 = a_3$$

But instead of assuming the equilibrium conditions appropriate to Marx's reproduction schemes, he assumes merely that when a_1 varies by x (the price-value ratio for means of production), then c_1, c_2 and c_3 also vary by x, and that when a_2 varies by y (the price-value ratio for workers' consumption goods), then v_1, v_2 and v_3 also vary by y. Thus he arrives at the following simple equational system:

$$\text{I.}\quad c_1x + v_1y + S_1 = a_1x$$
$$\text{II.}\quad c_2x + v_2y + S_2 = a_2y$$
$$\text{III.}\quad c_3x + v_3y + S_3 = a_3z$$

By putting $\dfrac{a_1x}{c_1x + v_1y} = \dfrac{a_2y}{c_2x + v_2y}$ (each of these expressions being equal to $1 + r$), solutions for $x:y$ and for r are easily obtained. A further set of relationships between x, y and z must then be postulated in order to determine the price level for the system as a whole. From a purely logical point of view, it obviously does not matter what relationships are postulated, but Winternitz puts

$$a_1x + a_2y + a_3z = a_1 + a_2 + a_3$$

(i.e., sum of prices = sum of values) because in his opinion this is "the obvious proposition in the spirit of the Marxian system".[1] x, y and z are then yielded immediately without any special difficulty. When applied to various sets of figures, these solutions naturally bring out the sum of prices equal to the sum of values, but total profit normally diverges from total surplus value.

Winternitz's solution, although in essence very similar to Bortkiewicz's, is evidently simpler, and therefore more acceptable from a purely mathematical point of view. Indeed, it is the special merit of Winternitz to have exposed the triviality of the whole problem as so posed—a triviality which tended to be hidden by Bortkiewicz's over-elaborate and confusing method. The Winternitz solution is an effective reply to those who said that it was not formally possible to transform values into prices when elements of input as well as output were involved. But it seems to me that something more is required before a transformation of the Bortkiewicz-Winternitz type can properly be used to *illustrate* the second stage of Marx's Volume III

[1] *Economic Journal*, June 1948, p. 279.

argument. The essential point for Marx, as we have seen, was that after aggregate surplus value had been converted into profit, and values consequently transformed into prices, the fundamental ratio between the value of labour power and the value of commodities in general, upon which profit depended, could be regarded as remaining un-altered as a result of the transformation. I have argued elsewhere[1] that it is quite possible to effect a transformation in which this ratio in fact remains unaltered—provided we assume that the organic composition of capital in Department II is equal to the social average—and that such a transformation can provide us with a suitable arith-metical illustration for use in connection with the second stage of Marx's argument.

It may well be, as Sweezy has suggested, that Marx would have dealt with this problem in more detail if he had lived to work over Volume III again.[2] On the other hand, the relative importance of the problem in Marx's general theoretical scheme is hardly very great, and my own feeling is that he would probably have left most of the relevant passages much as they are. In any event, I do not think he would have felt himself either obliged to provide an amended set of calculations to illustrate the second stage of his argument or embarrassed by any inability to do so. The function of the simple arithmetical illustrations in *Capital* is much the same as their function in Ricardo's *Principles*—and entirely different from their function in much of the work of modern mathematical economists. They are designed to illustrate arguments (or steps in arguments), and not to prove them; and they are usually designed to do this only on a very elementary level. To suggest that any argument in *Capital* stands or falls by Marx's arith-metical illustrations (or by the lack of them) is to betray a serious misunderstanding of his method. As Kenneth May has said, Marx "used calculations primarily as illustrations to accompany verbal arguments which combined process and cross-section analysis in a way which could hardly be fitted to the mathematical techniques available even to-day".[3] It would be a mistake, wrote Engels, to assume

> "that one may look in Marx's work at all for fixed and universally applicable definitions. It is a matter of course that when things and their mutual interrelations are conceived not as fixed, but as

[1] *Economic Journal*, March 1956.

[2] See Sweezy's introduction to his edn. of Böhm-Bawerk and Hilferding, p. xxiv.

[3] *Economic Journal*, December 1948, p. 598.

changing, that their mental images, the ideas concerning them, are likewise subject to change and transformation; that they cannot be sealed up in rigid definitions, but must be developed in the historical process of their formation."[1]

In concluding this chapter, reference should be made to one problem which is of importance, as we shall see later, in connection with the task of reapplying the basic Marxian categories to the monopoly stage of capitalism. I have argued above that Marx was primarily concerned to show how the operation of the law of value under simple commodity production, where the normal exchange was one of "value" for "value", was modified by the introduction of capitalism. But the assumption that commodities sold "at their values" under simple commodity production was not, I think, at least in most of the relevant contexts, intended to imply that commodities had in fact normally tended to sell "at their values" in any specific form of pre-capitalist society. Marx's assumption had reference not so much to actual exchange relations in this or that specific pre-capitalist society, but rather to exchange relations under commodity production *as such* in pre-capitalist society *as such*. In other words, he was talking about the way in which exchange ratios would be determined under a sort of "pure" pre-capitalist commodity production, unalloyed by elements of monopoly, etc. In what sense exactly, then, can the *logical* transformation of values into prices of production be said to reflect a real *historical* transformation?

In one passage in Volume III of *Capital*, Marx seems to suggest that the logical transformation of values into prices of production reflects a historical transformation of exchange ratios *which were in actual fact normally equal to embodied labour ratios* into exchange ratios which were equal to price of production ratios. "The exchange of commodities at their values, or approximately at their values", he writes,

"requires . . . a much lower stage than their exchange at their prices of production, which requires a relatively high development of capitalist production. . . .
"Aside from the fact that prices and their movements are dominated by the law of value, it is quite appropriate, under these circumstances, to regard the value of commodities not only theoretically, but also historically, as existing prior to the prices

[1] *Capital*, Vol. III, p. 24. Cf. Marshall's preface to the 1st edn. of his *Principles of Economics*. Marx was not the only great economist who learned much from Hegel.

of production. This applies to conditions, in which the labourer owns his means of production, and this is the condition of the land-owning farmer and of the craftsman in the old world as well as the new. This agrees also with the view formerly expressed by me that the development of product into commodities arises through the exchange between different communes, not through that between the members of the same commune. It applies not only to this primitive condition, but also to subsequent conditions based on slavery or serfdom, and to the guild organisation of handicrafts, so long as the means of production installed in one line of production cannot be transferred to another line except under difficulties, so that the various lines of production maintain, to a certain degree, the same mutual relations as foreign countries or communistic groups."[1]

Engels, referring to this passage in his important "Supplement" to Volume III of *Capital*,[2] said that "if Marx had had an opportunity to work over the third volume once more, he would doubtless have extended this passage considerably. As it stands it gives only the sketchy outline of what is to be said on the point in question." Engels therefore proceeded to amplify it along the lines which he thought Marx would have followed, arguing that during the whole period of pre-capitalist commodity production "prices gravitate towards the values fixed by the Marxian law and oscillate around these values".[3]

Now if "prices" here refers to actual market prices, as the context would certainly indicate, it does not seem to me that Engels's generalisation can possibly be regarded as valid, owing to the prevalence of various forms of monopoly, the low degree of factor mobility, etc., in most pre-capitalist societies. But if "prices" be taken to refer to *supply prices* the generalisation becomes much more true.[4] Broadly speaking, there are two main types of supply price to be found in the history of commodity exchange—first, that of the producer who thinks of his net receipts as a reward for his labour, and, second, that of the producer who thinks of his net receipts as a profit on his capital. It seems to me quite reasonable to assume that supply prices of the first type will tend to be proportionate to quantities of embodied

---

[1] *Capital*, Vol. III, pp. 208-9. Cf. *ibid.*, pp. 207-8 and 212.

[2] *Engels on "Capital"*, p. 102.   [3] *Ibid.*, p. 106.

[4] I am using the term "supply price" in a broad sense (divorced from its familiar Marshallian connotations) to mean the price which, as Marx put it, "is in the long run a prerequisite of supply, of the reproduction of commodities in every individual sphere" (*Capital*, Vol. III, p. 233). It is simply the price which a producer must receive for his commodity if he is to continue producing it.

labour, and that such supply prices are typical of commodity exchanges in pre-capitalist societies. Thus even if the barriers standing in the way of an automatic adaptation of market prices to supply prices in pre-capitalist societies are too important to be assumed away or classified as mere "frictions", it can at least be said that *the supply prices themselves* "gravitate towards the values fixed by the Marxian law". What Marx actually did, in effect, was to assume that the first type of supply price was characteristic of commodity exchanges in pre-capitalist society, and to demonstrate how the introduction of capitalism brought about the transformation of the first type of supply price into the second type. This, I think, is the historical transformation of which the logical transformation considered above must be regarded as the "corrected mirror-image".

CHAPTER SIX

THE CRITIQUE OF THE MARXIAN LABOUR THEORY

1. *Introduction*

BY the time of the publication of Volume III of *Capital* in 1894, Marxism had become the official doctrine of the majority of the leading European socialist parties, and a new stage in the development of the labour theory had begun. Thenceforth attacks upon or defences of the labour theory assumed direct political significance to a much greater degree than ever before. Under such circumstances, it was probably inevitable that the labour theory should enter upon new paths of development, rather different in character from those which it had followed during the past century, and very different in character from those which the marginal utility theory was following more or less contemporaneously.

Indeed, it may appear to many non-Marxists that the word "development" is a misnomer when used to describe the vicissitudes of the labour theory during the next sixty years. At first sight, the salient features of its history during this period may appear to be simply a series of well-aimed attacks upon it on the one hand, and a series of dogmatic defences of it on the other. Numerous critics, it may appear, have assailed the theory from every conceivable angle and refuted it a dozen times from each of them, but "official" Marxism continues obstinately to uphold it in its original form as laid down in the gospels of the Master. It sticks to it so dogmatically, we are often told, simply because it serves to "demonstrate the exploitation of the working class under Capitalism".[1] In other words, it insists on all this "Hegelian stuff and nonsense",[2] and on the "rigmarole"[3] of the transformation of values into prices, simply because "the fact of exploitation lies behind the phenomena of the market".[4]

No one will deny, of course, that many of the basic propositions of Marxism have often been accepted dogmatically by Marxists in

[1] O. Lange, "Marxian Economics and Modern Economic Theory", in *The Review of Economic Studies*, Vol. II, No. 3, June 1935, p. 195, footnote 3.
[2] Joan Robinson, *On Re-Reading Marx* (1953), p. 20.
[3] Joan Robinson, in the *Economic Journal*, June 1950, p. 360.　　　[4] *Ibid.*, p. 363.

the past, and that "vulgar Marxism" is to some extent still with us today. Given the circumstances in which Marxism was diffused and developed, this could hardly have been otherwise. No one will deny, either, that some of the popular appeal of the labour theory still lies (as it did in the days of the Ricardian socialists) in the political and ethical implications which are sometimes read into it. But this is not at all to imply that the view I have just been describing is a correct one. To say nothing of the "unworthy contempt of opponents"[1] which it expresses, this view is based on a complete misconception of the role of the labour theory in the Marxian system as a whole. As a result of this misconception, the reasons for the "official" retention of the leading elements of Marx's value theory are misunderstood, and the extent to which the theory has in fact been developed since Marx's time is greatly underestimated.

Marx's value theory has been retained not because it is believed to be good propaganda, but because it is believed to be good science. Marxists have indeed opposed the numerous suggestions which have been made from both inside and outside their ranks to purge the labour theory from the body of Marxism, or to "reconcile" it with the marginal utility theory. But they have not done this for religious reasons, or out of obtuseness. They have done it because in their view the labour theory is an essential tool for the scientific analysis of capitalist reality. They have been encouraged in this view by the fact that many of those within their own ranks who have criticised the labour theory have eventually shown themselves to be interested not so much in purging the labour theory from Marxism as in purging Marxism itself from the ideology of the labour movement. This does not mean, however, either that there has been no development of the labour theory at all since 1894, or that there is not room for much more development within the broad Marxian framework. It means simply that development has not normally taken the form of the out-and-out rejection of any of the basic principles of the original theory (as has been the case with the marginal utility theory), but has rather taken the form of the *reapplication* of the theory to new circumstances. It is true, of course, that there are still gaps in the working-out of the theory, but this is not due to any superstitious reverence on the part of Marxists for the original Marxian doctrines. It is due rather to the fact that the attention of Marxists has so often had to be turned to other theoretical problems (e.g., the problem of the "breakdown"

---

[1] A. D. Lindsay, *Karl Marx's "Capital"* (1925), p. 54.

of capitalism) which are of more direct and immediate relevance to the policy of the working-class movement; and also, of course, to the fact that since the 'thirties the political conditions in many countries have hardly been conducive to the development of serious research into the theroretical principles of Marxism.

One way of illustrating the rationale of the Marxists' defence of the theory, and the nature of the development it has undergone,[1] is to consider in turn the various types of attack which critics have made upon it. The attacks can be conveniently divided into three types. First, there is what might be called the pure Böhm-Bawerkian attack, which starts unambiguously from the standpoint of the marginal utility theory of value. This type of attack recognises that a theory of value of some sort must lie at the foundation of any general theoretical system in economics, but complains that Marx has chosen an invalid theory which does not square with the facts and does not penetrate sufficiently below the surface,[2] and that his whole system therefore falls to the ground. The second type of attack accepts the same view about the necessity for some sort of theory of value, and agrees that Marx's theory of value is invalid, but does not accept the view that his whole system falls to the ground because of this. In the opinion of some of the critics who make this type of attack, a number of Marx's leading propositions still remain true (at least in substance) when the labour theory of value is replaced by or reconciled with the marginal utility theory. In the opinion of others, Marx's theory of value, although technically invalid, performs a special role in Marx's system quite different from that which other theories of value play in their systems. The third type of attack rejects the view that a theory of value (at least in the traditional sense of that expression) is necessary at all, and concentrates on demonstrating that the labour theory is a useless excrescence upon Marx's system. At the worst it is a mere Hegelian mystification, and at the best it makes no statement which is not made by the leading propositions of the materialist conception of history.

These three types of attack, of course, do not exist in separate

---

[1] The development of the labour theory in the U.S.S.R. is dealt with in the following chapter.

[2] The Böhm-Bawerkians often complain of the Marxist theory in terms which are rather similar to those in which the Marxists complain of the Böhm-Bawerkian theory. Each argues that the other does not penetrate below the surface to the "real" or "ultimate" determinant or motive force in society. But in the Marxist view this determinant is the social relations entered into between men and men in the production of commodities, whereas in the Böhm-Bawerkian view it is the mental relations between individual men and the finished goods which they demand and consume.

watertight compartments. The second is in a sense a variant of the first; and the assumption that many of Marx's propositions are independent of the labour theory is common to the second and third. And some critics do not confine themselves to any one of these approaches, but use arguments appropriate to two or even all three of them. The more intelligent critics, however, have generally adopted an approach which is fairly distinctly aligned with one, and one only, of the three which I have distinguished, and in what follows I shall deal in turn with writers whose main arguments seem to me to be typical of each standpoint.

2. Pareto's Critique

So far as the first type of critique is concerned, I have perhaps said enough in the preceding chapters about Böhm-Bawerk's approach to render any further detailed reference to his own work unnecessary. But it might be useful to say a little about the attitude of Pareto, whose attack upon Marx[1] can most conveniently be regarded as the Lausanne variant of Böhm-Bawerk's. Although Pareto's critique is rather similar in content to Böhm-Bawerk's, it is on the whole much less competent.[2] All too often sneers about the religious character which Marx's work has allegedly assumed in the eyes of his followers take the place of reasoned criticism. And all too often the imaginary Marxists with whom Pareto argues are made to put forward interpretations of the labour theory which are suspiciously simple-minded. It is not very difficult, for example, to show that the "Marxist" method of reducing skilled to simple labour is absurd when the "Marxists" are made to say that the reduction can be effected simply by referring to the values of the products.[3] And it is easy enough to show that the labour theory does not apply to rare pictures, etc.,[4] since (as Pareto well knew) it was never intended to apply to anything other than freely reproducible goods.[5] Nor is it sufficient, when the Marxist characterises as exceptional the case of the picture whose price increases when its painter becomes famous without anything having happened to the quantity of labour embodied in it, to reply that it is by no means

---

[1] Pareto's main criticisms of Marx are contained in his introduction to *Extracts from Karl Marx's "Capital"* (Paris, 1893), and in a special section of his *Les Systèmes Socialistes* (Paris, 1902). The quotations from the latter work appearing below are from the 2nd edn. of 1926, edited by G.-H. Bousquet.

[2] Cf., *per contra*, T. W. Hutchison, *A Review of Economic Doctrines*, p. 228.

[3] *Les Systèmes Socialistes*, Vol. II, pp. 381-2.   [4] *Ibid.*, Vol. II, pp. 377-9.

[5] Cf. *Extracts*, p. xxiii, footnote.

exceptional because the prices of *all* commodities may vary without anything happening to the quantity of labour embodied in them— e.g., on account of a change in the tastes and incomes of their consumers.[1]

From the main body of Pareto's critique we may select three arguments which are typical of the general character of the critique as a whole. The first of these relates to Marx's statement that "however ... productive power may vary, the same labour, exercised during equal periods of time, always yields equal amounts of value".[2] This implies, of course, that if the productivity of labour in, say, the tailoring industry is doubled, so that two coats can be produced with the same expenditure of labour as was previously necessary to produce one, then "two coats are only worth as much as one was before".[3] Now Marx also says that means of production "never transfer more value to the product than they themselves lose during the labour-process by the destruction of their own use-value".[4] If this were in fact so, Pareto asks, why should a manufacturer ever wish to introduce a new machine designed to increase productivity, since the only result would be that the unit value of the commodity produced would fall in proportion to the increase in productivity? One way of explaining his action in introducing such a machine, Pareto argues, would be to say that it is only when prices have reached a stable equilibrium level that the machine does not transfer more value than it itself loses during the labour process. But since prices do not reach this level immediately after the introduction of a new machine,

> "there will be a certain lapse of time during which the value transferred will be greater than the depreciation (*usure*) of the machine, i.e., during which the simple capital which it represents will produce a certain value, and it is this surplus of value which serves as the reward which stimulates the producer to employ the machine."[5]

But if we take this line, Pareto continues, it is a case of out of the frying pan into the fire. If capital can produce exchange value during the period when prices have not reached their stable equilibrium level, it can always produce it, "for this stable equilibrium of prices is a pure abstraction, which does not exist in nature". Therefore, if

[1] The Marxist (and Classical) reply to this, of course, is that the long-run equilibrium prices of freely reproducible commodities (as distinct from their day-to-day market prices) will not in fact be affected by a change in demand unless it is accompanied by a change in the conditions of production.

[2] *Capital*, Vol. I, pp. 13-14.   [3] *Ibid.*, Vol. I, p. 13.

[4] *Ibid.*, Vol. I, p. 186.   [5] *Extracts*, p. xlvii.

we are going to argue on the assumption that the exchange value of a commodity is proportionate to the quantity of socially-necessary labour required for its production, we must also assume that this phenomenon of capital producing surplus value either does not exist, or is of no more than negligible importance. And we shall then have to admit that the manufacturer would have no incentive to introduce a new machine designed to increase productivity.[1]

If it were normally the case that the new machine were introduced simultaneously in all firms in the industry,[2] it is perfectly true that one might well have to consider the problem of incentive in terms of a temporary discrepancy between market and equilibrium prices. But it would not follow even then that the surplus profits received could be explained only in terms of the production of exchange value *by the new machine*; and even if we accepted such an explanation in this particular case of a discrepancy between market and equilibrium prices, it would certainly not follow that because the equilibrium price was never actually reached capital could *always* produce exchange value. However, Pareto's argument is academic as well as illogical, since in actual fact the new machine would not normally be introduced simultaneously in all firms in the industry. It would be introduced first by one or a few firms in an endeavour to steal a march on their competitors. The explanation of this process given by Marx himself, which does not assume the existence at any time of any divergence between value and price, seems quite satisfactory. "The real value of a commodity", Marx writes. "is . . . not its individual value, but its social value; that is to say, the real value is not measured by the labour-time that the article in each individual case costs the producer, but by the labour-time socially required for its production."[3] Thus an individual capitalist who introduces a new method which increases the productivity of labour in his establishment will be able, for a time, to sell his commodity above its individual value, thereby obtaining an extra surplus value. "The exceptionally productive labour", Marx writes, "operates as intensified labour; it creates in equal periods

[1] *Extracts*, pp. xlvii–xlix.

[2] Pareto discusses the problem in the setting of "a society without appropriated capital", in which it is decreed that all exchanges should take place in accordance with quantities of embodied labour (*ibid.*, p. xlv). In such a society, it *might* in fact normally be the case that a new machine would be introduced simultaneously in all firms in the industry. But Pareto quite clearly intends the conclusions he reaches from an examination of the problem in this special setting to be applicable to an ordinary capitalist society (see, e.g., *ibid.*, p. lx).

[3] *Capital*, Vol. I, p. 306.

of time greater values than average social labour of the same kind."[1] Eventually, however, when the new method of production has been generally applied in the industry, "the difference between the individual value of the cheapened commodity and its social value" will disappear, and the extra surplus value received by the original innovator will be squeezed out.

The argument I have just considered was framed by Pareto in 1893, prior to the appearance of Volume III of *Capital*. The second and third arguments which I wish to consider were put forward in 1902, and relate to the alleged "contradiction" between Volume I and Volume III. The second argument is as follows: From the statements at the beginning of the first chapter of Volume I of *Capital*, says Pareto, it is perfectly clear that

> "the fundamental proposition of Marx's work, the proposition which establishes the equality between the measure of *value* and the quantity of labour, is demonstrated precisely for a ratio of exchange (1 quarter of corn = a kilos of iron), that is, for a *price*, if in this example the iron is regarded as money. If now there is another *value* which does not coincide with prices, there is nothing to indicate that the preceding demonstration can be applied to it, and consequently we cannot know whether or not it is *crystallised labour*. Marx demonstrates a proposition for a particular entity and applies it to another."[2]

In Volume III, Pareto proceeds, Marx lays down three conditions which have to be fulfilled if the prices at which commodities are exchanged are to correspond approximately with their values:

> "(1) The exchange of the various commodities must no longer be accidental or occasional; (2) So far as the direct exchange of commodities is concerned, these commodities must be produced on both sides in sufficient quantities to meet mutual requirements, a thing easily learned by experience in trading, and therefore a natural outgrowth of continued trading; (3) So far as selling is concerned, there must be no accidental or artificial monopoly which may enable either of the contracting sides to sell commodities above their value or compel others to sell below value. An accidental monopoly is one which a buyer or seller acquires by an accidental proportion of supply to demand."[3]

This is all very well, Pareto argues, but nobody warned us about these essential conditions when the equation "1 quarter of corn = a

---

[1] *Capital*, Vol. I, pp. 307-8.   [2] *Les Systèmes Socialistes*, Vol. II, pp. 354-5.
[3] *Capital*, Vol. III, p. 209.

kilos of iron" was put forward, and it is by reasoning *exclusively* from this equation, without any other conditions, that Marx demonstrates (or believes that he demonstrates) that *value* is crystallised labour. Once this demonstration has been made, we cannot introduce into it *new* conditions which are not included in the original statement. Then again, what does Marx's second condition mean? Either it means that "requirements" are fixed (which is not true) or are assumed by hypothesis to be fixed (which is not legitimate); or it means simply that we have returned at last to the old law of supply and demand. Having started out by rejecting this law and affirming that value is nothing but crystallised labour, our theory is now reduced to the proposition that value is measured by labour *provided* that the conditions laid down by the law of supply and demand are satisfied. Thus "we see that it is always the same process of reasoning. When certain circumstances get in our way we suppress them *by hypothesis*, doing our best to make this hypothesis pass for reality."[1]

At bottom, this is a criticism of Marx's economic method, which has already been commented upon fairly extensively above. What Pareto says, in effect, is that it is illegitimate to begin by postulating embodied labour as the substance of value, to go ahead and base one's system on this proposition, and then subsequently to make it clear that exchange ratios are actually equal to embodied labour ratios only when supply is equal to or balanced by demand. Exchange ratios are in fact determined by a whole crowd of factors, of which embodied labour is one and the relation of supply and demand is another. It is easy enough to "prove" that exchange ratios are determined by one of these factors alone if you simply assume that the other factors do not vary. And according to Pareto this is in fact all that Marx does.

But this criticism is surely not valid in the case of an economist who sets out quite consciously, as Marx did, to frame a theory of value which will apply not to all exchange ratios under all conditions but only to equilibrium exchange ratios under conditions of free competition. Marx's theory of value, like Ricardo's, was designed to explain nothing more than the level at which supply and demand tended to fix exchange ratios under such conditions. And Marx was entitled, I think, writing in 1867, to take it for granted that his readers would understand from the beginning that this was his purpose.[2] There is

---

[1] *Les Systèmes Socialistes*, Vol. II, pp. 358-9.
[2] In his more popular expositions Marx makes the point perfectly clear. See, e.g., *Value, Price and Profit* (in *Selected Works*, Vol. I, pp. 310-11).

certainly nothing in Volume I of *Capital*, whether in the "equations" which Pareto mentions or elsewhere, to suggest that he ever intended anything else. Marx began, as did Ricardo, by postulating that exchange ratios were determined by embodied labour ratios, but this postulate, naturally enough, was not unrelated to the task which the law based upon it was designed to perform. Had Marx wished to develop a "law of value" which would explain all exchange ratios under all conditions he would clearly not have been able to begin with the same postulate. Much of the confusion which has arisen on this point is due to a difference between Ricardo's terminology and that of Marx. As we have seen, Ricardo usually identified the "value" of a commodity with its equilibrium price, and argued that relative "values" in this sense were determined by relative quantities of embodied labour. Marx, on the other hand, defined the "value" of a commodity as the quantity of labour embodied in it, and argued that relative equilibrium prices were determined by relative "values" in this sense. In essence, both economists were laying down the same proposition; but Marx's terminology, being less familiar, is more liable to misinterpretation.

The third argument is as follows: In Volume I, Pareto writes, Marx assumes that the amount of profit which each capitalist receives (given the rate of exploitation) is uniquely dependent upon the quantity of variable capital which he employs. In Volume III, on the other hand, Marx tells us that in actual fact each capitalist shares in the social "pool" of profit in accordance with the total quantity of capital which he employs. How then does he resolve this apparent contradiction? Pareto's answer is somewhat surprising. Marx, he says, argues that "under the pressure of competition" the organic composition of all capitals tends towards the average, so that it is roughly equal in all branches of production. Thus "it amounts to exactly the same thing whether we say that the surplus value which the capitalist appropriates is proportionate to the variable capital which he employs, or that it is proportionate to the fraction of social capital which he puts into operation."[1]

In actual fact, of course, Marx does not argue in this way at all. Indeed, it can be said that the whole problem of the transformation of surplus value into profit (and hence of values into prices of production) which Marx dealt with in Volume III arises precisely because "the pressure of competition" does *not* tend to equalise organic

[1] *Les Systèmes Socialistes*, Vol. II, p. 369.

compositions. However, Pareto has unearthed a "proof" of his interpretation in the shape of a single sentence from chapter 10 of Volume III of *Capital*. At the beginning of this chapter, Marx draws attention to the fact that "one portion of the spheres of production has an average composition of their capitals, that is to say, their capitals have exactly or approximately the composition of the average social capital". In these spheres of production, the prices of production of commodities coincide exactly or approximately with their values as expressed in money. "Competition", Marx proceeds, "distributes the social capital in such a way between the various spheres of production that the prices of production of each sphere are formed after the model of the prices of production in these spheres of average composition, which is . . . cost-price plus the average rate of profit multiplied by the cost-price." Since this average rate of profit is simply the percentage of profit in the sphere of average composition, where profit is identical with surplus value, the rate of profit is the same in all spheres of production "It is evident", Marx writes, "that the balance between the spheres of production of different composition must tend to equalise them [i.e., put them on an equal footing in this respect—R.L.M.] with the spheres of average composition." This argument is then repeated, in a slightly different way, in the following paragraph:

"In the case of capitals of average, or approximately average, composition, the price of production coincides exactly, or approximately with the value, and the profit with the surplus-value produced by them. All other capitals, of whatever composition, tend toward this average under the pressure of competition. But since the capitals of average composition are of the same, or approximately the same, structure as the average social capital, all capitals have the tendency, regardless of the surplus-value produced by them, to realise in the prices of their commodities the average profit, instead of their own surplus-value, in other words, to realise the prices of production."[1]

Pareto tears the second sentence of this paragraph from its context, interprets it to mean that competition tends to equalise all organic compositions, and affirms that this was Marx's solution of the "contradiction". But it is perfectly clear from the context that Marx is here simply repeating the idea, which he has just expressed immediately before, that competition brings it about that prices in all spheres are

[1] *Capital*, Vol. III, pp. 204-5.

formed after the model of prices in the spheres of average composition. Pareto's interpretation, which is inconsistent with everything which precedes and everything which follows the disputed sentence,[1] is clearly quite mistaken. The most charitable conclusion to which one can come is that Pareto, in spite of his extremely arrogant tone,[2] had simply not attempted to understand Marx's argument in Part 2 of Volume III.

3. Bernstein's Critique

I pass now to the second type of attack distinguished above, dealing first with those critics who have endeavoured to improve Marx's system either by replacing the labour theory by the marginal utility theory or by "reconciling" the two theories. The most conspicuous upholders of this view were the so-called revisionists, who set the tone for much of the subsequent criticism of Marx. The name "revisionists" is something of a misnomer: it appears to imply that these critics were concerned merely to re-examine the Marxist system with a view to amending relatively minor faults. In actual fact, it is more correct to regard the revisionist movement, in effect if not in intention, as the continental counterpart of the Fabian movement in Britain— i.e., as a revolt against Marxism rather than a "revision" of it.[3] This is

[1] One need look no further than the same page for evidence of this inconsistency. In the last sentence but one before the disputed sentence, Marx speaks of the way in which equal masses of capital, "whatever may be their composition", receive aliquot shares of the total surplus value; and in the sentence which immediately follows the disputed one the phrase "regardless of the surplus-value produced by them" shows clearly that no amendment of this basic notion was intended.

[2] "It is true", Pareto writes (not uncharacteristically), "that the exegesis of the experts can always have recourse to the argument that Marx, when he said that 'all other capitals of whatever composition, tend toward this average', really meant to say that they did not tend at all toward it. Perhaps, who knows, he did not even want, in these passages, to put forward a theory of the composition of capitals; perhaps he did not want to put forward a theory of value. Nothing is impossible. It has been discovered that the *Iliad* was a prophecy about the coming of the Messiah, and that Dante's *Divine Comedy* was a kind of cryptography for the use of the Ghibellines. Similar discoveries can be made in the work of Marx. It is clear that if one admits that words can change their meaning entirely, interpretation has no longer any limits" (*Les Systèmes Socialistes*, pp. 370-1).

[3] Sweezy, in an interesting essay on Fabian Political Economy (reprinted in *The Present as History*, 1953), draws attention (pp. 319-20) to the fact that the relation between Fabianism and revisionism was rather more direct than is generally appreciated. He quotes the following passage from *The History of the Fabian Society* by E. R. Pease: "The revolt [on the Continent] came from England in the person of Edward Bernstein, who, exiled by Bismarck, took refuge in London, and was for years intimately acquainted with the Fabian Society and its leaders. Soon after his return to Germany he published in 1899 a volume criticizing Marxism and thence grew up the Revisionist movement for free thought in Socialism which has attracted all the younger men, and before the war [World War I] had virtually, if not actually, obtained control over the Social Democratic Party. In England, and in Germany through Bernstein, I think the Fabian Society may claim to have led the revolt."

certainly true of the revisionist attitude towards the labour theory of value, of which the views of Bernstein, who was generally looked upon as the leader of the movement, can perhaps be regarded as typical.

Bernstein's essay "On the Meaning of the Marxist Theory of Value", reprinted in his famous book *Die Voraussetzungen des Sozialismus und die Aufgaben der Sozialdemokratie*,[1] sets out the main line of approach which he adopted in all his writings on this subject.[2] Marx, says Bernstein, begins by stating that the value of commodities consists in the socially-necessary labour spent on them, measured according to time. But "with the analysis of this measure of value quite a series of abstractions and reductions is necessary", as a result of which (at least so far as "single commodities or a category of commodities" are concerned) "value loses every concrete quality and becomes a pure abstract concept". But what becomes of the Marxian theory of surplus value under these circumstances? It is evident, Bernstein argues, "that at the moment when labour value can claim acceptance only as a speculative formula or scientific hypothesis, surplus value would all the more become a pure formula—a formula which rests on an hypothesis".[3] One cannot escape, as Engels tried to do, by arguing that the law of value had a general historical validity from the beginnings of commodity exchange to the beginnings of capitalism,[4] since a whole series of facts ("feudal relations, undifferentiated agriculture, monopolies of guilds, etc.") "hindered the conception of a general exchange value founded on the labour time of the producers".[5] The "fact of surplus labour", however, was much clearer during this early period than it is today, and even on the threshold of the capitalist period this clarity still prevailed. On the basis of the new theory of labour as the measure of value, Adam Smith was able to represent profits and rent as deductions from labour value. But with

---

[1] The quotations below are taken from the English translation of this work which was published (under the title *Evolutionary Socialism*) by the Independent Labour Party in 1909.

[2] For other commentaries on Bernstein's critique of the Marxian system, see Robert Guihéneuf, *Le Problème de la Théorie Marxiste de la Valeur* (1952); William J. Blake, *Elements of Marxian Economic Theory and its Criticism* (1939); Louis B. Boudin, *The Theoretical System of Karl Marx in the Light of Recent Criticism* (1915); and Paul M. Sweezy, *The Theory of Capitalist Development* (1946).

[3] *Evolutionary Socialism*, pp. 28-30.

[4] *Engels on "Capital"*, pp. 101 ff. It should be noted that Engels claimed validity for the law of value only so far as *commodities* were concerned, and, as he put it, only "to the extent that economic laws are valid at all" (*ibid.*, pp. 105-6).

[5] *Evolutionary Socialism*, pp. 30-1. Cf. above, pp. 199-200, and below, pp. 288 ff.

Smith "labour value is already conceived as an abstraction from the prevailing reality", fully applicable only in the "early and rude state of society"; and "labour value serves Smith only as a 'concept' to disclose the division of the products of labour—that is the fact of surplus labour". And "in the Marxist system it is not otherwise in principle".[1] In Volume III of *Capital* "the value of individual commodities or kinds of commodities becomes something quite secondary, since they are sold at the price of their production—cost of production plus profit rate. What takes the first place is the *value of the total production of society*, and the excess of this value over the total amount of the wages of the working classes—that is, not the individual, but the total social surplus value." But "the amount of this surplus value is only realised in proportion to the relation between the total production and the total demand—*i.e.*, the buying capacity of the market." Thus taking production as a whole,

"the value of every single kind of commodity is determined by the labour time which was necessary to produce it under normal conditions of production to that amount which the market—that is the community as purchasers—can take in each case.[2] Now just for the commodities under consideration there is in reality no exact measure of the need of the community at a given moment; and thus value conceived as above is a purely abstract entity, not otherwise than the value of the final utility of the school of Gossen, Jevons, and Böhm-Bawerk. Actual relations lie at the foundation of both; but both are built up on abstractions."[3]

The Marxian concept of value, then, according to Bernstein, is "nothing more than a key, an abstract image, like the philosophical atom endowed with a soul"—a key which in Marx's hands has "led to the exposure and presentation of the mechanism of capitalist economy as this had not been hitherto treated, not so forcibly, logically, and clearly", but which in the hands of Marx's disciples has nearly always

[1] *Evolutionary Socialism*, pp. 31-3.

[2] Bernstein's point here is related to a question which, as he says, was "passionately discussed" by Marxists prior to the appearance of Volume III—"whether the attribute of 'socially necessary labour time' in labour value related only to the *manner* of the production of the respective commodities or included also the relation of the *amount* produced of these commodities to effective demand". Volume III, according to Bernstein, "gave quite a different complexion to this and other questions, forced it into another region, on to another plane" (p. 33).

[3] *Ibid.*, p. 34. Cf. p. 36, footnote, where Bernstein argues that a passage from Volume III of *Capital*, p. 745 (quoted above, p. 179) "makes it impossible to make light of the Gossen-Böhm theory with a few superior phrases."

led to disastrous results, since it "refuses service over and above a certain point".[1] Marx used the key, as did Adam Smith, to disclose the empirical fact of surplus labour. But this is a fact which is "demonstrable by experience" and "needs no deductive proof". Thus "whether the Marxist theory is correct or not is quite immaterial to the proof of surplus labour. It is in this respect no demonstration but only a means of analysis and illustration."[2]

In Bernstein's view, then, if I have interpreted his extremely diffuse argument correctly, Marx's "value" is a "pure abstract concept", quite incapable of serving as the basis for an adequate theory of exchange ratios. It must therefore be either replaced or supplemented by the marginal utility theory.[3] But the "proof of surplus labour", fortunately, does not depend upon the correctness or otherwise of the Marxist theory of exchange ratios. The fact that some people live on the labour of others is a simple fact of experience, which needs no theory of value to prove it. In the analysis and illustration of this fact of experience, however, the Marxian concept of value as embodied labour can usefully be employed as a sort of expository device.

It is certainly true that the Marxian theory of exchange ratios, like all such theories, is based on an "abstract concept", and that it coincides only approximately with reality. But this fact in itself does not prevent it from being an adequate theory, since it is of the very nature of *all* concepts that they should coincide only approximately with reality.[4] Nor does it seem to me that the suggestion that "socially-necessary labour" includes the relation of supply to effective demand is any more true when we consider the totality of commodities than when we

---

[1] *Evolutionary Socialism*, pp. 38-9.   [2] *Ibid.*, p. 35.

[3] Bernstein does not make clear the exact nature of the amendments which are required. (Cf. Guihéneuf, *op. cit.*, p. 133.) Lenin's statement that the revisionists had contributed nothing to the theory of value "apart from hints and sighs, exceedingly vague, for Böhm-Bawerk" (*Selected Works*, Vol. XI, p. 708) is certainly true of Bernstein.

[4] "The reproaches you make against the law of value", wrote Engels to Schmidt in March 1895, "apply to *all* concepts, regarded from the standpoint of reality. The identity of thought and being, to express myself in Hegelian fashion, everywhere coincides with your example of the circle and the polygon. Or the two of them, the concept of a thing and its reality, run along side by side like two asymptotes, always approaching each other and yet never meeting. This difference between the two is the very difference which prevents the concept from being, forthwith and immediately, reality, and reality from being immediately its own concept. Though a concept has the essential nature of a concept and cannot therefore *prima facie* coincide with reality forthwith, from which it must first be abstracted, it is still something more than a fiction, unless you are going to declare all the results of thought fictions because reality has to make a long detour before it corresponds to them, and even then only with asymptotic approximation" (*Engels on "Capital"*, pp. 137-8). Cf. *ibid.*, p. 100: "The law of value has a far greater and more definite significance for capitalist production than that of a mere hypothesis, not to mention a fiction, even though a necessary one."

consider individual commodities[1]—in which case the fact that "there is in reality no exact measure of the need of the community at a given moment" cannot properly be adduced as a factor removing the law of value one stage further from reality. Then again, while it is perfectly true that the existence of unearned income is a fact of experience which needs no theory of value to prove it, it does not by any means follow that a *theory of distribution* can do without a theory of value. A "theory of distribution" which said only that unearned income was the fruit of the surplus labour of those employed in production would hardly qualify as a *theory* at all; and the mere fact that it ex- pressed input and output in terms of embodied labour would not make it any more likely to qualify as one. At the best, such a "theory" could be little more than a generalised description of the appropriation by the owners of the means of production, in all types of class society, of the product of the surplus labour of the exploited classes. But surely there are two salient points which a theory of distribution appropriate to our own times should concentrate on explaining: First, how is it that unearned incomes continue to be received in a society in which the prices of the great majority of commodities are determined on an impersonal market by the forces of supply and demand, and in which the relation between the direct producer and his employer is based on contract rather than on status? And second, how are the respective shares of the main social classes in the national income determined in such a society? Unless one is content to rely on some sort of explanation in terms of "force" or "struggle" (in which case again one could only with difficulty speak of a *theory* of distribution), it is impossible to give adequate answers to these questions without basing one's account on a theory of value.[2]

4. *The Critiques of Lindsay and Croce*

Something must now be said about those critics who argue that the labour theory of value, although invalid when considered as a theory of actual market prices, performs a special role in Marx's system quite different from that which other theories of value perform in

[1] See above, pp. 167-8 and 178-9.

[2] Cf. the interesting comments made by Croce on a book by Graziadei, who also apparently proposed "to examine profits independently of the theory of value." The fallacy of such a course, Croce maintains, "ought to be clearly evident at a glance, without its being necessary to wait for proof from the results of the attempt. A system of economics from which *value* is omitted, is like logic without the *concept*, ethics without *duty*, æsthetics without *expression*. It is economics . . . cut off from its proper sphere" (*Historical Material- ism and the Economics of Karl Marx*, London, 1914, p. 138).

theirs. Some critics, for example, of whom Lindsay may perhaps be taken as typical, have suggested that the labour theory of value is primarily a theory of natural right rather than a theory of prices. It is true, Lindsay agrees, that the labour theory of value "claims to be in some degree at least a theory of how market prices are determined. But the careful reader will soon find out that the market prices so explained are not actual existing prices, but the prices which would prevail under highly abstract conditions."[1] These assumed conditions are those which would prevail in a society so organised that things would fetch what they were "really" worth—a society, that is, "where a *man* gets what he is worth". The labour theory, in other words, is "concerned not with actual but with ideal prices"; it is "primarily interested in what a man ought to get in reward for his labour".[2]

One difficulty standing in the way of this interpretation has to be disposed of by Lindsay at the outset. If the labour theory was for Marx a "natural rights theory", just as it was for the individualists, how does this square with the fact that Marx's economic method was "historical" in character? "A natural rights theory and historical method", says Lindsay, "do not go well together."[3] Lindsay's answer is based upon an interpretation of part of the following sentence in chapter 1 of *Capital*: "The secret of the expression of value, namely, that all kinds of labour are equal and equivalent because, and so far as, they are human labour in general, cannot be deciphered *until the notion of human equality has already acquired the fixity of a popular prejudice*."[4] This shows, according to Lindsay, that "the labour theory of value was the application to economics of the principle of human equality". Now "Marx's case for the inevitable transformation of capitalism into collectivism entirely depends upon the assumption that the notion of human equality will be strong enough to overcome the inequalities produced by the buying and selling of labour power". Thus Marx "is able at one and the same time to use the labour theory

---

[1] A. D. Lindsay, *Karl Marx's "Capital"* (London, 1925), pp. 57-8.

[2] *Ibid.*, p. 61. (My italics.)   [3] *Ibid.*, p. 66.

[4] *Capital*, Vol. I, p. 29 (my italics). The sentence occurs in the course of a comment on Aristotle's failure to see that "to attribute value to commodities, is merely a mode of expressing all labour as equal human labour, and consequently as labour of equal quality". Greek society, says Marx, "was founded upon slavery, and had, therefore, for its natural basis, the inequality of men and their labour powers". The "deciphering" mentioned in the sentence quoted in the text "is possible only in a society in which the great mass of the produce of labour takes the form of commodities, in which, consequently, the dominant relation between man and man, is that of owners of commodities."

of value as a natural rights theory and as an account of what is actually happening, because the claim of right which the theory embodies is one of the elements operative in the actual situation which he, as an economic historian, is describing".[1]

Marx's statement of the theory in the first six chapters of *Capital*, according to Lindsay, although it is taken over from that of his "individualist" predecessors, differs in at least one important respect from theirs—in Marx's "insistence that [the labour which creates value] must be socially necessary labour, and his reiterated statement that value is a social product".[2] The concept of social necessity "transforms the labour theory of value into something not unlike the ordinary theory of the interplay of supply and demand", since the quantity of labour "socially necessary" for the production of a commodity depends (*inter alia*) upon the varying success with which the producers have "anticipated the amount and the kind of the demand for commodities".[3] And the idea that "value is a social product and comes into being only as a result of all the processes necessary to the production of wealth in society" allegedly takes Marx further and further away from "the conception of the individual labourer stamping value on his commodity[,] so much value for every minute of work".[4] Marx's "main discovery", in fact, was "that value was a social product, and that in that social product the social relations involved in production are as important as, but essentially different from, the social relations involved in exchange".[5] In modern society, the economic unit which makes and exchanges commodities is no longer the individual labourer, but what Marx calls the "collective labourer"—i.e., a group of labourers, of different specialities, involved in a series of integrated processes.[6] This means, according to Lindsay, that

"some of the value produced is produced by the association, not by its separate members, and the attempt to represent the price of the commodity as an amount of separate values created by the labour of the separate individuals concerned must break down. Some at least of the total value is created in common and, on the principle of justice which inspired the labour theory of value, ought to find a common, not a distributed reward. The labour theory of value and Marx's doctrine that value is a social product

[1] Lindsay, *op. cit.*, p. 66. [2] *Ibid.*, p. 71.

[3] *Ibid.*, p. 79. I omit here Lindsay's consideration of the question of the reduction of skilled to unskilled labour, which is based on the familiar assumption that Marx "look[s] up the answer at the end of the book, and then cook[s] the sum to fit" (p. 75).

[4] *Ibid.*, p. 78. [5] *Ibid.*, p. 95. [6] See *Capital*, Vol. I, pp. 333 ff.

are not really consistent with one another. Once the latter doctrine is taken seriously, the assumptions essential for the former no longer hold. The labour theory of value, regarded as a principle for determining the just reward of individuals, ends, like the good dialectical principle that it is, in transcending itself, in showing that there cannot be justice for individuals unless their claim to be regarded as separate individuals, each with an absolute right to a definite reward, is given up."[1]

Thus the claim of right which the individualistic theory of value embodies "can only be realized according to Marx when the anarchy of individualism is exchanged for a true society".[2]

In view of the number of occasions on which Marx insisted that the labour theory was actually "the scientific expression of the economic relations of present-day society", and *not* "the regenerating formula of the future" which Proudhon and others were claiming it to be,[3] it is surprising that so little evidence is offered by Lindsay to support the view that Marx in fact meant the exact opposite of what he so frequently said. One wonders, too, why Marx should have gone to such trouble to demonstrate that relative quantities of embodied labour still ultimately determined equilibrium exchange ratios even under developed capitalism, if his theory of value was for him "a statement of the conditions under which the producer would get his just reward".[4] It is difficult not to feel sympathetic towards Lindsay's sincere attempt to make sense out of an idea which must have appeared to him at first sight as nonsensical, but it has to be recognised that his account is based on a whole series of serious misinterpretations. For example, to support his basic idea that Marx's labour theory was a "natural rights theory", Lindsay lays considerable stress on a passage in which Marx describes simple commodity production as "a very Eden of the innate rights of man", in which "alone rule Freedom, Equality, Property and Bentham", and in which all "work together to their mutual advantage", in accordance with "the pre-established harmony of things, or under the auspices of an all-shrewd providence".[5] Marx could hardly have done more here than he actually did to warn his readers against taking this obviously ironical passage too literally, but apparently he did not do enough. Suffice it to say that Marx's belief in the "innate rights of man", in the

[1] Lindsay, *op. cit.*, pp. 106-7.   [2] *Ibid.*, p. 117.
[3] Marx, *The Poverty of Philosophy* (English edn.), p. 59.
[4] Lindsay, *op. cit.*, pp. 79-80.   [5] *Capital*, Vol. I, p. 155.

"pre-established harmony of things", and in an "all-shrewd providence" was scarcely strong enough to warrant the conclusion which Lindsay draws from this passage. Then again, the passage referred to above[1] where Marx says quite clearly that the discovery of the law which regulated the relative exchange values of commodities could not precede the development of "the notion of human equality" is interpreted by Lindsay to mean that Marx makes the principle of human equality "a standard operative within the economic facts themselves".[2] Lindsay's exact meaning here is not quite clear. If he means that Marx believed that the actual exchange of commodities in accordance with embodied labour ratios was the result (at least in part) of a conscious application of the principle of human equality to the determination of exchange ratios, then it must be said that this does not follow at all from what Marx wrote, and is quite inconsistent with his whole attitude. If, on the other hand, Lindsay means simply that Marx was here giving overt expression to the view that the labour theory tells us only under what conditions a commodity will fetch what it is really worth, then once again this does not follow from what Marx actually said. To say that a particular economic law could not have been discovered prior to the development of a particular ethico-political concept is by no means to say that the law itself is an analysis of what ought to be rather than what is.[3] Similarly, Lindsay's interpretations of the concepts of socially-necessary labour and of value as a social product seem to me to be quite mistaken. The notion that Marx admitted that the quantity of socially-necessary labour required to produce a unit of any commodity was dependent upon demand conditions has already been sufficiently discussed above.[4] And Marx's concept of value as a social product surely means something quite different from what Lindsay suggests. Lindsay in effect takes it to mean that the value of a commodity is something conferred upon it not by an individual labourer but rather by the "collective labourer". "The value-producing qualities, which in the simple abstract theory of Locke's theme and the individualists' variation upon it are concentrated in the individual producer, are in a developed society distributed. The skill, the foresight, and the direction, which

[1] P. 216.

[2] Lindsay, op. cit., p. 66. Cf. Engels, Anti-Dühring, p. 119, footnote.

[3] The typical situation assumed by Marx is one in which exchange ratios are determined by the operation of objective economic forces which work independently of the will of man, and not by feelings on the part of the individuals concerned as to what constitutes a "just reward" for productive activities.

[4] See above, pp. 167-8 and 178-9.

were once its accompaniment, are now divorced from labour."[1] The "social relation" which Marx primarily had in mind when he spoke of value as a social relation, however, was undoubtedly the simple relation which exists between commodity producers as such—in other words, the relation lying behind what Lindsay curiously refers to as the "very slight social bond" constituted by exchange in a commodity-producing society.[2] And finally, the replacement of the individual by the collective labourer does not necessitate any basic amendment of the labour theory, any more than does, say, the introduction of a new machine or any other innovation which results in an increase in productivity. The collective labourer produces the same quantity of value as the individual labourers formerly did in the same time, but this value is now distributed among a greater output of commodities. In other words, when productivity increases the unit value of commodities falls.

Croce's critique of the labour theory has important elements in common with that of Lindsay,[3] but seems to me to be very much more competent. *Capital*, says Croce, so far as its *method* is concerned, is "without doubt an *abstract* investigation"—in other words, the capitalist society studied by Marx is not this or that historically existing society, but "an ideal and formal society, deduced from certain hypotheses, which could indeed never have occurred as actual facts in the course of history", but which "correspond to a great extent to the historical conditions of the modern civilised world".[4] And so far as its *scope* is concerned, Marx's investigation is limited to "one special economic system, that which occurs in a society with private property in capital". But "even when these two points are settled, the real essence of Marx's investigation is not yet explained".[5] The main difficulty arises because Marx began by assuming a proposition "outside the field of pure economic theory"—i.e., "the proposition that the value of the commodities produced by labour is equal to the quantity of labour socially necessary to produce them"—and never explicitly stated the connection between this proposition and the laws of capitalist society.[6] After reviewing briefly the suggestions made in this connection by such writers as Sombart, Schmidt, Engels,

---

[1] Lindsay, *op. cit.*, p. 96.   [2] *Ibid.*, p. 101.

[3] The important element of *difference* is that Croce (in Lindsay's words) "maintains that Marx's theory of value is economic and not moral". See Lindsay's preface to Croce's *Historical Materialism and the Economics of Karl Marx* (London, 1914), p. xxi. Croce's main statement on this point will be found on pp. 58-9.

[4] Croce, *op. cit.*, p. 50.   [5] *Ibid.*, pp. 50-1.   [6] *Ibid.*, pp. 52-3.

Sorel, and Labriola, Croce summarises his own views as follows:

"Marx's labour-value is not only a logical generalisation, it is also *a fact conceived and postulated as typical*, *i.e.* something more than a mere logical concept. Indeed it has not the inertia of the abstract but the force of a concrete fact,[1] which has in regard to capitalist society, in Marx's investigation, the function of a term of comparison, of a standard, of a *type*.

"This standard or type being postulated, the investigation, for Marx, takes the following form. Granted that value is equal to the labour socially necessary, it is required to show *with what divergencies from this standard* the prices of commodities are fixed in capitalist society, and how labour-power itself acquires a price and becomes a commodity. To speak plainly, Marx stated the problem in unappropriate language; he represented this typical value itself, postulated by him as a standard, as being the *law* governing the economic phenomena of capitalist society. And it is the law, if he likes, but in the *sphere of his conceptions*, not *in economic reality*. We may conceive the divergencies from a standard as the revolt of reality when confronted by this standard which we have endowed with the dignity of law."[2]

This method is *formally* justifiable, Croce continues, but this is not enough: the *standard itself* needs justification—"*i.e.* we need to decide what meaning and importance it may have for us".[3] It is absurd to suggest, as some (e.g., Lindsay) have done, that "the equivalence of value and labour is an ideal of social ethics, a *moral ideal*". Nothing could be imagined, says Croce, "more mistaken in itself and farther from Marx's thought than this interpretation".[4] The real meaning of Marx's standard is described by Croce as follows:

"Let us . . . take account, in a society, only of what is properly economic life, *i.e.* out of the whole society, only of *economic society*. Let us abstract from this latter all goods which cannot be increased by labour. Let us abstract further all class distinctions, which may be regarded as accidental in reference to the general concept of economic society. Let us leave out of account all modes of distributing the wealth produced, which, as we have said, can only be determined on grounds of convenience or perhaps of justice, but

---

[1] Croce adds the following footnote at this point: "It must be carefully noticed that what I call a *concrete fact* may still not be a fact which is empirically real, but a fact made by us hypothetically and *entirely imaginary*, or a fact *partially empirical*, *i.e.* existing partially in empirical reality. We shall see later on that Marx's typical premise belongs properly to this second class."

[2] *Ibid.*, pp. 56–7.   [3] *Ibid.*, p. 58.   [4] *Ibid.*

in any case upon considerations belonging to society as a whole, and never from considerations belonging exclusively to economic society. What is left after these successive abstractions have been made? Nothing but *economic society in so far as it is a working society*. And in this society without class distinctions, *i.e.* in an economic society as such and whose only commodities are the products of labour, what can value be? Obviously the sum of the efforts, *i.e.* the quantity of labour, which the production of the various kinds of commodities demands. And, since we are here speaking of the economic social organism, and not of the individual persons living in it, it follows that this labour cannot be reckoned except by averages, and hence as labour *socially* (it is with society, I repeat, that we are here dealing) *necessary*.

"Thus labour-value would appear as that determination of value peculiar to economic society as such, when regarded only in so far as it produces commodities capable of being increased by labour.

"From this definition the following corollary may be drawn: the determination of labour value *will have a positive conformity with facts as long as a society exists, which produces goods by means of labour*. . . .

". . . But, of what kind is this conformity? Having ruled out (1) that it is a question of a moral ideal, and (2) that it is a question of scientific law; and having nevertheless concluded that this equivalence is a *fact* (which Marx uses as a type), we are obliged to say, as the only alternative, that *it is a fact, but a fact which exists in the midst of other facts; i.e. a fact that appears to us empirically as opposed, limited, distorted by other facts*, almost like a force amongst other forces, which produces a resultant different from what it would produce if the other forces ceased to act. *It is not a completely dominant fact but neither is it non-existent and merely imaginary.*"[1]

Thus Marx, "in postulating as *typical* the equivalence between value and labour and in applying it to capitalist society, was, as it were, making a comparison between capitalist society and a part of itself, isolated and raised up to an independent existence: *i.e.* a comparison between capitalist society and economic society as such (but only in so far as it is a working society)".[2] It was by virtue of this method that Marx was able to discover and define the social origin of surplus value. "Surplus value in pure economics is a meaningless word, as is evident from the term itself; since a *surplus value* is an *extra value*, and thus falls outside the sphere of pure economics. But it rightly has meaning and is no absurdity, as a *concept of difference*, in comparing

[1] Croce, *op. cit.*, pp. 60-2.   [2] *Ibid.*, p. 64.

one economic society with another, one fact with another, or two hypotheses with one another."[1] It was also by virtue of the same premise that Marx was able to arrive at the proposition that under capitalism *"value* does not correspond with *price"* in the great majority of cases.[2] It follows from all this, according to Croce, that "alongside . . . of the Marxian investigation, there can, or rather must, exist and flourish a general economic science, which may determine a concept of value, deducing it from quite different and more comprehensive principles than the special ones of Marx."[3] Nevertheless it must be admitted that Marx "teaches us, although it is with statements approximate in content and paradoxical in form, to penetrate to what society is in its *actual truth"*, whereas in the case of many of the economic purists "concrete reality, *i.e.* the very world in which we live and move, and which it concerns us somewhat to know, slips out, unseizable, from the broad-meshed net of abstractions and hypotheses".[4]

Now it is certainly true, and important, that Marx began by considering commodity-producing society as such, in abstraction from "all class distinctions"; and it is also true that there is a certain sense—although only a rather tenuous one—in which his subsequent analysis can be described as a sort of "comparison" between this abstract society and a fully-fledged (though "ideal") capitalist society. As I have suggested above,[5] Marx's enquiry into the way in which the labour theory operated was in essence an enquiry into the way in which the basic relation between men as producers of commodities (a relation conceived as persisting throughout the whole period of commodity production) exerts its influence on relations of exchange as the capitalist economic system succeeds those systems which went before it. It will be evident, however, that my own interpretation differs in certain important respects from that of Croce. It seems to me, for example, that Croce's analysis of Marx's method is fundamentally defective. Marx's researches, he says, "are not historical, but hypothetical and abstract, *i.e.* theoretical".[6] He finds it "strange" that Engels should in one and the same chapter (of *Anti-Dühring*) state both that economics in the Marxian sense is "essentially a *historical* science" and that Marx wrote *"theoretical economics"*.[7] But the two statements are surely quite consistent with one another when considered in the

---

[1] Croce, *op. cit.*, pp. 64-5. Cf. pp. 125 ff.   [2] *Ibid.*, p. 65.

[3] *Ibid.*, p. 68. Cf. pp. 76 and 124-5.   [4] *Ibid.*, p. 118.

[5] Pp. 151 ff.   [6] *Ibid.*, p. 67.

[7] *Ibid.*, p. 67, footnote. Croce's quotations from *Anti-Dühring* appear on pp. 165 and 169 of the English edn. of the latter work.

light of the accounts given by Engels himself of the logical-historical method which he and Marx followed.[1] Croce's failure to see this pervades—and up to a point invalidates—his whole thesis. In particular, if he had realised that Marx's logical analysis was intended to be a sort of "corrected mirror-image" of an actual historical process of development, he would not have spoken as if Marx had done little more than make a mere *comparison* between the determination of value in a "working society" and in a capitalist society. According to Croce, Marx postulates "labour-value" as fundamental, since it is the determination of value peculiar to economic society as such (when regarded only as a "working society"), and then shows "*with what divergencies from this standard* the prices of commodities are fixed in capitalist society".[2] A vital fact is here omitted from consideration— that Marx not only "compared" the one form of society with the other, but argued that the law of value which was *directly* operative in the first was still *indirectly* operative in the second. It was not just a question of demonstrating that values diverged from prices under capitalism, but of showing that the very extent of these divergencies was itself determined in terms of the original theory. In other words, what was involved was not a logical *comparison* between values and prices of production, but a logical (and historical) *transformation* of values into prices of production.

Most of the other criticisms which can be made of Croce's interpretation spring from this source. For example, there is his suggestion that surplus value (a "meaningless word", allegedly, in pure economics) rightly has meaning in Marx's system "as a *concept of difference*, in comparing one economic society with another". The law of surplus value, Croce argues, together with the law of value, the law of average profit, etc., are not to be "looked upon as *laws actually working in the economic world*, but as *the results of comparative investigations into different possible* forms of economic society".[3] If a capitalist society is considered "by itself" ("which is precisely what the pure economists do and ought to do"), the profits of the capitalists appear as "a result of mutual agreement, arising out of different comparative degrees of utility". You can only assert the "expropriatory character of profit", Croce

---

[1] See, e.g., pp. 148-9 above.

[2] "It is a usual method of scientific analysis," writes Croce, "to regard a phenomenon not only as it exists, but also as it would be if one of its factors were altered, and, in comparing the hypothetical with the real phenomenon, to conceive the first as diverging from the second, which is postulated as fundamental, or the second as diverging from the first, which is postulated in the same manner" (p. 57).

[3] *Ibid.*, p. 143.

argues, when you apply to a capitalist society, "almost like a chemical reagent, the standard, which, on the other hand, is characteristic of a type of society founded on human equality".[1] It is true, I suppose, that when one speaks of the "expropriatory character" of a class income, meaning thereby to condemn its receipt, one is often implicitly comparing the state of affairs in which this income exists with another state of affairs in which it does not or would not exist. But it does not follow from this that the concept of profit as the product of surplus labour is a "concept of difference" in any sense other than that in which *all* concepts can be described as "concepts of difference".[2] This concept has been accepted in the past by many thinkers who were far from "comparing" (in any special sense of this word) the state of society to which it seemed appropriate with any other state of society. They looked at capitalism "by itself", and saw that certain people received an income without working for it. If they made any "comparison", it was not between this state of society and another in which nobody received any "unearned" income, but rather between the situation of the majority of people under capitalism (who had to work for their income) and that of the minority (who did not). The fact that the rich lived off the labour of the poor seemed to them self-evident—and, incidentally, a matter for congratulation rather than for condemnation. It is certainly true, as Croce says, that in the "pure economics" of our own times surplus value is a meaningless phrase, but it has only become so because this "pure economics" has tended to abstract from those social relations of production with which Classical (and Marxian) political economy began. The concepts of profit in "pure economics" do not differ in *status* from the concept of profit as surplus value: no one of them is any more a "concept of difference" than any other. If one employs the concept of surplus value, one is certainly approaching the phenomenon of profit from a point of view different from that of the "pure economists", but one is not trying to solve an essentially different problem.

5. *The Critiques of Lange, Schlesinger and Joan Robinson*

Finally we come to the third type of critique, which is particularly fashionable at the present time—the type which rejects the view that a "theory of value" in the Classical, Marxian or Mengerian sense is

---

[1] Croce, *op. cit.*, pp. 126-7.

[2] The concepts of "bigness", "badness", "X-ness", etc., are "concepts of difference" in the sense that their meaning is dependent upon an implicit comparison with the concepts "smallness", "goodness", "not-X-ness", etc.

necessary (whether in Marx's system or anyone else's), and which concentrates on demonstrating that the labour theory, so far from being the indispensable tool which many Marxists claim it to be, is in fact a useless and even harmful excrescence upon Marx's system. It is admitted by most of those who adopt this line that Marxian economics is greatly superior to "bourgeois" economics in explaining the phenomena of economic *evolution*, but this superiority is said to be not at all due to the "outdated" labour theory of value, which is in fact (to quote Lange) "the cause of the inferiority of Marxian economics in many fields".[1] It is due rather to what Lange calls "an exact specification of the institutional (or, if the reader prefers the expression, sociological) data which form the framework in which the economic process works in Capitalist society".[2]

Lange's argument is roughly as follows. The superiority of Marxian economics, he claims, is only a partial one. There are some problems before which Marxian economics is "quite powerless", while "bourgeois" economics "solves them easily". Clearly the relative merits of the two systems belong to different "ranges". "Marxian economics", Lange says, "can work the economic evolution of capitalist society into a consistent theory from which its necessity is deduced, while 'bourgeois' economists get no further than mere historical description. On the other hand, 'bourgeois' economics is able to grasp the phenomena of the every-day life of a capitalist economy in a manner that is far superior to anything the Marxists can produce."[3] Further, "the anticipations which can be deduced from the two types of economic theory refer to a different range of time"—Marxism to the long period and "bourgeois" economics to the short period. This difference between the explanatory value of the two systems of thought is accounted for by the fact that modern "bourgeois" economic theory is "essentially a *static* theory of economic equilibrium analysing the economic process under a system of constant *data* and the mechanism by which prices and quantities produced adjust themselves to changes in these data". The data themselves, which are psychological, technical and institutional, are regarded as outside the scope of economic theory. Further, "the institutional data of the theory are not specified". In fact,

---

[1] O. Lange, "Marxian Economics and Modern Economic Theory" (*Review of Economic Studies*, June 1935), p. 196. Judging from Lange's recent article on *The Economic Laws of Socialist Society in the Light of Joseph Stalin's Last Work* (translated in *International Economic Papers*, No. 4, 1954), it seems likely that he no longer holds the views expressed in his 1935 article. The latter remains, however, one of the best short statements of an attitude which has achieved considerable popularity.

[2] *Ibid.*, p. 189.   [3] *Ibid.*, p. 191.

"in so far as the theory of economic equilibrium is merely a theory of distribution of scarce resources between different uses it does not need any institutional data at all, for the relevant considerations can be deduced from the example of Robinson Crusoe". Marxian economics, on the other hand, is distinguished by making the specification of a particular institutional datum—"the existence of a class of people who do not possess any means of production"—the very corner-stone of its analysis; and by providing "not only a theory of economic equilibrium, but also a theory of economic evolution".[1] The real source of the superiority of Marxian economics lies in the field of explaining and anticipating a process of economic evolution; and "it is not the specific economic concepts used by Marx, but the definite specification of the institutional framework in which the economic process goes on in capitalist society that makes it possible to establish a theory of economic evolution different from mere historical description".[2]

Most orthodox Marxists, however, according to Lange, "believe that their superiority in understanding the evolution of Capitalism is due to the economic concepts with which Marx worked, i.e. to his using the labour theory of value. They think that the abandonment of the classical labour theory of value in favour of the theory of marginal utility is responsible for the failure of 'bourgeois' economics to explain the fundamental phenomena of capitalist evolution."[3] But in this they are wrong. For the labour theory is "nothing but a static theory of general economic equilibrium". In essence, it is "as static as the modern theory of economic equilibrium, for it explains price and production equilibrium only under the assumption of certain data (i.e. a given amount of labour such as is necessary to produce a commodity—an amount determined by the technique of production)".[4] Nor is the theory "based on more specialised institutional assumptions than the modern theory of economic equilibrium; it holds not only in a capitalist economy, but in any exchange economy in which there is free competition".[5] Thus the labour theory "cannot possibly be the source of the superiority of Marxian over 'bourgeois' economics in explaining the phenomena of economic *evolution*".[6]

---

[1] O. Lange, *op. cit.*, pp. 191-2.   [2] *Ibid.*, p. 194.

[3] *Ibid.*, p. 194.   [4] *Ibid.*

[5] *Ibid.*, pp. 194-5; and see also pp. 197-8. In a capitalist economy the theory is of course subject, as Lange notes, to "certain modifications due to differences in the organic composition of capital".

[6] *Ibid.*, p. 195.

A Marxist must of course recognise that Lange's suggestion that "'bourgeois' economics" can deal with "the phenomena of the every-day life of a capitalist economy" in a superior manner to "Marxian economics" contains an important element of truth.[1] It is perfectly true that "bourgeois" economists have in general been more diligent and perceptive in writing about such matters as money, credit, taxation, etc., than Marxian economists. One sometimes wonders, however, whether those "bourgeois" economists who try to "provide a scientific basis for rational measures to be taken in the current administration of the capitalist economy"[2] normally gain a great deal of inspiration from the *general* theory of "bourgeois" economics—i.e., from the "static theory of economic equilibrium" which Lange so accurately describes. One wonders, too, whether it would not be more useful, even when dealing only with these every-day short-period phenomena, to start with a theory which makes the specification of "the existence of a class of people who do not possess any means of production" the very corner-stone of its analysis, rather than with a theory which omits altogether to specify this rather vital "institutional datum".[3] But even if we accept Lange's implicit denial of the relevance of the "institutional datum" to these short-term problems, is it quite so easy to deny its relevance to *the problem of distribution*? This, it seems to me, is the really important point here. Lange claims, in effect, that a number of the familiar propositions concerning *the evolution of capitalism* can be deduced without the intervention of the labour theory of value (or, indeed, of any theory of value), provided that the "institutional datum" is exactly specified— a claim which may, I think, at least up to a point, be conceded. From this Lange concludes that "the superiority of Marxian economics *in analysing Capitalism* is not due to . . . the labour theory of value".[4] But Marx's analysis of capitalism consists of much more than those

---

[1] Some of the instances which Lange gives of the alleged inferiority of Marxian to "bourgeois" economics, however, seem to me to be illusory. For example, to Lange's question (p. 191) "What can Marxian economics say about monopoly prices?", a Marxist may justifiably answer that so far as *general* laws of monopoly price are concerned it can say just as much—or as little—as "bourgeois" economics. And to his question "What can Marxian economics contribute to the problem of the optimum distribution of productive resources in a socialist economy?", a Marxist might answer that it can at least contribute a knowledge of the fact that this would probably not be the basic economic problem in a socialist economy. Similarly, one cannot accept Lange's some-what cavalier brushing aside of the Marxian theory of crisis, and his suggestion that its "failure" is due to the fact that the labour theory of value cannot explain deviations from equilibrium prices (p. 196).

[2] O. Lange, *op. cit.*, p. 191, footnote.   [3] Cf. *ibid.*, p. 200.

[4] *Ibid.*, p. 201. (My italics.)

propositions concerning the evolution of capitalism which Lange discusses. It would be misleading to say that it consists of a "static" part, in which the anatomy of capitalism as such is considered, and a "dynamic" part, in which the "laws of motion" of capitalism are revealed. Any such sharp distinction between the statics and the dynamics of the subject would have been just as alien to Marx's method as it was to Ricardo's. But it does consist of a general study of a developing organism, in which a consideration of what may be called the essential structure of that organism plays an important part. The study includes, in other words, an account of the laws of production and distribution characteristic of capitalism in its various stages of development. And a theory of distribution, if it is to be useful, must be based upon some sort of theory of value. What kind of considerations, then, should guide our choice of an appropriate theory of value? Surely one of the main criteria is that it should be capable of serving as the basis for a theory of distribution which does not abstract from the vital fact of "the existence of a class of people who do not possess any means of production". It is precisely this fact which the "bourgeois" theories of distribution do tend to abstract from; and it is precisely this fact which the Marxian theory, based as it is upon the labour theory of value, brings right to the forefront of the analysis. It is not a sufficient answer to this to say, as Lange does, that the "fact of exploitation" can be deduced without the help of the labour theory of value.[1] If the relations of production specific to capitalism do indeed determine the forms of distribution under capitalism, one's results are much more likely to be useful if one starts by considering distribution *in terms of* these relations of production, than if one starts from a theory which abstracts from them, and then, having arrived at a broad general result applicable to any type of economy, simply tacks on to it the "institutional datum" peculiar to capitalism.

In so far as "most orthodox Marxists" believe that the superiority of Marxian economics is "due to" its use of the labour theory of value, then, this is no doubt one of the main considerations which they have in mind. But it is not quite correct to ascribe to Marxists (whether "orthodox" or otherwise) the view that "the abandonment of the classical labour theory of value in favour of the theory of marginal utility is *responsible for* the failure of 'bourgeois' economics to explain the fundamental phenomena of capitalist evolution".[2] Rather, Marxists

[1] O. Lange, *op. cit.*, p. 195, footnote 3.   [2] My italics.

think that the marginal utility theory was the generalised expression of a new approach to economic phenomena, the essence of which was a tendency to abstract from the relations of production; and that it was this new approach which was responsible for the failure of the new "bourgeois" economics adequately to explain the "fundamental phenomena" both of distribution under capitalism and of the evolution of the capitalist system as a whole. The labour theory, on the other hand, is the generalised expression of an approach which emphasises the determining role of the relations of production in economic processes, and which therefore regards it as quite unsafe to abstract from them; and it is precisely this, in the Marxian view, which explains the relative success of Marxian economics in dealing with the "fundamental phenomena" of distribution and evolution under capitalism.

A more sophisticated (although less comprehensible) variant of Lange's theme has recently been put forward by Rudolf Schlesinger. The argument of the founders of Marxism, Schlesinger suggests, is burdened with "assumptions on the theory of prices which were current in their days but unnecessary for the argument itself".[1] Like Lange, he maintains that all the really valuable and essential tenets of *Capital* can be derived without the assistance of the labour theory of value. In his famous letter to Kugelmann,[2] says Schlesinger, "Marx dealt with the theory of value in a way which hardly implies more than the conception of social labour as the basic relation existing between the members of a society founded upon commodity exchange; and the basic tenets of Vol. I of *Capital* can be derived from that conception".[3] Similarly, speaking more specifically of "the fundamental Marxist tenets about the trend of capitalist development", Schlesinger argues that these are based on "a few fairly safe assumptions", viz:

"(1) The distribution of social labour between the various industries represents the basic relation existing between the members of a society based upon commodity exchange.

"(2) The various products of human labour are exchanged against each other at rates (prices) which tend to an equilibrium state which can be defined as a function of (though it is not necessarily proportionate to) the average productivity of labour applied in the different spheres of production.

[1] Schlesinger, *Marx: His Time and Ours* (London, 1950), p. 110.
[2] Quoted above, p. 153.   [3] Schlesinger, *op. cit.*, p. 119.

"(3) Competition puts a premium upon application of above-average means of production, and threatens with destitution the producer who does not succeed in keeping pace."

The first of these assumptions, Schlesinger continues, "is identical with the definition of the subject of economics, and is backed by the consideration that changes in the technique and productivity of human labour are a much more promising subject for investigating the trends in history than alleged changes in the scarcity of diamonds or artistic qualifications. It does *not* imply the assumption that this basic relation is the only one affecting prices. Nor is the second assumption dependent upon the derivation of the function in a way satisfactory from the economic and mathematical point of view; no more need be assumed than the fact, admitted as much by Marshall as by Marxists, that the long-term trends of prices are dominated by costs, and that labour is by far the most important element of costs." Given these assumptions, Schlesinger argues, the "fundamental Marxist tenets about the trend of capitalist development" follow "from elementary data".[1]

Schlesinger is much more specific than Lange on the question of the actual role which the labour theory plays, and ought to play, in Marx's system. We should not drop the argument of the founders as unnecessary, he argues, simply because in our own time certain non-Marxists "can recognise many facts predicted by Marx and draw from them inferences as to the need for social change, although they do not accept the Marxist methodology which enabled those facts to be forecast. What appears essential to me in this methodology is the definition of the subject of economics contained in the so-called theory of value and the dynamic approach to it."[2] The point Schlesinger appears to be trying to make here is better expressed in another place as follows: "If economics is defined as the material relations existing between men working for each other, the amount of work done for each other is the basic economic fact linking them, and any other economic fact has to be derived from it."[3] In other words, the "qualitative" aspect of the Marxian labour theory (to use Sweezy's expression) constitutes the essence of the Marxian methodology, and should on no account be "dropped as unnecessary" —although Marxists should cease using the term "value" to describe something which is really nothing more than a definition of the subject of economics. But the "quantitative" aspect of the theory, according

[1] Schlesinger, *op. cit.*, pp. 110-11.　　[2] *Ibid.*, p. 110.　　[3] *Ibid.*, p. 106.

to Schlesinger, is much more shaky. Marx, as we know, endeavoured to show that the "amount of work done for each other" actually determined the relative equilibrium prices of the commodities produced—even under capitalism, when commodities admittedly no longer tend to sell "at their values". Marx evidently believed that it was very important to be able to demonstrate this. According to Schlesinger, however, he was mistaken both in his belief that it was necessary to demonstrate it, and in his belief that his own demonstration of it was satisfactory. From the point of view of Marx's fundamental analysis of the laws of motion dominating the changing relations between the different classes of society, Schlesinger argues, "it is irrelevant whether the assumed substance of economic relations (that is to say, the chosen abstraction) is sufficient to explain the actual levels of prices".[1] And Marx's endeavour to show that the abstraction was in fact sufficient to explain these price levels ran up against three great (and probably insuperable) difficulties. First, there is the skilled-unskilled labour problem, which according to Schlesinger is "certainly the most serious difficulty met by an inherent criticism of Marxist economics".[2] Second, there is the problem arising because of "the incorrectness of Marx's derivation of production prices from values"— i.e., the "transformation problem".[3] And third, there is the difficulty of adapting the labour theory of value, in the form in which Marx propounded it, to "the stage of modern monopoly capitalism".[4] All in all, Schlesinger suggests, it would be better if Marxists dropped the "quantitative" aspect of the Marxian value theory entirely, and retained the concept of "value" (suitably re-named) only as "a methodological approach which by mere incident (*sic*) coincides with the law of prices actually valid in a past stage of society".[5]

This argument, while more imposing than Lange's, suffers from the same fundamental defect. If the "quantitative" aspect of the Marxian theory of value is dropped, nothing will remain of the Marxian theory of distribution but a sort of sociological skeleton. Is any attempt to be made to fill the gap, and if so along what lines should it be made? Schlesinger, looking at the problem through

---

[1] Schlesinger, *op. cit.*, p. 107.

[2] *Ibid.*, p. 129. "Should no one succeed in solving the problem", Schlesinger suggests, "we should be left with no alternative other than describing Marx's continued use of the term 'value' as an abstraction from the conditions of a disintegrating society of small craftsmen and peasants, simple producers of commodities with the corresponding ideology."

[3] *Ibid.*, p. 139.   [4] *Ibid.*, p. 149.   [5] *Ibid.*, p. 119.

the spectacles of a sociologist, would probably not admit the existence of any real gap: the "basic tenets" of *Capital*—i.e., those basic for him as a sociologist—could be derived easily enough from the sociological skeleton. Lange, looking at the problem as an economist, certainly recognises the existence of a gap, and suggests in effect that it be filled with the aid of the "bourgeois" theory of distribution. For reasons which I have described elsewhere in this book, neither of these two answers to the question appears to me to be satisfactory. But if Schlesinger were correct in thinking that it is impossible to demonstrate the existence of the kind of quantitative connection between "values" and prices which Marx had in mind, the whole matter would obviously have to be reconsidered. In relation to the first two of the difficulties which Schlesinger names, the skilled-unskilled labour problem and the "transformation problem", I hope I have already said enough to suggest that these obstacles are not as serious as he thinks. The third difficulty, however, the adaptation of the theory to monopoly capitalism, is indeed a more serious one, although (as I shall try to indicate later) I do not think it calls for a really fundamental reconstruction of the Marxian theory.

Why did Marx think it necessary to demonstrate the existence of a quantitative connection between "values" and prices? Why, in other words, did he consider it so important to show that "the material relations existing between men working for each other" ultimately determined the relative prices of the products of their work? Schlesinger suggests that this was a "logical mistake": it does not follow from "the fundamental importance of social labour as the factor dominating economic events", he says, that "it must be possible to derive prices exclusively from this factor".[1] But surely

[1] Schlesinger, *op. cit.*, pp. 96-7. Schlesinger's phrase "the fundamental importance of social labour as the factor dominating economic events" is evidently a compound of two others which appear in inverted commas on the same page (96) of his book. In the context, it appears as if these were quotations from Engels. In actual fact, they are quotations from a summary by Engels of an argument by Sombart. Sombart (according to Engels) argued that "the concept of value in its material definiteness in Marx is nothing but the economic expression for the facts of the social productive force of labour as the basis of economic existence; in the final analysis the law of value dominates economic events in a capitalist economic system, and for this economic system quite generally has the following content: the value of commodities is the specific and historical form in which the productive force of labour, in the last analysis dominating all economic transactions, determiningly asserts itself". Engels comments that although it cannot be said that this concept of the significance of the law of value for the capitalist form of production is wrong, "it does seem to me to be too broad, and capable of a narrower, more precise formulation; in my opinion it by no means exhausts the entire significance of the law of value for the economic stages of society's development dominated by this law" (*Engels on "Capital"*, pp. 99-100).

Marx began with something rather more concrete than a mere recognition of "the fundamental importance of social labour as the factor dominating economic events". He began, first, with a hypothesis which was to be tested—the hypothesis that men's relations of production ultimately determined their other economic relations (including their exchange relations) throughout the whole period of commodity production; and, second, with the assumption that (as Schlesinger puts it) "the distribution of social labour between the various industries represents the basic relation between the members of a society based upon commodity exchange". How, then, does this basic relation between men who work for one another operate to determine relations of exchange? It operates, Marx answered, through the amount of work which they do for each other, which directly or indirectly determines the exchange ratios of the goods in which this work is embodied. The question of whether or not prices can be derived from "values", then, can hardly be said to be "irrelevant" to Marx's fundamental analysis in *Capital*. So long as we exclude the possibility of the relations of production generating "extra-economic" forces which cause prices to deviate from "values" or "prices of production" in a way which is not quantitatively determinate, the demonstration that prices can be derived from "values" ("even if such derivation should give no more than a first approximation")[1] is a necessary and important part of the testing of the hypothesis with which Marx began.

The great merit of Schlesinger's critique is that it draws special attention to the "qualitative" aspect of the value problem. The main distinguishing feature of Mrs. Robinson's numerous digs at the labour theory (they can scarcely be said to constitute an integrated critique)[2] is that she ignores this aspect almost entirely. She sees Marx's definition of "value" as nothing more than a "purely dogmatic statement".[3] The labour theory, "according to Marx's own argument, . . . fails to provide a theory of prices"; "none of the important ideas which he expresses in terms of the concept of *value* cannot be better expressed without it"; and its function is therefore reduced to that of providing the "incantations" which Marx uses (in conjunction with the "arsenic" of his "penetrating insight and bitter hatred of

[1] Schlesinger, *op. cit.*, p. 119.

[2] Cf. Guihéneuf, *op. cit.*, p. 171: "L'interprétation de Mrs. Robinson ne saurait constituer une critique sérieuse de la théorie marxiste de la valeur. Elle ne va même pas sans une certaine naïveté."

[3] *An Essay on Marxian Economics*, p. 12.

oppression") to slay "the complacent apologists of capitalism".[1] So far as the theory of exchange ratios is concerned, all we can take from Marx is the " 'quite ordinary' theory of cost of production"[2] put forward in Volume III. Marx's attempt at a "reconciliation" of his Volume I theory of value with his Volume III theory of prices is "purely formalistic and consists in juggling to and fro with averages and totals".[3] Thus in Marx's system, Mrs. Robinson tells us, "*value* precedes price, because the fact of exploitation lies behind the phenomena of the market".[4] In the concept of value are concentrated "the mystical elements in Marxian thought, which give it a significance quite beyond its definable meaning".[5] Nowhere does Mrs. Robinson give any real consideration to the meaning of Marx's dictum that value is a social relation, or to the connection between the Marxian concept of value and the materialist conception of history.

In her *Open Letter from a Keynesian to a Marxist*, however, Mrs. Robinson argues that she understands Marx better than the Marxists, since she has Marx in her bones whereas the Marxists only have him in their mouths. As an example, she takes "the idea that constant capital is an embodiment of labour power expended in the past". To the Marxists, she argues, "this is something that has to be proved with a lot of Hegelian stuff and nonsense. Whereas I say (though I do not use such pompous terminology): 'Naturally—what else did you think it could be?' "[6] And in the following passage she makes her point rather more explicit:

"For Ricardo the Theory of Value was a means of studying the distribution of total output between wages, rent and profit, each considered as a whole. This is a big question. Marshall turned the meaning of Value into a little question: why does an egg cost more than a cup of tea? . . . Keynes changed the question back again. He started thinking in Ricardo's terms: output as a whole and why worry about a cup of tea? When you are thinking about output as a whole, relative prices come out in the wash—including the

---

[1] *An Essay on Marxian Economics*, pp. 17, 20 and 22. Cf. the following statement by Mrs. Robinson in the *Economic Journal*, June 1950, p. 360: "The theory of *value*, in the narrow sense of a theory of relative prices, is not the heart of Marx's system (though both he and Böhm-Bawerk believed that it was), and nothing that is important in it would be lost if *value* were expunged from it altogether."

[2] Sombart, quoted by Böhm-Bawerk, quoted by Mrs. Robinson in the *Economic Journal*, June 1950, p. 359.

[3] *Economic Journal*, June 1950, p. 360.   [4] *Ibid.*, p. 363.

[5] *Science and Society*, Spring 1954, p. 145.

[6] *On Re-reading Marx* (Cambridge, 1953), p. 20.

relative price of money and labour. The price level comes into the argument, but it comes in as a complication, not as the main point. If you have had some practice on Ricardo's bicycle you do not need to stop and ask yourself what to do in a case like that, you just do it. You assume away the complication till you have got the main problem worked out. So Keynes began by getting money prices out of the way. Marshall's cup of tea dissolved into thin air. But if you cannot use money, what unit of value do you take? A man hour of labour time. It is the most handy and sensible measure of value, so naturally you take it. You do not have to prove anything, you just do it.

"Well there you are—we are back on Ricardo's large questions, and we are using Marx's unit of value. What is it that you are complaining about?"[1]

If the final question is intended to mean: "How does this differ in essence from what Marx did?", the answer is surely fairly evident. In the first place, as we have seen, the Marxist concept of value was not put forward to provide a handy unit of account, but to provide the basis for a theory showing how exchange ratios were determined, which is of course an entirely different matter. And in the second place, Keynes certainly changed the question back from a little one to a big one, but he did not change it back to *Ricardo's* question. Keynes was concerned, as Mrs. Robinson states, with the question of the determinants of output as a whole. He was not concerned (or at least not directly concerned) with "the distribution of total output between wages, rent and profit, each considered as a whole". It is perfectly true that in Keynes's question "relative prices come out in the wash". But they do not do so, and cannot legitimately be made to do so, in Ricardo's question—nor in Marx's question, which in this respect is a sort of compound of Ricardo's and Keynes's.[2] Ricardo and Marx, in dealing with *their* questions, found that it was necessary to begin with a theory showing how relative prices were determined. They found, too, that since their questions were big rather than small their theory of the determination of relative prices had to be rather different in character from that which was later to serve Marshall in connection with his cup of tea problem. They found, in other words, that they needed a *theory of value* in the traditional sense

---

[1] *On Re-reading Marx*, pp. 22-3.

[2] In the case of Marx's question, however, it is perfectly true that the problem of the relative prices of individual commodities such as an egg and a cup of tea was of distinctly secondary importance when compared with that of the relative prices of broad *groups* of commodities such as wage-goods, capital goods, etc.

if they were going to be able to solve the problem of distribution. The fact that Mrs. Robinson does not appear to see this, and thus misconstrues entirely the role which the labour theory played in Marx's system, is no doubt one of the things that the Marxists are "complaining about".

It is nevertheless true, as Henri Denis has said, that "each of the studies in which Mrs. Robinson develops and refines her criticism of the labour theory of value brings us a great variety of new insights, which are always very suggestive".[1] But the suggestive character of her studies is somewhat diminished by the fact that she often appears to take her stand upon an aggressive "common sense" which rejects abstractions such as "value" and "surplus value" on the grounds that we should deal only with the hard, elementary facts of direct experience. For example, Marx puts forward the idea that prices can usefully be explained in terms of a "value" which underlies and ultimately determines them. Mrs. Robinson argues that the problem of the transformation of values into prices is unreal because "the *values* which have to be 'transformed into prices' are arrived at in the first instance by transforming prices into *values*".[2] Then again, Marx puts forward the idea that profits can usefully be explained in terms of a "surplus value" which underlies and ultimately determines them. Mrs. Robinson argues that "what is important is the total amount of surplus which the capitalist system succeeds in acquiring for the propertied classes, and there is no virtue in dividing that total by the amount of labour employed, to find the rate of exploitation, rather than by the amount of capital, to find the rate of profit".[3] In other words, according to Mrs. Robinson, the derivation of prices from values, and of profits from surplus values, only makes sense if the values and surplus values with which we start are themselves directly derived from empirically-perceived prices and profits—that is, only if the "derivation" amounts to nothing more than the statement of a tautology. If the values and surplus values with which we start are conceived to be arrived at by any other means, then according to Mrs. Robinson we are immediately transported to the sphere of metaphysics.[4] Thus *Capital*, in so far as it does not consist of tautologies, inevitably appears to Mrs. Robinson as a collection of mutually

[1] *Science and Society*, Spring 1954, p. 160.

[2] *Economic Journal*, June 1950, p. 362.   [3] *Essay*, p. 16.

[4] A similar argument to that which Mrs. Robinson employs here could be used to show that Adam Smith's "natural price" does not exist—all that is "real" is market prices, since these alone enter directly into our experience.

inconsistent propositions, some sound (i.e., corresponding to the "common-sense" view of market phenomena), and others unsound or metaphysical (i.e., not so corresponding), which Marx vainly endeavours to "reconcile" with one another.

But one who really had Marx in his bones could hardly help seeing what he was actually trying to do in *Capital*. Broadly, as we have seen, he was trying to penetrate to the essence which lay below the appearances of the market place. The appearances which were accessible to simple observation, he believed, were often deceptive: it *appeared*, for example, as if exchange ratios were determined by nothing more than "supply and demand", and as if profit was simply an amount, proportionate to the total quantity of capital employed, which was "added on" to their costs by the capitalists. If one wanted a *theory* of value and distribution, in any real sense of the word, one could not be content with the crude facts and superficial generalisations which simple observation revealed, but must try to explain these facts in terms of the operation of deeper and more fundamental causes. There was nothing metaphysical about Marx's approach, however much his "coquetting" with Hegelian modes of expression[1] might make it appear otherwise. He was simply trying to ascertain the *basic causes* of the phenomena observable in the market—a reasonable enough enquiry, surely, under conditions where "there is no conscious social regulation of production", and "the reasonable and the necessary in nature asserts itself only as a blindly working average". The vulgar economist, said Marx,

> "thinks he has made a great discovery, when, as against the disclosure of the inner connection, he proudly claims that in appearance things look different. In fact, he is boasting that he holds fast to the appearance, and takes it for the last word. Why, then, any science at all?"[2]

This, I think, is the type of consideration which has to be borne in mind when assessing Mrs. Robinson's suggestion that "if there is any hope of progress in economics at all, it must be in using academic methods to solve the problems posed by Marx".[3] Now that academic economists have turned their attention to the problems of capitalist crisis and economic development, it seems to me perhaps rather more true to say that the hope of progress lies in using Marx's methods to solve the problems posed by academic economists.

[1] *Capital*, Vol. I, p. xxx.
[2] *Letters to Kugelmann*, p. 74. Cf. *Engels on "Capital"*, p. 127.   [3] *Essay*, p. 95.

6. *Conclusion*

It is not easy to sum up the work of the critics considered in this chapter. The quality of their contributions and the viewpoints from which they start are so diverse that they seem at first sight to have very little in common. But I think there are two points which may usefully be made by way of general comment.

In the first place, what mainly worries most of the critics is the fact that prices do not directly correspond with Marxian "values" in the capitalist economy which Marx was primarily concerned to analyse. To Böhm-Bawerk and Pareto, this "contradiction" is absolutely fatal to the whole Marxian theory, since it appears to them that Marx's "solution" is logically unsound. To Bernstein, the "contradiction" reduces the Marxian concept of value to nothing more than an "abstract image" which cannot possibly serve as the basis for a "theory of value" in the traditional sense. To Lindsay and Croce, it means that the labour theory cannot legitimately be interpreted as a scientific tool for the analysis of capitalist reality, but only as a theory of natural right or as a mere standard for comparing one type of society with another. To Schlesinger, it means that the "quantitative" aspect of the labour theory must be dropped entirely, and to Mrs. Robinson it reduces the theory to mystification and metaphysics. There is no need to recapitulate my reasons for believing that these conclusions are quite unwarranted. All that I wish to emphasise here is that what most of the critics are really confused about, at heart, is the nature of Marx's *economic method*.

Second, the arguments of most of the critics suggest, either directly or impliedly, that the gap left by Marx's alleged failure to provide a scientific theory must be filled, if it is to be filled at all, by one or another of the modern theories of value or price. In the case of Böhm-Bawerk and Pareto this is of course the main theme. To Bernstein, both the Marxian theory and the marginal utility theory are equally "purely abstract entities", and if a choice has to be made between them it should probably be made in favour of the latter rather than the former. To Lindsay and Croce, it seems that a "general economic science", deducing the concept of value from quite different principles, must exist alongside the Marxian investigation. To Lange and Mrs. Robinson, the gap must be filled by an explanation of commodity and factor prices couched in terms of the conceptual apparatus of modern equilibrium theory. Taken as a whole, then, and quite apart from the subjective intentions of any individual writer, the criticisms we have considered must be regarded as constituting not only an attack on the Marxian approach to economic phenomena but also a defence of the type of approach which abstracts from the relations of production.

There is one other matter which should be mentioned before this chapter is concluded. The writers I have dealt with are not only typical representatives of the different standpoints distinguished above, but also among the most competent representatives of these standpoints. If the labour theory is to be defended, it must obviously be defended against the attacks of its most mature and intelligent critics. But it would leave the reader with an entirely false impression of the quality of the general run of Marx-criticism in the West today if I did not say at least a little about the lesser critics.

There is no doubt that the average standard of Marx-criticism, both in academic circles and elsewhere, is quite extraordinarily low. Let us take as a not untypical example a recent book entitled *The Theory and Practice of Communism* by R. N. Carew Hunt—an author who begins by specifically accepting the healthy assumption that Marxism "is not to be refuted by attributing to its best exponents positions which they have not adopted",[1] and then proceeds to do precisely this. From the seven pages in which Mr. Hunt discusses the labour theory of value we may select the following statements: The Classical economists "had adopted the theory of value first outlined by Locke, who had defended private property on the grounds that a man was entitled to that to which he had given value by his labour, and they had thus made labour the criterion of value". Ricardo put forward, with certain reservations, a theory of value according to which the value of a commodity depended on the relative quantity of labour required to produce it; and he held what Lassalle was later to call the "Iron Law of Wages", according to which the value of labour itself similarly depended upon the cost of the labourer's subsistence. Marx and others seized upon this theory, using it to suggest that the whole value of a commodity, since it was due to labour, ought to be paid to labour. In Volume I of *Capital* Marx certainly gives the impression that he is seeking to relate value to price; but in actual fact Marx "never sought to establish any such connection, as he did not believe that value could be related even to the normal price of the classical economists, much less to market prices". In Marx's account of the reduction of skilled to unskilled labour the

[1] P. vi.

"coefficient of reduction" is not stated, and Marx's argument is therefore circular. "Socially-necessary labour" is the amount of time a labourer works for himself (i.e., to reproduce the value paid to him as wages). According to Marx, labour alone is entitled to the value it is alleged to create. When Marx came across the famous "contradiction", "he did not face it at the time, and set it aside for further treatment". Present-day Marxist economists maintain that the derivation of average profit from surplus value is "a technical and esoteric process, and that in drawing attention to it Marx had revealed further contradictions within Capitalism that had hitherto escaped his notice". But Marx's explanation is in fact "a manifest trespass, as it is inconsistent with his premise that labour alone determines value". In the end, Marx is "driven to admit that exchange value is governed by the market, that is, by the law of supply and demand, which makes nonsense of his theory that it is derived from labour only".[1] It seems to me, for reasons which I have sufficiently explained above, that these statements involve so many half-truths, superficial interpretations and errors of fact that the picture presented of the Marxian theory is simply a travesty. And it should be remembered that Mr. Hunt's book is far from being the worst of the popular accounts of Marxism which have appeared in recent years.

If I take only this one example of relatively uninformed criticism, this is by no means because a dozen similar examples do not lie ready to hand. We occasionally read even yet that Marx accepted the Malthusian theory of population, and that he wrote Volume III of *Capital* in order to extricate himself from the difficulties in which he had got himself involved in Volume I. There are many variations on the theme that Marxian economic theory is an "unscientific" and "metaphysical" construction erected upon "the quicksands of an obsolete Ricardian dogma".[2] All too often, writers seem to assume that when dealing with Marx it is permissible to relax academic standards to a degree which they themselves would regard as quite illegitimate if they were dealing with any other economist.

The present writer would not of course maintain that Marx's theory of value is in all respects complete and perfect. Apart altogether from the fact that Volume III was not fully revised by its author, Marx worked out his theory of value with the primary aim of analysing a particular stage in the development of commodity production—

---

[1] *The Theory and Practice of Communism*, pp. 52-8.
[2] G. D. H. Cole, *Marxism and Anarchism, 1850-1890*, p. 296.

the competitive capitalist stage; and much more work still remains to be done on the application of the theory to the pre-capitalist, monopoly capitalist and socialist stages. Naturally Marxists always have an obligation to develop their theories in the face of changing concrete circumstances. There are a dozen important problems still to be solved, but one of the essential preconditions for solving them is to obtain a proper understanding of Marx's original theory. And such an understanding, unfortunately, the work of the critics considered above—in spite of the sincerity and ingenuity which much of it displays—is very far indeed from giving us.

Chapter Seven

THE REAPPLICATION OF THE MARXIAN LABOUR THEORY

1. The "Marginal Revolution" and its Aftermath

"THE critique of Marx's book", wrote Pareto, "no longer remains to be carried out. It is to be found not only in the special monographs which have been published on this subject, but also and above all in the improvements made by Political Economy in the theory of value."[1] The best reply to Marx's theory of value, Pareto believed—and many others from Böhm-Bawerk onwards have shared his belief—was constituted by the new theories of value which arose as the direct or indirect result of the "marginal revolution" of the 1870's.

I think it may be useful, therefore, before proceeding to discuss the problem of the reapplication of the Marxian labour theory, to give a short account of the "improvements" of which Pareto speaks. If the new theories are in fact improvements on the old ones, if they are more "scientific" and give a more useful and meaningful explanation of economic reality, then obviously there is no need to bother our heads about the problem of reapplying the Marxian theory. If, however, the apparent advance in the understanding of economic reality is actually a retreat, if the superiority of the new theories is merely technical and formal, then it is evidently the duty of economists to re-examine some of the older tools which have perhaps been too hastily discarded.

The so-called "marginal revolution", as every student knows, was ushered in by Jevons, Menger and Walras in the early 1870's. But the term "revolution" here is something of a misnomer. The change in the general atmosphere was real enough, but the leading ideas of the "revolutionaries" were by no means as novel as they sometimes liked to contend. Many of these ideas had already been put forward—often in a surprisingly "advanced" form—in the years before 1870, particularly in the course of the debates on the Ricardian theory which took place in the 1820's and '30's. And, even more important, the work of certain writers like John Stuart Mill, who

---

[1] Introduction to *Extracts from Karl Marx's "Capital"*, p. iii.

believed themselves to be writing in the broad Ricardian tradition, had paved the way for the later developments to a far greater extent than the "revolutionaries" themselves suspected.

Under the influence of Jevons,[1] Marshall,[2] Keynes[3] and others, the idea has grown up that the Ricardian system was taken over more or less in its entirety by John Stuart Mill, whose amendments and additions allegedly related only to inessentials. But this is so only if we regard the theory of value as an inessential, since nothing is more certain than that Mill decisively rejected Ricardo's concept of real or absolute value and the theory which he had based upon it. And we surely cannot regard the theory of value as an inessential. The particular theory of value with which an economist begins, as we have already seen, is almost invariably a sort of shorthand expression of the basic attitude which he is going to adopt towards the phenomena he seeks to analyse and the problems he seeks to solve.[4] This was as true of Mill as it was of Ricardo and Jevons. Mill's role in relation to the opponents of Ricardo was actually very similar to Marshall's role in relation to the opponents of Mill half a century later. From the point of view of the development of economic thought, the real significance of Mill's system lay in the extent to which the ideas of Ricardo's opponents were in fact absorbed into it, thereby clearing the path for the subsequent development of these ideas.

Let us examine Mill's theory of value with this point in mind. To begin with, Mill insists in the first of the propositions constituting his "summary of the theory of value" that "value is a relative term", thus implicitly acknowledging the correctness of Bailey's criticism of Ricardo's concept of absolute value.[5] Then again, although his own theory of value cannot properly be described as a supply-and-demand

[1] Jevons, *Theory of Political Economy*, p. li.
[2] Marshall, *Principles*, Appendix I.   [3] Keynes, *General Theory*, pp. 32-3.
[4] Cf. J. S. Mill, *Principles* (People's Edn.), pp. 264-5: "In a state of society . . . in which the industrial system is entirely founded on purchase and sale, . . . the question of Value is fundamental. Almost every speculation respecting the economical interests of a society thus constituted, implies some theory of Value: the smallest error on that subject infects with corresponding error all our other conclusions; and anything vague or misty in our conception of it, creates confusion and uncertainty in everything else." Cf. also Wieser, *Natural Value* (English edn., 1893, ed. W. Smart), p. xxx.: "As a man's judgment about value, so, in the last resort, must be his judgment about economics. Value is the essence of things in economics. Its laws are to political economy what the law of gravity is to mechanics. Every great system of political economy up till now has formulated its own peculiar view on value as the ultimate foundation in theory of its applications to practical life, and no new effort at reform can have laid an adequate foundation for these applications if it cannot support them on a new and more perfect theory of value."
[5] Mill, *Principles*, p. 290. Cf. *ibid.*, pp. 266-7 and 278-9.

theory, Mill did on occasion use expressions which suggested that "the law of demand and supply" was in fact (as he put it in one place) "a law of value anterior to cost of production, and more funda-mental".[1] So far as the utility theory of value was concerned, Mill cannot be said to have given much encouragement to its development, except to the extent that his emphasis on the role of demand was greater than that of most of his "Ricardian" predecessors; and he explicitly rejected the theory that profit "depends upon the productive power of capital".[2] If he protected the Ricardian fortress against this attack, however, he yielded it completely to another, that of the "cost of production" theorists. Having begun his analysis of value in the *Principles* by accepting the traditional idea that the equilibrium price of a commodity tends to be equal to its money costs of produc-tion, including profit at the average rate, Mill went on to undertake what he called the "ultimate analysis of cost of production".[3] This, however, turned out to be little more than a statement to the effect that costs of production consisted of wages, profits, and (occasionally) taxes. It could still be said that "the value of commodities . . . depends principally . . . on the quantity of labour required for their production" —but only, it appeared, in the absurdly restricted sense that wages usually made up the principal part of money costs.[4] This was clearly not Ricardo's theory of value, but an out-and-out rejection of it.

It would be wrong to suggest, however, as some have done, that Mill's analysis of cost of production was couched exclusively in money terms. A real cost underlies the money cost in Mill's system. Behind wages, of course, lies the expenditure of labour—but what lies behind profits? "As the wages of the labourer are the remuneration of labour", Mill replies,

"so the profits of the capitalist are properly, according to Mr. Senior's well-chosen expression, the remuneration of abstinence. They are what he gains by forbearing to consume his capital for his own uses, and allowing it to be consumed by productive labourers for their uses. For this forbearance he requires a recompense."[5]

It is clear that the distance is not so very great between this rather vague labour-plus-abstinence theory of Mill's and the "real cost"

[1] Mill, *Principles*, p. 345.
[2] *Essays on Some Unsettled Questions of Political Economy* (1844), p. 90. Cf. *Principles*, p. 252.
[3] *Principles*, pp. 277 ff.   [4] *Ibid.*, pp. 277-8; and cf. p. 291.
[5] *Ibid.*, p. 245.

theory put forward by Marshall.[1] And it is also clear that the very juxtaposition of labour (which Ricardo had always regarded as something purely objective) and abstinence (which had necessarily to be regarded as something subjective) must have encouraged the growing tendency to conceive economic categories in subjective terms, in abstraction from the relations of production[2]—if, indeed, it was not itself an expression of this tendency.

Two other features of Mill's work which paved the way for the subsequent developments may be briefly described. The first of these, his well-known distinction between production and distribution, was of course made for the very best of reasons.[3] But the idea that "the laws and conditions of the production of wealth, partake of the character of physical truths", whereas the distribution of wealth is "a matter of human institution solely",[4] can be taken to imply (as Marx put it) that "distribution exists side by side with production as a self-contained, independent sphere".[5] Smith, Ricardo and Marx, as we have seen, tended to visualise production and distribution as two aspects of a single economic process in which production was regarded as the dominant and determining factor.[6] Once the ties binding production and distribution together have been broken, however, it becomes much easier to escape from the Classical tradition in this respect and to begin to consider the laws of distribution in abstraction from the relations of production.

Second, there was Mill's famous distinction between statics and dynamics,[7] and his analysis of the stationary state.[8] To Smith and Ricardo, the distinction between static and dynamic analysis would probably have seemed an arbitrary and unnecessary one. The main topic with which Ricardo, for example, was concerned, was "the progress of a country in wealth and the laws by which the increasing produce is distributed";[9] and in his analysis of this essentially dynamic problem the static parts could hardly be separated out from the other parts. Reading Ricardo's work with Mill's distinction in mind, one becomes very conscious of the fact that the distinction cannot really

---

[1] Cf. Schumpeter, *History of Economic Analysis*, p. 604, footnote 33: "It would be almost though not quite correct to say that Mill (and Cairnes) transformed the Ricardian labour quantity theory into the Marshallian 'real-cost' theory."

[2] Cf. M. H. Dobb, *Political Economy and Capitalism*, pp. 140-1.

[3] Cf. Mill's *Autobiography* (1873), pp. 246-8.   [4] *Principles*, p. 123.

[5] *Critique of Political Economy*, p. 276.   [6] Cf. *ibid.*, p. 282.

[7] *Principles*, p. 421.   [8] *Ibid.*, Book IV, Chapter 6.

[9] Ricardo, *Works*, VII, p. 24.

be applied at all to Ricardo's analysis. The fact that Mill isolated "the Dynamics of political economy" in a special section of his book and contrasted it so sharply with "the Statics of the subject"[1] can no doubt be explained by his passion for logical systematisation; but the fact that the section dealing with dynamics constitutes only about one-tenth of the *Principles* requires further explanation. The basic reason for Mill's pre-occupation with statics, I think, is that he believed that it would not be very long before the advanced countries arrived at the stationary state,[2] in the analysis of which dynamics would naturally be of little use. In this state, Mill believed, "the mere increase of production and accumulation" which now unfortunately "excites the congratulations of ordinary politicians"[3] would by definition be no longer a matter of concern, and men would be able to concentrate upon securing something which in the advanced countries is much more needed—a "better distribution".[4] It would of course be too much to say that Mill is here delineating that problem of the distribution of a given set of scarce resources among competing ends upon which so many of his successors have concentrated. By "better distribution" Mill clearly meant a better distribution of *income*. But it at least seems very probable that Mill's general approach helped appreciably to bring this problem to the forefront.

That this is so can perhaps be seen from the example of Jevons, who appears to have started with a somewhat similar set of presuppositions concerning the progress of society—except that for him the main obstacle to further advance was the impending exhaustion of Britain's coal reserves rather than the law of diminishing returns. "The momentous repeal of the Corn Laws", he wrote in his early work on *The Coal Question*, "throws us from corn upon coal",[5] and this is bound to mean sooner or later "the end of the present progressive condition of the kingdom."[6] Now a man who displays such a "readiness to be alarmed and excited by the idea of the exhaustion of resources"[7] as Jevons did is quite likely to visualise the fundamental economic problem as one of making the best possible

[1] *Principles*, p. 421.

[2] Mill was careful to refrain from making any concrete prophecies, but the whole tone of his argument (see particularly p. 452) suggests that in his opinion the end of material progress in the advanced countries could not be long delayed.

[3] *Principles*, p. 453.   [4] *Ibid.*, p. 454.

[5] *The Coal Question* (2nd edn., 1866), p. 173.   [6] *Ibid.*, p. vi.

[7] J. M. Keynes, "William Stanley Jevons, 1835-1882", in *Journal of the Royal Statistical Society*, Part III, 1936, p. 522.

use of these scarce resources; and a man whose "vigorous individual-ism"[1] and fear of the working-class movement[2] are as manifest as Jevons's were will not be likely to envisage the proper solution of this problem as involving any fundamental change in the relations of production or even in the distribution of wealth and income.[3] "The problem of Economics", wrote Jevons,

> "may, as it seems to me, be stated thus:—*Given, a certain population, with various needs and powers of production, in possession of certain lands and other sources of material: required, the mode of employing their labour which will maximise the utility of the produce."*[4]

The problem with which Jevons thought economics ought to be mainly concerned, then, was how to allocate a given set of resources among competing uses so that a given set of desires (or demands) would be most effectively satisfied.[5]

Jevons himself did not carry this through. In particular, his optimum-allocation formulae did not quite extend to the problem of the entre-preneur's demand for producers' goods. But he did at least manage to outline the basic features of the new type of analysis which was soon to be developed to deal with the new problem of "scarcity". In the first place, he made it clear that this was essentially a static rather than a dynamic problem.[6] In the second place, he established once and for all that it was a problem in which marginal techniques might be expected to be useful. And in the third place, he pointed out thas since the problem was one of satisfying a given set of individual demands "the theory of Economics must begin with a correct theory of consumption".[7]

[1] T. W. Hutchison, *A Review of Economic Doctrines*, p. 46.
[2] Anyone who reads Jevons's *Introductory Lecture on the Importance of Diffusing a Know-ledge of Political Economy* (1866) will not, I think, feel inclined to question this phrase. Jevons was acutely aware of the fact that "erroneous and practically mischievous" (p. 32) views on political economy were becoming popular among the lower orders. It is worth while reading some of the edifying works whose diffusion he recommended in order to stop the rot setting in, particularly Whateley's *Easy Lessons on Money Matters*, which is interesting not only in itself but also because Jevons himself was brought up on it and praised it very highly. It is only fair to add, however, that a much more moderate view was expressed by Jevons in his *The State in Relation to Labour* (1882).
[3] Cf. *The Coal Question*, p. xxv: "Reflection will show that we ought not to think of interfering with the free use of the material wealth which Providence has placed at our disposal, but that our duties wholly consist in the earnest and wise application of it."
[4] *Theory of Political Economy*, p. 267.
[5] Cf. Hutchison, *op. cit.*, pp. 34-6, for an interesting discussion of certain other factors which may have led Jevons to see "pure economic problems as optimum-allocation problems."
[6] *Theory of Political Economy*, pp. vii and 93-4.
[7] *Ibid.*, p. 40. Cf. also, on the same page, the statement that "human wants are the ultimate subject-matter of Economics."

It seems to me that the increasing popularity of the new type of analysis in the years which followed can be at least partly explained by the fact that the basic problem of "scarcity" with which it was designed to deal actually began to emerge to prominence in the real world. In the 1870's and 1880's, as Wesley Mitchell pointed out, "on the whole the rate of progress was believed by contemporaries to have been checked";[1] and in spite of the subsequent recovery the general situation has still apparently been such as to induce many economists to begin by assuming (at least provisionally) that "there is no further possibility of increasing the total quantity of resources" and therefore to concentrate on "the possibilities of increasing economic welfare by a more efficient allocation of the *given* resources".[2] In addition, of course, the new type of analysis was found to be particularly useful in connection with the task of opposing the labour theory of value—a task which became more and more urgent as Marxist ideas began to grow in popularity.

The marginal utility theory of value, of course, was much more than an alternative method of explaining price ratios. It also expressed an alternative general approach to economic phenomena. First and foremost, it was an expression of the idea that the whole of economics ought to be based on the investigation of "the condition of a mind". "The general forms of the laws of Economics", wrote Jevons,

> "are the same in the case of individuals and nations; and, in reality, it is a law operating in the case of multitudes of individuals which gives rise to the aggregate represented in the transactions of a nation."[3]

What we must start with, Jevons in effect argued, was the mental relation between the individual and finished goods, rather than the social relation between men and men in the production of commodities.[4] And this implied that the basic laws and techniques of economics had a much greater degree of generality than had usually been

---

[1] Wesley C. Mitchell, *Lecture Notes on Types of Economic Theory* (New York, 1949), Vol. II, p. 59.

[2] Hla Myint, *Theories of Welfare Economics* (London, 1948), p. xii. If my interpretation is correct, it follows that Bukharin, in *The Economic Theory of the Leisure Class*, was wrong in characterising the theory of marginal utility as the ideology of a new *rentier* class, but right in associating it with a particular stage in the development of capitalism.

[3] *Theory of Political Economy*, p. 15. Cf. J. S. Mill, *System of Logic* (People's Edn., 1891), p. 573.

[4] Cf. *Theory of Political Economy*, p. 43: "Utility, though a quality of things, is *no inherent quality*. It is better described as *a circumstance of things* arising out of their relation to man's requirements."

assumed: they were in fact adequate to deal not only with the optimum-allocation problems to be found in all forms of exchange economy, but also with those of the isolated individual.[1] This amounted, of course, to a complete rejection of the Classical idea that economic phenomena could only be properly understood if one started with the relations of production peculiar to the particular economic formation under consideration. It was widely contended, however, that because of its "scientific" character[2] the new type of approach was capable of giving a much more satisfactory answer to all the main economic problems which the Classical economists had tackled.

The chief developments ushered in by the Austrians proceeded within this framework. Indeed, most if not all of these developments are to be found (at least in embryo) in the work of Jevons himself. It is true that Jevons never worked out at all fully anything which could properly be called a marginal productivity theory of distribution, and that he still tended to think in terms of some sort of independent "real cost" lying behind supply. But there is some justification for the view that his theories of interest and wages were essentially "in agreement with the modern theory of marginal productivity";[3] and in his preface to the second edition of the *Theory of Political Economy* the foundations of a co-ordinated marginal productivity theory of distribution and a generalised doctrine of opportunity cost were quite clearly mapped out.[4] And Jevons made it clear from the beginning that the "real cost" lying behind supply, although it could often be said to be the "determining circumstance" in the process whereby values were fixed, could never be said to be so directly, but only through the medium of its effect (through supply) on marginal utility—a view summarily expressed as follows in his famous table:

"Cost of production determines supply:
Supply determines final degree of utility:
Final degree of utility determines value."[5]

If he had ever had time to reformulate this argument in the light of the ideas put forward in his preface to the second edition, there is

[1] Cf. *Theory of Political Economy*, pp. 75 and 222.

[2] The belief that the new developments had at last turned political economy into a real science was expressed (*inter alia*) by what Jevons described as "the substitution for the name Political Economy of the single convenient term *Economics*" (*ibid.*, p. xiv).

[3] *Ibid.*, Appendix I (by H. S. Jevons), p. 279. It is certainly true, at any rate, that Jevons's theory of interest substantially anticipated that of Böhm-Bawerk.

[4] *Ibid.*, pp. xlvi ff.   [5] *Ibid.*, p. 165.

little doubt that Jevons would have come much closer to the Austrian approach, with its rejection of the whole concept of "real cost".

To many of the later writers in this new tradition, the refutation of the Marxian version of the labour theory appeared as a particularly urgent task. There seems little doubt, for example, that Böhm-Bawerk set out more or less deliberately to provide alternative solutions to the problems of value and surplus value which Marx had dealt with in so unpalatable a fashion.[1] Wieser, again, was well aware of the fact that in Germany "there has of late years been a widening acceptance of the labour theory", and that many socialists were basing their "crusade against interest" on Ricardo's system; and he therefore found himself, as he put it, "obliged again and again to speak against the socialists".[2] The "key fact" about J. B. Clark's marginal productivity theory of distribution, as his son has recently reminded us, was probably that "his statements are oriented at Marx, and are best construed as an earnest, and not meticulously-qualified, rebuttal of Marxian exploitation theory".[3] Cassel and Pareto, again, wrote extensively on the Marxian system, and there can be little doubt that many of their leading theoretical statements too were "oriented at Marx". And Wicksteed, in "co-ordinating" the laws of distribution and attacking the Ricardian theory of rent, was well aware of the fact that "any diagram of distribution that represents the share of the different factors under different geometrical forms is sure to be misleading, and is likely to be particularly mischievous in its misdirection of social imagination and aspiration".[4]

[1] There is an interesting parallel here between Böhm-Bawerk and Schumpeter. Both men agreed that Marx had posed a particular problem correctly (in Böhm-Bawerk's case the problem of surplus value, and in Schumpeter's case the problem of economic development), and both set out to give an alternative answer to the problem as posed by Marx.

[2] *Natural Value*, pp. xxxi, xxix and 64. The extent to which *Natural Value* was, in intention and effect, a sustained polemic against the Marxist and Rodbertian systems has not been sufficiently commented upon. See, e.g., Book II, chapter 7, on "The Socialist Theory of Value"; Book III, chapter 3, on the socialist approach to the "problem of imputation"; Book V, chapters 8-10, on "labour" theories of cost. It is worth noting, I think, that Wieser's most important and distinctive contributions to economics, the theory of imputation and the "law of costs", were put forward, at least in this work, as arguments against and alternatives to the Ricardian and Marxian theories. Cf. Hutchison, *op. cit.*, p. 157, who speaks of Wieser's "constant preoccupation" with attacks on the labour theory.

[3] J. M. Clark, in an essay in *The Development of Economic Thought* (ed. H. W. Spiegel, New York, 1952), p. 610. Cf. p. 605: "The readiness of thinkers to accept such a theory [as the marginal utility theory of value] at this time is probably explainable as a result of the use Marx had made of the Ricardian theory, turning it into a theory of exploitation, and leaving liberal economists predisposed to adopt a theory of a basically different sort." Cf. also p. 599.

[4] *The Common Sense of Political Economy* (ed. L. Robbins, London, 1933), Vol. II, p. 792.

For obvious reasons, the desire to use the new theories to attack Marx was not nearly so manifest in the case of the British writers as it was in the case of their continental colleagues.[1] To Marshall, for example, it was evidently a very minor consideration indeed. Marshall's main aim, so far as the theory of value was concerned, was to correct certain excesses of Jevons and the Austrians (notably their over-emphasis on the "demand side" and their dilution or rejection of the concept of real cost), and, while accepting what he regarded as the important element of truth in their doctrines, to emphasise the essential continuity between these doctrines when so corrected and those of the Classical economists. The appearance of continuity was maintained by Marshall on the basis of a somewhat shallow inter-pretation of Ricardo's value theory. Setting the modern fashion for "generous" interpretations of Ricardo, Marshall argued that Ricardo's theory of value, "though obscurely expressed, . . . anticipated more of the modern doctrine of the relations between cost, utility and value than has been recognized by Jevons and some other critics".[2] Marshall's own theory of value, however, was not in fact very much closer to Ricardo's than Jevons's had been. It is true that Marshall argued that the theory of consumption was *not* the scientific basis of economics;[3] but his theoretical exposition in the *Principles* nevertheless began with an outline of what was in effect such a theory.[4] It is true, too, that he insisted on the "real" character of costs, and the importance of their role in the process whereby values were determined, much more strongly than Jevons had done, and that he specifically attacked the Austrian idea that cost could be better explained in terms of foregone utilities than in terms of "real" sacrifices.[5] But it must be emphasised that the elements of "real cost" in terms of which Marshall's analysis was framed were essentially subjective, and therefore very different from Ricardo's;[6] and also that certain important ambiguities in his concept of waiting brought his analysis of cost rather nearer to that of the Austrians (at least in a formal sense) than he himself probably

[1] But the example of Sir Louis Mallet shows that the desire did indeed exist, particularly in Cobdenite circles. See his essays on "The Law of Value and the Theory of the Un-earned Increment", in *Free Exchange* (ed. B. Mallet), London, 1891.

[2] Marshall, *Principles of Economics* (8th edn.), p. xxxiii.

[3] *Principles*, p. 90.

[4] Similarly, although Marshall always insisted on the importance of dynamics (upon which his numerous incidental comments were often very valuable), and although he was suspicious of "stationary state" models, his own analysis remained essentially static.

[5] *Principles*, pp. 527-8, footnote.

[6] Cf. Schumpeter, *History of Economic Analysis*, p. 924, footnote 10.

suspected.[1] Indeed, as we shall shortly see, there is an important sense in which Marshall's theory of value was actually further away from Ricardo's than Jevons's had been.

From the point of view of the subsequent development of value theory, the most important feature of Marshall's *Principles* was possibly the encouragement which it gave to the general equilibrium approach to value theory and that pre-occupation with form at the expense of content which is today so often associated with it. This encouragement was given in part directly, by means of Marshall's Mathematical Note XXI and the "intermittent attention" given to "the wider conception of the general interdependence of all economic quantities" in the *Principles*;[2] and in part indirectly, by means of his insistence on the principle (which he ascribed to Cournot) that

> "it is necessary to face the difficulty of regarding the various elements of an economic problem,—not as determining one another in a chain of causation, A determining B, B determining C, and so on—but as all mutually determining one another. Nature's action is complex: and nothing is gained in the long run by pretending that it is simple, and trying to describe it in a series of elementary propositions."[3]

Nothing is indeed gained by pretending that nature's action (or the action of men in society) is simple, or that there is not an important sense in which everything can be said to be determined by everything else. But unless it is held possible to isolate some particular factor in a given situation, and to treat it in some significant sense as a "cause" or "determinant", it is difficult to see how any science can ever advance very far beyond the classificatory stage. Jevons's *catena* of causes was not quite as silly as Marshall made it out to be. Marshall's attitude, however, would—and in fact did—encourage economists to believe that it was neither possible nor necessary to make any causal statements

---

[1] Cf. M. H. Dobb, *Political Economy and Capitalism*, pp. 143 ff.

[2] Schumpeter, *History of Economic Analysis*, p. 836. Cf. *Memorials of Alfred Marshall* (ed. A. C. Pigou, London, 1925), p. 417: "My whole life has been and will be given to presenting in realistic form as much as I can of my Note XXI."

[3] *Principles*, pp. ix-x. This principle was of course the basis of what Marshall described as his "greatest objection" to Jevons's tabular statement of his doctrine—that "it does not represent supply price, demand price and amount produced as mutually determining one another (subject to certain other conditions), but as determined one by another in a series. It is as though when three balls A, B and C rest against one another in a bowl, instead of saying that the position of the three mutually determines one another under the action of gravity, he had said that A determines B, and B determines C. Someone else however, with equal justice might say that C determines B and B determines A" (*Principles*, p. 818).

at all in the field of value theory.[1] The Classical economists
and the leaders of the "marginal revolution", it began to be said,
had alike been misled into a false enquiry. There was in fact no need
whatever to seek for an "independent" determining constant. All
that was really necessary was that the conditions of the mutual interdependence of economic quantities should be expressible in a mathematically determinate form—i.e., roughly, in the form of an equational
system in which the number of unknowns was equal to the number
of equations. It will be clear that the particular idea of "determinate-
ness" which lies behind this approach is radically different from that
which lay behind the Classical, Marxian and Mengerian theories of
value. To solve the value problem in this way is to solve it only in a
purely formal sense—i.e., it is not to solve it at all.

To Walras, who is generally regarded as the founder of this type
of approach, utility was still a significant factor—although its role
appeared by no means as important to him as it did to Jevons and the
Austrians. To his followers, however, it gradually began to appear
less and less important. Pareto, for example, noted that "the whole
theory of economic equilibrium is independent of the notions of
utility (economic), use value, or ophelimity". He himself, like most
of his immediate predecessors, had started by establishing the theory
of economic equilibrium on the basis of these notions, but he later
came to the conclusion that it was possible to do without them and to
develop instead "the theory of choice, which gives more rigour and
more clarity to the whole theory of economic equilibrium".[2] Utility
gradually became more and more suspect, partly because of the
hedonist presuppositions allegedly involved in the concept, partly
because under certain circumstances it was unmeasurable, and partly,
no doubt (in some instances), because in certain hands it had proved
more capable of lending support to equalitarian proposals than many
of its progenitors had expected or desired. In any event, utility began
to be regarded as an unsatisfactory and superfluous concept. Its place
came more and more to be taken by the concept of preference
schedules, from which all hedonist presuppositions had allegedly been
expelled. To some economists this latter concept at first appeared
capable of fulfilling the same function as utility had previously done—
i.e., the function of serving as the "independent" factor which could
in the last analysis be regarded as determining value. Today, however,

[1] Cf. Cassel, *Fundamental Thoughts in Economics*, pp. 93-6.
[2] Pareto, *Manuel d'Économie Politique* (French edn., tr. A. Bonnet, Paris, 1927), p. 543.
Cf. Schumpeter, *op. cit.*, p. 918.

the preference schedules have increasingly come to be interpreted as simply reflecting a consumer's empirically observed behaviour in the market place, and it is widely held that all that needs to be postulated concerning the mental attitudes of the consumer is that his choices should be *consistent*—i.e., that in a given price-and-income situation he chooses to buy in a way that is uniquely determined. In effect, this has meant giving up entirely the search for a value theory properly so-called. "The theory of price", says Mr. Little, "can begin on the demand side quite legitimately with the demand curve. That one's 'ultimate' data should be statistical can no longer be considered a shocking idea."[1] Prices can be made formally "determinate" by setting up an equational system in which the number of equations is equal to the number of unknowns; and the ground has been so well prepared by men like Pareto, Cassel, Fisher and Barone that this type of approach has come to command a wide measure of approval without the majority of economists realising that anything at all is missing. Modern economists, like modern artists and poets, seem all too often to feel quite at home in

"... a world where the form is the reality,
Of which the substantial is only a shadow."

The fact that value and distribution theory has developed in this direction does not in itself give grounds for complaint: one cannot properly object to people engaging in a pleasing aesthetic activity. But the new approach is often quite solemnly put forward as an alternative to the Classical theory, and is used to give answers to the same vital questions with which that theory was designed to deal. Indeed, it is frequently claimed that the new doctrines, being more "scientific" and precise than the old, and less limited to particular economic formations, are much more capable of giving useful answers to these questions than the "crude" Classical theories were. Thus the fact that the Classical theories of distribution gave "separate" accounts of rent, wages and profits has been widely held to be evidence of their "unscientific" character.[2] If one objects that a theory which explains the origin of the wages of labour and the rent of land on precisely the same basis is not likely to be a very useful guide to practice, the upholders of the theory may concede that it is in fact

[1] I. M. D. Little, *A Critique of Welfare Economics*, p. 52.

[2] Cf. Schumpeter, *op. cit.*, p. 934; J. F. Bell, *A History of Economic Thought* (New York, 1953), p. 424; and G. J. Stigler, *Production and Distribution Theories* (New York, 1946), pp. 1-3.

purely formal, but insist that this does not matter because there is nothing at all to stop an economist going on to distinguish between these two forms of income on moral or political grounds if he wishes. Was not Walras a land reformer? All one can really say in reply to this is that it used to be conceived as a major task of economic theory to give information which people concerned with economic practice would at least regard as *relevant* to the decisions they were obliged to reach; and that if economic theory has now ceased to regard this as part of its function, so much the worse for it.

The real point here, I think, is that the expulsion of utility from value theory has not meant the expulsion of the presuppositions which were brought in with the utility theory. So far from meaning a return to the Classical emphasis on relations of production, the expulsion of utility has usually if anything meant a further retreat from it. Welfare economics and the so-called "economics of socialism" remain to a large extent in the grip of the old presuppositions, and even Keynes was by no means unaffected by them. And the theory of distribution, broadly speaking, is still weighed down by the notion —the first-fruit of the utility approach—that no "factor" which is customarily regarded as necessary for production can possibly receive (at least in the absence of monopoly or development) anything in the nature of a true surplus as part of its income.[1] The Marxian labour theory of value is not a magic wand which needs only to be waved to transform the barren desert of "pure theory" into fertile land. But it is, I think, a signpost pointing to the direction which must be followed if a way out of the desert is to be found.

2. *The Operation of the "Law of Value" under Socialism*

In his well-known letter to Kugelmann of July 1868,[2] Marx described the "necessity of distributing social labour in definite proportions" as a "natural law", which "cannot be done away with by the *particular form* of social production, but can only change the *form it assumes*". And "the form in which this proportional division of labour operates, in a state of society where the interconnection of social labour is manifested in the *private exchange* of the individual products of labour, is precisely the *exchange value* of these products". A clear implication of this careful statement is that in a state of society where

[1] "That one cannot get something for nothing" has recently been described by Mr. Harrod as "the most basic law of economics" (*Towards a Dynamic Economics*, p. 36).

[2] See above, p. 153.

the interconnection of social labour was *not* manifested in the private exchange of the individual products of labour, the form in which the proportional division of labour operated would *not* be the exchange value of the products. The economic category "value", and the question of the manner in which the "law of value" operates, in other words, have relevance only to what Marx and Engels called "commodity production". ("Commodities", it will be remembered, are "products made in a society of private producers more or less separate from each other, and therefore in the first place private products. These private products, however, become commodities only when they are made, not for use by their producers, but for use by others, that is, for social use; they enter into social use through exchange."[1] There is no doubt that Marx and Engels visualised their "law of value" as being uniquely associated with systems of commodity production, coming into operation as commodity production developed and ceasing to operate when commodity production ended.

There is no lack of references to support this interpretation. Engels, for example, in a letter to Kautsky of September 1884, wrote as follows: "[You say that] value today is associated with commodity production, but that with the abolition of commodity production value too will be 'changed', that is *value as such* will remain, and only its form will be changed. In actual fact, however, economic value is a category peculiar to commodity production, and *disappears* together with it (cf. 'Dühring', pp. 252-262), just as it did not exist before it. The relation of labour to its product did not manifest itself in the form of value before commodity production, and will not do so after it."[2] The passages from *Anti-Dühring* to which Kautsky was here being referred are those in the chapter on Distribution in which Engels elaborates on this point. "Commodity production", he writes,

" . . . is by no means the only form of social production. In the ancient Indian communities and in the family communities of the southern Slavs, products are not transformed into commodities. The members of the community are directly associated for production; the work is distributed on the basis of tradition and requirements, and likewise the products in so far as they are destined for consumption. Direct social production and direct distribution

[1] Engels, *Anti-Dühring*, p. 336, and cf. *ibid.*, p. 221. Cf. also *Capital*, Vol. I, p. 9.

[2] *K. Marx i F. Engels, Sochineniya* (ed. V. Adoratsky, Moscow, 1935), Vol. XXVII, p. 406.

exclude all exchange of commodities, therefore also the transformation of the products into commodities (at any rate within the community) and consequently also their transformation into *values*.

"From the moment when society enters into possession of the
means of production and uses them in direct association for production, the labour of each individual, however varied its specifically useful character may be, is immediately and directly social
labour. The quantity of social labour contained in a product has
then no need to be established in a roundabout way; daily experience
shows in a direct way how much of it is required on the average.
Society can calculate simply how many hours of labour are contained
in a steam-engine, a bushel of wheat of the last harvest, or a hundred
square yards of cloth of a certain quality. It could therefore never
occur to it still to express the quantity of labour put into the products,
which it will then know directly and in its absolute amount in a
third product, and moreover in a measure which is only relative,
fluctuating, inadequate, though formerly unavoidable for lack of a
better, and not in its natural, adequate and absolute measure, *time*. . . .
On the assumptions we have made above, therefore, society will
also not assign values to products. It will not express the simple
fact that the hundred square yards of cloth have required for their
production, let us say, a thousand hours of labour in the oblique
and meaningless way, that they have the *value* of a thousand hours
of labour. It is true that even then it will still be necessary for society
to know how much labour each article of consumption requires
for its production. It will have to arrange its plan of production
in accordance with its means of production, which include, in particular, its labour forces. The useful effects of the various articles of
consumption, compared with each other and with the quantity
of labour required for their production, will in the last analysis
determine the plan. People will be able to manage everything
very simply, without the intervention of the famous 'value'.[1]

"The concept of value is the most general and therefore the most
comprehensive expression of the economic conditions of commodity
production. Consequently, the concept of value contains the germ,
not only of money, but also of all more developed forms of the
production and exchange of commodities. . . . The value form of
products . . . already contains in embryo the whole capitalist form of

---

[1] A footnote here reads as follows: "As long ago as 1844 I stated that the above-
mentioned balancing of useful effects and expenditure of labour would be all that would
be left, in a communist society, of the concept of value as it appears in political economy
(*Deutsch-Französische Jahrbücher*, p. 95). The scientific justification for this statement,
however, as can be seen, was only made possible by Marx's *Capital*." Engels's reference
here is to a passage in his *Outlines of a Critique of Political Economy* which will be found
in F. Engels, *Stati i Pisma, 1838-1845* (Moscow, 1940), at p. 301.

production, the antagonism between capitalists and wage workers, the industrial reserve army, crises. To seek to abolish the capitalist form of production by establishing 'true value' is therefore equivalent to attempting to abolish catholicism by establishing the 'true' Pope, or to set up a society in which at last the producers control their products by the logical application of an economic category which is the most comprehensive expression of the subjection of the producers by their own product.

" . . . The 'exchange of labour against labour on the principle of equal value', in so far as it has any meaning, that is to say, the exchangeability against each other of products of equal social labour, that is to say, the law of value, is precisely the fundamental law of commodity production, hence also of its highest form, capitalist production. It manifests itself in existing society in the only way in which economic laws can manifest themselves in a society of individual producers: as a law of Nature inherent in things and in external conditions, independent of the will or intentions of the producers, working blindly. By elevating this law into the basic law of his economic commune, and demanding that the commune should apply it with full consciousness, Herr Dühring makes the basic law of existing society into the basic law of his imaginary society."[1]

That this was also Marx's view is beyond doubt. The argument which Engels here advances against Dühring was in essence the same as that which Marx had advanced thirty years before against Proudhon.[2] Marx consistently denied that the law of value would operate after the end of commodity production. In his notes on a book by Adolf Wagner, for example, in which the latter had apparently suggested that Marx's theory of value constituted "the cornerstone of his socialist system", Marx unequivocally replied that his investigations into the theory of value had reference to bourgeois relations and not to the application of the theory to a socialist state.[3] And in his *Critique of the Gotha Programme*, one of the few works in which he went into any detail concerning the characteristics of socialist society, Marx again made his opinion quite clear:

"Within the co-operative society based on common ownership of the means of production, the producers do not exchange their products; just as little does the labour employed on the products

---

[1] *Anti-Dühring*, pp. 339-43.   [2] See above, pp. 143-4.

[3] *Sochineniya*, Vol. XV, pp. 456 and 459. In his argument here Marx is referring more particularly to the ideas of Schäffle. See, e.g., the latter's *The Quintessence of Socialism* (English edn., London, 1898), chapters 6 and 7, and *passim*.

appear here *as the value* of these products, as a material quality possessed by them, since now, in contrast to capitalist society, individual labour no longer exists in an indirect fashion but directly as a component part of the total labour."[1]

Nevertheless, attempts are frequently made to prove that Marx in fact did hold the view which Wagner apparently imputed to him. The passages from Marx's works which are usually cited in this connection are of two types. First, there are those in which Marx briefly touches upon the possibility that under socialism "the producers may eventually receive paper cheques, by means of which they withdraw from the social supply of means of consumption a share corresponding to their labour-time".[2] Here there appears to be at least a *formal* similarity with the principle which regulates the exchange of commodities under capitalism, so far as this is an exchange of equal "values". But in the *Critique of the Gotha Programme*, in which Marx's clearest treatment of this point is to be found, he explains (*a*) that the share which the producers withdraw will be subject to a deduction for the "common fund"; (*b*) that when society proceeds from the first stage of communism (now usually called "socialism") to the second stage of communism (now usually called "communism" *simpliciter*), this principle of distribution will be replaced by an entirely different one; and (*c*) that even in the first stage both "content and form" of the capitalist principle will be changed, because "under the altered circumstances no one can give anything except his labour, and because, on the other hand, nothing can pass into the ownership of individuals except individual means of consumption".[3] It is quite clear that all this has extremely little to do with the "law of value". Second, there are several passages in which Marx discusses the "balancing of useful effects and expenditure of labour" in a planned socialist society. For example, in the course of a discussion on the relations between supply, demand and value under capitalism, he remarks in parenthesis:

"(Only when production will be under the conscious and prearranged control of society, will society establish a direct relation between the quantity of social labour time employed in the production of definite articles and the quantity of the demand of society for them.)"[4]

[1] *Critique of the Gotha Programme* (English edn.), p. 11.
[2] *Capital*, Vol. II, p. 412. Cf. Vol. I, p. 50.
[3] *Critique of the Gotha Programme*, pp. 10 ff.   [4] *Capital*, Vol. III, p. 221.

But it is surely illegitimate to cite statements such as this as evidence for the view that Marx thought that the law of value would "come into its own" under socialism.[1] Nowhere does Marx say, or imply, that exchange ratios under socialism would be made equal to embodied labour ratios. The "law of value" for Marx was a blind and elemental law, operating independently of the will of man to determine exchange ratios under commodity production and under commodity production alone. Marx always refrained, quite deliberately, from going into any detail concerning the principles according to which the authorities ought to fix prices under socialism.

There is only one passage that is really at all equivocal. Towards the end of Volume III of *Capital*, Marx quotes the following statement by Storch:

"The salable products, which make up the national revenue, must be considered in political economy in two ways. They must be considered in their relations to individuals as values and in their relations to the nation as goods. For the revenue of a nation is not appreciated like that of an individual, by its value, but by its utility or by the wants which it can satisfy."

Marx replies, first, that "it is a false abstraction to regard a nation, whose mode of production is based upon value and otherwise capitalistically organised, as an aggregate body working merely for the satisfaction of the national wants"; and second, that

"after the abolition of the capitalist mode of production, but with social production still in vogue, the determination of value continues to prevail in such a way that the regulation of the labour time and the distribution of the social labour among the various groups of production, also the keeping of accounts in connection with this, become more essential than ever."[2]

The meaning of this statement, read in its context, seems fairly clear. To Storch's suggestion that a nation, as distinct from an individual, is indifferent to the *value* of commodities (i.e., to their cost in terms of labour), and interested only in their *utility*, Marx replies (a) that a capitalist nation cannot properly be regarded as indifferent to value, and (b) that even after the abolition of capitalism the nation will still be vitally interested in the labour cost of the goods it produces. Marx

[1] Unless, of course, like Mrs. Robinson (*Essay on Marxian Economics*, p. 23), one removes the brackets from the statement just quoted and juxtaposes it with a subsequent remark clearly referring to the operation of the law of value under commodity production.

[2] *Capital*, Vol. III, pp. 991-2.

is no doubt thinking here of the idea, which he and Engels shared, that the "balancing of useful effects and expenditure of labour would be all that would be left, in a communist society, of the concept of value as it appears in political economy".[1] For the purpose of his criticism of Storch, Marx emphasises the "expenditure of labour" side of this balance. But there is no suggestion at all that prices will be or ought to be made equal to "values" under socialism. It is quite clear from the context that Marx is using the word "determination" here to mean something like "calculation" or "estimation", and does not intend to refer to the rule of the law of value as an automatic and objective social force.

In all their statements concerning the disappearance of value and the law of value under socialism, however, Marx and Engels clearly had in mind a socialist society *in which commodity production had been abolished*. Value and the law of value were economic categories peculiar to commodity production; commodity production would disappear with the coming of socialism; therefore value and the law of value would also disappear with the coming of socialism. To Marx and Engels, evidently, socialism and commodity production were mutually exclusive terms, since the very aim of socialism was to transfer the means of production, now operated by "private producers more or less separate from each other", into the hands of society as a whole. Socialism would necessarily destroy the basis of commodity production, and thereby enable the end of the reign of the law of value to be brought about. "The seizure of the means of production by society", said Engels, "puts an end to commodity production, and therewith to the domination of the product over the producer."[2]

Marx and Engels were of course aware that the socialist revolution might take place under conditions where the seizure of *all* the means of production by the victorious proletariat would not be politically or economically possible. For example, in his article on *The Peasant Question in France and Germany*, written in 1894, Engels spoke as follows of the policy which the proletariat should adopt towards the peasantry:

> "When we are in possession of state power we shall not even think of forcibly expropriating the small peasants (regardless of whether with or without compensation), as we shall have to do in the case of the big landowners. Our task relative to the small peasant consists, in the first place, in effecting a transition of his

[1] See above, p. 258.   [2] *Anti-Dühring*, p. 311.

private enterprise and private possession to co-operative ones, not forcibly but by dint of example and the proffer of social assistance for this purpose."[1]

Under such circumstances, in a country with a substantial peasant population, the fact that the victorious proletariat would be unable to seize *all* the means of production might conceivably mean the continuance, in a limited sphere but possibly for some considerable time, of "commodity production" in the technical Marxian sense, and therefore of the reign of the law of value. Marx and Engels themselves do not seem to have given specific attention to this possibility—partly, no doubt, because they usually assumed that the typical socialist revolution would occur in a fairly advanced capitalist country which had no really serious "peasant problem", but more particularly because they deliberately framed their comparisons between capitalism and socialism in very general terms, without making much attempt to distinguish between the different conditions under which socialism might be established and developed in different countries and at different times. They were mainly concerned to contrast capitalism with socialism *as such*—with the *essence* of socialism, as it were, rather than with socialism in this or that country at this or that stage of development. After the Russian revolution, however, for obvious reasons, the problem of the "operation of the law of value" in Soviet society came to be the subject of intense and prolonged debates in the U.S.S.R. The fact that the theoretical question was necessarily bound up with the practical question of the policy to be adopted towards the peasantry goes far to explain not only the great importance which has been attached to it in the U.S.S.R. during the whole period from 1917 to the present day, but also the violent disagreements and changes of attitude which have marked the gradual emergence of the particular set of ideas on the subject which has now come to be generally accepted.

Bukharin, in his *Economics of the Transition Period*, published in 1920, wrote as follows:—

"*Theoretical* political economy is the science of a social economy based on the production of *commodities*, i.e., the science of an *unorganised* social economy. . . . The end of capitalist-commodity society will also be the end of political economy."[2]

---

[1] *Marx and Engels: Selected Works*, Vol. II (English edn., Moscow 1951), p. 393.

[2] Translated from Lenin's *Zamechaniya na Knigu N. Bukharina "Ekonomika Perekhodnovo Perioda"*, 2nd edn. (Moscow, 1932), p. 6.

This view, which the experience of War Communism in the U.S.S.R. must have done much to encourage, was of course based on the traditional idea that many of the leading categories of Marxian political economy—commodity, value, profit, wages, etc.—would have no relevance in an "organised" socialist economy, where the conscious planning of economic life had replaced the operation of the blind laws of the market characteristic of "unorganised" capitalism. It was perfectly true, of course, as Lenin pointed out in one of his marginal notes to Bukharin's book, that the definition of political economy given by Bukharin represented "a step backwards from Engels".[1] Engels, it will be remembered, had defined political economy (in what he called the "wider sense") as "the science of the conditions and forms under which *the various human societies* have produced and exchanged and on this basis have distributed their products".[2] But he had hastened to add that "political economy in this wider sense has still to be brought into being", since "such economic science as we have up to the present is almost exclusively limited to the genesis and development of the capitalist mode of production".[3] And in 1920 there was still no real sign of that wider and more general political economy whose development Engels had prophesied. "Political economy", to all intents and purposes, still meant the political economy of capitalism. In addition, there was an evident and natural desire on the part of Soviet intellectuals and publicists at this time to lay special emphasis on the importance of the *differences* between a planned and an unplanned economy. For these reasons, Bukharin's thesis appeared sufficiently plausible in 1920 to command a wide measure of acceptance among Marxist economists both inside and outside the U.S.S.R. In a planned socialist economy, it was often said, political economy would disappear. Its place might be taken by some other science—"social engineering" was one of the terms used by Bukharin, Preobrazhensky and others[4]—but whatever it was, this new science would not be political economy.[5]

Lenin, commenting on Bukharin's statement that "the end of of capitalist-commodity society will also be the end of political economy", asked whether the relation $v_1 + s_1 = c_2$ would not hold

---

[1] *Zamechaniya*, p. 6.   [2] *Anti-Dühring*, p. 168. (My italics).
[3] *Ibid*., pp. 168-9.
[4] See the article by Adam Kaufman, "The Origin of 'The Political Economy of Socialism' ", in *Soviet Studies*, January 1953, pp. 245 ff.
[5] See e.g., *An Outline of Political Economy*, by I. Lapidus and K. Ostrovitianov (English edn., 1929), p. 4.

even under pure communism.[1] The comment is pertinent enough, but it raises an important problem which in one form or another was to cause considerable controversy in the subsequent years. It is evident that under "pure communism" the relation $v_1 + s_1 = c_2$ (or at least the similar relation appropriate to expanded reproduction) would be established in quite a different way from that in which it is normally established in a "capitalist-commodity society". Under capitalism, the various balances between different economic quantities, in so far as they are established at all, are established unconsciously, elementally, as a sort of net resultant of the conflict of millions of different decisions and actions. It makes good sense under such circumstances to speak of these balances being established as the result of the operation of objective "economic laws" which act independently of the will of man. But under "pure communism", the balances would presumably be established by the conscious action of the planning authorities, who, recognising that the smooth development of the economy required the maintenance of these balances, would take deliberate steps to bring this about. If, then, as Lenin's comment implied, certain "economic laws" would continue to operate under pure communism, must it not be said that these "laws" would differ *in kind*—i.e., in their general character—from those which now operate under capitalism?

Certain aspects of this problem were brought to the forefront of the discussions during the N.E.P. period, when the Soviet economy was manifestly divided into two sectors—a state-owned sector characterised up to a point by the "planning principle", and a private sector characterised up to a point by the operation of "economic laws" in the traditional elemental sense. Exchange relations having been re-established between town and country—i.e., roughly, between state-owned industry and peasant-owned agriculture—one of the basic questions under discussion soon became that of the extent to which the state-owned sector was bound by the laws of the market. The main question at issue, in other words, was that of the extent to which the "law of value" could be said to be the chief regulator of the Soviet economy considered as a whole. During the earlier period of N.E.P., apparently, the majority of writers "underlined the preponderance of the market as a supreme arbiter in the struggle between plan and spontaneity". During the later period, naturally

[1] *Zamechaniya*, p. 6. The equation expresses Marx's basic condition of equilibrium between the two main departments of the economy under conditions of simple reproduction.

enough, "plan and market change their place of importance; the market becomes a corrective to the plan".[1] The debates on this subject were often violent, closely linked as they were to the practical problem of the policy to be adopted towards the peasantry and to the related problem of whether economic planning should be "genetic" or "teleological" in character.[2] In this stormy period, controversies over the most academic-seeming problems, such as that between the so-called "mechanists" and "idealists" over the interpretation of Marx's concept of abstract labour,[3] had important political implications, of which the participants in the discussions were usually fully conscious. Looking back on this period from the standpoint of the controversies which have taken place in the U.S.S.R. during the decade just past, we can see the emergence of certain notions which were destined to play an important role in these controversies— notably the idea (mentioned in the last paragraph) that the "economic laws" of socialism differ *in kind* from those of capitalism; the idea that the category "value" might continue to exist in a different form even under full socialism; and the idea that in a system where some "private" elements still exist the socialist state "uses" the law of value to serve its purposes.

As an example of one type of approach which was fairly widely adopted at this time, we may take the textbook *An Outline of Political Economy*, by Lapidus and Ostrovitianov, an English edition of which appeared in 1929. The authors, in addition to giving a summary of the traditional Marxist analysis of capitalism (as developed by Lenin), also make an attempt to study "the laws of Soviet economy" in its then stage of development. "The peculiar feature of Soviet economy", they write,

"lies in the fact that it is in transition from capitalism to socialism. In it are combined planned and anarchic features, socialist elements and the most varied of economic forms, from primitive and simple commodity relationships to private capitalist production. These factors confront us with a number of new problems, such as the extent to which the laws of capitalist economy still operate in Soviet economy; the extent to which these laws are being replaced by planned regulation; the mutual relationships that are being established between the planned and the anarchic basis in Soviet economy; their specific weight (importance), the tendencies of their development, and so on. All these are problems not only of enormous

---

[1] Kaufman, *op. cit.*, p. 264.   [2] *Ibid.*, pp. 266–8.   [3] *Ibid.*, pp. 254–6.

theoretical interest, but also problems which are inseparably bound up with the burning questions of the current practical policy of the Soviet State."[1]

The key to the authors' attitude towards these problems is to be found in their account of the manner in which the law of value operates in the Soviet economy. In all societies, they argue, the requisite equilibrium between production and consumption must be brought about somehow—i.e., the distribution of labour among the different branches of production must somehow be made to correspond with society's needs. In capitalist society, this correspondence is achieved (in so far as it is achieved at all) through the elemental operation of the law of value. In communist society, on the other hand, the necessary "labour balance" will be regulated "not blindly by means of exchange on the market by independent commodity-producers, but by the conscious will of all society".[2] But the Soviet economy in its present stage of development is essentially *transitional* in character—"taking it as a whole it is no longer capitalist, but at the same time it has not yet been transformed into a wholly socialist economy". At the present time, therefore, the law of value continues to operate, but "it does not operate in the form in which it operates in the capitalist system, since it is passing through the *process of withering away*, the process of transformation into the law of 'expenditure of labour' that operates in socialist society".[3]

[1] Lapidus and Ostrovitianov, *op. cit.*, p. 4. [2] *Ibid.*, p. 169.

[3] *Ibid.*, pp. 169–70. Cf. the following summary of this argument on p. 471: "This law of proportionality in labour investment is a law of every society, whatever the form of its productive relations. The only difference is that in different social formations its operation is manifested in different ways. In capitalist production it operates independently of the will and consciousness of man, through the law of value; in Communist society it operates exclusively through the will and consciousness of the people and finds its expression in the planned measures of the organs concerned. What do we find in Soviet society? In Soviet society, as in any other, the law of labour expenditure is the basis of the equilibrium in productive relations. But how and in what form does the law of value enforce its regulating influence on the productive relations of Soviet society? In accordance with the transitional character of Soviet economy, the two forms of regulation, the mechanism of the law of value and planned guidance, are merged, the active principle being planned control, which makes use of the law of value. In so far as the planning principle is gaining strength, the law of value is transformed directly into the law of labour expenditure." Cf. also *ibid.*, pp. 469–70: "The principle of planning presupposes conscious guidance in, or at least conscious influence on, the economic processes on the part of public or State organs or individuals. This, of course, must not be taken to mean that the planning organ which guides the economic processes can do what it likes. The actions of such an organ are also conditioned by certain causes and are subject to certain laws. But it is not a blind toy of these laws; on the contrary, the laws operate through the agency of its will and consciousness. Anarchy, on the other hand, presupposes a regulation of productive relations by means of the blind law of value, regardless, and sometimes in spite, of the will and conscious desire of man."

What, then, is the exact nature of the connection which the authors believe to exist between the simple commodity producers, the capitalist enterprises and the socialist State enterprises? Private and State enterprises are connected with one another through the market. But the authors emphasise that

"despite the relative independence of the State and private enterprises communicating with one another through the market, none the less they cannot be considered as absolutely equal commodity owners, like two capitalists in capitalist society. . . . *The fundamental and characteristic feature of Soviet economy taken as a whole is the leading role of State industry*, its predominance in the national economy, which corresponds to the predominance of the proletariat in the political sphere."[1]

In order to illustrate this "leading role of State industry", the authors give a number of examples of "the influence which State enterprises may bring to bear on the most essential sector of private enterprise, namely on peasant production".[2] But "the struggle which the Soviet State carries on with the blind forces of the market" must not be over-simplified. "In Soviet production", the authors state, "the planned element does not mechanically restrict and squeeze out the law of unconscious regulation. . . . The Soviet State realises its influence on market relations through *the operation of the blind laws of the market*, and by forcing them to operate along lines desirable to the State."[3] For example, if an extension of flax sowing is desired, this can be achieved under present conditions "only by raising the price of flax, and so making its production more profitable".[4] Such an action, the authors argue,

"will not be equivalent to the elimination of the law of value, but only an intelligent manipulation of that law by the State.
"Thus the deliberate and planned regulation of the Soviet State amounts to its taking into account the law of value and availing itself of it, directing its operation along the way of strengthening and developing the socialist economic elements."[5]

So far as exchanges between State enterprises are concerned there will usually be a "superficial form of sale and purchase" here, but the same productive relationships will not lie beneath this form as lie beneath value, since the State enterprises are not "independent

---

[1] Lapidus and Ostrovitianov, *op. cit.*, p. 172.   [2] *Ibid.*
[3] *Ibid.*, p. 175.   [4] *Ibid.*, p. 175.   [5] *Ibid.*, p. 176.

owners". Nevertheless, the relative prices of commodities exchanged between State enterprises cannot be fixed arbitrarily, since "it is obvious that here the influence of the market is felt, though indirectly". The price of a locomotive, for example,

> "will largely depend on the wages of the workers, and the level of those wages, even with their deliberate regulation, depends on the prices of articles of prime necessity, on which the anarchy of market exerts great influence. In determining the price of the locomotive the reaction of that price on the cost of transport of commodities sold to the peasantry, and consequently on the price of those commodities, etc., has also to be taken into account."

The authors emphasise, however, that "the influence of value will here be purely superficial and will not strike at the very essence of the relations between the various parts of the Soviet State economy".[1]

The launching of the first Five-Year Plan and the collectivisation campaign, together with the necessity for defending these measures against the "geneticists" and others, made the atmosphere unfavourable for the further development of ideas concerning the "operation of the law of value" in the Soviet economy. After the official declaration in 1936 that a socialist form of organisation had at last been achieved in the U.S.S.R., the main emphasis shifted to a study of the regularities observable in a socialist economy in which the "principle of planning" definitely predominated.[2] Little more was heard of the *limitations* to which the actions of the planners were necessarily subject (whether due to the "operation of the law of value" or to anything else) in an economy of the type which existed in the U.S.S.R.

In 1943 an important unsigned article entitled *Some Questions on the Teaching of Political Economy* appeared in a Soviet journal.[3] This article, which endeavoured to establish a basic distinction of kind between the economic "laws" of capitalism and the economic "laws" of socialism, indicated the main lines which published discussion was to follow in the U.S.S.R. for almost a decade. Following Engels's "wider" definition of political economy, the authors of the article

[1] Lapidus and Ostrovitianov, *op. cit.*, pp. 176–7.

[2] Cf. J. Miller, in *Soviet Studies*, April 1953, pp. 412 ff.

[3] The article will be found in *Pod Znamenem Marksizma* ("Under the Banner of Marxism"), No. 7–8, 1943. The quotations below are taken from an English translation which was published in the *American Economic Review* of September 1944, pp. 501 ff. The article caused a great deal of discussion abroad, particularly in the United States. See, e.g., the numerous articles in Vols. 34 and 35 (1944 and 1945) of the *American Economic Review*.

state that "*political economy is the science of the development of men's social-productive, i.e., economic relations. It explains the laws which govern production and distribution of the necessary articles of consumption—personal as well as productive—in human society in the different stages of its development.*"[1] What, then, are the essential differences, if any, between the economic "laws" which operate in the capitalist stage of development and the economic "laws" which operate in the socialist stage? "It is an elementary truth", the article states,

> "that a society, whatever its form, develops in accordance with definite laws which are based on objective necessity. This objective necessity manifests itself differently under different forms of society. Under capitalism objective necessity acts as an elemental economic law manifesting itself through an infinite number of fluctuations, by means of catastrophes and cataclysms and disruption of productive powers. Under the conditions of the socialist method of production, objective necessity acts quite differently. It operates as an economic law which is conditioned by the entire internal and external state of the particular society, by all the historical prerequisites of its evolution; but it is an objective necessity known to, and working through the consciousness and will of men, as represented by the builders of a socialist society, by the guide and leading force of the society—the Soviet state and the Communist Party, which guides all the activity of the toiling masses.
>
> "Thus the economic laws of socialism emanate from the real conditions of the material life of socialist society, from the total internal and external conditions of its development. But these laws are not realized spontaneously, nor of their own accord, but operate as recognized laws consciously applied and utilized by the Soviet state in the practice of socialist construction."[2]

This distinction, which as we have already seen was quite familiar to the disputants of the 'twenties, leads the authors to the conclusion that the economic laws of socialism "in their character, content, method of action are fundamentally different from the economic laws of capitalism".[3] This view pervades the whole of the rest of the article. Having described industrialisation and the collectivisation of agriculture as "laws of the socialist development of our society"—industrialisation

---

[1] *American Economic Review*, September 1944 (hereafter AER), p. 504. This definition is substantially the same as that later adopted in the official Textbook of Political Economy published in Moscow in 1954 (p. 10). Cf. Stalin's interesting discussion of the latter definition in his *Economic Problems of Socialism in the U.S.S.R.* (English edn., 1952), pp. 78–82.

[2] AER, p. 514.   [3] AER, p. 518.

and collectivisation being "economic necessities" which were "recognized in time by our Party and the working class"[1]—the authors proceed to discuss the question of the operation of the "law of value" under socialism. "There is no basis", they state,

> "for considering that the law of value is abrogated in the socialist system of national economy. On the contrary, it functions under socialism but it functions in a transformed manner. Under capitalism the law of value acts as an elemental law of the market, inevitably linked with the destruction of productive forces, with crises, with anarchy in production. Under socialism it acts as a law consciously applied by the Soviet state under the conditions of the planned administration of the national economy, under the conditions of the development of an economy free from crises."[2]

The basic arguments by which this conclusion is reached are by no means clear. Under socialism, it is stated, "the guiding principle of social life is distribution according to and based upon the quantity and quality of work performed. That means that labour continues to be the measure in economic life. Naturally, it follows that the law of value under socialism is not abrogated but continues to exist, although it functions under different conditions, in a different environment and, when compared with capitalism, reveals most radical differences."[3] From this and the argument which follows, one gathers that in the opinion of the authors the Soviet state is "using the law of value" when it distributes the national product "to each according to his labour". For such a distribution, we are told, requires the comparison of different *qualities* of labour, and this comparison can only be made indirectly "by means of accounting and comparison of the products of labour, of commodities".[4] It is "using the law of value", too, when it "sets as its goal the establishment of commodity prices based on the socially-necessary costs of their production",[5] even though these prices are fixed "with certain deviations from their values, corresponding to the particular objectives of the Soviet state,

---

[1] AER, p. 517. As J. Miller remarks (*op. cit.*, p. 419), "from economic necessity to law is a step taken without any argumentation whatever."

[2] AER, p. 525. The idea that the law of value is abrogated under socialism, the authors state, was "widely current" in former years. "In former teaching practices", they write, "there was widely current in the curricula and textbooks an entirely erroneous idea that from the first day of the socialist revolution all laws and categories of the economics of capitalism lose their force and cease to function. It is evident that the matter is much more complex. In particular, in our instruction and textbook literature the incorrect idea took root that in the economics of socialism there is no place for *the law of value*" (p. 519).

[3] AER, p. 521.   [4] AER, p. 522.   [5] AER, p. 523.

and the quantity of commodities of various kinds which can be sold under the existing scale of production and the needs of society".[1] "Cost accounting", again, is "based on the conscious use of the law of value."[2] The facts that "in the Soviet economy there exist . . . two markets and two kinds of prices",[3] and that "a struggle goes on between the organized market, which is in the hands of the Soviet state, and the elemental forces of the unregulated market",[4] are mentioned but not emphasised; and one definitely gets the feeling that in the opinion of the authors the operation of the "law of value" (in the rather amorphous sense in which they use that expression) under socialism is not at all dependent, or at least not directly dependent, upon the co-existence of these "two markets". It is only when a transition from distribution according to labour to distribution according to need becomes possible, the authors insist, that the reign of the "law of value" will cease.[5] Behind this argument, no doubt, lies the idea that the Soviet state, in its distributive and pricing activities, is recognising certain "objective necessities" which can usefully be described in terms of the operation of a "transformed law of value". But the logic of the argument is dubious; the use of the term "commodities" to describe the products of labour under socialism is arbitrary and inconsistent;[6] and the burden of the argument as a whole is exceedingly obscure.

It is easy to conceive of circumstances in which the main thesis of the 1943 article might become politically dangerous. The authors' insistence on the fact that the economic laws of socialism, as distinct from those of capitalism, "work . . . through the consciousness and will of men", etc., leads them, as we have seen, to classify such things

---

[1] AER, pp. 523-4.   [2] AER, p. 524.   [3] AER, p. 523.

[4] AER, p. 524. "In order to be the complete master over the market", the authors add here, "and to be able completely to dictate market prices, the Soviet state would have to have at its disposal enormous masses of commodities, enormous reserves of all sorts of goods." But this point is not followed up.

[5] AER, pp. 526-7.

[6] According to the Marxian account, as we have seen, the "law of value" and commodity production are inseparably connected. The authors of the article therefore probably felt themselves obliged, when arguing that the "law of value" (in a transformed form) still operated in the U.S.S.R., to define the products of labour as commodities. Nevertheless, at the close of the section on the law of value, they remark that "labour power, land, and the most important means of production (equipment of factories, plants, machine tractor stations, state farms, etc.) are no longer commodities in a socialist society" (p. 527). Does the law of value, then, not apply to the means of production? The sentences which follow the statement just quoted suggest that in the view of the authors it does so apply, but the explicit statement that the most important means of production are not commodities tends to undermine the main argument of the preceding section. Cf. Miller, *op. cit.*, p. 421.

as industrialisation, collectivisation, and even planning itself[1] as "laws" of socialist development. This comes very close indeed to a virtual identification of "economic law" under socialism with government economic policy. And such an identification was in fact more or less openly made by a number of economists and publicists during the years after the publication of the 1943 article. "The state plan", wrote Voznesensky in 1948, "has the force of a law of economic development because it is based on the authority and practice of the entire Soviet people organized into the state. . . . Socialist planning, based on the rational utilization and application of the economic laws of production and distribution, is in itself a social law of development and as such a subject of political economy."[2] Such a view is evidently the product of an over-optimistic period in which, as Stalin was later to put it, people "begin to imagine that Soviet government can 'do anything', that 'nothing is beyond it', that it can abolish scientific laws and form new ones".[3] But it is a dangerous view, because it may encourage the advocacy of economic policies which take too little account of the limitations imposed by objective reality. And there is some evidence to suggest that it did in fact come to be associated with the advocacy of "adventurist" policies, particularly in relation to agriculture, in the early post-war period of reconstruction and development in the U.S.S.R.[4]

The authors of the 1943 article were in effect trying to pursue two more or less separate aims. In the first place, they were attacking the doctrine, which had apparently achieved a certain amount of popularity during the previous decade, that "under the conditions of the proletarian dictatorship it would be possible to set up laws of economic development arbitrarily, without taking economic factors and material prerequisites into consideration, in isolation from the totality of the conditions which determine the level of economic development".[5] The 1943 article pointed out, albeit not very emphatically, that although the "necessities" which the socialist state recognised worked

---

[1] "For socialism planned administration of the economy is not a question of volition or caprice but an objective economic necessity" (AER, p. 518).

[2] N. Voznesensky, *War Economy of the U.S.S.R. in the Period of the Patriotic War* (English edn., Moscow, 1948), pp. 115 and 120.

[3] *Economic Problems of Socialism in the U.S.S.R.* (hereafter EP), p. 13.

[4] See my article "Stalin as an Economist", in *Review of Economic Studies*, Vol. XXI (3), 1953-54, at pp. 234-5.

[5] K. Ostrovitianov, in an article in *Bolshevik*, No. 23-24, December 1944. The quotation is from an English translation of the article appearing in *Science and Society*, Summer 1945, p. 234.

through and not independently of the will and consciousness of man, they were none the less *objective* necessities for that.[1] In the second place, the authors were trying to give theoretical expression to the fact that the Soviet economy was now basically a *planned* economy, and that the power of the state to influence the development of the economy directly and consciously in predetermined directions, although by no means unlimited, was far greater in the U.S.S.R. than it was in capitalist countries. Unfortunately, however, as we have seen, some of the theoretical concepts which they put forward in order to give expression to this fact, when taken to their logical conclusion, tended to give encouragement to the further growth of that very "voluntarism" which it seems to have been one of their aims to attack. Evidently a new approach to the problem was called for. In November 1991 a conference of Soviet economists was held at which the various problems involved were debated. The materials of the conference, including a "Memorandum on Disputed Issues", were apparently sent to Stalin, who wrote a set of "Remarks" on these issues. These "Remarks" seem to have been widely circulated among those concerned. A number of economists submitted criticisms of Stalin's "Remarks", and in October 1952 Stalin's replies to some of these criticisms, together with the "Remarks" themselves, were published under the title *Economic Problems of Socialism in the U.S.S.R.* In essence, what Stalin did in this interesting work was to reinforce the attack on "voluntarism" by giving a more realistic account of the "laws" which limited the activities of the Soviet planners, and in particular by emphasising the importance of the limitations caused by the continued existence of a semi-private agricultural sector alongside the state sector. But to say no more than this would be to minimise both the theoretical and the practical importance of Stalin's conclusions, and a fuller account of his analysis must be given.

Stalin begins by rehabilitating the normal commonsense concept of "law". "Marxism", he argues, "regards laws of science—whether they be laws of natural science or laws of political economy—as the reflection of objective processes which take place independently of the will of man. Man may discover these laws, get to know them, study them, reckon with them in his activities and utilize them in the

[1] Cf. AER, p. 514: "To deny the existence of economic laws under socialism is to slip into the most vulgar voluntarism which may be summarized as follows: in place of an orderly process of development there is arbitrariness, accident and chaos. Naturally, with such an approach every standard of judgment of one doctrine or another or one practice or another is lost; there is lost the comprehension of the conformity of phenomena in our social development to established laws."

interests of society, but he cannot change or abolish them. Still less can he form or create new laws of science."[1] Under socialism as well as under capitalism, Stalin maintains, "the laws of economic development, as in the case of natural science, are objective laws, reflecting processes of economic development which take place independently of the will of man".[2] It is true, he agrees, that the majority of economic laws (as distinct from the laws of natural science) are impermanent, operating only for a definite historical period and then giving place to new laws. However, "these laws are not abolished, but lose their validity owing to the new economic conditions and depart from the scene in order to give place to new laws, laws which are not created by the will of man, but which arise from the new economic conditions".[3] Stalin then goes on to refer to Engels's statement that under socialism "man will obtain control of his means of production, that he will be set free from the yoke of social and economic relations and become the 'master' of his social life". Engels calls this freedom "appreciation [or 'recognition'—R.L.M.] of necessity". "What can this 'appreciation of necessity' mean?", asks Stalin. "It means that, having come to know objective laws ('necessity'), man will apply them with full consciousness in the interest of society. . . . Engels's formula does not speak at all in favour of those who think that under socialism economic laws can be abolished and new ones created. On the contrary, it demands, not the abolition, but the understanding of economic laws and their intelligent application."[4] Nor is it true, Stalin proceeds to argue, "that economic laws are elemental in character, that their action is invertible and that society is powerless against them"; or that "the specific role of Soviet government in building socialism . . . enables it to abolish existing laws of economic development and to 'form' new ones";[5] or that economic laws can be "transformed" under socialism.[6] In his reply to a criticism by Notkin, again, Stalin opposes the view that his postulate concerning the utilisation of economic laws in the interests of society "cannot be extended to other social formations, that it holds good only under socialism and communism, that the elemental character of the economic processes under capitalism, for example, makes it impossible for society to utilize economic laws in the interests of society".[7]

[1] EP, p. 6.   [2] EP, pp. 7–8.   [3] EP, p. 8.
[4] EP, pp. 8–9.   [5] EP, p. 9.
[6] EP, pp. 11-12. "If they can be transformed", Stalin argues, "then they can be abolished and replaced by other laws. The thesis that laws can be 'transformed' is a relic of the incorrect formula that laws can be 'abolished' or 'formed'."
[7] EP, p. 54.

And in his reply to Sanina and Venzher he attacks the view that "only because of the conscious action of the Soviet citizens engaged in material production do the economic laws of socialism arise".[1]

Leaving no loopholes, then, Stalin decisively rejects the main thesis of the 1943 article—the idea that the economic laws of socialism differ from those of capitalism in their *general character* as well as in their specific content. *All* economic laws are truly "objective" in character, and reflect processes taking place independently of the will of man. It is important to note, however, that Stalin in effect agrees with the authors of the 1943 article that it is "quite un-Marxist" to include in the category "economic law" only those laws which operate elementally, "after the fashion of a house falling down on your head".[2] He is quite prepared to include under the term "law" certain "objective necessities" which the authors of the 1943 article would have classified as "working through the consciousness and will of men". He speaks, for example, of the "objective economic law of balanced, proportionate development of the national economy". This law, he says, "arose from the socialisation of the means of production, after the law of competition and anarchy of production had lost its validity. It became operative because a socialist economy can be conducted only on the basis of the economic law of balanced develop-ment of the national economy."[3] In other words, the planning authorities are confronted with the "objective necessity" of securing and maintaining certain balances and proportions between different branches of the economy—and this "objective necessity", arising as it does from the very nature of the socialist economy, ought to be regarded as a "law" which operates independently of the will of man. What Stalin is primarily concerned to emphasise is that it is improper to base a distinction between "laws" of this type and "laws" which operate elementally *on the alleged fact that the former "work through the consciousness and will of men" whereas the latter do not.* Such a distinc-tion can legitimately be made only on the basis of differences in *the degree to which men get to know economic laws and utilise them in the interests of society.* And "laws" do not differ in *general character* merely because in one case they are utilised in the interests of society and in another case are not so utilised. Whether they are allowed to manifest their effects elementally, or whether they are utilised in the interests of society, they remain *objective* laws, which must be conceived as existing and operating independently of the will of man. Nor can an

[1] EP, p. 93.   [2] AER, p. 513.   [3] EP, p. 11.

absolute distinction be made in this respect between the economic laws of socialism and those of capitalism, since economic laws "are in one degree or another utilized in the interests of society not only under socialism and communism, but under other formations as well".[1] It was no doubt very important that these points should be made in a document which seems to have been largely designed to counteract a certain "dizziness with success" which had apparently been manifesting itself in various ways in the U.S.S.R. since the end of the war.

Proceeding to the question of commodity production under socialism in the U.S.S.R., Stalin draws attention in the following passage to the chief factor in the situation:

"Today there are two basic forms of socialist production in our country: state, or publicly-owned production, and collective-farm production, which cannot be said to be publicly owned. In the state enterprises, the means of production and the product of production are national property. In the collective farm, although the means of production (land, machines) do belong to the state, the product of production is the property of the different collective farms, since the labour, as well as the seed, is their own, while the land, which has been turned over to the collective farms in perpetual tenure, is used by them virtually as their own property, in spite of the fact that they cannot sell, buy, lease or mortgage it.

"The effect of this is that the state disposes only of the product of the state enterprises, while the product of the collective farms, being their property, is disposed of only by them. But the collective farms are unwilling to alienate their products except in the form of commodities, in exchange for which they desire to receive the commodities they need. At present the collective farms will not recognize any other economic relation with the town except the commodity relation—exchange through purchase and sale. Because of this, commodity production and trade are as much a necessity with us today as they were thirty years ago, say, when Lenin spoke of the necessity of developing trade to the utmost."[2]

Stalin is apparently using the terms "commodity production" and "commodity relation" in something very closely approximating to their original Marxian sense. "Commodity production" in this sense requires two main conditions: first, separate ownership of such of the means of production, or such separate rights of productive use over them, as are necessary to provide a basis upon which productive activity can be carried on by units which are more or less independent

[1] EP, p. 55   [2] EP, pp. 19-20.

of one another; and, second, separate ownership of the products of this activity. A "commodity relation" is the basic socio-economic relation which exists between the producers of "commodities" (as so defined), and which is reflected in the relations manifested between the commodities themselves in the markets where they are exchanged. What Stalin is doing is to apply this concept of a "commodity relation" to the existing economic relationships between the collective-farm sector and the state sector in the U.S.S.R. today, and also, by implication, to the relationships between the separate productive units within the collective-farm sector. The collective farms, although they do not actually own the land on which they work, have been granted separate rights of productive use over it, and on this basis they carry on productive activity more or less independently of one another, each unit having a substantial degree of freedom to decide what it is going to produce and on which of the available markets it is going to sell its surplus. And the produce of each collective farm, of course, is its own property. Thus the surplus products of the collective farms (and of the private plots of individual farmers), and the manufactured goods for which they are directly or indirectly exchanged, are alike *commodities*, and the relation between their producers is essentially a *commodity relation*.[1] Stalin's reapplication of these traditional Marxist categories to a type of socialist society which Marx and Engels did not specifically analyse constitutes the most original—and most controversial—part of the *Economic Problems*.

"Wherever commodities and commodity production exist", Stalin writes at the beginning of his section on "The Law of Value under Socialism", "there the law of value must also exist." In the U.S.S.R., he continues,

"the sphere of operation of the law of value extends, first of all, to commodity circulation, to the exchange of commodities through purchase and sale, the exchange, chiefly, of articles of personal consumption. Here, in this sphere, the law of value preserves, within certain limits, of course, the function of a regulator."[2]

And the sphere of operation of the law of value also extends to production. It has no *regulating* function here, but it nevertheless *influences* production, since (as Lapidus and Ostrovitianov had already emphasised

[1] Stalin emphasises, however, that "*our* commodity production is not of the ordinary type, but is a special kind of commodity production, commodity production without capitalists". Its sphere of action is relatively narrow, and it "cannot possibly develop into capitalist production" (EP, pp. 20-1).

[2] EP, p. 23.

in the '20's)[1] the prices of commodities produced by state industry will depend largely upon wage-costs, which will in turn depend largely upon the prices of wage-goods—i.e., upon the prices of commodities which come under the operation of the law of value.[2] The trouble, however, Stalin says, is not that production in the U.S.S.R. is influenced by the law of value, but that "our business executives and planners, with few exceptions, are poorly acquainted with the operations of the law of value, do not study them, and are unable to take account of them in their computations".[3] The exact manner in which the law of value operates, however, is by no means made as clear as it might have been—at least to a western economist who was not present at the discussion of November 1951;[4] but the statement just quoted, and the horrific practical example which Stalin then goes on to give of what he calls "the confusion that still reigns in the sphere of price-fixing policy", seems to suggest that what he is in effect saying here is that the relative prices of certain commodities which are exchanged between town and country in the U.S.S.R. are still determined by economic forces which in present conditions are to some extent at least outside the control of the planning authorities; that in so far as the prices of commodities are directly or indirectly controlled or influenced by the state, they must be controlled or influenced with a careful eye to the incentives which depend upon them, to the overall balance of the economy, and, generally, to what we might call the "economic realities"; and, finally, that the influence which the state exerts on collective-farm market prices should be economic rather than administrative in character.[5] The law of value, then,

---

[1] See above, p. 269.

[2] This, at any rate, is my interpretation of the following statement by Stalin: "The law of value has no regulating function in our socialist production, but it nevertheless influences production, and this fact cannot be ignored when directing production. As a matter of fact, consumer goods, which are needed to compensate the labour power expended in the process of production, are produced and realized in our country as commodities coming under the operation of the law of value. It is precisely here that the law of value exercises its influence on production. In this connection, such things as cost accounting and profitableness, production costs, prices, etc., are of actual importance in our enterprises. Consequently, our enterprises cannot, and must not, function without taking the law of value into account" (p. 23).

[3] EP, p. 24.   [4] Cf. *Economic Journal*, September 1953, p. 722.

[5] Cf. A. I. Mikoyan, *Measures for the Further Expansion of Trade, etc.* (English edn., Moscow 1954), p. 77: "To some extent the anarchy of the market exists in the collective-farm market. If the regulating economic influence of the state is relaxed, collective-farm prices in this or that market may rise. We exercise, and must exercise, economic influence upon collective-farm market prices, but not administrative influence. The employment of the economic lever is a somewhat more complicated matter than the exercise of the administrative lever, but it fully guarantees for us a normal price level in the collective-farm market, provided the state uses the economic lever properly, in a flexible manner,

according to Stalin, is *not* "transformed" under socialism, as had been widely suggested since the 1943 article,[1] but operates in much the same way as it does under capitalism, though the conditions in which it operates are different and its operation is therefore restricted. In the U.S.S.R. its sphere of operation is "strictly limited and placed within definite bounds"[2] by virtue of the fact that the means of production in both town and country have been socialised. This means that the law of value does not function in the U.S.S.R. as "the regulator of production"[3] or as the regulator of "the 'proportions' of labour distributed among the various branches of production".[4]

The continued operation of the law of value in the U.S.S.R., then, according to Stalin, is due to the continued existence of a "commodity relation" between agriculture and industry. It was precisely this feature of present-day Soviet economic organisation which much of the published writing of the previous decade on the law of value had tended to ignore or to play down. The assumption implicit in the *Economic Problems* that this basic economic relation between town and country would continue to exist substantially unaltered for some time to come was no doubt based on a major policy decision which it was part of the function of Stalin's work to announce and popularise. Stalin argues firmly against the proposal made by "some comrades" to "nationalize collective-farm property", and suggests that the job of "raising collective-farm property to the level of public property" should rather be tackled by a gradual extension of the so-called "products-exchange" system, the rudiments of which already exist in the U.S.S.R.[5] The abolition of commodity production by the use of this method is postulated by Stalin as one of the essential preconditions of the transition from socialism to communism.[6] Once the two basic production sectors which exist side by side today have been replaced by "one all-embracing production sector",[7] commodity production and circulation will disappear, and with them will also disappear value and the law of value. It is incorrect, Stalin argues, to suggest that under communism the law

and takes the situation in the collective-farm market into account." For some recent examples of the influence which the approach described in the text is having on price-fixing policy in the U.S.S.R., see my article in the October 1955 issue of *Oxford Economic Papers*.

[1] The post-1943 literature frequently claimed Stalin's authority for the view that the law of value had been "transformed". But there does not appear to be anything in Stalin's *published* work to support such a claim, and it seems very likely that this invocation of Stalin's authority was purely conventional.

[2] EP, p. 25.   [3] EP, p. 26.   [4] EP, p. 27.
[5] EP, pp. 20, 96, 103-4 and *passim*.   [6] EP, pp. 75-6.   [7] EP, p. 20.

of value will retain "its function as a regulator of the relations between the various branches of production". Value, like the law of value, Stalin maintains, is "a historical category connected with the existence of commodity production. With the disappearance of commodity production, value and its forms and the law of value will also disappear." And his description of the state of affairs which will exist under communism is also completely within the traditional Marxian framework:

> "In the second phase of communist society, the amount of labour expended on the production of goods will be measured not in a roundabout way, not through value and its forms, as is the case under commodity production, but directly and immediately— by the amount of time, the number of hours, expended on the production of goods. As to the distribution of labour, its distribution among the branches of production will be regulated not by the law of value, which will have ceased to function by that time, but by the growth of society's demand for goods. It will be a society in which production will be regulated by the requirements of society, and computation of the requirements of society will acquire paramount importance for the planning bodies."[1]

It will be seen from the above account, then, that there has been little dispute among Marxists regarding the question of the operation of the law of value under *communism*. With few exceptions, all Marxists from Marx himself to Stalin have agreed that the law of value will not operate under communism. The only dispute has been over the question of its operation under *socialism* in countries like the U.S.S.R., where collective-farm property exists side by side with state property and important obstacles therefore exist to "the full extension of government planning to the whole of the national economy, especially agriculture".[2] The question as to whether the law of value would continue to operate under socialism in countries like Britain, where there would presumably be no need for a "collective-farm compromise" such as that which was found necessary in the U.S.S.R., has not yet been seriously debated. If we assume, as Marx did, that the law of value can operate only on the basis of commodity production, the problem of the status of goods entering into international trade (abstracted from in the above survey)[3] becomes all-important. If such goods were classified as "commodities" in the technical Marxian sense—as presumably they would have to be, at least initially—then

---

[1] EP, pp. 26-7.   [2] EP, p. 76.
[3] But not abstracted from by Stalin—see EP, pp. 14-15 and 59.

the law of value would to some extent continue to operate so far as these goods were concerned. Strictly speaking, therefore, one probably ought to say that commodity production (and therefore the operation of the law of value) would finally disappear only when an internal "all-embracing production sector" had been achieved inside all countries like the U.S.S.R., *and* when, in addition, *world* production was controlled by a single international economic organisation.

The main theoretical propositions in the *Economic Problems* which I have considered above were probably intended by Stalin not as final answers to the problems involved, but rather as indications of the new paths which he believed that further research into these problems should follow. It cannot be said, however, that Marxist economists, either inside or outside the U.S.S.R., have yet been particularly diligent in following these paths. Part of the reason for this, no doubt, is the position of unique authority which Stalin's statements on theory and policy assumed in the U.S.S.R. during the last twenty years of his life. With one or two not very important exceptions, the published Soviet discussions on Stalin's *Economic Problems* which I have so far seen consist of little more than extended repetitions of Stalin's propositions, often in the identical words of the original, adding little or nothing by way of clarification or elaboration. This also applies to the official textbook on political economy which was eventually published in 1954. The section of the textbook dealing with the socialist mode of production, while it undoubtedly represents a great advance over previous accounts, makes no real attempt to answer the important questions which Stalin's *Economic Problems* had raised. In the field of economic theory, as in other fields, it is becoming fairly evident that the particular method of developing Marxism adopted in the U.S.S.R. during the 'thirties and 'forties, however necessary it may then have been, is now hindering progress rather than promoting it.

*As this book goes to press, however, it is becoming clear that a welcome and radical change in Soviet intellectual life is taking place. The speeches made at the Twentieth Congress of the Soviet Communist Party indicate that in the opinion of the leadership the time is now ripe for a critical reassessment of past work, including the work and position of Stalin himself, and for an end to the exaggerated respect for authority which has so often disfigured Soviet work in such fields as economic theory. Take, for example, the following extract from a speech by Suslov:

"Dogmatism and doctrinairism have become widespread because part of the economists and philosophers held aloof from practical life. The essence of the evil disease called doctrinairism is not simply that those infected with it cite quotations all the time whether they fit in or not; they consider as the supreme criterion of their correctness not practical experience but the pronouncements of authorities on one or another question. They lose the taste for studying concrete life. Everything is replaced by the culling of quotations and their artful manipulation. The slightest deviation from a quotation is regarded as a revision of fundamental principles. This activity of the doctrinaires is not merely futile, it is harmful.

"There is no doubt that the cult of the individual greatly promoted the spread of dogmatism and doctrinairism. Worshippers of the cult of the individual ascribed the development of the Marxist theory only to certain personalities and fully relied on them. As for all the other mortals, they had allegedly to assimilate and popularize what was created by these personalities. The role of the collective thought of our Party and that of fraternal parties in developing revolutionary theory, the role of the collective experience of the popular masses, was, thus, ignored."[1]

The only specific reference at the Congress to Stalin's *Economic Problems* (apart from a number of statements from it which were quoted approvingly by speakers without acknowledgment to Stalin) seems to have been that made by Mikoyan, who condemned one of Stalin's less important propositions as incorrect,[2] and added the following carefully-phrased remark:

"Incidentally, it must be pointed out that if they are strictly examined some other statements in the *Economic Problems* also need deep study and critical re-examination by our economists from the point of view of Marxism-Leninism."[3]

Apart from this open invitation to the economists to join in the work of developing Marxian economic theory, nothing further was said on this subject. A passage from Suslov's speech, however, indicates one of the "other statements" which the leadership may have had in mind:

[1] *For a Lasting Peace*, 24 February 1956, p. 11.

[2] The proposition concerned is that on p. 36 of the *Economic Problems*, where Stalin suggests that following the division of the world market into two the volume of production in the U.S.A., Britain and France would contract.

[3] *Pravda*, 18 February 1956.

"Economists inadequately study the operation of the law of value in socialist production. That our architects, carried away by extravagances, gave little thought to what that would cost the people and that MTS and collective-farm personnel still very often do not figure the cost of a ton of grain or meat is undoubtedly in some measure due to the fact that our economists have not elaborated the problem of exactly how the law of value operates in our economy."[1]

All in all, whatever devices may temporarily be adopted within the U.S.S.R. to emphasise the importance of the changes which are taking place, I do not think that in the long term it will be seriously disputed that Stalin's position in history, both as political leader and as Marxist theoretician, is a very great one. The *Economic Problems* may well remain the basis for serious scientific work on the problem of the operation of the law of value under socialism for some time to come.

3. *The Operation of the "Law of Value" under Monopoly Capitalism*

Hilferding once wrote that "the realization of Marx's theory of concentration, of monopolistic merger, seems to result in the invalidation of Marx's value theory".[2] Under conditions of free competition, as we have seen, the law of value can be said ultimately to determine prices even after values are transformed into prices of production, since the very deviations of prices of production from values can be explained in terms of the Volume I analysis. But under monopolistic conditions, as Marx himself fully appreciated, the price of a commodity is "determined only by the eagerness of the purchasers to buy and by their solvency, independently of the price which is determined by the general price of production and by the value of the products".[3] The deviations of monopoly prices from values, therefore, are not explicable in terms of the Volume I analysis.

The fact that the labour theory of value as the Classical economists and Marx developed it cannot explain monopoly prices has been held against it ever since Ricardo's time, but so long as reasonably free competition was the rule and monopoly the comparatively rare exception this did not constitute a very serious objection. Today, however, when monopolistic conditions are becoming more and more widespread (as Marx himself forecast), and when it is frequently

---

[1] *For a Lasting Peace, loc. cit.*
[2] Quoted in Sweezy, *The Theory of Capitalist Development*, p. 270.
[3] *Capital*, Vol. III, p. 900.

suggested that the traditional analyses of price based on the assumption of free competition ought properly to be *replaced* (and not merely supplemented) by an analysis based on the assumption of "imperfect" or "monopolistic" competition, the problem clearly becomes much more important.

Marx himself, in an interesting passage in the closing section of Volume III of *Capital*, suggested that even though the actual prices of monopolised commodities might be higher than their prices of production, the *limits* within which monopoly conditions could cause actual prices to deviate from prices of production were still fairly strictly determined in accordance with the Volume I analysis:

> "If the equalization of the surplus-value into average profit meets with obstacles in the various spheres of production in the shape of artificial or natural monopolies, particularly of monopoly in land, so that a monopoly price would be possible, which would rise above the price of production and above the value of the commodities affected by such a monopoly, still the limits imposed by the value of commodities would not be abolished thereby. The monopoly price of certain commodities would merely transfer a portion of the profit of the other producers of commodities to the commodities with a monopoly price. A local disturbance in the distribution of the surplus-value among the various spheres of production would take place indirectly, but they would leave the boundaries of the surplus-value itself unaltered. If a commodity with a monopoly price should enter into the necessary consumption of the labourer, it would increase the wages and thereby reduce the surplus-value, if the labourer would receive the value of his labour-power, the same as before. But such a commodity might also depress wages below the value of labour-power, of course only to the extent that wages would be higher than the physical minimum of subsistence. In this case the monopoly price would be paid by a deduction from the real wages (that is, from the quantity of use-values received by the labourer for the same quantity of labour) and from the profit of the other capitalists. The limits, within which the monopoly price would affect the normal regulation of the prices of commodities, would be accurately fixed and could be closely calculated."[1]

The question arises, however, of whether this type of approach is useful in a world in which "artificial or natural monopolies" have become far more widespread and powerful than they were in Marx's

[1] *Capital*, Vol. III, pp. 1,003-4.

day, and in which the possession of monopoly power is becoming increasingly associated with the use of what we might call "extra-economic" methods of maintaining and enlarging profits.[1] In such a world, it does not seem to me to be reasonable to assume any longer that the *sole* source of profit is the surplus labour of the workmen employed by the capitalist. For example, there are now many cases in which a part of the excess profit received by certain monopoly capitalists should properly be regarded as something like the old "profit upon alienation" characteristic of the Mercantilist period.[2] In such a world, "the limits imposed by the value of commodities" do indeed appear to be "abolished", and under such conditions the type of approach adopted by Marx in the passage just quoted is not capable of giving anything much more than a purely formal answer to the problem of monopoly price. If total profits diverge from total surplus value, then it can no longer really be said that the limits within which deviations of actual prices from prices of production may occur under monopoly are determined in accordance with the Volume I analysis. This is the setting within which the problem of the reapplication of the Marxian theory of value to present-day conditions must be considered.

One must be careful, however, not to exaggerate the extent to which the coming of monopoly capitalism has invalidated the traditional analyses based on the assumption of free competition. Monopoly does not mean the end of competition, and may even at times (e.g., during periods of price war) mean an intensification of competition. And even when actual competition is slight, the fear of potential competition may in many cases induce a monopolist to keep his price at a level which affords him not much more than the "normal" or "average" rate of profit. These are points which have recently been emphasised by a number of commentators on the so-called "theory of monopolisitic competition" which was developed in the early 'thirties. Mr. Guillebaud, for example, has argued that "except in those relatively few cases where there is a *high* degree of restriction of entry and demand is very inelastic, the notion of normal value in Marshall's sense . . . has a large measure of applicability".[3] Such con-

---

[1] Cf. my article in *The Modern Quarterly*, Summer 1953, at pp. 152 ff.

[2] Cf. *ibid.*, pp. 155-6.

[3] "Marshall's Principles of Economics in the Light of Contemporary Economic Thought", in *Economica*, May 1952, at p. 122. Cf. p. 118. Marshall's concept of "normal value" was in essence the same as the Classical concept of "natural price", although his analysis of the forces lying behind and determining this price was of course very different from the Classical analysis.

siderations certainly suggest that a theory of monopoly price must be regarded as a supplement, rather than as an alternative, to a theory of competitive price. But naturally they do not exempt us from the obligation to work out such a theory.

It should be clear from what I have said above that Marx's theory of value cannot be *mechanically* extended to the new historical circumstances. Marx's theory was developed in the context of a given stage in the development of capitalism and a given set of problems, and the essence of what he said has to be disentangled from this context before it can be reapplied to present-day conditions. Nor can his theory be properly reapplied without a much more careful study of contemporary exchange phenomena in capitalist countries than Marxists have yet engaged in. It is not my purpose in this concluding section to undertake any such study, but rather to outline very sketchily a new conceptual framework within which research into the operation of the law of value in different historical systems, including monopoly capitalism, might profitably proceed.

What Marx was above all concerned to show in his discussion of the value problem was that *relations of exchange were ultimately determined by relations of production*—using the latter expression here to include not only the basic relation between men as producers of commodities which persists throughout the whole period of commodity production, but also the specific set of relations of subordination or co-operation within which commodity production is carried on at each particular stage of its development. And the particular *form* which Marx's demonstration of this proposition assumed was largely determined, as we have seen, by the aim which he had in view when writing *Capital*. His main object, it will be remembered, was to enquire into the modifications which took place in the general laws of commodity production and exchange when the capitalist system of commodity production replaced the earlier systems. In this enquiry, Marx abstracted from the differences between various forms of pre-capitalist commodity production, and assumed that capitalism impinged upon a system of "simple" commodity production in which the normal exchange was one of "value" for "value". Thus the task of showing how relations of exchange were ultimately determined by relations of production presented itself to Marx as the task of showing how the production relations specific to capitalist commodity production modified the influence which the basic relation between men as producers of commodities could be assumed to have exerted upon exchange ratios under "simple" commodity production.

Now if we wish to demonstrate that relations of exchange are ultimately determined by relations of production at any given stage in the development of commodity production, we must of course show that the *actual prices* at which commodities produced under conditions typical of that stage tend to sell are ultimately determined by the prevailing relations of production. But the labour theory of value as Marx developed it afforded an explanation of actual prices only in so far as these were equal to *supply prices*.[1] In the particular context in which Marx considered the problem, however, this did not raise any special difficulty, since in the case of each of the two systems of commodity production with which he was primarily concerned the deviations of actual prices from supply prices could be regarded as negligible. Under capitalist commodity production—at least in its competitive stage, in which Marx was mainly interested—actual exchange ratios do in fact tend automatically towards equality with ratios of supply prices. And under "simple" commodity production as Marx defined it exchange ratios could at least be legitimately *assumed* to be equal to ratios of supply prices. In this context, then, in order to show that relations of exchange were ultimately determined by relations of production, it was quite sufficient for Marx to show (*a*) that under "simple" commodity production ratios of supply prices were *directly* determined by embodied labour ratios, and (*b*) that under capitalist commodity production ratios of supply prices were *indirectly* determined by embodied labour ratios. The main subject of Marx's enquiry was the manner in which capitalist relations of production caused "prices of production" to deviate from "values" —i.e., the manner in which they caused the supply prices characteristic of capitalist commodity production to deviate from the supply prices characteristic of "simple" commodity production. The question of the causes of *deviations of actual prices from supply prices* could quite properly be abstracted from.

But if we change the perspective from which we look at the problem, and begin to concern ourselves with examining and comparing the way in which the law of value operates over a rather wider range of historical situations than that which Marx considered, it becomes clear that our approach must to some extent be different from his. Suppose, for example, that we wish to compare the way in which

[1] Cf. above, pp. 199-200.

the law of value operated under slavery or feudalism with the way in which it operated under competitive capitalism. Or suppose, again, that we wish to compare the way in which it operated under competitive capitalism with the way in which it operates today under monopoly capitalism. In such an enquiry, evidently, the question of the causes of deviations of actual prices from supply prices would assume much more importance than it did in the case of Marx's enquiry. The task of showing that relations of exchange are ultimately determined by relations of production could not be carried out in quite the same way as Marx carried it out.

It would still be possible, however, I believe—and in fact essential— to begin with Marx's concept of "value" as embodied labour, and to regard the "values" of commodities as reflecting or expressing the basic relation between men as producers of commodities which persists throughout the whole period of commodity production. In other words, it would still be necessary to begin by assuming that

"the exchange, or sale, of commodities at their value is the rational way, the natural law of their equilibrium. It must be the point of departure for the explanation of deviations from it, not vice versa the deviations the basis on which this law is explained."[1]

How, then, are these deviations from "value" determined? There are two useful generalisations which it seems possible to make in this connection. The first is that the typical[2] deviations of price from "value" at each stage in the development of commodity production are determined by the specific set of relations of subordination or co-operation in production which characterises that stage. Exchange relations at each stage, then, as manifested in the ratios in which commodities typically tend to exchange for one another on the market, are determined by the whole complex of production relations which characterise that stage—not only by the simple relation between men as producers of commodities which is common to all commodity-producing societies and which is expressed in the "values" of these commodities, but also by the particular set of relations of subordination or co-operation in production which is specific to the stage under consideration and which determines the nature and order of magnitude

[1] *Capital*, Vol. III, p. 221.

[2] I use the word "typical" here primarily in order to exclude from consideration those accidental deviations of price from value which are due to temporary discrepancies between supply and demand. Such discrepancies may of course cause deviations of price from value in any form of commodity-producing society.

of the typical deviations from these "values".[1] The second generalisation is that the relations of subordination or co-operation in production specific to the stage under consideration may cause two different types of deviation of prices from "values". In the first place, they may cause a deviation of supply prices from "values"; and in the second place, they may cause a deviation of actual prices from supply prices.

The nature of this conceptual framework may become a little clearer if I give a brief—and necessarily somewhat schematic—outline of the way in which it might be used as a guide to the concrete investigation of exchange relations in the different stages of commodity production. We begin, as I have suggested, with the Marxian concept of the *value* of a commodity as the quantity of socially-necessary labour embodied in it, and we then proceed to enquire into the nature of the typical deviations of prices from values at each stage, explaining these deviations in terms of the particular set of relations of subordination or co-operation in production specific to that stage.

So far as pre-capitalist societies are concerned, we assume, as Marx did, that the supply prices of commodities (though not necessarily the actual prices) are more or less directly proportionate to values throughout the whole pre-capitalist period. We then examine the manner in which the particular set of relations of subordination or co-operation in production specific to each stage of pre-capitalist development influences the typical deviations of actual prices from supply prices (i.e., from values) at that stage.[2]

[1] These two types of production relation are of course interconnected, the second being in fact the *form* in which the first appears at any given stage, but for the purpose of tracing out "how the law of value operates" in different historical stages it seems advisable to distinguish between their effects in the manner indicated in the text.

[2] It is interesting to note that Adam Smith examined certain deviations of price from value caused by the existence of guild regulations in almost precisely the manner which I am suggesting. The following passages seem to be worth quoting in this connection: (The italics are mine.)

"The government of towns corporate was altogether in the hands of traders and artificers; and it was the manifest interest of every particular class of them, to prevent the market from being over-stocked, as they commonly express it, with their own particular species of industry; which is in reality to keep it always understocked. Each class was eager to establish regulations proper for this purpose, and, provided it was allowed to do so, was willing to consent that every other class should do the same. In consequence of such regulations, indeed, each class was obliged to buy the goods they had occasion for from every other within the town, somewhat dearer than they otherwise might have done. But in recompence, they were enabled to sell their own just as much dearer; so that so far it was as broad as long, as they say; and in the dealings of the different classes within the town with one another, none of them were losers by these regulations. But in their dealings with the country they were all great gainers; and in these latter dealings consists the whole trade which supports and enriches every town.

"Every town draws its whole subsistence, and all the materials of its industry, from

So far as capitalism is concerned, we assume that the really crucial features of the transition from pre-capitalist to capitalist forms of society are (a) the conversion of the great majority of products, including labour power, into commodities—i.e., the rise to almost complete dominance over social production of that basic relation between men as producers of commodities which was present to some extent in all preceding forms of society but which had never hitherto succeeded in dominating more than a relatively small part of production; and (b) as a result of the conversion of labour power into a commodity and the extension of competition, the historical transformation of the pre-capitalist type of supply price, which was *directly* determined by value, into a new type of supply price which is *indirectly* determined by value. The *main* effect upon exchange relations of the new relations of production specific to capitalism, as Marx demonstrated, is to cause supply prices to deviate from values, in a quantitatively determinate way. But the new relations of production also have an important effect, at certain stages of capitalist development, in causing actual prices to deviate from supply prices, and this effect must be specifically examined. In this connection, it is convenient to consider capitalism as developing through three more or less consecutive stages:

(a) *The Transitional Stage.* In this stage, when capitalism is just beginning to transform production, the new relations of production bring about deviations of prices from values of both the types distinguished above. On the one hand, they set forces to work which begin to transform values into "prices of production"—i.e., to cause *supply*

the country. It pays for these chiefly in two ways: first, by sending back to the country a part of those materials wrought up and manufactured; in which case their price is augmented by the wages of the workmen, and the profits of their masters or immediate employers: secondly, by sending to it a part both of the rude and manufactured produce, either of other countries, or of distant parts of the same country, imported into the town; in which case too the original price of these goods is augmented by the wages of the carriers or sailors, and by the profits of the merchants who employ them. In what is gained upon the first of these two branches of commerce, consists the advantage which the town makes by its manufactures; in what is gained upon the second, the advantage of its inland and foreign trade. The wages of the workmen, and the profits of their different employers, make up the whole of what is gained upon both. Whatever regulations, therefore, tend to increase those wages and profits beyond what they otherwise would be, *tend to enable the town to purchase, with a smaller quantity of its labour, the produce of a greater quantity of the labour of the country.* They give the traders and artificers in the town an advantage over the landlords, farmers, and labourers in the country, *and break down that natural equality which would otherwise take place in the commerce which is carried on between them.* The whole annual produce of the labour of the society is annually divided between these two different sets of people. By means of these regulations a greater share of it is given to the inhabitants of the town than would otherwise fall to them; and a less to those of the country" (*Wealth of Nations*, Vol. I, pp. 126-7).

prices to deviate from values; and on the other hand, they cause *actual prices* to deviate from supply prices. Because of the prevalence of various forms of monopoly, etc., in this early stage of development, the latter effect is possibly more important at this stage than at any other.[1]

(b) *The Competitive Stage.* In this stage—the one which Marx was primarily concerned to analyse—the deviations of prices from values, broadly speaking, are almost exclusively of the first type distinguished above. The effect of the relations of production specific to this stage is spent, as it were, in making supply prices deviate (in a quantitatively determinate manner) from values, and they have comparatively little effect in making market prices deviate from supply prices.

(c) *The Monopoly Stage.* In this stage, the relations of production once again take a hand, as they did in the earlier transitional stage, in causing prices to deviate from supply prices. They make it possible for the monopolist to restrict the total supply of his commodity and thus to raise its price above the competitive level, in the manner with which we are nowadays made familiar in every economics textbook. But the relations of production may also have other effects which are rather more difficult to generalise about and which have so far attracted little attention from the writers of textbooks. Most notably, they make it possible for certain groups of monopoly capitalists to tap sources of profit other than the "pool" of surplus value created by wage-labour— in other words, to employ what would formerly have been looked upon as "abnormal" or "extra-economic" methods of profit-making.[2] If, as seems probable, the use of such methods normally results in a rise in the rate of profit which accrues to the groups of capitalists concerned, the latter will come to regard the higher rate of profit as the norm and will resist any reduction in it by all the means, both old and new, which are at their disposal. If one accepted the view that the concept of supply price was still applicable in such cases, one could then say that the

---

[1] Thus Böhm-Bawerk's suggestion (*op. cit.*, p. 49) that if Marx's analysis were correct "there must be traces of the actual fact that *before* the equalization of rates of profit the branches of production with the relatively greater amounts of constant capital have won and do win the smallest rates of profit, while those branches with the smaller amounts of constant capital win the largest rates of profit", cannot be accepted. Marx's analysis was concerned only with the broad historical transformation of one type of supply price into another, and the importance of deviations of actual prices from supply prices during the transitional period is such that it is extremely unlikely that evidence of the type asked for by Böhm-Bawerk could in fact be found.

[2] This seems to me to be the rationale of the useful but rather confusing distinction made by Stalin (EP, pp. 42 ff.) between "average" and "maximum" profits. The word "maximum" is perhaps ill-chosen, since there is obviously an important sense in which *all* capitalists, whether monopolists or otherwise, seek "maximum" profits.

relations of production peculiar to the monopoly stage resulted in the formation of a modified supply price which included profit derived not only from surplus value but also from certain other sources. Or, alternatively, one could simply consider these new phenomena in terms of the manner in which actual prices deviated from the supply prices peculiar to *competitive* capitalism.[1]

So far as socialism is concerned, the groundwork for the analysis of exchange relations has been laid by the Soviet work discussed in the second section of this chapter. Under socialism in a country like the U.S.S.R., where a semi-private agricultural sector continues to exist alongside the state sector, commodity production (and therefore the law of value) will also continue to exist, although in a relatively restricted sphere. In a socialist society of this sort, the supply prices of agricultural products can reasonably be assumed to be proportionate to values. Agricultural producers in such a society will usually tend to think of their net receipts as a reward for their labour rather than as a profit on their "capital",[2] and will tend to shift over to another line of production if the one in which they are at present engaged does not appear to offer a return proportionate to the quantity of that labour expended. Thus at least so far as agricultural products are concerned, the introduction of socialist relations of production brings about a transformation of the supply prices peculiar to the previous capitalist stage into supply prices of a similar character to those which prevailed in pre-capitalist societies. So far as manufactured goods are concerned, their situation is somewhat anomalous, since although they are technically "commodities" the concept of a supply price is not really applicable to them, and I cannot see that there is much point in attempting to analyse their prices in terms of our conceptual apparatus. This is not of course to say that when manufactured goods come into the picture relations of production no longer determine

---

[1] For an interesting discussion of some of the important issues involved here, see the article by R. Bellamy in *The Marxist Quarterly* of January 1956. Stalin (EP, pp. 43-4) seems to suggest that monopoly capitalism needs a higher rate of profit than competitive capitalism in order to meet the requirements of "more or less regular extended reproduction". What Stalin had in mind here is by no means clearly stated, and the question obviously needs further discussion. What he *may* have been wanting to emphasise is the fact that under modern conditions, in which new investment projects often require the tying-up of much larger quantities of capital for a much longer period of time than was formerly the case, the capitalists concerned are not going to run the risk of losing their capital (which must always exist in this uncertain world) unless they can reasonably expect to receive a relatively high rate of profit on their investment.

[2] Most of the important items of capital equipment required in Soviet agriculture are in fact owned by the State and hired out to the collective farms by the Machine and Tractor Stations.

relations of exchange: it is simply to say that the task of showing that relations of production determine relations of exchange can no longer usefully be carried out by analysing the nature and causes of "typical deviations of prices from values".

When we consider the picture of the development of exchange relations just outlined, two questions immediately arise. Even assuming that the deviations of price from value typical of a given stage of development can actually be said to be determined by the relations of production specific to that stage, it may first be asked, what grounds have we for beginning our research with the assumption that "the exchange, or sale, of commodities at their value is the rational way, the natural law of their equilibrium"? The majority of commodities do not in fact tend to sell at these "values" in capitalist society, or in socialist society, and it seems rather unlikely that they very often tended to do so in pre-capitalist societies. What right have we to expect, then, that a consideration of the value problem in terms of the determination of deviations from these apparently quite hypothetical "values" will lead to useful results? And further, second, if we adopt an approach of this type are we not in effect giving up all hope of obtaining any *quantitatively* determinate laws of price?

So far as the first question is concerned, the essential point is that for the major part of the period of commodity production as a whole, *supply prices* have in actual fact been directly or indirectly determined by "values" in Marx's sense. And these supply prices are by no means hypothetical: for most of the period of commodity production they have been firmly rooted in the consciousness of the producers themselves. Even in primitive societies one can see the beginnings of the idea that the exchange of commodities "at their values" in the Marxian sense is "the rational way, the natural law of their equilibrium". In quite a few cases, apparently, the prices asked and received for commodities in primitive markets are based on production costs.[1] The introduction of money, which "materially simplifies the determination of equivalence",[2] and the gradual extension of commodity production and exchange within the community, contribute substantially to the growth of this idea in the consciousness of the producers. After a while, the producers of commodities come quite naturally to think of the actual price they happen to receive for their commodity in terms of the extent to which this price deviates from

[1] Cf. M. J. Herskovits, *Economic Anthropology* (New York, 1952), pp. 220-1 and 234-5. Cf. also Paul Einzig, *Primitive Money* (London, 1949), Book III, Part 3, chapter 21.

[2] Herskovits, *op. cit.*, p. 211.

the supply price—i.e., roughly, from the *value* of the commodity in Marx's sense. The value of the commodity, although the market price may not often "tend" to conform to it at any particular stage of development owing to the existence of certain specific forms of monopoly, state interference, etc., characteristic of that stage, is regarded by the producers themselves as a sort of basis from which the deviations caused by these factors may legitimately be measured.

The idea that the exchange of commodities "at their values" represents the "natural" way of exchanging them was of course often expressed in ethical terms. In other words, it often took the form of an idea concerning the manner in which exchanges *ought* to be conducted if justice was to be done. But ideas as to what constitutes a "fair" exchange come into men's minds in the first instance from earth and not from heaven. When the small capitalist who is faced with the competition of a powerful monopolist says that he has a right to receive a "fair" profit on his capital, or when the peasant who exchanges his produce for that of a guildsman on disadvantageous terms says that he has a right to receive a "fair" return for his labour, the standard of "fairness" erected by each of the complainants actually has reference to the way in which exchanges *would in fact be conducted in the real world* if the particular form of monopoly to which he is objecting did not exist. In pre-capitalist times, there must always have been some commodities which were exchanged more or less at their values, and some times and localities in which deviations of price from value were relatively small, so that the "natural" method of exchanging commodities could actually be seen in operation. For obvious reasons, this "natural" method was regarded as the only really "fair" one. Thus the persistence of the concept of a "just price"[1] throughout the major part of the pre-capitalist period seems to me to

[1] For a short history of this concept see Rudolf Kaulla, *Theory of the Just Price* (London, 1940), chapter I. Kaulla's interpretation (pp. 151-2) of the celebrated passage in Aristotle's *Nichomachean Ethics* dealing with reciprocity in exchange (Book V, 5) does not seem to me to be very convincing. What Aristotle was in fact saying, I think, was simply that the exchange of commodities at their "values", weighted according to differences in skill and status, was the "natural" (and "just") method of exchanging them. If a builder and a shoemaker are exchanging their commodities, Aristotle argues, "there is nothing to prevent the work of the one being better than that of the other; they must therefore be equated". And "there will . . . be reciprocity when the terms have been equated so that as farmer is to shoemaker, the amount of the shoemaker's work is to that of the farmer's work for which it exchanges" (*The Works of Aristotle*, ed. W. D. Ross, Oxford, 1925, Vol. IX, 1133a), W. D. Ross interprets the passage much as I do. If A's "worth" is *n* times that of B, he says, then a "fair" exchange will take place "if A gives what it takes him an hour to make, in exchange for what it takes B *n* hours to make."

afford evidence in favour of the objective (and not merely hypo-thetical) existence of supply prices proportionate to values during that period.

Thus although Adam Smith's picture of an "early and rude state of society" in which deer and beaver hunters exchanged their products strictly in accordance with embodied labour ratios was indeed a "Robinsonade",[1] it did at least contain this element of truth—that in pre-capitalist societies the supply price of a commodity, which had an objective existence even though the actual prices of the majority of commodities usually deviated from their supply prices for one reason or another, could be regarded as directly determined by the value of the commodity. And we have seen that in socialist societies like that which exists in the U.S.S.R. the supply prices of the bulk of agricultural produce (whether its producers be individual peasants or collective farms) can plausibly be said to be determined in a similar way. In between the pre-capitalist and socialist stages, there lies the relatively short capitalist stage, in which supply prices differ in character from those prevalent in pre-capitalist and socialist society. But at least for the major part of the capitalist period, supply prices, although not directly proportionate to values, can be shown to be ultimately determined by them. All in all, then, it surely seems reasonable to begin one's re-searches into the problem of the determination of prices by defining value in terms of embodied labour, and then to proceed to consider actual prices in terms of their deviations (if any) from these "values". If we do not adopt this approach, it seems to me that we shall be reduced either to a sort of *ad hoc* empiricism or to a superficial explan-ation in terms of "supply and demand", thereby cutting ourselves off completely from any possibility of discovering the *laws* which govern the development of exchange relations.

But would the adoption of the approach I have recommended in fact mean giving up all hope of obtaining any *quantitatively determin-ate* laws of price? Dr. Schlesinger has suggested (with reference to the monopoly capitalist stage) that once we take the interweaving of the "economic" and "political" aspects for granted, "the predictability of economic events . . . is reduced to that of political ones", so that "economics can be no more an exact science than politics".[2] But this is surely to prejudge the results of an investigation which has not yet taken place. It is true that at the present level of our knowledge

---

[1] Marx, *Critique of Political Economy*, p. 266.
[2] *Marx: His Time and Ours*, p. 149.

REAPPLICATION OF THE LABOUR THEORY   297

we are not able to make very many useful generalisations concerning the extent (as distinct from the nature and causes) of the typical deviations of prices from values in respect of any stage in the development of commodity production other than the competitive capitalist stage. But this is not at all to say that there are no more such generalisations to be made. For example, there does not seem to me to be any *a priori* reason why present-day Marxists should not eventually be able to discover laws of monopoly price which are "quantitative" in the same sense as Marx's laws of competitive price were "quantitative".[1]

In addition, it should be noted in this connection that the approach which I am suggesting—the explanation of typical deviations of price from value in terms of the specific set of relations of production characteristic of the particular stage under consideration—would not have the effect of making certain prices indeterminate where they were determinate before. All that the labour theory as Marx developed it can do is to make the *supply prices* characteristic of pre-capitalist and capitalist society determinate. Where actual prices deviate from these supply prices it cannot by itself provide us with any generalisations which would serve as a basis for exact quantitative predictions concerning the extent of these deviations. The point is that the suggested approach has been designed precisely in order to help make the deviations *more* predictable than they are now. If there are in fact any new "quantitative" laws of price to be found, such an approach should assist to discover them.

Finally, let us suppose that it turns out that such new generalisations as the approach enables us to discover are *not* strictly "quantitative" in character. This would not at all imply that "economics can be no more an exact science than politics". For—leaving aside here the question of whether politics cannot in fact be made a far more exact science than it is at present—the quantitative indeterminacy, broadly speaking, would affect only the deviations from the supply prices and not the supply prices themselves; and the predictions which the new generalisations would enable us to make concerning these deviations would surely be at least as "exact" as those which the science of politics at present enables us to make. A Marxian theory of price

1 It is already possible, on the basis of the Marxian approach, to make certain generalisations of the "more or less" type concerning the deviations of monopoly prices from supply prices, and concerning the deviations of prices under socialism from values. Cf. Sweezy, *Theory of Capitalist Development*, chapter 15, and M. H. Dobb, *Political Economy and Capitalism*, pp. 321 ff.

worked out along the lines indicated above might indeed appear to be "inexact" if it were placed alongside, say, the general equilibrium theory of price. But the apparent "exactness" of the latter theory has been purchased only at the expense of realism and relevance: the equations of which the theory consists have very little of the real world of men in them. To consider the laws of commodity exchange in terms of the relations of production, instead of in abstraction from them, might mean some sacrifice of elegance and precision. But the gain in real scientific understanding of the society in which we live would far outweigh this cost. And unless economics in fact takes this course—unless it becomes once more *political* economy—there is indeed little hope for it.

APPENDIX

KARL MARX'S ECONOMIC METHOD

I

Most of the great "heroic" economic models of a dynamic character which have been put forward in the course of the history of economic thought—those of Quesnay, Smith, Ricardo and Marx, for example—possess certain important characteristics in common. The model-builder usually begins, on the basis of a preliminary examination of the facts, by adopting what Schumpeter has called a "vision" of the economic process. In other words, he begins by orienting himself towards some key factor or factors which he regards as being of vital causal significance so far as the structure and development of the economic system as a whole are concerned. With this vision uppermost in his mind, he then proceeds to a more thorough examination of the economic facts both of the present situation and of the past situations which have led up to it, and arranges these facts in order on what might be called a scale of relevance. Their position on this scale will depend upon such factors as the particular vision which the model-builder has adopted, his political and social sympathies, and the extent to which the facts display uniformities and regularities which promise to be capable of causal analysis in terms of the postulation of "laws" and "tendencies".

Taking the facts which he has placed at the top of the scale as his foundation, the model-builder proceeds to develop certain concepts, categories and methods of classification which he believes will help him to provide a generalised explanation of the structure and development of the economy. In this part of his work he has necessarily to rely to some extent on concept-material inherited from the past, but he also tries to work out new analytical devices of his own. The particular analytical devices which he employs—his tools and techniques, as it were—are thus by no means arbitrarily chosen. To quite a large extent they are dependent upon the nature of his vision, the nature of the primary facts which they are to be used to explain, and the nature of the *general* method of analysis which he decides to adopt. The degree of their dependence upon these factors, however, varies from one device to another. Whereas some of the devices may be useless or even harmful when the facts to be analysed and the orientation, aim and general method of analysis of the model-builder are radically different, others may have a greater degree of general applicability. Some may well prove useful when applied to other forms of market economy, and some may even be "universal" in the sense in which, say, statistical techniques are "universal".

With the aid of these devices, then, the model-builder proceeds to the theoretical analysis of the particular economic facts which he has placed at the top of his scale of relevance. He endeavours to give a causal explanation of the uniformities and regularities which he has observed in these facts; he affords these explanations the status of "laws" or "tendencies"; and he gathers together these laws and tendencies into his first theoretical approximation. He then takes into account the facts next in order on the scale of relevance, from which he has hitherto abstracted, enquires into the extent to which their introduction into the picture requires a modification of the laws and tendencies of the first approximation, and thus arrives at his second approximation. He may well then proceed to a third, fourth, etc., approximation, progressively taking into account facts which he has placed lower and lower on the scale of relevance; but obviously there must come a time when it is not worth while to proceed any further down the scale. At the point where the basic laws and tendencies begin to be submerged beneath the exceptions and qualifications, he usually stops. The facts further down in the scale of relevance are simply abstracted from.

The final task is to use the model for the purpose of making concrete predictions—a task which is carried out largely by extrapolating the laws and tendencies into the future, on the express or implied assumption that the economic facts will continue to maintain their assumed position on the scale of relevance. The model which finally emerges is therefore compounded of elements not only of the past and present but also of the future.

This description of the model-building process is necessarily somewhat schematic, and I certainly do not mean to imply that all the great model-builders *consciously* adopted this intricate methodological approach. In essence, however, this was the method which most of them did in actual fact adopt, whether or not they were fully aware of what they were doing. It does help, I think, to have this general scheme in mind when we are analysing the economic work of a thinker like Marx—particularly if we are analysing it with a view to discovering whether and in what sense it is still relevant today.

II

The application of this general scheme to Marx's model is easier than in the case of most of the other great models, because Marx was more conscious of what he was doing than most of his predecessors in the field. The key causal factor towards which Marx began by orienting himself was the socio-economic production relation between the class of capital-owners and the class of wage-earners. This relation, he believed, gave birth to the main contemporary forms of unearned income and to the possibility of the large-scale accumulation of capital; and this accumulation led in turn to rapid technological progress, which interacted with the capital-labour relation to determine the main features of the structure of capitalism and the main lines of the development of the system of a whole.

This was in effect Marx's "vision" of the capitalist economic process. With this vision uppermost in his mind, he made a thorough examination of the economic facts both of the past and the present. The most relevant fact appeared to him to be the existence in all forms of class society of a mass of unearned income, which in capitalist society mainly took the form of net profit on capital, rent of land, and interest. Associated with this were certain other important facts or tendencies of a historical character which Marx's study of capitalist development in the past revealed to him—notably the progressive decline in the rate of profit; the increasing subordination of formerly independent workers to the capitalist form of organisation; the increasing economic instability of the system; the growth of mechanisation with its accompanying changes in the industrial structure; the emergence of various forms of monopoly; the growth of the "reserve army of labour"; and the general deterioration in the condition of the working class. It is important to emphasise that these facts, by and large, were regarded by Marx simply as the *data* of his problem. As anyone can see by glancing at his *Economic and Philosophic Manuscripts of 1844*, Marx had placed these facts at the top of his scale of relevance long before he came to work out the detailed tools and techniques required to analyse them.

The next stage—conceptually if not chronologically—was the development of Marx's *general* method of analysis, which was intimately associated with his vision of the economic process. Three aspects of this general method are worthy of note in the present connection.

In the first place, Marx had begun, as Lenin put it, "by selecting from all social relations the 'production relations', as being the basic and prime relations that determine all other relations".[1] In *Capital*, where he sets out to deal with "one of the economic formations of society—the system of commodity production", Marx's analysis is "strictly confined to the relations of production between the members of society: without ever resorting to factors other than relations of production to explain the matter, Marx makes it possible to discern how the commodity organisation of social economy develops, how it

[1] V. I. Lenin, *Selected Works* (London, 1939), Vol. II, p. 418.

becomes transformed into capitalist economy, creating the antagonistic
. . . classes, the bourgeoisie and the proletariat, how it develops the
productivity of social labour and how it thereby introduces an element
which comes into irreconcilable contradiction to the very foundations
of this capitalist organisation itself".[1] In the context of the particular
range of enquiry encompassed in *Capital*, it is evident that "relations
of production" must be taken to include not only the specific set of
relations of subordination or co-operation within which commodity
production is carried out at each particular stage of its historical
development (e.g., the capitalist stage), but also the broad basic relation
between men as producers of commodities which persists throughout
the whole period of commodity production.[2]

In the second place, within the framework of the methodological
approach just outlined and in close association with it, Marx developed
a highly idiosyncratic method of enquiry—it might perhaps be called
the "logical-historical" method—which was one of the more interesting
and significant of the fruits of his early Hegelian studies. The description which Engels gave of this method in a review of Marx's *Critique of
Political Economy* in 1859 has not been bettered, and the following
extract can be reproduced without apology:

> The criticism of economics . . . could . . . be exercised in two ways: histori-
> cally or logically. Since in history, as in its literary reflection, development
> as a whole proceeds from the most simple to the most complex relations,
> the historical development of the literature of political economy provided a
> natural guiding thread with which criticism could link up and the economic
> categories as a whole would thereby appear in the same sequence as in the
> logical development. This form apparently has the advantage of greater clear-
> ness, since indeed it is the *actual* development that is followed, but as a matter
> of fact it would thereby at most become more popular. History often proceeds
> by jumps and zigzags and it would in this way have to be followed every-
> where, whereby not only would much material of minor importance have
> to be incorporated but there would be much interruption of the chain of
> thought; furthermore, the history of economics could not be written without
> that of bourgeois society and this would make the task endless, since all
> preliminary work is lacking. The logical method of treatment was, therefore,
> the only appropriate one. But this, as a matter of fact, is nothing else than
> the historical method, only divested of its historical form and disturbing
> fortuities. The chain of thought must begin with the same thing that this

---

[1] V. I. Lenin, *Selected Works*, Vol. II, pp. 420-1. Lenin adds that Marx, "while
'explaining' the structure and development of the given formation of society 'exclusively' in terms of relations of production, . . . nevertheless everywhere and always
went on to trace the superstructure corresponding to these relations of production and
clothed the skeleton in flesh and blood" (*ibid.*, p. 421).

[2] "Commodity production" in the Marxist sense means roughly the production of
goods for exchange on some sort of market by individual producers or groups of producers who carry on their activities more or less separately from one another.

history begins with and its further course will be nothing but the mirror-image of the historical course in abstract and theoretically consistent form, a corrected mirror-image but corrected according to laws furnished by the real course of history itself, in that each factor can be considered at its ripest point of development, in its classic form.[1]

This then was another important aspect of Marx's general method of analysis. No doubt this "logical-historical" approach was sometimes carried to excess (for reasons which Marx himself partly explained in his "Afterword" to the second German edition of *Capital*),[2] but in his hands it proved on the whole to be very fruitful. It was particularly important, as will shortly be seen, in connection with the theory of value developed in *Capital*.

In the third place, and again closely associated with the two other aspects just described, there was the important notion that if one wished to analyse capitalism in terms of relations of production the best way of doing this was to imagine capitalism suddenly impinging upon a sort of generalised pre-capitalist society in which there were as yet no separate capital-owning or land-owning classes. What one ought to do, in other words, was to begin by postulating a society in which, although commodity production and free competition were assumed to reign more or less supreme, the labourers still owned the whole produce of their labour. Having investigated the simple laws which would govern production, exchange and distribution in a society of this type, one ought then to imagine capitalism suddenly impinging upon this society. What difference would this impingement make to the economic laws which had operated before the change, and why would it make this difference? If one could give adequate answers to these questions, Marx believed, one would be well on the way to revealing the real essence of the capitalist mode of production. In adopting this kind of approach, Marx was of course following—and developing further—a long and respectable tradition which had been established by Smith and Ricardo. Marx's postulation of an abstract pre-capitalist society based on what he called "simple" commodity production was not essentially different in aim from Adam Smith's postulation of an "early and rude" society inhabited by deer and beaver hunters. Neither in Marx's case nor in that of Smith was the postulated pre-capitalist society intended to be an accurate representation of historical reality in anything more than the very broadest sense. Nor was it intended as a picture of an ideal form of society, a sort of golden age of the past which the coming of the wicked capitalists and land-lords was destined rudely to destroy. It was clearly part of a quite complex analytical device, and in its time a very powerful one. I am

---

[1] Cf. above, pp. 148–9.   [2] *Capital*, Vol. I, pp. 19–20.

accustomed to tell my students that it was not a *myth*, as some critics maintain, but rather *mythology*.

This, then, was the nature of Marx's *general* method of economic analysis, in the context of which his other tools and techniques were developed and employed. Some of these were inherited by Marx from his predecessors—the concept of equilibrium, for example, and the particular classification of social classes and class incomes which he adopted. Others were newly developed, such as the important distinctions between abstract and concrete labour, labour and labour-power, and constant and variable capital. As his analysis proceeded, certain other concepts, relations and techniques emerged—notably the concept of surplus value, the distinction between relative and absolute surplus value, the ratios representing the rate of surplus value, the rate of profit and the organic composition of capital, and the techniques associated with his famous reproduction schemes.

In so far as it is possible to distinguish *methods* and *tools* of analysis from the *results* of analysis, then, these were some of the main methods and tools which Marx employed to analyse the economic facts which he had placed at the top of his scale of relevance. The uniformities and regularities which he believed he could detect in these facts were analysed in terms of the relations of production, with the aid of these methods and tools; and causal explanations emerged which were generalised in the form of tendencies and laws, modified in the second and subsequent approximations, and eventually extrapolated into the future in the form of more or less concrete predictions.

III

The most important field of application of Marx's general economic method was of course the *theory of value* elaborated in *Capital*. Indeed, Marx's theory of value is perhaps best regarded as being in essence a kind of generalised expression, or embodiment, of his economic method. In his analysis of value, as Engels noted, Marx "proceeds from the simple production of commodities as the historical premise, ultimately to arrive from this basis [at] capital". In other words, he begins with the "simple" commodity, and then proceeds to analyse its "logically and historically secondary form"—the "capitalistically modified commodity".[1] The first part of his analysis of value therefore consists of a set of statements concerning the way in which relations of production influence the prices of goods in that abstract pre-capitalist form of society of which I have just spoken above. The second part of his analysis consists of a further set of statements concerning the way in which this basic causal connection between prices and relations of pro-

[1] *Capital*, Vol. III, p. 14.

duction is modified when *capitalist* relations of production impinge upon those appropriate to "simple" commodity production—i.e., when the "simple" commodity becomes "capitalistically modified". This process of capitalistic modification is conceived to take place in two logically separate stages. In the first stage, it is assumed, capital subordinates labour on the basis of the technical conditions in which it finds it, and does not immediately change the mode of production itself. In the second stage, it is assumed, the extension of capitalist competition brings about a state of affairs in which profit becomes proportional not to labour employed but to capital employed and in which a more or less uniform rate of profit on capital comes to prevail. Thus Marx's theory of value can conveniently be considered under the three headings of Pre-capitalist Society, Early Capitalism, and Developed Capitalism.[1] To each of these forms of society there may be conceived to correspond certain basic economic categories and certain basic logical problems. The task of the analysis of value as Marx understood it was to solve these basic problems in terms of the relations of production appropriate to the particular "historical" stage which was under consideration.

In Volume I of *Capital*, then, Marx proceeds "from the first and simplest relation that historically and in fact confronts us"[2]—the broad socio-economic relation between men as producers of commodities. In so far as economic life is based on the private production and exchange of goods, men are related to one another in their capacity as producers of goods intended for each other's consumption: they work for one another by embodying their separate labours in commodities which are destined to be exchanged on some sort of market. Historically, this "commodity relation" reached its apogee under capitalism, but it was also in existence to a greater or lesser extent in almost all previous forms of society. If we want to penetrate to the essence of a society in which the commodity relation has become "capitalistically modified", then, one possible method of procedure is to begin by postulating an abstract pre-capitalist society in which the commodity relation is assumed to be paramount but in which there are as yet no separate classes of capital-owners and land-owners. Having analysed the commodity relation as such in the context of this generalised pre-capitalist society, one can then proceed to examine what happens when capitalist relations of production impinge upon it.

[1] A word of caution may be appropriate here, in order to forestall possible criticisms involving the fallacy of misplaced concreteness. The three forms of society mentioned here do not necessarily represent actual historically identifiable forms: they are merely the "historical" counterparts of the three main stages in Marx's logical analysis of the value problem. In Marx's view, it will be remembered, the course of logical analysis is a *corrected* mirror-image of the actual historical course.

[2] Cf. above, p. 149.

Marx's *logical* starting-point in *Capital*, then, is the commodity relation as such, and his *historical* starting-point is an abstract pre-capitalist
society of the type just described. In such a society, great importance
clearly attaches to the fact that commodities acquire the capacity to
attract others in exchange—i.e., that they come to possess *exchange
values*, or *prices*. The basic logical problem to be solved here is simply
that of the determination of these prices. For Marx, no solution of this
problem could be regarded as adequate which was not framed in terms
of the appropriate set of relations of production. And for Marx, too,
no solution could be regarded as adequate which did not possess as it
were two dimensions—a qualitative one and a quantitative one. The
qualitative aspect of the solution was directed to the question: Why
do commodities possess prices at all? The quantitative aspect was
directed to the question: Why do commodities possess the particular
prices which they do? This distinction between the qualitative and
quantitative aspects of Marx's analysis of value is of considerable
importance, if only because it crops up again in the second and third
stages of his enquiry.

In the context of the postulated pre-capitalist society, the answers to
both the qualitative and the quantitative questions are fairly simple.
The quality of exchange value is conferred upon commodities precisely
because they are commodities—i.e., because a commodity relation
exists between their producers. The price relations between commodities which manifest themselves in the sphere of exchange are essentially
reflections of the socio-economic relations between men as producers
of commodities which exist in the sphere of production. And just as it
is the fact that men work for one another in this particular way which
is responsible for the *existence* of commodity prices, so in Marx's view
it is the amount of work which they do for one another which is
responsible for the *relative levels* of commodity prices. The amount of
labour laid out on each commodity, Marx argued, will determine (in
the postulated society) the *amount* of exchange value which each comes
to possess relatively to the others. In other words, in a society based on
simple commodity production the equilibrium prices of commodities
will tend to be proportional to the quantities of labour normally used
to produce them. This is a familar proposition which Marx of course
took over from Smith and Ricardo, and *given the particular set of
assumptions upon which it is based* it is almost self-evidently true. It is
this proposition which is usually abstracted from Marx's analysis and
labelled "the labour theory of value"—a procedure which is of course
quite illegitimate and which has had most unfortunate consequences.

Having thus proclaimed right at the beginning the general way in
which he intends to unite economic history, sociology and economics
in a kind of *ménage à trois*, Marx now proceeds to the second logical

stage of his analysis. The "historical" counterpart of this second stage is a society based on commodity production which has just been taken over by capitalists. The formerly "independent" labourers now have to share the produce of their labour with a new social class—the owners of capital.[1] But nothing else is at this stage assumed to happen: in particular, it is supposed that capital subordinates labour on the basis of the technical conditions in which it finds it, without immediately changing the mode of production.[2] It is also assumed that commodities for the time being continue to sell "at their values" in the Marxian sense—i.e., at equilibrium prices which are proportionate to quantities of embodied labour. In such a society, the crucial differentia is the emergence of a new form of class income, profit on capital, and the basic logical problem as Marx conceived it was to explain the origin and persistence of this new form of income under conditions in which free competition was predominant and both the finished commodity and the labour which produced it were bought and sold on the market at prices which reflected their Marxian "values". The conditions of the problem were carefully posed by Marx in such a way as to rule out explanations in terms of anything other than the relations of production appropriate to the new stage.

Qualitatively speaking, the Marxian answer to the problem is obvious enough. The basic feature of the new situation is that a new social class has arisen and obtained a kind of class monopoly of the factor of production capital, the other side of this medal being that labour has itself become a commodity which is bought and sold on the market like any other commodity. The existence of this class monopoly of capital means that the capitalists are able to "compel the working-class to do more work than the narrow round of its own life-wants prescribes".[3] The produce of this extra or surplus labour of the workers constitutes in effect the profit of the capitalists—or, as Marx calls it at this stage, the surplus value. But once again Marx was not content with an explanation couched solely in qualitative terms: he considered it necessary to derive in addition a *quantitative* explanation from the basic socio-economic relation between capitalists and wage-earners.[4] The "law of value" is therefore applied by Marx to the commodity labour

[1] At this stage, the existence of a separate class of land-owners is abstracted from—a fact which throws further light on Marx's conception of the relation between the logical and the historical in analysis. The land-labour relation was historically prior to the capital-labour relation. But *under capitalism* it is the capital-labour relation which is primary, and the land-labour relation which is secondary. Since the analysis as a whole is oriented towards capitalism, the logical analysis must in Marx's view proceed from the capital-labour relation to the land-labour relation, and not vice versa.

[2] Cf. *Capital*, Vol. I, pp. 184 and 310.   [3] *Capital*, Vol. I, p. 309.

[4] Or, rather, from the broad relation between men as producers of commodities *as modified by* the impingement upon it of the class relation between capitalists and wage-earners.

—or rather labour-power—itself, the value of labour-power being in effect defined as the amount of labour required to produce wage-goods for the labourers at subsistence level. The surplus value received by any individual capitalist can then be regarded as determined and measured by the difference between the number of hours of work which his labourers perform and the number of hours of other men's work which are embodied in the wage-goods which he is in effect obliged to pay his labourers. This "law", as Marx noted in Volume I, implies that profits are proportional to quantities of labour employed rather than to quantities of capital employed, and thus "clearly contradicts all experience based on appearance";[1] but the solution of this "apparent contradiction" is reserved for a later logical-historical stage in the analysis.

This later stage occurs in Volume III, where Marx deals with commodity and value relations which have become "capitalistically modified" in the fullest sense. His "historical" starting-point here is a fairly well developed capitalist system in which the extension of competition between capitalists has made profit proportional not to labour employed but to capital employed, and in which a more or less uniform rate of profit on capital prevails. In this new situation, which Marx speaks of as one in which "surplus value has been transformed into profit", it is easy to see that the equilibrium prices at which commodities normally tend to sell must diverge appreciably from their Volume I "values": clearly commodities can continue to sell at these "values" only so long as the profit constituent in the price remains proportional to the quantity of labour employed.[2] Once commodities come to sell not at their Volume I "values" but at their Marshallian "costs of production" (or "prices of production", as Marx called them) a new logical problem arises for solution—that of the determination of prices of this new type. In particular, the question arises as to whether these Volume III "prices of production" can be explained in terms of the relations of production postulated as determinants in Volume I (suitably modified, of course, to reflect the transition to the new historical stage), or whether Adam Smith was correct in thinking that an entirely new type of explanation of prices was necessary in the stage of developed capitalism.

Qualitatively speaking, Marx's answer was that the "capitalistically modified" commodity relation was still of primary importance in determining prices even in this final stage, when actual equilibrium prices obviously diverged appreciably from Volume I "values". In a commodity-producing society of the modern capitalist type, the labour-

---

[1] *Capital*, Vol. I, p. 307.
[2] Given, of course, that what Marx called the "organic composition of capital" varies from industry to industry—which it does in fact do under developed capitalism.

capital production relationship still determined the distribution of the national income between wages and profits—i.e., it determined the total amount of profit available over the economy as a whole for allocation among the individual capitalists. As capitalism developed, changes certainly occurred in the *mode* of allocation of this profit between industries and enterprises, but these changes were logically and historically secondary. The socio-economic production relation between workers and capitalists, determining as it did the proportion of the national income available for allocation in the form of profit, was still in a meaningful sense the primary and determining relation. Given the total amount of profit, and given the amount of capital employed in producing each commodity, the profit constituent in the price of each commodity, and therefore its "price of production", was automatically determined.

Once again, however, Marx was not content with a mere qualitative statement of this kind: he felt it necessary to translate the socio-economic relations involved in this analysis into quantitative terms. The result was his famous and much-criticised statement to the effect that under developed capitalism "the sum of the prices of production of all commodities produced in society . . . is equal to the sum of their values",[1] together with the equally famous arithmetical illustrations of this proposition. What these statements and illustrations really amounted to was an assertion that under developed capitalism there was still an important functional relationship between embodied labour and individual equilibrium prices, which may be expressed in the following symbolic form:

$$\text{Price of commodity} = c + v + \frac{c + v}{\Sigma(c + v)} (\Sigma s)$$

Here c is the value of used-up machinery and raw materials; v is the value of labour-power; s is surplus value; $\Sigma(c + v)$ is the aggregate amount of capital employed over the economy as a whole; and Σs is the aggregate amount of surplus value produced over the economy as a whole. The formula expresses the idea that the profit constituent in the price of an individual commodity represents a proportionate share of the total surplus value produced over the economy as a whole, the proportion being determined by the ratio of the total capital employed in the enterprise concerned to the aggregate amount of capital employed over the economy as a whole. Since all the items on the right-hand side of the formula are expressible in terms of quantities of embodied labour, it can plausibly be maintained that there is still a causal connection, however indirect and circuitous, between Volume I "values" and Volume III "prices of production"—i.e., between

[1] *Capital*, Vol. III, p. 157.

socio-economic production relations and the prices at which commodities actually tend to sell under developed capitalism.

This causal connection is clearly a rather complex one, particularly when it is borne in mind that for the sake of simplicity I have deliberately abstracted from the complications caused by the existence of different turnover periods for the two elements of capital, and also from the very difficult issues associated with the so-called "transformation problem". It is understandable that the above formula should not have appeared very often in popular Marxist writing: clearly no revolution would ever have been achieved if this formula had been inscribed on the red banners. Much more suitable for this purpose was the familiar proposition put forward in the first stage of the development of Marx's theory of value in Volume I of *Capital*. But it must be strongly emphasised that neither the Volume I analysis nor the Volume III analysis, taken by itself, can properly be said to constitute the Marxian theory of value. The theory of value as Marx developed it was a subtle and complex compound of the Volume I and Volume III analyses, and we cut ourselves off from all hope of understanding it if we consider it as anything less.

If this interpretation of Marx's theory of value is correct, it follows that any criticism of the theory based on the assumption that it is a crude and primitive over-simplification is entirely misconceived. The only really valid criticism of it which can be made, I would suggest, is one of precisely the opposite type—that for our present purposes today it is unnecessarily complex and refined. I am thinking here of two aspects of the theory in particular. First, there is the quite extraordinary way in which it draws upon and unites certain basic ideas of sociology, economic history, economics, and (up to a point) philosophy. In Marx's hands, the theory of value is not simply a theory which sets out to explain how prices are determined: it is also a kind of methodological manifesto, embodying Marx's view of the general way in which economics ought to be studied and calling for a restoration of the essential unity between the different social sciences. In Marx's time there was much to be said for the adoption of this line of approach, given certain points of view which were then current in the field of economics. It was indeed vitally important at that time to reassert the essential unity between economics and the other social sciences (particularly sociology) which Adam Smith had established but which the "vulgar" economists who followed Ricardo had gone far to destroy; and the theory of value had traditionally been regarded as an appropriate vehicle for the promulgation of methodological recommendations of this type. Today, of course, it remains as important as it ever was to call for inter-disciplinary co-operation in the social sciences. But I am not convinced that it would any longer be practicable to achieve that very high degree of integration which Smith and Marx still found possible. Nor am I convinced that the theory of value would any longer be the proper medium for the embodiment of an integrationist methodology. The role of the theory of value (in the traditional sense of a theory of price determination) in the general body of economic analysis is much more modest today than it was in Marx's time, and there is no longer any very compelling reason why a theorist wishing to bring sociology or economic history into his economics should feel obliged to start by reforming the theory of value.

If he *did* decide to start in this way, however, and set out to bring sociology into the picture by demonstrating the existence of a qualitative and quantitative relationship of a causal character between relations of production and relative prices, should he make the quantitative link-up in the particular way that Marx did? This is the second aspect of Marx's theory which I had in mind when stating that it seemed too complex and refined for present-day use. Joan Robinson has recently suggested[1] that it was an "aberration" for Marx to tie up the problem of relative prices with the problem of exploitation in the way that he did. I am not myself convinced that it was in fact an "aberration": as I have just stated, there were very good reasons, given the particular views against which Marx had to fight, for the adoption of this particular method of tying them up. Today, however, it does seem to me that Marx's method of making the quantitative tie-up between economics and sociology tends to obscure the importance of the infusion of sociology rather than to reveal it. Certainly, at any rate, generations of Marx-scholars have felt that they have proved something important about the real world when they have shown that in some moderately meaningful mathematical sense the "sum of the prices" *is* equal to the "sum of the values". I am now persuaded that this was in some measure an illusion. In my more heretical moods, I sometimes wonder whether much of real importance would be lost from the Marxian system if the quantitative side of the analysis of relative prices were conducted in terms of something like the traditional supply and demand apparatus— *provided* that the socio-economic relationships emphasised by Marx were fully recognised as the basic cause of the existence of the prices whose level was shown to vary with variations in supply and demand, and *provided* that these Marxian sociological factors, where relevant, were also clearly postulated as lying behind the supply and demand schedules themselves.[2]

[1] J. Robinson, *Collected Economic Papers* (Oxford, 1965), Vol. III, p. 176.
[2] In many cases, of course, Marxian postulates would have to *replace* those commonly employed today. A Marxist, for example, in analysing the forces lying behind the demand curve, could hardly base his analysis on the assumption that the consumer acted (in some more or less sophisticated way) so as to maximise the net income or utility he received from his purchases.

IV

Marx's theory of value, as we have seen, was a complex piece of analysis, replete with profound methodological implications, which depicted in a general way the process whereby the causal relationship between relations of production and relative prices was gradually modified as "simple" commodity production was transformed into capitalist commodity production. For the purposes of this theory, the only change *within capitalism* which it was necessary for Marx to take into account was the emergence of an average or normal rate of profit as a result of the extension of competition between capitalists. When Marx turned to the task of elucidating the "laws of motion" of capitalism, however, it was of course precisely the changes taking place within capitalism as the system developed which assumed paramount importance. And here Marx laid considerable emphasis on the *technological* changes associated with the development of capitalism, particularly in its so-called "Modern Industry" phase. "Modern Industry", wrote Marx, "never looks upon and treats the existing form of a process as final. The technical basis of that industry is therefore revolutionary, while all earlier modes of production were essentially conservative."[1] The really significant difference between the "laws of motion" put forward by Smith and Ricardo and those put forward by Marx is that in the case of the latter technological change appears as a crucial determining factor. It was indeed in terms of the mutual interaction of technological change and changes in the relations of production that Marx endeavoured to explain the main "innate tendencies" of the capitalist system. In the short period, Marx argued, the "constant revolution in production" associated with technological change, taking place as it did within a social framework which continually limited and restricted it, would be accompanied by "sudden stoppages and crises in the production process".[2] And in the long period, the mutual interaction of technological change and relations of production would produce certain other equally unpleasant consequences. In order to illustrate the general method of analysis used by Marx in this part of his enquiry, let us consider, first, the law of the falling tendency of the rate of profit, and, second, the so-called "law of increasing misery".

---

[1] *Capital*, Vol. I, p. 486. In a footnote to this passage, Marx quotes a well-known passage from the *Communist Manifesto*: "The bourgeoisie cannot exist without continually revolutionising the instruments of production, and thereby the relations of production and all the social relations. Conservation, in an unaltered form, of the old modes of production was on the contrary the first condition of existence for all earlier industrial classes. Constant revolution in production, uninterrupted disturbance of all social conditions, everlasting uncertainty and agitation, distinguish the bourgeois epoch from all earlier ones . . ."

[2] *Capital*, Vol. III, p. 244.

The basic assumptions lying behind both these laws can best be explained with the aid of Marx's three basic ratios, viz.:

$$\frac{c}{v} = \text{organic composition of capital}$$

$$\frac{s}{v} = \text{rate of surplus value}$$

$$\frac{s}{c+v} = \text{rate of profit}$$

As capitalism develops, according to Marx's account, c/v tends to rise as a result of technological changes, which Marx assumed would normally take a predominantly labour-saving form. This rise in c/v is associated with an increase in productivity in (*inter alia*) the wage-goods industries, which in its turn induces a tendency for s/v to rise. The mutual interaction of technological change and relations of production, in terms of which Marx explained the developmental process, operates primarily through the changes which it brings about in these two key ratios and in their relation to one another.

According to Marx, these changes in the ratios will lead to a long-term tendency for the rate of profit on capital to decline. As we see from the simple identity:

$$\frac{s}{c+v} = \frac{\dfrac{s}{v}}{1 + \dfrac{c}{v}}$$

the rate of profit will tend to rise if s/v rises and to fall if c/v rises. Now both these ratios, on Marx's assumptions, will in fact rise as capitalism develops, so that the net effect upon the rate of profit would seem at first sight to be indeterminate. For reasons I have explained elsewhere,[1] however, Marx believed that the effect upon the rate of profit of the rise in c/v would eventually win out over that of the rise in s/v, so that the rate of profit would in fact tend to fall over time. In other words, the advance of capitalism would itself tend to weaken the very spring and stimulus of capitalism—as Smith and Ricardo, although for very different reasons, had already maintained.

The changes in the two key ratios would also, Marx argued, contribute to an important historical process which has been variously called "increasing misery", "impoverishment", and "social polarisation". The rise in c/v means the displacement of labour by machinery, which swells the pool of unemployed and exercises a substantial downward

---

[1] *Economics and Ideology*, pp. 133-4.

pressure on the level of real wages. The effect of this pressure, together with that exercised by the formerly independent artisans and peasants whom capitalism throws on to the labour market, is such that real wages per head rise, if indeed they rise at all, only very slowly and inconsiderably. The rise in s/v means, by definition, an increase in the share of the national income going to the capitalists and a decrease in the share going to the workers, so that even if the workers' real wages rise absolutely they still suffer *relatively* to the capitalists. The social polarisation which results from these processes is accentuated by the growth of monopoly in the ownership of capital; and the misery-increasing effects of all this are enhanced by the growing degradation of the labourers in manufacture to the level of the appendage of a machine.

Naturally Marx's analysis of these "laws of motion" was much more sophisticated and much less schematic than I may have suggested in this very brief account. But Marx did, I think, really believe that these "laws" and "tendencies" (as well as certain others, such as the "law" of the increasing severity of cyclical crises), would, in spite of the various qualifications and modifications and "counteracting influences" which he was usually careful to insert, in fact reveal themselves on the surface of economic reality in the course of time as capitalism developed. If they never did so, why should the expropriators ever be expropriated?

Now it is a simple fact that most of Marx's "laws of motion of capitalism" have *not* revealed themselves on the surface of economic reality, at any rate during the last quarter of a century and at any rate in the advanced capitalist countries. The rate of profit in the Marxian sense, so far as one can gather from the rather inadequate data which is available, has not tended to fall; only some of the predictions embodied in the "increasing misery" doctrine—and those probably not the most important ones—have been fulfilled; and economic crises of the classical type, so far from increasing in severity as they indeed appeared to be doing in the 30s, seem to have virtually disappeared. Clearly we should not "blame" Marx for this, any more than we should "blame" Ricardo for the even worse failure of most of his predictions. In Marx's time the tendencies which he described and analysed had in fact been revealing themselves on the surface of economic reality—or at any rate were commonly believed to have been doing so—for some considerable time. All Marx really did was to extrapolate these tendencies into the future, on the implied assumption that the relevant economic facts would remain substantially the same and retain the same relative positions on the scale of relevance, and he cannot be blamed if the tendencies he analysed have in fact been offset by the emergence of various new factors which he could not possibly have foreseen. But to say this is not of course to dispose of the problem of what now remains of Marxian economics, as a result of the emergence of these new factors.

It is obvious that the particular "laws of motion" developed by Marx can no longer be used today as a guide to what is actually going to happen as capitalism develops further. This does not mean, however, that they may not still be useful, even as they stand, for other and more modest purposes. They may still be useful, for example, as aids to the understanding of the development of capitalism up to Marx's time. They may still be useful in some of the less advanced countries as a guide to the actual situation there. And even in the more advanced capitalist countries, they may still be useful as a sort of awful warning of what might happen if the tempo of social legislation and trade union activity were allowed to slacken. But these are extremely limited uses compared with those which Marx himself had in mind when he designed his model. Broadly speaking, and subject to a number of qualifications which will be made below, it can properly be said that all that really remains of Marxian economics today is the body of general methods and tools of analysis which Marx employed to analyse the facts of his time.

V

The most effective way of demonstrating the validity and utility of these methods and tools, of course, would be to use them to construct a completely new model of capitalist development in which the postulated "laws of motion" reflected tendencies which were actually manifesting themselves on the surface of reality. Pending the construction and testing of a new Marxian model of this type, however, all we can really do is to attempt to introduce certain basic Marxian ideas into orthodox economic theory, particularly those parts of it where there appear to be deficiencies due to a neglect of the sociological factors which Marx emphasised. In recent years, it is true, something of this kind has in fact been occurring on quite a large scale: we have indeed been witnessing, as Mrs. Robinson has pointed out, "the same sort of infiltration of Marxian ideas into economic theory as had already occurred in history".[1] Sometimes this infiltration has been conscious, as in the case of Kalecki, Lange, Sraffa, and Mrs. Robinson herself. More often it has been unconscious, as in the case of Harrod's growth model and Richardson's *Information and Investment*. It is only natural that the recent rediscovery of the importance of certain typically Marxian problems should have been accompanied by the rediscovery

---

[1] *Collected Economic Papers*, Vol. III, p. 149.

of certain typically Marxian methods and techniques. But there still remains a great deal of room for further useful infiltration.

Take, for example, the theory of monopoly. Marx's general analysis of value and distribution, it is true, was worked out primarily with reference to a world of more or less free competition. But his discussion of the interrelations between the growth of monopoly on the one hand and the growth of economic instability on the other was far-reaching and acute, and he foresaw with remarkable accuracy some of the basic features of our contemporary world of monopolies. Thus, starting from what we know of his vision and general method of analysis, it is fairly easy to reconstruct the line of approach which he would probably have adopted in an examination of the contemporary trends. In the first place, he would certainly have emphasised that individual monopolies in different industries should be looked at not in isolation but in the context of a new monopolistic *stage* in the development of capitalism—a stage in which monopoly had become intimately connected with imperialism and the new functions of the state, and in which the interrelations between monopoly, accumulation and instability had to some extent taken on new forms. In the second place, he would probably have insisted that monopolistic price-phenomena should be studied in close connection with the main characteristics of this new stage of development; that attention might more profitably be directed to analysing the effects of monopoly on the prices of broad *groups* of goods and services (wage goods and labour-power, for example) than to analysing its effects on the prices of individual goods and services in isolated markets; and that priority should be given to the analysis of the *leading* forms of monopoly, notably oligopoly. He would almost certainly have criticised the tendency of many monopoly theorists to lay their main emphasis on the qualitative *resemblance* between the "monopoly position" of the small tobacconist at the corner and the monopoly position of a firm like I.C.I. Such an approach, he might have said, which starts off by saying in effect that all men are monopolists, is likely to discourage economists from going on to make the vitally necessary distinction between weak monopolists and strong ones. The infiltration of this kind of attitude into orthodox monopoly theory would, I think, be likely to effect an appreciable improvement in the realism and relevance of the theory.

The same can be said of the infiltration of a Marxian attitude into the theory of wages. Here it is true that the orthodox theory has certain important achievements to its credit, particularly in the field of the analysis of short-run wage levels in individual industries under monopolistic conditions of various kinds; and it is also true that the general laws which Marx himself formulated concerning long-run trends in wages have been largely invalidated by the unexpected concurrence and increase in intensity of certain "counteracting influences". But this does not mean that some of the key factors upon which Marx's theory of wages depended are not still operative in the modern world. In particular, any new theory of long-run trends in wages which neglected to lay emphasis on the accumulation of capital, and the technological changes and market problems which it brings about, would be likely to possess little interest or relevance.[1] In an important sense, it is still true to say in our modern world that "relative surplus-population is . . . the pivot upon which the law of demand and supply of labour works".[2] And it should also be borne in mind that the above-mentioned "counteracting influences" have as yet been unable to eliminate economic instability or to prevent the growth of monopoly, both of which in themselves may have significant effects on wage levels. Once again there would seem to be a decided advantage in bringing the relations of production in, as Marx always did, on the ground floor.

Finally, a brief mention may be made of one of the most important areas of all—the theory of profit. Surely in this field nothing would be lost, and much might be gained, by an attempt to explain the origin and persistence of net profit in terms of, rather than in abstraction from, the existence under capitalism of a class monopoly of capital. And surely Marx's theory of the falling rate of profit, in spite of the failure of the prediction which Marx based on it, may have something to offer those modern theorists who are concerned with the problem of secular changes in the rate of profit. Whatever else may be said about it, at least it puts before us the interesting suggestion that changes in the rate of profit may depend not on technological factors alone but rather on the interaction of these with sociological factors.

What I am trying to say here, putting it in general terms, is simply that many modern Western economists have still to learn one fundamental lesson from Marx—that the analysis of economic categories ought so far as possible to be conducted in terms of, rather than in abstraction from, "relations of production" in Marx's sense. The really original and essential aspects of Marx's economic model are the vision and general method of analysis which Marx employed in building it. Everyone pays lip-service nowadays to the aim of bringing sociology back into economics, but somehow no one ever manages actually to achieve this aim, particularly in sensitive spheres like that of the theory of distribution where we most need to achieve it. Whatever one may think about Marx, at least he *did* achieve it—and by no means least in the sphere of distribution theory. We cannot simply reproduce his

---

[1] Cf. Rogin, *The Meaning and Validity of Economic Theory* (New York, 1956), pp. 407-8. See also *ibid.*, p. 405.

[2] *Capital*, Vol. I, p. 639.

achievements today: "official" textbooks of Marxian political economy are coming to look more and more antediluvian with every year that passes. But we *can* experiment with the use of Marx's general economic method. A vision and method which produced such interesting results when applied to the capitalism of Marx's day are surely capable of producing at least *some* useful results when applied to the not so very different capitalism of our own day.

INDEX